Multicultural Education in a Pluralistic Society

Sixth Edition

DONNA M. GOLLNICK

National Council for Accreditation of Teacher Education
Washington, DC

PHILIP C. CHINN

California State University
Los Angeles

Merrill
Prentice Hall

Upper Saddle River, New Jersey
Columbus, Ohio

Library of Congress Cataloging in Publication Data

Gollnick, Donna M.
  Multicultural education in a pluralistic society / Donna M. Gollnick, Philip C. Chinn.—6th ed.
    p. cm.
  Includes bibliographical references and index.
  ISBN 0-13-019618-5
  1. Multicultural education—United States. 2. Social sciences—Study and teaching
(Elementary)—United States. 3. Pluralism (Social sciences)—Study and teaching
(Elementary)—United States. 4. Social sciences—Study and teaching (Secondary)—United
States. 5. Pluralism (Social sciences)—Study and teaching (Secondary)—United States I.
Chinn, Philip C. - II. Title.

LC1099.3 .G65 2002
370.117—dc21   00-069107

Vice President and Publisher: Jeffery W. Johnston
Acquisitions Editor: Debra A. Stollenwerk
Editorial Assistant: Penny S. Burleson
Development Editor: Heather Doyle Fraser
Production Editor: Kimberly J. Lundy
Production Coordination: Carlisle Publishers Services
Design Coordinator: Diane C. Lorenzo
Photo Coordinator: Sandy Lenahan
Cover Designer: Thomas Mack
Cover Image: SuperStock
Production Manager: Pamela D. Bennett
Director of Marketing: Kevin Flanagan
Marketing Manager: Krista Groshong
Marketing Services Manager: Barbara Koontz

This book was set in Palatino by Carlisle Communications, Ltd. It was printed and bound by R. R.
Donnelly & Sons Company. The cover was printed by Phoenix Color Corp.

Photo Credits: Bill Aron, pp. 196, 211; Victor Bracamontes, p. 211; Keith Brofsky, p. 302; Peter Buckley, p. 65; Scott Cunning-
ham, pp. 2, 177, 318, 347; Laima Druskis, p. 49; The Fo Kuang Shan Hsi Lai Temple, p. 215; Larry Hamill, p. 724; Louisiana Office of Tourism, p. 36; Anthony Magnacca, p. 751; New York Convention & Visitors Bureau, pp. 8, 244; Pearson Education, pp.
97, 285; PhotoDisc, Inc., p. 178; Mark Richards, p. 180; Barbara Schwartz, p. 112; SW Productions, p. 131; Anne Vega, p. 23, 136,
160, 212, 240, 260, 333; Todd Yarrington, p. 76; Shirley Zeiberg, pp. 274, 286.

Prentice-Hall International (UK) Limited, *London*
Prentice-Hall of Australia Pty. Limited, *Sydney*
Prentice-Hall Canada, Inc., *Toronto*
Prentice-Hall Hispanoamericana, S.A., *Mexico*
Prentice-Hall of India Private Limited, *New Delhi*
Prentice-Hall of Japan, Inc., *Tokyo*
Prentice-Hall Singapore Pte. Ltd.
Editora Prentice-Hall do Brasil, Ltda., *Rio de Janeiro*

10 9 8 7 6 5 4 3 2 1
ISBN 0-13-019618-5

To Marva Atwater, Pam Magasich, Wendy Wiggins, and Denise Thomas
—Colleagues whose support makes this book possible
DMG

To Mary Shepherd
PCC

Preface

DIVERSITY IN THE NEW MILLENNIUM

As we begin the new millennium, we find the United States considerably more diverse than it was at the beginning of the last century. The country is a multicultural nation comprised of indigenous peoples, such as the American Indians, Aleuts, Eskimos, and Hawaiians, and those who themselves or whose ancestors arrived as immigrants from other countries. These groups of individuals represent different classes, religions, and native languages. In addition, the people differ in gender, sexual orientation, age, and physical and mental abilities. As we move further into the new millennium, the population will become increasingly more diverse. By 2040, the U.S. Census Bureau predicts that children of color will comprise 50 percent of the school-aged population. As the ethnic composition of the United States changes, so will the religious landscape as new immigrants bring their religions from abroad. They will also bring diverse languages, values, and ideas that will help reshape U.S. society.

We are all exposed to a social curriculum that makes positive and negative statements about these differences through radio, television, newspapers, and magazines, as well as through family attitudes. Often, distorted messages about people who are ethnically or religiously different from the listener or observer are portrayed stereotypically. We hear that Italian Americans are involved in organized crime, African Americans are on welfare, the homeless are dangerous, women are weak, and individuals with disabilities are helpless. These stereotypes and gross generalizations influence educators, employers, politicians, and neighbors who make important decisions based on such misconceptions. As educators, we are faced with the responsibility of helping our students sift through and honestly analyze the cultural cues forced on them daily.

While poverty levels have dropped in recent years, poverty still affects African Americans, Native Americans, Latinos, and families headed by single parents at disproportionately high levels. While the economy of the United States has experienced an unprecedented period of growth, the population is becoming less middle class and more representative of two classes—those who are financially secure and those who, at best, live from paycheck to paycheck. Our race, gender, and class determine how privileged we are. We live in very different worlds in which most individuals from the dominant group do not recognize (or acknowledge) the privileges that are automatically extended to them. Many persons of color, with disabilities, or of low income, in contrast, experience firsthand the slights and discrimination of the dominant society.

Events in Laramie, Wyoming; Jasper, Texas; and Littleton, Colorado at the end of the last decade remind us that hate still exists in this country. There are many other reminders. It is estimated that there are now over 500 hate groups in the United States. These groups are reaching thousands with their hate-filled websites, many of which are creative and contain recruitment materials and links for children. Revisionists among the hate groups contend that the Jewish Holocaust never occurred. Some declare on their websites that Jesus was not a Jew. Others declare that the HIV virus is God's retribution against homosexuals.

The culture and the society of the United States are dynamic. They are in a continuous state of change. Unless teachers are able to understand the diverse needs of their students, it will be difficult if not impossible to teach them effectively.

What Impact Does Multicultural Education Have on Teaching?

Education that is multicultural provides an environment that values diversity and portrays it positively. Gender, age, race, ethnicity, native language, religion, class, or disability should not limit students' educational and vocational options. Educators have the responsibility to help students contribute to and benefit from our democratic society. Effective instructional strategies for all students in the classroom should not evolve solely from the teacher's culture; they should be drawn primarily from the cultures of students and communities. The integration of multicultural education throughout the curriculum helps students and teachers think critically about institutional racism, classism, sexism, ageism, and homophobia. Hopefully, educators will help their students develop both individual and group strategies to overcome the debilitating effects of these society scourges.

Teaching to Understand Microcultures

We approach multicultural education with a broad perspective of the concept. Using culture as the basis for understanding multicultural education, we present descriptions of seven microcultures to which students and teachers belong. Of course, these are not the only microcultures to which individuals belong. However, we feel that these microcultures are among those most critical to understanding pluralism and multicultural education at this time. We recognize the importance of studying ethnicity; however, we, as many other authors, have chosen to focus on the complex nature of pluralism in the United States. An individual's cultural identity is not limited to his or her ethnicity, but is based also on class, religion, gender, language, abilities, age, and geographical background. To further complicate our understanding of a student in a classroom, the degree to which he or she identifies with a microcultural membership may vary considerably. Two sixteen year old Italian American female students from an upper middle class Roman Catholic home are in the same classroom and even have a similar physical appearance. One strongly identifies with her Italian heritage and her Roman Catholic religion while the other doesn't; one strongly identifies with her privileged social class while the other doesn't. In spite of their similar backgrounds, these students differ in their values and the way they view the world.

The complexity and pluralism in the United States makes it difficult for educators to develop expectations of students solely on the basis of one or more of their group memberships. The interaction of these memberships within a sexist and racist society defines who we are. This text is designed to examine these group memberships and the ways in which educators can develop education programs to meet the needs of diverse groups and the nation.

Teaching to Create Equitable Environments

We also believe that educators can deliver an equitable education for all students. Schools can eradicate discrimination in their own policies and practices if educators are willing to confront and eliminate their own racism and sexism. We believe that educators cannot attack sexism without also fighting racism, classism, homophobia, and discrimination based on abilities, age, and religion. To rid our schools of such practices takes a committed and strong faculty. It is a task that can no longer be ignored.

We have tried to present different sides of a number of issues in the most unbiased manner possible. We are not without strong opinions or passion on some of the issues. However, in our effort to be equitable, we do attempt to present different perspectives on the issues and allow the reader to make his or her own decisions. There are some issues related to racism, sexism, handicapism, etc., that are so important to the well-being of society that we do provide our positions, which we recognize to be our biases.

HOW THE TEXT IS ORGANIZED

Multicultural Education in a Pluralistic Society provides an overview of the different microcultures to which students belong. The first chapter examines the pervasive influence of culture and the importance of understanding our own cultural backgrounds and experiences, as well as those of our students. The following seven chapters examine the microcultures of class, ethnicity and race, gender, exceptionality, religion, language, and age. The final chapter contains recommendations for the portrayal and use of diversity, equity, and social justice in the implementation of multicultural education. All of the chapters in this edition have been revised and reorganized to reflect current thinking and research in the area. In particular, the first chapter provides the foundational framework that supports our thinking about multicultural education. The final chapter integrates critical pedagogy with research on teaching effectively. Each chapter opens with a scenario to place the topic in an educational setting. At the end of most chapters are critical incidents in education based on our experiences or those of our colleagues. These are real incidents, and you are asked what you would do in a similar situation.

Critical Incidents in Teaching

Critical incidents appear at the end of some chapters. Some reflect real-life situations that have occurred in schools or classrooms; others combine parts of different incidents to provide you with a problematic situation that could very well take place in your school. These incidents provide you with an opportunity to examine your feelings, attitudes, and possible actions or reactions. In some respects, they are not realistic for you as a potential problem solver. In many real situations, decisions must be made quickly, and you may not have even five minutes to ponder your options and decide on an appropriate action. However, these exercises in problem solving will facilitate and sharpen your critical thinking skills, which may enhance your functioning in various school situations and help you better meet the diverse needs of your students.

These critical incidents and the responses that you, your classmates, and even your instructor make to them will provide you with some insights. A similar situation but with different players and different personalities may require different responses. In some instances, more than one response could be acceptable. Your career as a teacher will be filled with critical incidents and critical responses. At times, after reflecting, you will wish that you could do it all over again differently. You may well make some mistakes during your career. What is important is that you make informed decisions. When you make an error in judgment, reflect on it. Most important, learn from your mistakes and resolve not to make the same mistakes again. The names of the individuals and the schools in the critical incidents have been changed for obvious reasons.

New to This Edition

New, additional *Critical Incidents* have been added. The Critical Incidents have been moved from the end of the text to the end of each chapter. New Video Insight features have been added to each chapter. These features summarize the videos that accompany the text and ask thought-provoking, critical thinking questions for the reader to address. A greater emphasis has been placed on the effects of geographical location on culture. Discussions on geographical influences are imbedded in a number of chapters. We have added new sections on hate groups, school violence, social justice, culturally responsive teaching, and teaching for democracy and social justice.

An Attention to Language

Readers should be aware of several caveats related to the language used in this text. Although we realize that the term *American* is commonly used to refer to the U.S. population, we view *American* as including other North Americans as well. Therefore, we have tried to limit the use of this term when referring to the United States. Although we have tried to use the terms *black* and *white* sparingly, data about groups often have been categorized by the racial identification, rather than by national origin such as African or European American. In many cases, we were not able to distinguish ethnic identity and have continued to use *black, white,* or *persons of color.* We have limited our use of the term *minority* and have focused more on the power relationships that exist between groups. In previous editions we used the term *Hispanic.* In this edition we have tried to use *Latino,* which appears to be the preferred term for individuals from a group with many ethnic origins.

WHAT IS THE MOST IMPORTANT PURPOSE OF THIS TEXT?

Students in undergraduate, graduate, and in-service courses will find this text helpful in examining social and cultural conditions that influence education. This most important purpose is designed to assist students in understanding diversity and how to use this knowledge effectively in the classroom and schools. Other professionals in the social services will find it helpful in understanding the complexity of cultural backgrounds and experiences as they work with families and children.

ACKNOWLEDGMENTS

The preparation of any text involves the contributions of many individuals in addition to those whose names are found on the cover. We wish to thank the following reviewers, whose recommendations were used to improve this edition: Gregory Dmitriyev, Georgia Southern University; Beatrice Fennimore, Indiana University of Pennsylvania; Robert Gustafson, University of Central Florida; Les Irwin, Arizona State University West; Anthony A. Koyzis, University of Wisconsin-Oshkosh; Jane Lehmann, Elgin Community College; and Elizabeth Offutt, Samford University.

We wish to thank William Howe, Sandra Winn, and Pauline Chinn for their contributions to the critical incidents. The research assistance of Maria Gutierrez is also acknowledged and very much appreciated. The assistance, patience, encouragement, and guidance of our editors, Debra A. Stollenwerk and Heather Doyle Fraser, are sincerely appreciated.

Discover the Companion Website Accompanying This Book

 THE PRENTICE HALL COMPANION WEBSITE

A Virtual Learning Environment

Technology is a constantly growing and changing aspect of our field that is creating a need for content and resources. To address this emerging need, Prentice Hall has developed an online learning environment for students and professors alike—Companion Websites—to support our textbooks.

In creating a Companion Website, our goal is to build on and enhance what the textbook already offers. For this reason, the content of each user-friendly website is organized by chapter and provides the professor and student with a variety of meaningful resources.

For the Professor—

Every Companion Website integrates **Syllabus Manager**™, an online syllabus creation and management utility.

- **Syllabus Manager**™ provides you, the instructor, with an easy, step-by-step process to create and revise syllabi, with direct links into the Companion Website and other online content without having to learn HTML.
- Students may log on to your syllabus during any study session. All they need to know is the web address for the Companion Website and the password you've assigned to your syllabus.
- After you have created a syllabus using **Syllabus Manager**™, students may enter the syllabus for their course section from any point in the Companion Website.
- Clicking on a date, the student is shown the list of activities for the assignment. The activities for each assignment are linked directly to actual content, saving time for students.

- Adding assignments consists of clicking on the desired due date, then filling in the details of the assignment—name of the assignment, instructions, and whether or not it is a one-time or repeating assignment.
- In addition, links to other activities can be created easily. If the activity is online, a URL can be entered in the space provided, and it will be linked automatically in the final syllabus.
- Your completed syllabus is hosted on our servers, allowing convenient updates from any computer on the Internet. Changes you make to your syllabus are immediately available to your students at their next logon.

The Companion Website for this text also gives professors access to **PowerPoint™ transparencies** for every chapter.

For the Student—

Companion Website features for students include:

- **Chapter Summaries**
- **Interactive self-quizzes**—multiple choice questions with automatic grading provides immediate feedback for students
- After students submit their answers for the interactive self-quizzes, the Companion Website **Results Reporter** computes a percentage grade, provides a graphic representation of how many questions were answered correctly and incorrectly, and gives a question by question analysis of the quiz. Students are given the option to send their quiz to up to four email addresses (professor, teaching assistant, study partner, etc.).
- **Web Resources**—links to websites that relate to chapter content
- **Integration Activities**—projects and activities that connect chapter content with other resource information and technology
- **Message Board**—serves as a virtual bulletin board to post—or respond to—questions or comments to/from a national audience
- **Chat**—real time chat with anyone who is using the text anywhere in the country—ideal for discussion and study groups, class projects, etc.
- Students can log on to the Companion Website and answer questions from the text in the online modules **Pause to Reflect, Ask Yourself, Questions for Review,** and **Critical Incidents.** They can then share their responses with their professor or their peers.

To take advantage of the many available resources, please visit the Companion Website for *Multicultural Education in a Pluralistic Society, Sixth Edition* at

www.prenhall.com/gollnick

Brief Contents

Chapter 1 Foundations of Multicultural Education 2

Chapter 2 Class 36

Chapter 3 Ethnicity and Race 76

Chapter 4 Gender 124

Chapter 5 Exceptionality 160

Chapter 6 Religion 196

Chapter 7 Language 240

Chapter 8 Age 274

Chapter 9 Education That Is Multicultural 318

Subject Index 356

Name Index 360

Contents

Chapter 1   *Foundations of Multicultural Education*   **2**

Diversity in the Classroom   4

Culture   6

    Characteristics of Culture   7

    Manifestations of Culture   9

    Ethnocentrism   10

    Cultural Relativism   10

Pluralism in Society   11

    The Dominant Culture   11

    Cultural Pluralism   15

    Cultural Borders   16

    Biculturalism and Multiculturalism   17

    Microcultural Groups   18

Equality and Social Justice in a Democracy   21

    Individualism and Meritocracy   23

    Equality   24

    Social Justice   26

Multicultural Education   28

Summary   31

Questions for Review   32

Web Resources   32

References   32

Suggested Readings   33

Critical Incidents in Teaching   35

Chapter 2   *Class*   *36*

Class Structure   38

Social Stratification   40

Socioeconomic Status   40

> *Income   41*
>
> *Wealth   42*
>
> *Occupation   43*
>
> *Education   44*
>
> *Power   45*

Class Differences   46

> *The Underclass   48*
>
> *The Working Class   51*
>
> *The Middle Class   52*
>
> *The Upper Middle Class   53*
>
> *The Upper Class   54*

Interaction of Class with Race and Ethnicity, Gender, and Age   56

> *Race and Ethnic Inequality   57*
>
> *Gender Inequality   60*
>
> *Age Inequality   62*

Educational Implications   64

> *Teacher Expectations and Tracking   65*
>
> *Curriculum for Equality   68*
>
> *Financial Support for Schools   69*

Summary   70

Questions for Review   71

References   72

Suggested Readings   73

Critical Incidents in Teaching   74

Chapter 3   *Ethnicity and Race*   *76*

Ethnic and Racial Diversity   78

Ethnic and Racial Groups   83

> *Ethnic Groups   83*
>
> *Racial Groups   85*

Intergroup Relations   89

Prejudice and Discrimination   90
Racism   93
Hate Groups   95
Racial and Ethnic Identity   97
Degree of Ethnic and Racial Identity   98
Oppositional Identity   100
Educational Implications   102
Acknowledging Ethnic Differences   104
Curriculum Approaches   106
Student Achievement and Assessment   109
Desegregation and Intergroup Relations   111
Summary   113
Questions for Review   114
Web Resources   114
References   115
Suggested Readings   117
Critical Incidents in Teaching   119

Chapter 4   *Gender*   *124*

Gender and Society   126
Gender and Biology   128
Gender and Culture   130
Gender Identity   132
Impact of Perceived Differences   134
Stereotyping of Gender Roles   134
Sexism and Gender Discrimination   136
Jobs and Wages   138
Sexual Orientation   141
Sexual Harassment   143
Interaction of Gender with Ethnicity, Class, and Religion   144
Educational Implications   146
Women's Studies   147
Gender-Sensitive Education   148
Participation in Science, Mathematics, and Technology   151

Nondiscrimination and Title IX   *153*

Summary   154

Questions for Review   155

Web Resources   155

References   156

Suggested Readings   157

Critical Incidents in Teaching   158

Chapter 5   *Exceptionality   160*

Students with Disabilities and Those Who Are Gifted and Talented   162

Labeling   163

Historical Antecedents   165

Disproportionate Placements in Special Education   166

Litigation and Legislation   168

PARC v. the Commonwealth of Pennsylvania   169

Exceptionality and Society   173

Exceptional Microcultures   175

Individuals Who Are Gifted   175

Individuals with Mental Retardation   177

Individuals with Visual or Hearing Impairments   178

Individuals with Physical and Health Impairments   179

Individuals with Emotional Disturbance and with Delinquent Behaviors   180

Educational Implications   181

Communication Needs   183

Acceptance Needs   183

Freedom to Grow   184

Normalization and Mainstreaming   185

Summary   188

Questions for Review   188

References   189

Suggested Readings   190

Critical Incidents in Teaching   192

Chapter 6   *Religion   196*

Religion and Culture   198

Religion as a Way of Life   201

Religious Pluralism in the United States   203
Protestantism   206
   Similarities among Diversity   *206*
   Political Influence   *207*
Catholicism   209
Judaism   210
Islam   212
   Black Muslims   *213*
Buddhism   214
   Other Denominations and Religious Groups   *216*
   Cults and Other Groups   *218*
Religion and Gender   219
Religion and Homosexuality   220
Religion and Race   221
Beliefs: A Function of Class and Education   223
Individual Religious Identity   223
Influence of the Religious Right   224
Educational Implications   227
   School Prayer   *227*
   Tuition Tax Credits   *228*
   School Vouchers   *229*
   Censorship   *230*
   Classroom Implications   *232*
   Guidelines for Teaching about Religions   *232*
Summary   233
Questions for Review   233
References   234
Suggested Readings   235
Critical Incidents in Teaching   236

Chapter 7   ***Language   240***
Language and Culture   242
The Nature of Language   245
Language Differences   247
   Sign Language   *247*
   Bilingualism   *248*
   Accents   *249*

Dialect Differences   250
    Dialects   250
    Bi-dialecticism   252
    Standard English   253
    Perspectives on Black English   253
    Dialects and Education   254
Nonverbal Communication   258
Second Language Acquisition   259
    *Role of First Language in Second Language
    Acquisition   259*
    Language Proficiency   260
Official English (English Only) Controversy   261
Educational Implications   263
    Language and Educational Assessment   264
    Bilingual Education   265
    English as a Second Language   267
    Nonverbal Communications in the Classroom   269
Summary   269
Questions for Review   269
References   270
Suggested Readings   272
Critical Incidents in Teaching   273

Chapter 8   *Age*   **274**
Age and Culture   277
Critical Issues in Childhood   277
    Social Class and Poverty   277
    Immigrant Children   279
    Children, Ethnic Awareness, and Prejudice   279
    Child Abuse   281
Critical Issues in Adolescence   283
    Relationship with Parents   284
    At-Risk Youth and High-Risk Behavior   284
    *The Young African American Male: An Endangered
    Species   295*
Adulthood   298
    The Baby Boomers   299

Generation X   *300*

The Aged   *301*

Educational Implications   305

Summary   308

Questions for Review   308

References   309

Suggested Readings   312

Critical Incidents in Teaching   313

Chapter 9   *Education That Is Multicultural*   **318**

Multicultural Education   320

Public Support   *321*

Supporting Dispositions   *322*

Multiculturalizing the Curriculum   *323*

Culturally Responsive Teaching   325

High Teacher Expectations   *325*

Reflecting Culture in Academic Subjects   *327*

Multiple Perspectives   *329*

Student Voices   *330*

Student and Teacher Interactions   *331*

Student and Teacher Communications   *333*

Crossing Borders   334

Race   *336*

Poverty   *337*

Teaching Urban, Rural, and Suburban Schools   338

Rural Schools   *338*

Urban Schools   *339*

Suburban Schools   *341*

Teaching for Democracy and Social Justice   341

Critical Thinking   *342*

Student Engagement   *343*

School Climate   343

The Hidden Curriculum   *345*

Parent Involvement   *346*

Professional Growth   348

Becoming Multicultural   *348*

Teaching as a Political Activity   *349*

Summary   349

Questions for Review   350

Web Resources   351

References   352

Suggested Readings   353

Subject Index   *356*

Name Index   *360*

NOTE: Every effort has been made to provide accurate and current Internet information in this book. However, the Internet and information posted on it are constantly changing, so it is inevitable that some of the Internet addresses listed in this textbook will change.

Multicultural Education in a Pluralistic Society

Chapter 1

Foundations of Multicultural Education

Equality is the heart and essence of democracy, freedom, and justice.

A. Philip Randolph, 1942

You are just beginning your first teaching position in a nearby urban area. Like many new teachers in an urban area, you were offered the job only a few weeks before school started. You had never been to that part of the city but were sure you could make a difference in the lives of students there. Soon you learn that many students have single parents, many of whom work two jobs to make ends meet. More than half of the students are eligible for free lunch. The families of some students use a language other than English at home, but the principal says the students speak English. You are disappointed in the condition of the school, and your classroom in particular, but have been assured that it will be repainted during one of the vacation periods.

When students arrive on the first day, you are not surprised that a large proportion of them are from families that immigrated from Central America during the past two decades. The population includes some African American students and a few European American students. You did not realize that the class would include a student who had just moved from Bulgaria and spoke no English and that the native language of two students was Farsi. You have taken a few Spanish courses but know little or nothing about the language or cultures of Bulgaria and Iran. You wonder about the white boy with the black eye but guess that he has been in a fight recently.

What assumptions about these students did you make as you read this brief description? How has your own cultural background prepared you to teach this diverse group of students? What might you want to learn about students' cultural backgrounds to ensure that they learn? What kind of challenges are likely to confront you during this year? What do you wish you had learned in college to help you be a better teacher in this school? Where could you go for assistance in working with students who speak little English? Are you glad that you accepted this teaching assignment? Why or why not?

DIVERSITY IN THE CLASSROOM

Educators today are faced with an overwhelming challenge to prepare students from diverse cultural backgrounds to live in a rapidly changing society and a world in which some groups have greater societal benefits than others because of race, ethnicity, gender, class, language, religion, ability, or age. Schools of the future will become increasingly culturally diverse. Demographic data on birthrates and immigration indicate that there will be more Asian American, Latino (but not Cuban American), and African American children, but fewer children who are European American. Students of color comprise more than one third of the school population today. However, the race and sex of their teachers match neither the student population nor the general population; 86.5% of the teachers are white and 75% are female. By 2020, students of color will represent nearly half of the elementary and secondary population. Latino, Asian Americans, American Indians, and African Americans comprise more than half of the student population in California, the District of Columbia, Hawaii, Mississippi, New Mexico, New York, and Texas. Whites make up less than one fourth of the student population in the nation's largest cities. In addition, one of four children in the United States lives in poverty. Although the national data are sketchy, it appears that the number of children with physical and emotional disabilities is on the increase.

It is not only ethnic and racial diversity that is challenging schools. During the past 35 years, new waves of immigrants have come from parts of the world unfamiliar to many Americans. With them have come their religions, which seem even stranger to many Americans than these new people. While small groups of Muslims, Hindus, Buddhists, and Sikhs have been in the country for many decades, only recently have they and their religions become highly visible. Even Christians from Russia, Hong Kong, Taiwan, Korea, and the Philippines bring their own brand of worship to denominations that are well rooted in this country. The United States has not only become a multicultural nation, but it has also become a multireligious society. In earlier years, most religious minority groups maintained a low and almost invisible profile. As the groups have become larger, they have become more visible, along with their houses of worship (Eck, 2000).

These religious differences raise a number of challenges for educators. The holidays to be celebrated must be considered, along with religious codes related to the curriculum, appropriate interactions of boys and girls, dress in physical education classes, and discipline. Parents value the importance of education for their children, but they do not always agree with the school's approaches to teaching and learning. Working collaboratively with parents and communities will become even more critical in providing education equitably to all students.

To work effectively with the heterogeneous student populations found in schools, educators need to understand and feel comfortable with their own cultural backgrounds. They also must understand the cultural setting in which the school is located to develop effective instructional strategies. They must help their students become aware of cultural differences and inequalities in the nation and in the world. One goal is to help students affirm cultural differences while realizing that individuals across cultures have many similarities.

Teachers will find that students have individual differences, even though they may appear to be from the same cultural group. These differences extend far beyond intellectual and physical abilities. Students bring to class different historical backgrounds, religious beliefs, and day-to-day living patterns. These experiences guide the way students behave in school. The cultural background of some students will be mirrored in the school culture. For others, the differences between the home and school cultures will cause dissonance unless the teacher can integrate the cultures of the students into the curriculum and develop a supportive environment for learning. If the teacher fails to understand the cultural factors in addition to the intellectual and physical factors that affect student learning and behavior, it will be impossible to help students learn.

Multicultural education is the educational strategy in which students' cultural backgrounds are used to develop effective classroom instruction and school environments. It is designed to support and extend the concepts of culture, diversity, equality, social justice, and democracy in the formal school setting. An examination of the theoretical precepts and practical applications of these concepts will lead to an understanding of the development and practice of multicultural education.

CULTURE

Everyone has a *culture*. Until early in the twentieth century, the term culture was used to indicate the refined ways of the elite and powerful. People who were knowledgeable in history, literature, and the fine arts were said to possess culture.

No longer is culture viewed so narrowly. Anthropologists define culture as a way of perceiving, believing, evaluating, and behaving (Goodenough, 1987). It provides the blueprint that determines the way we think, feel, and behave in society. Our culture is "in us and all around us, just as the air we breathe" (Erickson, 1997, p. 33). What appears as the natural and only way to learn and to interact with others (e.g., respond to our grandparents) is determined by our culture. Generally accepted and patterned ways of behavior are necessary for a group of people to live together. Culture imposes order and meaning on our experiences. It allows us to predict how others will behave in certain situations.

Culturally determined norms guide our language, behavior, emotions, and thinking in different situations; they are the do's and don'ts of appropriate behavior within our culture. Whereas we are comfortable with others who share the same culture because we know the meaning of their words and actions, we often misunderstand the cultural cues of persons from different cultures. Culture is so much a part of us that we do not realize that not everyone shares our culture. This may be, in part, because we have never been in cultural settings different from our own. This lack of knowledge often leads to our responding to differences as personal affronts, rather than as cultural differences. These misunderstandings may appear insignificant to an observer, but they can be important to participants. Examples include how loud is too loud, how late one may arrive at an event, and how close one can stand to another without being rude or disrespectful.

PAUSE TO REFLECT

It is normal for people to experience some cultural discontinuity when they visit another country or a new city or a neighborhood in which the inhabitants are ethnically different from themselves. Have you ever found yourself in a setting in which you did not know the cultural norms and were at a loss as to how to fit in? How often are you in such settings? Why did you feel uncomfortable? How were you able to overcome your awkwardness?

To answer these questions online, go to the Pause to Reflect module for this chapter of the Companion Website.

Characteristics of Culture

We all have culture, but how did we get it? The first characteristic of culture is that it is learned, and the learning starts at birth. The way a baby is held, fed, bathed, and dressed is culturally determined. This process continues throughout life.

Two similar processes interact as one learns how to act in society: enculturation and socialization. *Enculturation* is the process of acquiring the characteristics of a given culture and generally becoming competent in its language and ways of behaving and knowing. *Socialization* is the general process of learning the social norms of the culture. Through this process, we internalize social and cultural rules. We learn what is expected in social roles, such as mother, husband, student, or child, and in the occupational roles of teacher, banker, plumber, custodian, or politician.

Enculturation and socialization are processes initiated at birth by others, including parents, siblings, nurses, physicians, teachers, and neighbors. These varied instructors may not identify these processes as enculturation or socialization, but they demonstrate and reward children for acceptable behaviors. We learn how to behave by observing and participating in society and culture. Thus, people are socialized and enculturated according to the patterns of the cultures in which they are raised.

The culture in which one is born becomes unimportant unless one is also socialized in that culture. Because culture is so much a part of us, we tend to confuse biological and cultural heritage. Our cultural heritage is learned. It is not innately based on the culture in which we are born. Vietnamese infants adopted by Italian American, Catholic, middle-class parents will share a cultural heritage with middle-class Italian American Catholics, rather than with Vietnamese in Vietnam. Observers, however, will continue to identify these individuals as Vietnamese Americans, because of physical characteristics and a lack of knowledge about their cultural experiences.

A second characteristic of culture is that it is shared. Shared cultural patterns and customs bind people together as an identifiable group and make it possible for them to live together and function with ease. An individual in the shared culture is provided with the context for identifying with the group that shares that culture. Although there may be some disagreement about certain aspects of the culture, there is a common acceptance and agreement about most aspects. Actually, most points of agreement are outside our realm of awareness. For example, we do not even realize that the way we communicate with each other and the foods we eat are part of culture.

Third, culture is an adaptation. Cultures accommodate environmental conditions and available natural and technological resources. Thus, the Eskimo who lived with extreme cold, snow, ice, seals, and the sea developed a culture different from that of the Pacific Islander, who has limited land, unlimited seas, and few mineral resources. The culture of urban residents differs from that of rural residents, in part, because of the resources available in the different settings. The culture of oppressed groups differs from that of the dominant group because of power relationships within society.

Finally, culture is a dynamic system that changes continuously. Some cultures undergo constant and rapid change; others are very slow to change. Some changes, such as a new word or new hairstyle, may be relatively small and have little impact on the culture as a whole. Other changes have a dramatic impact. The intro-

Urban workers have adapted their culture to an environment in which smog, crowded conditions, and public transportation are the norm.

duction of technology into a culture has often produced changes far broader than the technology itself. For example, the replacement of industrial workers with robots is changing the culture of many working-class communities. Such changes may also alter traditional customs and beliefs.

Manifestations of Culture

The cultural patterns of a group of people are determined by how the people organize and view the various components of culture. Culture is manifested in an infinite number of ways through social institutions, lived experiences, and the individual's fulfillment of psychological and basic needs. To understand how extensively our lives are affected by culture, let's examine a few of these manifestations.

Our values are initially determined by our culture. *Values* are conceptions of what is desirable and important to us or to our group. Our values influence prestige, status, pride, family loyalty, love of country, religious belief, and honor. Status symbols differ across cultures. For many families in the United States, accumulation of material possessions is a respected status symbol. For others, the welfare of the extended family is of utmost importance. These factors, as well as what is decent or indecent, what is moral or immoral, and how punishment and reward are provided, are determined by the value system of the culture.

Culture also manifests itself in the nonverbal communication used by individuals. The meaning of an act or an expression must be viewed in its cultural context. Raising the eyebrow is an example: "To most Americans this means surprise; to a person from the Marshall Islands in the Pacific it signals an affirmative answer; for Greeks, it is a sign of disagreement. The difference is not so much in how the eyebrows are raised but in the cultural meaning of the act" (Spradley & Rynkiewich, 1975, p. 7). Culture also determines the manner of walking, sitting, standing, reclining, and gesturing. We must remind ourselves not to interpret acts and expressions of people from a different cultural background as wrong or inappropriate just because they are not the same as our own.

Language itself is a reflection of culture and provides a special way of looking at the world and organizing experiences that is often ignored in translating words from one language to another. Many different sounds and combinations of sounds are used in the languages of different cultures. Those of us who have tried to learn a second language may have experienced difficulty in verbalizing the sounds that were not part of our first language. Also, diverse language patterns found within the same language group can lead to misunderstandings. For example, one person's "joking" is heard by others as serious criticism or abuse of power; this is a particular problem when the speaker is a member of the dominant group and the listener is a member of an oppressed group.

Although we have discussed only a few daily patterns determined by culture, they are limitless. Among them are relationships of men and women, parenting, choosing a spouse, sexual relations, and division of labor in the home and society. These patterns are shared by members of the culture and often seem strange and improper to nonmembers.

Ethnocentrism

Because culture helps determine the way we think, feel, and act, it becomes the lens through which we judge the world. As such, it can become an unconscious blinder to other ways of thinking, feeling, and acting. Our own culture is automatically treated as innate. It becomes the only natural way to function in the world. Even common sense in our own culture is naturally translated to common sense for the world. The rest of the world is viewed through our cultural lens; other cultures are compared with ours and are evaluated by our cultural standards. It becomes difficult, if not impossible, to view another culture as separate from our own—a task that anthropologists attempt when studying other cultures.

This inability to view other cultures as equally viable alternatives for organizing reality is known as *ethnocentrism*. It is a common characteristic of cultures, whereby one's own cultural traits are viewed as natural, correct, and superior to those of another culture, whose traits are perceived as strange, inferior, or wrong. Although it is appropriate to cherish one's culture, members sometimes become closed to the possibilities of difference. Feelings of superiority over other cultures often develop.

The inability to view another culture through its cultural lens, rather than through one's own cultural lens, prevents an understanding of the second culture. This inability can make it impossible to function effectively in a second culture. By overcoming one's ethnocentric view of the world, one can begin to respect other cultures and even learn to function comfortably in more than one cultural group.

Cultural Relativism

Never judge another man until you have walked a mile in his moccasins. This North American Indian proverb suggests the importance of understanding the cultural backgrounds and experiences of other persons, rather than judging them by our own standards. The principle of cultural relativism is to see a culture as if you are a member of the culture. In essence, it is an attempt to view the world through the other individual's cultural lens. It is an acknowledgement that another person's way of doing things, while perhaps not appropriate for us, may be valid for him or her. This ability becomes more essential than ever in the world today as countries and cultures become more interdependent. In an effort to maintain positive relationships with the numerous cultural groups in the world, the United States cannot afford to ignore other cultures or to relegate them to an inferior status.

Within our own boundaries are many cultural groups that historically have been viewed and treated as inferior to the dominant Western European culture that has been the basis for most of our institutions. These intercultural misunderstandings occur even when no language barrier exists and when large components of the major culture are shared by the people involved. These misunderstandings often occur because one cultural group is largely ignorant about the culture of another group and gives the second culture little credibility. One problem is that members of one group are, for the most part, unable to describe their own cultural system, let alone another. These misunderstandings are common among the various groups in this country and are accentuated by differential status based on race, gender, and class.

Cultural relativism suggests that people need to learn more about their own culture than is commonly required. That must be followed by study about, and interaction with, other cultural groups. This intercultural process helps one know what it is like to be a member of the second culture and to view the world from that point of view. To function effectively and comfortably within a second culture, that culture must be learned.

PLURALISM IN SOCIETY

Many similarities exist across cultures. At the same time, there is great diversity in the ways people learn, the values they cherish, their worldviews, their behavior, and their interactions with others. There are many reasonable ways to organize our lives, approach a task, and use our languages and dialects. It is when we begin to see our cultural norms and behaviors not just as one approach, but as superior to others, that differences become politicized.

These differences among and within groups sometimes lead to not only misunderstandings and misperceptions, but even conflict. Cultural differences become demarcated by lines of political differences that are further exacerbated by real and perceived realities of group domination or subordination (Erickson, 1997). These differences can become tied to strong feelings of nationalism and patriotism that expand into armed conflicts across nations, tribes, religious communities, and ethnic origins. They sometimes are manifested in anti-Semitic symbols and actions, cross burnings, gay bashing, and sexual harassment.

Conflicts between groups are usually based on the groups' differential status and value in society. The alienation and marginalization that many powerless groups experience can lead to groups accentuating their differences, especially to separate themselves from the dominant group. Groups sometimes construct their own identities in terms of others. Whites often do not think of themselves as white, except as different from black. Males define themselves in opposition to female. They see themselves as being at the center of a world in which they are privileging themselves in relation to others—women and African Americans.

In developing an understanding of differences and otherness, we can begin to change our simplistic binary approaches of us/them, dominant/subordinate, good/bad, and right/wrong. We may realize that a plurality of truths are as reasonable as our own. We seek out others for dialogue, rather than speak about, and for, them (McLaren, 1995). We move from exercising *power over* others to sharing *power with* others.

The Dominant Culture

U.S. political and social institutions have evolved from a Western European tradition. The English language is a polyglot of the languages spoken by the various conquerors and rulers of Great Britain throughout history. The legal system is derived from English common law. The political system of democratic elections comes from France and England. The middle-class value system has been modified from a European system. Even our way of thinking, at least the way it is rewarded in school, is based on Socrates' linear system of logic.

Formal institutions, such as governments, schools, social welfare, banks, and businesses, affect many aspects of our lives. Because of the strong Anglo-Saxon influence on these institutions, the dominant cultural influence on the United States also has been identified as Anglo-Saxon, or Western European. More specifically, the major cultural influence on the United States, particularly on its institutions, has been white, Anglo-Saxon, and Protestant (WASP). But no longer is the dominant group composed only of WASPs. Instead, most members of the ethnically diverse middle class have adopted these traditionally WASP institutions, which provide the framework for the traits and values that outsiders identify as U.S. culture. Although most of our institutions still function under the strong influence of their WASP roots, many other aspects of American life have been greatly influenced by the numerous cultural groups that make up the U.S. population.

Although we have an agrarian tradition, the population now is primarily located in metropolitan areas and small towns. The country has mineral and soil wealth, elaborate technology, and a wealth of manufactured goods. Mass education and mass communication are ways of life. We are regulated by clocks and calendars, rather than by seas and the sun. Time is used to organize most activities of life. Most of us are employees whose salaries or wages are paid by large, complex, impersonal institutions. Work is done regularly, purposefully, and sometimes grimly. In contrast, play is fun—an outlet from work. Money is the denominator of exchange. Necessities of life are purchased, rather than produced. Achievement and success are measured by the quantity of material goods purchased. Religious beliefs are concerned with general morality.

The overpowering value of the dominant group is *individualism,* which is characterized by the belief that every individual is his or her own master, is in control of his or her own destiny, and will advance and regress in society only according to his or her own efforts (Bellah, Madsen, Sullivan, Swidler, & Tipton, 1985). This individualism is grounded in the Western worldview that individuals can control both nature and their destiny. Traits that emphasize this core value include industriousness, ambition, competitiveness, self-reliance, independence, appreciation of the good life, and the perception of humans as separate from, and superior to, nature. The acquisition of such possessions as televisions, cars, boats, and homes measures success and achievement.

Another core value is freedom. *Freedom* is defined by the dominant group, however, as "being left alone by others, not having other people's values, ideas, or styles of life forced upon one, being free of arbitrary authority in work, family, and political life" (Bellah et al., 1985, p. 23). As a result, impersonality in relations with others is common. Communication is often direct or confrontive. Many members of the dominant group rely more on associations of common interest than on strong kinship ties. The nuclear family is the basic kinship unit. Values tend to be absolute (e.g., right or wrong, moral or immoral), rather than range along a continuum of degrees of right and wrong. Personal life and community affairs are based on principles of right and wrong, rather than on shame, dishonor, or ridicule. Youthfulness is also emphasized.

Many U.S. citizens, especially if they are middle-class, share these traits and values to some degree. However, not all members of the dominant culture value these traits or accept them as the most desirable traits for the culture. Nevertheless, they are patterns that are privileged in institutions such as schools. They are values to which the dominant society expects citizens to adhere.

Privilege.   Most male members of the dominant group do not usually think about themselves as white, financially secure, Christian, English-speaking, or heterosexual. They have not seen themselves as privileged in society and do not view themselves as oppressors of others. Most schools and teachers have made "little effort to make inequality, racism, or powerlessness problematic, open to discussion" (Giroux, 1994, p. 36). Most members of the dominant group have not had the opportunity to explore their own whiteness and other privileged positions in society. They often have not studied or interacted with groups to which they do not belong. Therefore, they have been unable to locate themselves within the problem of power and inequality (Boyd, 1996).

In contrast, members of oppressed groups are constantly confronted with the difference of their race, language, class, religion, gender, disability, and/or homosexuality. The degree of identification with the characteristics of the dominant culture depends, in part, on how much an individual must interact with society's formal institutions for economic support and subsistence. The more dependence on formal institutions, the greater the degree of sharing, or of being forced to adopt, the common traits and values of the dominant group.

These opposing perspectives are situated in one's real or perceived position of privilege or lack of privilege in society. They have led, in recent years, to public debates on college campuses about affirmative action to ensure diversity, and diversity in the common core of the college curriculum. Members of oppressed groups argue that their cultures are not reflected in a curriculum that includes only the great books of Western European thought. The traditionalists, who are predominantly representatives of the dominant group, often invoke nationalism and patriotism in their calls to retain the purity of the Western canon and promote homogeneity in society. Proponents of a common core curriculum that includes the voices of women, people of color, and religions other than Christianity also include many members of the dominant group who value differences and multiple perspectives.

The question appears to be whose culture will be reflected in the elementary and secondary, as well as college, curriculum. Those who call for a curriculum and textbooks that reflect only their history and experiences view their culture as superior to all others. Thus, they and their culture become privileged over others in schools and other institutions in society. They do not see themselves as different; to them, cultural diversity refers only to others in society. "Traditionally in [A]merican society, it is the members of oppressed objectified groups who are expected to stretch out and bridge the gap between the actualities of [their] lives and the consciousness of [their] oppressor" (Lorde, 1995, p. 191). The privileged curriculum once again requires members of oppressed groups to learn the culture and history of the dominant group without the opportunity to see or hear themselves or to validate the importance of their own history and lived experiences. It is as if they do not belong; this feeling often leads to marginalization and alienation from school.

Assimilation.   *Assimilation* is the process by which groups adopt or change the dominant culture. Cultural patterns that distinguished the two groups disappear, their distinctive cultural patterns become part of the dominant culture, or a combination of the two occurs. In the United States, the middle-class microculture reflects this process. In fact, the values and traits of this cultural group are often defined as the macroculture, with the characteristics that have the greatest influence on the lives of citizens. Many of the values and traits of the dominant middle-class microculture, however, are not universally accepted by all U.S. citizens.

According to Gordon (1964), the assimilation process develops through stages in which the new cultural group: (1) changes its cultural patterns to those of the dominant group, (2) develops large-scale primary-group relationships with the dominant group, (3) intermarries fully with the dominant group, (4) loses its sense of peoplehood as separate from the dominant group, (5) encounters no discrimination, (6) encounters no prejudiced attitudes, and (7) does not raise any issues that would involve value and power conflict with the dominant group. Each of these stages also represents a degree of assimilation. Stage 1 is acculturation, in which cultural patterns of the dominant group are adopted by the new or oppressed group. This is the most common pattern for many groups that have immigrated during the twentieth century. Although some groups have tried to maintain the original culture, it is usually in vain as children go to school and participate in the larger society. Continuous and firsthand contacts with the dominant group usually result in subsequent changes in the original cultural patterns of either or both groups.

The rapidity and success of the acculturation process depends on several factors, including location and discrimination. If a minority group is spatially isolated and segregated (whether voluntarily or not) in a rural area, as is the case with many American Indians on reservations, the acculturation process is very slow. Unusually marked discrimination such as that faced by oppressed groups, especially African Americans, Native Americans, and Mexican Americans, deprives group members of educational and occupational opportunities and primary relationships with members of the dominant group. The acculturation process may be retarded indefinitely (Gordon, 1964).

Structural assimilation occurs in Gordon's (1964) Stages 2 through 7. The two groups share primary group relationships, including membership in the same cliques and social clubs; they begin to intermarry; and they are treated equally within society. Only limited structural assimilation has occurred for any of the groups except white European immigrants. For most groups, success in becoming acculturated has not led to structural assimilation. It has neither eliminated prejudice and discrimination nor led to large-scale intermarriage with the dominant cultural group. If the assimilation process is effective, it leads to the disappearance of a cultural group that is distinct from the dominant group.

It is important to note that acculturation is determined, in part, by the individual; that is, the individual can decide how much he or she wants to dress, speak, and behave like members of the dominant group. Members of many groups, however, have had little choice if they wanted to share the American dream of success. They have had to give up native languages and behaviors or hide them at home. Even that has not guaranteed acceptance by the dominant group. Most members of oppressed groups, even those who adopted the values and behaviors of the dominant group, have not been permitted to assimilate fully into society.

Although some groups try to preserve their native cultures, others have assimilation as their goal. Nevertheless, assimilation does not characterize the contemporary U.S. scene. We are a nation of many cultural groups distinguished by our ethnicity, gender, class, language, and religion. At the same time, theories of assimilation have affected and continue to affect our political, social, and educational policies and practices.

Cultural Pluralism

Refusing or not being permitted to assimilate into the dominant American culture, many immigrants and ethnic groups have maintained their own unique ethnic communities and enclaves. For most oppressed ethnic and religious groups, primary-group contacts have been maintained within the group, rather than across cultural groups as required in structural assimilation. Cross-cultural contacts occur only at the secondary level—in work settings and in interaction with political and civic institutions. Members develop institutions, agencies, and power structures for services within their ethnic communities. These enclaves exist as Little Italy, Chinatown, Harlem, Korea Town, East Los Angeles, Amish and Hutterite communities, and some settlements in rural areas. In some places, the blind, the deaf, and the gay have established communities in which they feel comfortable with other members of the same microculture.

A society organized according to a theory of *cultural pluralism* allows two or more distinct groups to function separately without requiring any assimilation of one into the other. Pratte (1979) identifies three stringent criteria for the application of cultural pluralism to a society:

1. Cultural diversity, in the form of a number of groups—political, racial, ethnic, religious, economic, or age—is exhibited in the society.
2. The coexisting groups approximate equal political, economic, and educational opportunity.
3. There is a behavioral commitment to the values of cultural pluralism as a basis for a viable system of social organization. (p. 141)

Most observers of U.S. society would agree that the condition of cultural diversity is met. Data on the income inequities that exist between men and women or between blacks and whites indicate that the condition for relative parity and equality between groups is not met. The commitment to the value of cultural pluralism is not supported broadly by individuals and groups in society. Native American nations within the United States probably come closest to a reflection of cultural pluralism in that some of them have their own political, economic, and educational systems. For most Native Americans, however, the economic, political, and educational opportunities do not approach equality with the dominant group. For cultural pluralism to be a reality, the nation would recognize many ethnic and/or religious groups that could coexist. It would require that power and resources be shared somewhat equitably across those groups.

The dominant group will not very willingly share its power and wealth with others. Some critics of the system believe that the dominant group uses a strategy of divide and conquer to keep ethnic groups segregated and fighting among themselves for the few resources available. Others believe that a societal goal should be integration of cultural groups and the promotion of more equality across groups through a united front. Still others believe that individuals should be able to maintain their ethnic identities while participating in the macroculture. These beliefs are not necessarily discrete from one another; for example, society could be integrated, but members would not be required to relinquish their ethnic identities. At the same time, an integrated society can lead to greater assimilation in that primary contacts across cultural groups are more likely.

Cultural Borders

"Culture develops within unequal and dialectical relations that different groups establish in a given society at a particular historical point" (Giroux, 1988, p. 116). These differing and unequal power relations have a great impact on "the ability of individuals and groups to define and achieve their goals" (Giroux, 1988, p. 117). The dynamics of those power relationships and the effect they have on the development of groups must also be an integral part of the study of culture.

A *cultural border* is a "social construct that is political in origin" and "involves differences in rights and obligations" (Erickson, 1997, p. 42). Each of us belongs to multiple microcultures (e.g., ethnic, religious, and socioeconomic groups) that help define us. As long as those differences have no status implications in which one group is treated differently from another, conflict among groups is minimal. Unfortunately, borders are often erected between groups, and crossing them can be easy or difficult. What is valued on one side of the border may be denigrated on the other side. Speaking both Spanish and English may be highly rewarded in the community, but using Spanish in some schools may not be tolerated.

Educators establish cultural borders in the classroom when all activity is grounded in the teacher's culture alone. As we learn to function comfortably in different microcultures, we may be able to move away from a single perspective linked to cultural domination. We may be able to cross cultural borders.

Biculturalism and Multiculturalism

Individuals who have competencies in, and can operate successfully in, two or more different cultures are border crossers; they are bicultural or multicultural and are often multilingual as well. Having proficiencies in multiple cultures allows a broad range of abilities on which to draw at any given time, as determined by the particular situation.

Goodenough (1987) defines *multiculturalism* as the normal human experience. All Americans participate in more than one cultural group or microculture. Thus, most persons have already become proficient in multiple systems for perceiving, evaluating, believing in, and acting according to the patterns of the various microcultures in which they participate. We often act and speak differently when we are in the community in which we were raised than when we are in a professional setting. We behave differently on a night out with members of our own sex than we do at home with the family. People with competencies in several microcultures develop a fuller appreciation of the range of cultural competencies available to all people.

Many members of oppressed groups are forced to become bicultural to work or attend school and to participate effectively in their own ethnic community. Different behaviors are expected in the two settings. To be successful on the job usually requires proficiency in the ways of the dominant group. Because most schools

LINK TO THE CLASSROOM

Crossing a Border

The families of many students use language patterns and intonations that may be dramatically, but often subtly, different from the teacher's. In a preschool in a Northeastern city, a North American teacher found that her Haitian students were more unruly than those in classrooms with Haitian teachers. Through studying Haitian culture, learning Creole, studying sociolinguistics, and observing Haitian and North American teachers, she learned that the way children were corrected for misbehavior differed between the two groups of teachers. North American teachers, on the one hand, attached consequences to their corrections (e.g., "You may be hit by a car if you cross on a red light"). Haitian teachers, on the other hand, referred to misbehaviors as bad (e.g., "Your parents would not approve"). Once the North American teacher learned these cultural differences, she was able to cross a cultural boundary. Students responded differently to her interactions with them.

Source: Ballenger, C. (1992, Summer). Teaching and practice. *Harvard Educational Review, 62*(2), 199–208.

reflect the dominant society, students are forced to adjust if they are going to be academically successful. In contrast, many European Americans find almost total congruence between the culture of their family, schooling, and work. Most remain monocultural throughout their lives. They do not envision the value and possibilities of becoming competent in a different culture.

In our expanding, culturally diverse nation, it is critical that educators themselves become at least bicultural. Understanding the cultural cues of several ethnic groups, especially oppressed groups, improves our ability to work with all students. It also helps us to be sensitive to the importance of these differences in teaching effectively.

Microcultural Groups

Subsocieties within the United States contain cultural elements, institutions, and groups in which cultural patterns are shared. Unlike the Western view that humans control the world, "Navajo Indians are said to have a passive view of man, for they see the world as 'doing things to people' " (Pai, 1990, p. 23). Even the fundamental value of individualism is questioned by many. Although it may help build character, it also has the "potential for creating personal isolation" (Lasley, 1996, p. 363).

Groups in the United States have been called *subsocieties* or *subcultures* by sociologists and anthropologists because they exist within the context of a larger society and share political and social institutions, as well as some traits and values of the macroculture. These cultural groups are also called *microcultures* to indicate that they have distinctive cultural patterns but share some cultural patterns with all members of the U.S. macroculture. People who belong to the same microculture share traits and values that bind them together as a group. At the same time, there is no essential or absolute identity as female or male, or American or recent immigrant or Buddhist or Jew. Our identities in any single microcultural group are influenced by our historical and lived experiences and membership in other microcultural groups.

Numerous microcultures exist in most nations, but the United States is exceptionally rich in the many distinct cultural groups that make up the population. Cultural identity is based on traits and values learned as part of our ethnic origin, religion, gender, age, socioeconomic status, primary language, geographic region, place of residence (e.g., rural or urban), and abilities or exceptional conditions, as shown in Figure 1–1. Each of these groups has distinguishable cultural patterns shared with others who identify themselves as members of that particular group. Although they share certain characteristics of the macroculture with most of the U.S. population, members of microcultures also have learned cultural traits, discourse patterns, ways of learning, values, and behaviors characteristic of the microcultures to which they belong.

Individuals sharing membership in one microculture may not share membership in other microcultures. For example, on the one hand, all men are members of the male microculture, but not all males belong to the same ethnic, religious, or

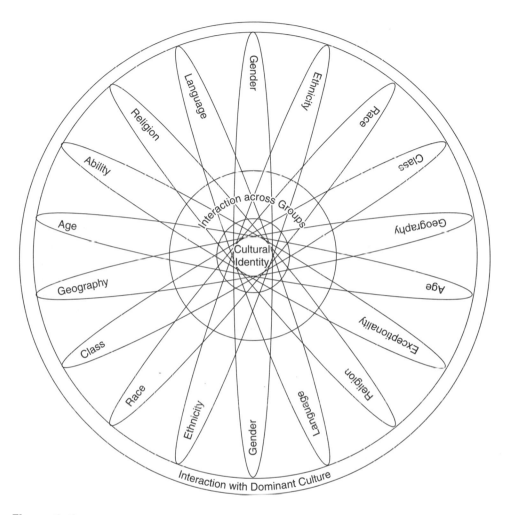

Figure 1–1
Cultural identity is based on membership in microcultural groups that continuously interact and influence each other. Identity within these groups is also affected by the interaction with the dominant group and within power relations in society.

class group. On the other hand, an ethnic group is composed of both males and females with different religious and socioeconomic backgrounds.

The interaction of these various microcultures within the macroculture begins to determine an individual's cultural identity. Membership in one microculture can greatly influence the characteristics and values of membership in other microcultures. For instance, some fundamentalist religions have strictly defined expectations for women and men. Thus, membership in the religious group influences, to a great extent, the way a female behaves as a young girl, teenager, bride, and wife, regardless of her ethnic group. One's class level will greatly affect the quality of life for families, especially for children and the elderly in that group.

This interaction is most dynamic across race, ethnicity, class, and gender relations. The feminist movement, for example, was primarily influenced early on by white, middle-class women. The labor movement had an early history of excluding minorities and women, and their causes; in some areas, this antagonism continues. Membership in one microculture often conflicts with the interests of another.

One microculture may have a greater influence on identity than others. This influence may change over time and depends on life experiences. We can shed aspects of our microcultures that no longer have meaning, and we can also adopt or adapt aspects of other microcultures that were not inherent in our upbringing. Identity is not fixed; we can learn alternative views of self and culture (Hoffman, 1996).

The region of the country in which we have lived provides a cultural context for living. Our culture also may adjust differently to living in urban, rural, and suburban areas. Because we have grown up in the same or similar geographic areas does not mean we have experienced the places in the same ways as our neighbors or friends. Some members of the community have lived there for much longer than others. The area takes on a different meaning based on a member's race, ethnicity, religion, age, and language, and how membership in those groups is viewed by other members of the community. One's job and educational background may take on different significance in one geographic area as compared to another.

Different individuals and groups interpret places differently (Massey, 1997). Some find a locale to be the ideal place to live and raise a family; others feel isolated, crowded, or entrapped. Mountains are critical to the well-being of some; others feel the need to be near bodies of water or the desert or greenery. Wide-open spaces where one can live for long periods of time with little interaction with others provide freedom for some, but boredom and confinement for others. Cities can be exciting and stimulating places for some, but stifling and impersonal for others. Thus, places provide complex multiple identities for the people who live in them. Although the place helps us understand students and families, we cannot assume that it has the same meaning from person to person or group to group.

Regional differences become apparent to educators as they move from one area to another to work. Sometimes local and regional differences will be hardly noticeable. At other times, they will lead to a number of adjustments in the way one lives, the content that can be taught in the classroom, and interactions in the community. Not only do teachers move around the country and globe, but so do students and their families, especially if they are in the military or on the fast track at a multinational corporation. Students may experience cultural shock that should be considered as they settle into a new school. To meet the needs of students, educators must be aware of the influences of geography and space on the culture of the people who live there.

The degree to which individuals identify with their microcultural memberships and the related cultural characteristics determines, to a great extent, their individual cultural identities. For example, a 25-year-old, middle-class, Catholic, Polish American woman in Chicago may identify strongly with being Catholic and Polish American when she is married and living in a Polish American community. However, other microcultural memberships may have a greater impact on her identity after she has divorced and becomes totally responsible for her financial

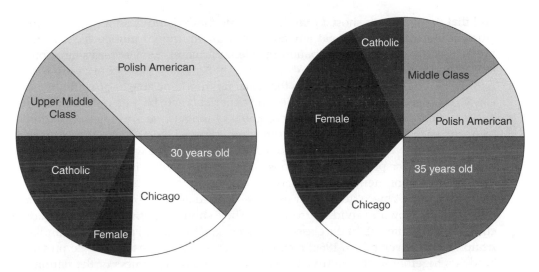

Figure 1–2
Cultural identity is adapted and changed throughout life in response to political, economic, educational, and social experiences that either alter or reinforce one's status or position in society. Membership in some microcultural groups may take on more importance than others at different periods of life, as shown here for a woman when she was 30 years old and married, and again when she was 35, divorced, and a single mother.

well-being. Her femaleness and class status may become the most important representations in her identity. This change in identity is characterized in Figure 1–2.

The interaction of these microcultures within the macroculture is also important. Most political, business, educational, and social institutions (e.g., the courts, the welfare system, the city government) have been developed and controlled by the dominant group. The values and practices that have been internalized by the dominant group also are inherent within these institutions. Members of oppressed groups are usually beholden to the dominant group to share in that power.

The interaction of these microcultures with each other and with the dominant culture begins to answer the questions "Who am I?" and "Who are my students?" The various microcultures that educators are likely to confront in a classroom are examined in detail in Chapters 2 through 8.

EQUALITY AND SOCIAL JUSTICE IN A DEMOCRACY

Schools and the mass media teach us that the United States is a democracy to be emulated by the rest of the world. The democracy was designed to promote the good of all its citizens. Thus, the Constitution was fashioned with a coherent set of "checks and balances" to limit the systematic abuse of power. We are told that egalitarianism is a key principle on which democracy is based. We learn that everyone has a voice and that no one group should forever dominate the economic, political, social, and cultural life of the country. Society and government, though not perfect, are promoted as allowing mass participation and steady advancement toward a more prosperous and egalitarian society.

One strength of a democracy is that citizens should be able to bring many perspectives, based on their own histories and experiences, to bear on policy questions and practices. Thus, to disagree is acceptable as long as we are able to communicate with each other openly and without fear of reprisal. Further, we expect that no single right way will be forced on us. For the most part, we would rather struggle with multiple perspectives and actions and determine what is best for us as individuals within this democratic society.

At the same time, a democracy expects its citizens to be concerned about more than just their own individual freedoms. They should be involved in a broader community of interest. In the classic *Democracy and Education,* philosopher and educator John Dewey (1916/1966) suggested that our emphasis should be on what binds us together in cooperative pursuits and results, regardless of the nation or our group alliance and membership. He raised concern about our possible stratification into separate classes and called for "intellectual opportunities [to be] accessible to all on equitable and easy terms" (p. 88).

The emphasis on individualism in the dominant culture provides a dilemma for educators who promote democratic practice. In many classrooms, individualism is supported through competitive activities in which individual achievement is rewarded. A democratic classroom promotes working together across groups. Responsibility and leadership is shared by students and teachers as students practice being active participants in a democratic setting.

Both individualism and equality have long been central themes of political discourse in a democratic society. The meaning of equality within our society varies according to one's assumptions about humankind and human existence. At least two sets of beliefs govern the ideologies of equality and inequality. The first accepts inequality as inevitable and promotes meritocracy. It stresses the right of access to society's resources as a necessary condition for equal rights to life, liberty, and happiness. The focus is on individualism and the individual's right to pursue happiness and obtain personal resources. The second set of beliefs supports a much greater degree of equality across groups in society.

This dilemma forces some people to promote some equality while preventing any real equity from occurring. Affirmative action, for example, is viewed as evidence of group welfare gaining precedence over individual achievement. The outcry against affirmative action suggests that racism no longer exists and that decisions about employment, promotion, and so forth are no longer influenced by racism and sexism. Whites filing for reverse discrimination decisions believe that their individual rights to an education at a select school, a promotion, or a job should be based solely on their individual achievement. They believe that other factors such as income (or lack of), ethnicity, race, or gender should not be valued in the process. They overlook the fact that they have probably been advantaged throughout their lives because of their race and family income.

Even though egalitarianism is an often-espoused goal of democracy in the United States, the inequities that actually exist in society are continually over-looked. Thus, equality must be an essential tenet of multicultural education.

Individualism and Meritocracy

Proponents of *meritocracy* accept the theories of sociobiology or functionalism or both, in which inequalities are viewed as natural outcomes of individual differences. Oppressed groups usually are seen as inferior, and their hardships are blamed on their personal characteristics.

A society based on meritocracy ensures that the ablest and most meritorious, ambitious, hardworking, and talented individuals will acquire the most, achieve the most, and become society's leaders. Proponents accept the resulting inequalities as tolerable, fair, and just. They are viewed as a necessary consequence of equality of opportunity and roughly in proportion to inequalities of merit.

The belief system that undergirds meritocracy has at least three dimensions that are consistent with dominant values. First, the individual is valued over the group. The individual has the qualities, ambitions, and talent to achieve at the highest levels in society. Popular stories expound this ideology as they describe

Students do not start life with an equal chance to succeed. Because of family income and wealth, some students have access to resources and experiences in their homes, communities, and often schools that are not available to most low income students.

the poor immigrant who arrived on our shores with nothing, set up a vegetable stand to eke out a living, and became the millionaire owner of a chain of grocery stores.

The second dimension stresses differences through competition. IQ and achievement tests are used throughout schooling to help measure differences. Students and adults are rewarded for outstanding grades, athletic ability, and artistic accomplishment.

The third dimension emphasizes internal characteristics, such as motivation, intuition, and character, that have been internalized by the individual. External conditions, such as racism and poverty, are to be overcome by the individual; they are not accepted as contributors to an individual's lack of success.

Equal educational opportunity, or equal access to schooling, applies this principle to education. All students are to be provided with equal educational opportunities that supposedly will give them similar chances for success or failure. Proponents of this approach believe it is the individual's responsibility to use those opportunities to his or her advantage in obtaining life's resources and benefits. Critics of meritocracy would point out that children of low-income families do not start with the same chances for success in life as children from affluent families. Thus, competition is unequal from birth. The chances of the affluent child being educationally and financially successful are much greater than for the low-income child. Those with advantages at birth are almost always able to hold onto and extend those advantages throughout their lives.

Equality

With the persistence of racism, poverty, unemployment, chronic crisis, and inequality in major social systems such as education and health, many persons have found it difficult to reconcile daily realities with the publicized egalitarianism that characterizes the public rhetoric. These persons view U.S. society as comprised of institutions and an economic system that represents the interests of the privileged few, rather than the pluralistic majority. Even where institutions, laws, and processes have the appearance of equal access, benefit, and protection, they are almost always enforced in highly discriminatory ways. These patterns of inequality are not the product of corrupt individuals as such, but rather are a reflection of how resources of economics, political power, and cultural and social dominance are built into the entire political-economic system.

Even in the optimistic view that some degree of equality can be achieved, inequality is also expected. Not all resources can be redistributed so that every individual has an equal amount, nor should all individuals expect equal compensation for the work they do. The underlying belief, however, is that there need not be the huge disparities of income, wealth, and power that currently exist. Equality does suggest fairness in the distribution of the conditions and goods that affect the well-being of all children and families. It is fostered by policies for full employment, wages that prevent families from living in poverty, and child care for all children.

Critics decry the perceived socialism as being against the democratic foundations that undergird the nation. They believe that equality of resources and societal benefits would undermine the capitalist system that allows a few individuals to

VIDEO INSIGHT

School Busing

For decades the remedy for segregation has been school busing. The goals of integrating schools has been racial balance and access to better schools, new equipment, and new opportunities for all students. Now some African American families are criticizing the busing experiment as a failure and are requesting a "separate but equal" education for their children in their own neighborhoods.

In this video segment, you will see proponents of this movement in Oklahoma City and in other cities across the country say their children have been subjected to segregated settings within integrated schools. African American children are often assigned to remedial classes or lower academic tracks and do not get exposure to the services and resources that other students receive. In addition, because these schools are not close to home, it is difficult for parents to be involved or even present if there is a problem or an emergency at school.

After viewing this video segment, how have your views on busing changed? Are the people who support this movement to neighborhood schools forsaking the efforts of the countless individuals who have worked so hard for integration in our schools? History has shown us that "separate but equal" has not worked. Is this because separate, by definition, is not equal? What are your views on the issue of "separate but equal"? Do you think we now have the resources, support, and technology to make "separate but equal" a reality?

acquire the great majority of those resources. They warn that equality of results would limit freedom and liberty for individuals.

Equality should mean more than just providing oppressed group members with an equal chance. One proposal is that equal results should be the goal. These results might be more equal achievement by students of both oppressed and dominant groups and similar rates of dropping out of school, college attendance, and college completion by different ethnic, racial, gender, and class populations.

Traditionally, the belief has been that education can overcome the inequalities that exist in society. The role of education in reducing the amount of occupation and income inequality may be limited, however. School reform has not yet led to significant social changes outside the schools. Equalizing educational opportunity has had very little impact on making adults more equal. Providing equal educational opportunities for all students does not guarantee equal results at the end of a specific number of years in school. Equality requires financial support for providing quality instruction in environments that are conducive to learning to all students. More, not less, money may be needed to ensure equity in educational results by the children of dominant groups and other groups.

To establish equality, major changes in society must take place. This process is very difficult when power is held by those who believe in a meritocratic system. Those in power defend the status quo and are not anxious to relinquish the privileges they have gained. In contrast, the advocates for equality support the dictum: *from each according to his or her ability, to each according to his or her needs.*

To answer these questions online, go to the Pause to Reflect module for this chapter of the Companion Website.

PAUSE TO REFLECT

How do you view equality in society and schooling? Check the statements below that best describe your perceptions.

1. *The ablest and most meritorious, ambitious, hardworking, and talented individuals should acquire the most, achieve the most, and become society's leaders.*
2. *The individual is more important than the group.*
3. *The U.S. economic system represents the interests of a privileged few, rather than those of the pluralistic majority.*
4. *Huge disparities of income, wealth, and power should not exist in this country.*
5. *It is the student's responsibility to get as much out of school as possible.*
6. *Differences measured on standardized tests are more important than similarities.*
7. *External conditions, such as racism and poverty, should be overcome by the individual.*
8. *Students from all cultural groups can be academically successful.*
9. *Tracking of students promotes inequality.*
10. *Teachers can make a difference in the academic success of students.*

Which of these statements are most related to a belief in meritocracy, and which to a belief in equality?

Social Justice

Social justice is another element of democracy. It speaks to the care of those persons in society who are not as advantaged as others. To not ensure that they are treated equitably and with dignity is a disservice to democracy. Dewey (1966) called for social justice when he said, "What the best and wisest parent wants for his [or her] own child, that must the community want for all of its children. Any other ideal for our schools is narrow and unlovely; acted upon, it destroys our democracy" (p. 3). In schools, social justice requires "that schools provide equal access to and equal receipt of a quality education for all students. Any structures or practices that interfere with the simultaneous goals of equity and excellence, that perpetuate preexisting social and economic inequities, are subject to critique and elimination" (Sirotnik, 1990, p. 310). In a democratic society that is also capitalistic in nature, there are always inequities. In the United States, it would be difficult to recall a period of time when there were no individuals with enormous wealth and none who lived in abject poverty. Most who live in this country do so by choice. Two thirds of the world's immigrants come to this country. This is not surprising because the United States is perceived as the land of opportunities.

Enormous disparities exist, however, between the very wealthy and the very poor. The very wealthy have accumulated such vast resources that, for some, it would be difficult to spend all that they have. At the same time, the very poor cannot even meet their basic needs. They are often unable to obtain the barest essentials for shelter, food, or medical care. Some suffer from lack of heat in the winter and lack of cooling in the very hot summers. Every year, there are reports of elderly poor people who die from exposure to excessive heat or cold. This is inconceivable for many Americans who simply turn their thermostats to the precise temperature that will meet their comfort level. Every day, children from poor families come to school with insufficient sleep because of the physical discomforts of their homes, with inadequate clothing, and with empty stomachs. Tens of thousands suffer from malnutrition and no dental care. When they are sick, many go untreated. Under these conditions, it is difficult, at best, to function well in an academic setting.

Civil unrest has almost always been precipitated by the disenfranchised who have no realistic hope of extricating themselves from lives of despair. Children of affluent members of society do not form street gangs; they are typically much too busy enjoying the good life that prosperity brings. The street gangs of New York, Chicago, and Los Angeles are comprised almost exclusively of young individuals who are poor, embittered, and disenfranchised.

Those who have the power to bring about meaningful change in society are usually the more affluent. They have the resources and connections to make things happen. Yet, those who have such power are reluctant to make any significant changes that threaten to diminish their position in society. To bring about truly meaningful change requires paradigm shifts. Even the middle class may be reluctant to make changes if a change in the status quo diminishes their position. Individuals want changes only if the changes provide benefits to them or do not affect them negatively.

Meaningful change in society requires a universal social consciousness. It requires, to some extent, a willingness of the citizenry to explore the means of redistributing some of the benefits of a democratic society. Effective redistribution would require that some who have considerable wealth provide a greater share in the effort to eliminate poverty and its concomitant effects. Even the middle class would be expected to make proportionate sacrifices. The end result should be a society in which everyone has a decent place to sleep, no child comes to school hungry, and appropriate health care is available to all.

Those who possess special skills and talents will likely continue to accrue, in varying degrees, the benefits of a democratic society. In the United States, most citizens want incentives for achievements. In such a society, however, no one need be disenfranchised, and the allure of street gangs and other means of expressing discontent will be diminished.

One of the problems is that people of color, women, and low-income groups have long been recipients of institutional discrimination in the United States. As a result, many exhibit anger at, dissatisfaction with, and alienation from the system.

Racism, sexism, and class inequality characterize societies in which the disparities of income, wealth, and power are great. Competition over resources increases conflicts among the various groups. Thus, fundamental changes in the structure of society must accompany changes in attitudes if border crossings are to become a reality. Addressing issues of equality is a key to such changes.

MULTICULTURAL EDUCATION

Multicultural education is not a new concept. It has evolved from concepts that have existed since the 1920s, when educators began writing about and training others in intercultural education and ethnic studies. The movement during the first two decades had an international emphasis with antecedents in the pacifist movement. Some textbooks were rewritten with an international point of view. Proponents encouraged teachers to make their disciplines more relevant to the modern world by being more issue oriented. The goal was to make the dominant majority populations more tolerant and accepting toward first- and second-generation immigrants in order to maintain national unity and social control (Montalto, 1978).

In the 1960s, desegregation was being enforced in the nation's schools. At the same time, differences were being described as deficits. Students of color and whites from low-income families were described as culturally deprived. Their families were blamed for not providing them with the cultural capital that would help them succeed in schools. Programs like Head Start, compensatory education, and special education were developed to compensate for these shortcomings. Not surprisingly, those classes were filled with students of color, in poverty, or with disabilities.

By the 1970s, oppressed groups were described as culturally different to acknowledge that they did have a culture but that it was different from the culture of the dominant group. The goal of the approach to teach the exceptional and culturally different was to help them develop the cultural patterns of the dominant society so that they could fit into the mainstream (Sleeter , 1999).

The civil rights movement brought a renewed interest in ethnic studies, discrimination, and intergroup relations. Racial and ethnic pride emerged from oppressed groups, creating a demand for African American and other ethnic studies programs in colleges and universities across the country. Later, similar programs were established in secondary schools.

Students and participants in ethnic studies programs of the 1960s and early 1970s were primarily members of the group being studied. Programs focused on the various ethnic histories and cultures, with the main objective of providing students with insight and instilling pride in their own ethnic backgrounds. Most of these programs were ethnic-specific, and only one ethnic group was studied. Sometimes the objectives included an understanding of the relationship and conflict between the ethnic group and the dominant or majority population, but seldom was a program's scope multiethnic.

Concurrent with the civil rights movement and the growth of ethnic studies, emphasis on intergroup or human relations again emerged. Often, these programs accompanied ethnic studies content for teachers. The objectives were again to promote intergroup, and especially interracial, understanding and to reduce or eliminate stereotypes. This approach emphasized the affective level—teachers' attitudes and feelings about themselves and others (Sleeter, 1999).

With the growth and development of ethnic studies came a realization that those programs alone would not guarantee support for the positive affirmation of cultural diversity and differences in this country. Students from the dominant culture also needed to learn about the history, culture, and contributions of oppressed groups. Thus, ethnic studies expanded into multiethnic studies. Teachers were encouraged to develop curricula that included the contributions of oppressed groups along with those of the dominant group. Textbooks were to be rewritten to represent more accurately the multiethnic nature of the United States. Students were to be exposed to perspectives of oppressed groups through literature, history, music, and other disciplines integrated throughout the general school program.

During this period, other groups that had suffered from institutional discrimination called their needs to the attention of the public. These groups included women, persons with low incomes, persons with disabilities, English language learners, and the elderly. Educators responded by expanding multiethnic education to the more encompassing concept of *multicultural education*. This broader concept focused on the different microcultures to which individuals belong, with an emphasis on the interaction of membership in the microcultures, especially race, ethnicity, class, and gender. It also called for the elimination of discrimination against individuals because of their group membership. No longer was it fashionable to fight sexism without simultaneously attacking racism, classism, homophobia, and discrimination against children, the elderly, and persons with disabilities.

Still, after eight decades of concern for civil and human rights in education, educators struggle with the management of cultural diversity and provision of equality in schools. Some classrooms may be desegregated and mainstreamed, and both boys and girls may now participate in athletic activities. However, a disproportionate number of students who are African American, Mexican American, Puerto Rican, American Indian, and some Asian American groups score below European American students on national standardized tests. The number of female, students of color, and low-income students participating in advanced science and mathematics classes is not proportionate to their representation in schools. They too often are offered little or no encouragement to enroll in advanced courses that are necessary to be successful in college.

In a country that champions equal rights and the opportunity for an individual to improve his or her conditions, educators should be concerned with helping all students achieve academically, socially, and politically. It is impossible to teach all students in the classroom equally because they are not the same. They have different needs, skills, and experiences that must be recognized in developing educational programs. Each student is different because of physical and mental abilities, gender, ethnicity, race, language, religion, class, and age. Students behave differently in school and toward authority because of cultural factors and their relationship to the dominant society. As educators, we behave in certain ways toward students because of our own cultural experiences within the power structure of the country.

When educators are given the responsibilities of a classroom, they need the knowledge and skills for working effectively in a diverse society. An educational concept that addresses cultural diversity and equality in schools is multicultural education. This concept is based on the following fundamental beliefs and assumptions:

- Cultural differences have strength and value.
- Schools should be models for the expression of human rights and respect for cultural differences.
- Social justice and equality for all people should be of paramount importance in the design and delivery of curricula.
- Attitudes and values necessary for the continuation of a democratic society can be promoted in schools.
- Schooling can provide the knowledge, dispositions, and skills for the redistribution of power and income among diverse groups.
- Educators working with families and communities can create an environment that is supportive of multiculturalism.

Many concepts undergird multicultural education. The relationships and interactions among individuals and groups are essential to understanding and working effectively with different cultural groups. Educators should understand racism, sexism, prejudice, discrimination, oppression, powerlessness, power, inequality, equality, and stereotyping. Multicultural education includes various components that often manifest themselves in courses, units of courses, and degree programs. These components include ethnic studies, global studies, bilingual education, women's studies, human relations, special education, and urban education.

For multicultural education to become a reality in the formal school situation, the total environment must reflect a commitment to multicultural education. Sleeter (1999) refers to this commitment as *education that is multicultural.* What would be the characteristics of a school that is multicultural? The composition of the faculty, administration, and other staff would accurately reflect the pluralistic composition of the United States. Differences in academic achievement levels would disappear between males and females, dominant and oppressed group members, and upper-middle-class and low-income students. The school curriculum would incorporate the contributions of many cultural groups and integrate multiple perspectives throughout it. Instructional materials would be free of biases, omissions, and stereotypes. Cultural differences would be treated as differences, rather than as deficiencies that must be addressed in compensatory programs. Students would be able to use their own cultural resources and voices to develop new skills and to critically explore subject matter. Students would learn to recognize and confront inequities in school and society. The faculty, administrators, and other staff would see themselves as learners enhanced and changed by understanding, affirming, and reflecting cultural diversity. Teachers and administrators would be able to deal with questions of race and intergroup relations and controversial realities on an objective, frank, and professional basis.

Multicultural educators believe that all students have the right to learn and can learn. Each subject area is taught from a multicultural perspective. Teachers draw representations from students' cultures and experiences to engage them actively in learning. Skills to function effectively in different cultural settings are taught. For students to function effectively in a democratic society, they must learn about the inequities that currently exist. As teachers, counselors, and principals, we serve as the transmitters of our culture to children and youth. We should have the courage to try new methods and techniques, the courage to challenge ineffective and inequitable procedures and policies, and the strength to change schools to ensure learning and equity for all students.

Summary

Culture provides the blueprint that determines the way an individual thinks, feels, and behaves in society. We are not born with culture, but rather learn it through enculturation and socialization. It is manifested through societal institutions, lived experiences, and the individual's fulfillment of psychological and basic needs.

Historically, U.S. political and social institutions have developed from a Western European tradition and still function under the strong influence of that heritage. At the same time, many aspects of American life have been greatly influenced by the numerous cultural groups that make up the U.S. population. The dominant culture is based on its White, Anglo-Saxon, Protestant roots and the core values of individualism and freedom. Assimilation is the process by which groups adopt or change the dominant culture. Schools have traditionally served as the transmitter of the dominant culture to all students regardless of their cultural backgrounds and differences from the dominant group.

Individuals also belong to a number of microcultures with cultural patterns that differ from that of the dominant group. Cultural identity is based on the interaction and influence of membership in microcultures based on ethnic origin, race, religion, gender, age, class, native language, geographic region, and abilities. Membership in a single microculture can greatly affect one's identity with the others. Some religions, for example, dictate the norms for the behavior of men and women, children and adults, as well as the treatment of members of other groups. The theory of cultural pluralism promotes the maintenance of the distinct differences among cultural groups.

A democracy should recognize the differences in society and provide social justice for all of its people. Egalitarianism and equality have long been espoused as goals for society, but they are implemented from two perspectives. The emphasis on individualism is supported in a meritocratic system in which everyone is alleged to start out equally and the most deserving will end up with the most rewards. Equality, in contrast, seeks to ensure that society's benefits and rewards are distributed more equitably among individuals and groups.

Multicultural education is a concept that incorporates cultural differences and provides equality in schools. For it to become a reality in the formal school situation, the total environment must reflect a commitment to multicultural education.

The diverse cultural backgrounds and microcultural memberships of students and families are as important in developing effective instructional strategies as are their physical and mental capabilities. Further, educators must understand the influence of racism, sexism, and classism on the lives of their students and ensure that these are not perpetuated in the classroom.

Questions for Review

To answer these questions online, go to the Chapter Questions module for this chapter of the Companion Website.

1. What is culture? How is culture determined?
2. What are microcultures? Give examples of microcultural memberships that have the greatest impact on your identity.
3. What are the implicit and explicit differences between dominant and oppressed cultural groups?
4. What are cultural borders? How do they help us understand differences in classroom settings?
5. How do meritocracy and individualism conflict with the ideal of equality?
6. How does multicultural education differ from multiethnic studies and intercultural education?
7. What is the danger of stereotyping students on the basis of their membership in only one microculture?
8. Why is multicultural education as important to students of the dominant culture as to students of other cultures?

Web Resources

To link to the following websites, go to the Web Resources module for this chapter of the Companion Website.

The website of the Children's Defense Fund (CDF) includes data about the status of children in the United States and information on CDF's programs and activist work on the behalf of children.

The website of the National Association for Multicultural Education connects users to a network of teachers, parents, and others supporting the goals of multicultural education.

References

Bellah, R. N., Madsen, R., Sullivan, W. M., Swidler, A., & Tipton, S. M. (1985). *Habits of the heart: Individualism and commitment in American life.* New York: Harper & Row.

Boyd, D. (1996, Fall). Dominance concealed through diversity: Implications of inadequate perspectives on cultural pluralism. *Harvard Educational Review, 66*(3), 609–630.

Dewey, J. (1966). *Democracy and education: An introduction to the philosophy of education.* New York: Free Press. (Original work published 1916)

Eck, D. L. (2000). Religious pluralism in America in the year 2000. In E. W. Linder, *Yearbook of American and Canadian churches 2000.* Nashville, TN: Abingdon Press.

Erickson, F. (1997). Culture in society and in educational practices. In J. A. Banks & C. A. M. Banks (Eds.), *Multicultural education: Issues and perspectives* (3rd ed., pp. 32–60). Needham Heights, MA: Allyn & Bacon.

Giroux, H. A. (1988). *Teachers as intellectuals: Toward a critical pedagogy of learning.* Granby, MA: Bergin & Garvey.

Giroux, H. A. (1994). Living dangerously: Identity politics and the new cultural racism. In H. A. Giroux & P. McLaren (Eds.), *Between borders: Pedagogy and the politics of cultural studies* (pp. 29–55). New York: Routledge.

Goodenough, W. (1987). Multi-culturalism as the normal human experience. In E. M. Eddy & W. L. Partridge (Eds.), *Applied anthropology in America* (2nd ed.). New York: Columbia University Press.

Gordon, M. M. (1964). *Assimilation in American life: The role of race, religion, and national origins.* New York: Oxford University Press.

Hoffman, D. M. (1996, Fall). Culture and self in multicultural education: Reflections on discourse, text, and practice. *American Educational Research Journal, 33*(3), 545–569.

Lasley, T. J. (1996, October). The fabric of peace: Adults create the patterns. *Journal for a Just and Caring Education, 2*(4), 360–377.

Lorde, A. (1995). Age, race, class, and sex: Women redefining difference. In J. Arthur & A. Shapiro (Eds.), *Campus wars: Multiculturalism and the politics of difference* (pp. 191–198). Boulder, CO: Westview Press.

Massey, D. (1997). Space/power, identity/difference: Tensions in the city. In A. Merrifield & E. Swyngedouw, *The urbanization of injustice.* New York: New York University Press.

McLaren, P. (1995). *Critical pedagogy and predatory culture.* New York: Routledge.

Montalto, N. V. (1978). The forgotten dream: A history of the intercultural education movement, 1924–1941. *Dissertation Abstracts International, 39A,* 1061. (University Microfilms No. 78–13436)

Pai, Y. (1990). *Cultural foundations of education.* Upper Saddle River, NJ: Merrill.

Pai, Y. & Adler, S. A. (2001). *Cultural foundations of education.* (3rd ed.) Upper Saddle River, NJ: Merrill.

Pratte, R. (1979). *Pluralism in education: Conflict, clarity, and commitment.* Springfield, IL: Charles C. Thomas.

Sirotnik, K. A. (1990). Society, schooling, teaching, and preparing to teach. In J. I. Goodlad, R. Soder, & K. A. Sirotnik (Eds.), *The moral dimensions of teaching* (pp. 296–327). San Francisco: Jossey-Bass.

Sleeter, C. E. (1999). *Making choices for multicultural education: Five approaches to race, class, and gender* (3rd ed.). New York: John Wiley & Sons.

Spradley, J. P., & Rynkiewich, M. A. (Eds.). (1975). *The nacirema: Readings on American culture.* Boston: Little, Brown.

Suggested Readings

Arthur, J., & Shapiro, A. (1995). *Campus wars: Multiculturalism and the politics of difference.* Boulder, CO: Westview Press.

This collection addresses the most controversial issues with which colleges were struggling at the end of the last decade—the content of the curriculum, date rape, freedom of speech, and affirmative action.

Hooks, B. (1994). *Teaching to transgress: Education as the practice of freedom.* New York: Routledge.

Using passion and politics, this teacher promotes education that helps students cross racial, sexual, and class boundaries in the practice of freedom.

Rethinking our classrooms: Teaching for equity and justice. (1994). Milwaukee, WI: Rethinking Schools.

Teachers' narratives include teaching ideas and hands-on examples of ways teachers can promote values of community, justice, and equality while ensuring that students build academic skills. The book emphasizes critical thinking, critical practice, and effective classrooms.

Smelser, N. J., & Alexander, J. C. (1999). *Diversity and its discontents: Cultural conflict and common ground in contemporary American society.* Princeton NY: Princeton University Press.

Sociologists, political theorists, and social historians explore the issues of culture wars, multiculturalism, moral majority, and family values and their relationship to cultural conflict from their various perspectives.

CRITICAL INCIDENTS IN TEACHING

General Multicultural Education

Esther Greenberg is a teacher with Asian and African American students in an alternative education class. Ms. Greenberg's college roommate was Chinese American and she remembers fondly her visit to her roommate's home during the lunar New Year. She remembers how the parents and other Chinese adults had given all the children, including her, money wrapped in red paper, which was to bring all of the recipients good luck in the New Year. Ms. Greenberg thought that it would be a nice gesture to give the students in her class the red paper envelopes as an observance of the upcoming lunar New Year. Since she was unable to give the students money, she took gold-foil covered coins (given to Jewish children) and wrapped these coins in red paper to give to her students.

Unfortunately, on the lunar New Years Day, all of the African American students were pulled out of class for a full day of testing. All of the remaining students were her Asian students. When she passed out the red envelopes, the students were surprised and touched by her sensitivity to cherished custom.

When her administrator, who was not a person of color, was told what Ms. Greenberg had done, he became enraged. He accused her of favoritism to the Asian students and of deliberately leaving out the African American students. When she tried to convince him otherwise, he responded that she had no right to impose Asian customs on African American students. She responded that this was an important Asian custom, and that the Asian students had participated in the observance of Martin Luther King's birthday. However, he continued his attack saying that this was Asian superstition bordering on a religious observance. She was threatened with discipline.

To answer these questions online, go to the Critical Incidents module for this chapter of the Companion Website.

Questions for Discussion

1. Were Esther Greenberg's actions inappropriate for a public school classroom? If so, why? If no, why not? Was this a violation of the principles of church and state?
2. Did Ms. Greenberg create problems for herself by giving out the red envelopes when the African American students were absent from class? Did this create an appearance of favoritism of one racial group over the other?
3. How could Ms. Greenberg have handled the situation to make it a pleasing experience to all concerned?
4. Was the administrator the one who was out of line, and was Ms. Greenberg simply a victim?

Chapter 2

Class

According to our textbook rhetoric, Americans abhor the notion of a social order in which economic privilege and political power are determined by hereditary class. Officially, we have a more enlightened goal in sight: namely, a society in which a family's wealth has no relation to the probability of future educational attainment and the wealth and station it affords. By this standard, education offered to poor children should be at least as good as that which is provided to the children of the upper-middle class.

Jonathan Kozol, 1991

While he was still in college, Tomas Juarez had decided that he wanted to work with children from low-income families. He began his teaching career, however, in a culturally diverse suburban school. The school had been built only a few years before and included the most modern science labs. Students were expected to be proficient with computers; they even helped Mr. Juarez develop his skills. Most of the students participated in extracurricular activities, and their parents were active in school affairs. More than 90% of the previous graduating class had enrolled in post-secondary programs. It was a pleasure to work with a team of teachers who planned interesting lessons that were based on a constructivist approach, engaged students in the content, and developed higher-order thinking skills.

After a few years, Mr. Juarez decided that he was ready to take on the challenge of an inner-city school where most students were members of oppressed groups. As soon as he stepped into his new school, he realized that he had been spoiled in the suburbs.

First, the smell wasn't right and the halls were dirty even though it was the beginning of the school year. The room that was to be his classroom did not have enough chairs for all of the students who had been assigned to the class. Not only did the room look as if it had not been repainted for 20 years, but several window panes were covered with a cardboard-like material, and numerous ceiling tiles were missing. His first thought was that both he and the students would be exposed to asbestos and lead poisoning throughout the year. Outside, the playground was almost worse. There was no grass, the stench from local factories was overpowering, and the football field did not even have goalposts.

During Mr. Juarez's first few weeks, he found that the students were terrific. They were enthusiastic about being back in school, and they seemed to like him. He had only enough textbooks for half the class, however, and no money in the budget to purchase more. Chalk was limited, and most of the audiovisual equipment had been stolen the previous year and never replaced.

Why were conditions at Mr. Juarez's new school so much different from those in the suburban school? How can a teacher overcome environmental conditions that are not supportive of effective learning? What are the chances of the new students being academically successful in the same way as the students in the suburban school? Why are students in the urban school more likely to drop out, become pregnant, and not attend college? Why has society allowed some students to go to school under such appallingly poor conditions?

CLASS STRUCTURE

The two views of equality in U.S. society that were outlined in Chapter 1 suggest different class structures in the country. One view accepts the objective existence of different socioeconomic levels or classes in society. It also strongly supports the notion that one can be socially mobile and can move to a higher class by getting an education and working hard. Groups that have not yet achieved upper-middle-class status are usually seen as inferior. The hardships faced by low-income families are blamed on their lack of middle-class values and behaviors. It is the individual's fault for not moving up the class ladder—a phenomenon called *blaming the victim*.

In the second view of U.S. society, distinct class divisions are recognized. Those individuals and families who own and control corporations, banks, and other means of production comprise the privileged upper class. The professional and managerial elite "constitute a new class only in the sense that their livelihoods rest not so much on the ownership of property as on the manipulation of information and professional expertise" (Lasch, 1995, p. 34). Persons who earn a living primarily by selling their labor make up other middle and working classes. Another class includes those persons who are unable to work or who can find work only sporadically. Although some individuals are able to move from one class level to another, chances are limited. Those who control most of the resources and those who have few of the resources are dichotomous groups in a class struggle.

Most people are caught in the socioeconomic strata into which they were born, and the political-economic system ensures that they remain there. Certainly some individuals have been socially and economically mobile. Stories about athletes, coaches, movie stars, and singers are recounted during sporting events and in newspaper and television accounts. Few people, however, have abilities that translate into the high salaries of elite stars of the entertainment world. A college education is the most reliable means for moving from a low-income to a middle-class and higher status.

Family background has been found to account for a large part of the variation in educational and occupational attainment; the opportunity to achieve equally is thwarted before one is born. Individuals born into a wealthy family are likely to achieve wealth; individuals born into a low-income family will have difficulty achieving wealth no matter how hard they work. Therefore, families do everything possible to protect their wealth to guarantee that their children can have the *good life*. The inequalities that exist in society often lead to the perpetuation of inequalities.

Most people, if asked, could identify themselves by class. Whereas they do not strongly vocalize their identity with a specific class, they participate socially and occupationally within a class structure. Their behavior and value system may be based on a strong ethnic or religious identification, but that specific identification is greatly influenced by class. The first generation of a group that has moved to the middle class may continue to interact at a primary level with friends and relatives who are in the working class and underclass. Time and differences in circumstances, however, often lead to the reduction of those cross-class ties.

Most U.S. citizens exhibit and articulate less concern about class consciousness than many of their European counterparts. Nevertheless, many have participated in class actions, such as strikes or work stoppages to further the interests of the class to which they belong. Class consciousness, or solidarity with others at the same socioeconomic level, may not be so pronounced here because overall improvement in the standard of living has occurred at all levels, especially during the period from 1940 to the early 1970s and again in the 1990s. In addition, the dominant cultural values and belief systems emphasize the individual's personal responsibility for his or her class position.

SOCIAL STRATIFICATION

Social stratification ranks individuals and families on the basis of their income, education, occupation, wealth, and power in society. It is possible because consistent and recurring relationships exist between people who occupy different levels of the social structure. Many individuals accept and follow socially defined positions based on occupation, race, gender, and class, for which patterns of behavior have been institutionalized. However, civil rights organizations, including women's organizations, try to combat the institutionalized acceptance and expectation of status for specific groups of people.

Inequality results, in part, from differential rankings within the division of labor. Different occupations are evaluated and rewarded unequally. Some jobs are viewed as more worthy, more important, more popular, and more preferable than others. Finally, the rewards and evaluations of higher-ranking positions produce common interests among people who hold those positions, who then restrict others' chances of obtaining the same status—a key to establishing and maintaining a system of stratification.

Many people in the United States receive high or low rankings in the social stratification system on the basis of characteristics over which they have no control. Women, people with disabilities, the elderly, children, and people of color often receive low-prestige rankings. Ascribed status affects who is allowed entrance into the higher-ranking socioeconomic positions. Ascribed status does not ensure that all white, able-bodied men achieve a high-ranking position, however. They are found at all levels of the continuum, from a very low socioeconomic status to the highest socioeconomic status, but they and their families are overrepresented at the highest levels. Conversely, members of most oppressed groups can be found at all levels of the continuum, with a few at the top of the socioeconomic scale.

Such inequities are, in large part, a result of historical discrimination against some groups of people, as described in other chapters of this book. One's ascribed status affects one's social stratification from birth. It influences one's chances of choosing alternative courses of action, overcoming discrimination, and achieving one's goals.

SOCIOECONOMIC STATUS

How is the economic success or achievement of Americans measured? The U.S. Bureau of the Census measures the economic condition of individuals with a criterion called *socioeconomic status (SES)*. It serves as a composite of the economic status of a family or unrelated individuals on the basis of *occupation, educational attainment,* and *income*. Related to these three factors are *wealth* and *power,* which also help determine an individual's SES but are more difficult to measure through census data.

These five determinants of SES are interrelated. Although inequality has many forms, these factors are probably the most salient for the individual because they affect how one lives. A family's SES is usually observable—in the size of their home and the part of town in which they live, the schools their children attend, or the clubs to which the parents belong. Many educators place their students at specific SES levels on the basis of similar observations.

Income

Income is the amount of money earned in wages or salaries throughout a year. One way to look at income distribution is by dividing the population into fifths; the lowest one fifth earns the least income, and the highest one fifth earns the highest income. Figure 2–1 shows what percentage of total income earned in 1997 was earned by each fifth of the population, and the total wealth held by each fifth. The top 20% of the population earned 47.2% of the total income, whereas the bottom 20% earned 4.2% of the total income (U.S. Bureau of the Census, 1999). Five percent of the families in the United States earned 21% of the income received in 1997.

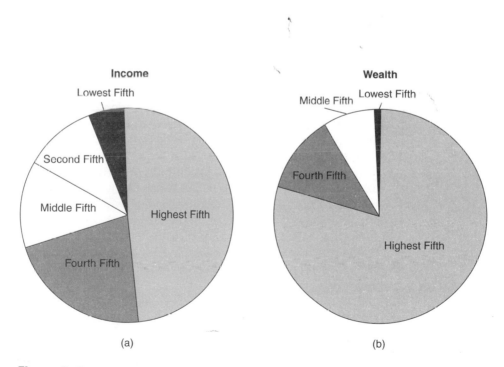

(a)   (b)

Figure 2–1
Distribution of family income and wealth in the United States by fifths of the population.

Source: (A) U.S. Census Bureau. (1999). *Statistical abstract of the United States* (119th edition). Washington, DC: U.S. Government Printing Office. (B) Rose, S. J. (2000). *Social stratification in the United States* New York: New Press.

Many people view this income inequity as a natural outcome of the American way. Because some people have achieved at a much higher level than most of the population, it is believed that they deserve to be paid more for their effort. People at the lower end of the continuum are either unemployed or work in unskilled jobs and thus are not expected to receive the same economic rewards. The degree of difference is quite large, however. The average salaries of 362 chief executive officers surveyed by *Business Week* was $2.3 million; when bonuses and long-term compensation such as stocks were included, the average salary grew to $12.4 million in 1999 (Anderson, Cavanagh, Collins, Hartman, & Yeskel, 2000). At the other end of the scale, people earning minimum wage received less than $11,000 annually. International studies are finding that the gap between high and low wages is greater in the United States than in most other industrialized countries. This situation is further exacerbated by the lack of tax policies to readjust somewhat the disparities.

Between World War II and 1973, the growth of the U.S. economy allowed incomes of workers at all levels to increase at a faster rate than expenditures. Many middle-income families were able to purchase homes, cars, boats, and luxuries for the home; often, money was left over for savings. During this period, the annual median income of all people 14 years of age and older nearly tripled, from $1,787 to $5,004. The standard of living for most of the population was markedly better in 1973 than in 1940. Beginning in 1973, however, the cost of living (the cost of housing, utilities, food, and other essentials) began to increase faster than income. Except for the wealthy, all families felt the financial pressure. No longer did they have extra income to purchase nonessentials. No longer was one full-time worker in a family enough to maintain the same standard of living. The 1990s brought another upswing in the economy. By 1997, the median annual income of a family was $44,568 (U.S. Bureau of the Census, 1999). When both husband and wife worked full-time and year-round, the median income of married couples was $69,507.

Income sets limits on the general lifestyle of a family, as well as on their general welfare. It controls the consumption patterns of a family—the number and quality of material possessions, housing, consumer goods, luxuries, savings, and diet. The house, the new car, the furnishings, the food, the clothes, and the entertainment portrayed in many television advertisements reflect an accepted pattern of living the *good life*. According to American mythology, almost every American lives this way; the few who have not attained such a lifestyle expect to do as soon as they "get on their feet." Only about 40% of the families in the United States, however, come close to that ideal.

Wealth

Although the difference in income among families is great, an examination of income alone does not indicate the vast differences in the way families live. Income figures show the amount of money earned by a family for their labors during one year, but the figures do not include the amount of money earned from investments, land, and other holdings. They do not present the net worth of a family. (Net worth is the amount of money remaining if all owned property were converted to cash and all debts were paid.) The wealth of a family includes savings accounts, insurance, corporate stock ownership, and property. Wealth provides a partial guarantee of future income and has the potential of producing additional income and wealth. However, for most families, the majority of family wealth comes from the equity value of homes and the residual value of household goods. "Almost 40 percent of the population has zero or negative net worth" (Rose, 2000, p. 40).

Whereas income can be determined from data gathered on federal income tax forms by the Internal Revenue Service, wealth is difficult to determine from these or any other standard forms. It is known, however, that the distribution of wealth is concentrated in a small percentage of the population. Ten percent of the population, with a median wealth of $483,000, holds 72% of the country's net worth, but the wealthiest clearly control the bulk of the financial assets. One percent of the population holds 38% of the assets (Rose, 2000). Figure 2–1 shows how wealth is distributed across fifths of the population. Of the richest 225 people in the world, 64% live in the United States, Canada, and Western Europe. The difference between the wealthiest and poorest in the world is shocking in its magnitude. "The combined wealth of the world's 225 richest people is the same as the annual income of the poorer half of the world population" (Smith, 2000, p. 22).

Wealth ensures some economic security for its holders even though the amount of security depends on the amount of wealth accumulated. It also enhances the power and prestige of those who possess it. Great wealth accrues power, provides an income that allows luxury, and creates values and lifestyles that are very different from most of the remainder of the population.

Occupation

Income, for most people, is determined by their occupation. Generally speaking, it is believed that income is a fair measure of occupational success—both of the importance of the occupation to society and of one's individual skill at the job. In addition to providing an income, a person's occupation is an activity that is considered important. Individuals who are unemployed often are stigmatized as noncontributing members of society who cannot take care of themselves. Even individuals with great wealth often hold a job, although additional income is unnecessary.

Just over half of today's workforce is comprised of white-collar workers—that is, people who do not do manual work. The percentage of service workers is growing, although the percentage of those who are private household workers continues to decline. Between now and 2006, the 10 fastest growing occupations will be database administrators and computer support specialists, computer engineers, systems analysts, personal and home care aides, physical and corrective therapy assistants and aides, home health aides, medical assistants, desktop publishing specialists, physical therapists, and occupational therapy assistants and aides. Special education teachers are thirteenth on the list; further down the list are speech-language pathologists and audiologists, and instructors and coaches for sports and physical training.

Within the working classes, the type of job one holds is the primary determinant of income received. The job provides a relatively objective indicator of a person's SES. It often indicates one's education, suggests the types of associates with whom one interacts, and determines the degree of authority and responsibility one has over others. It gives people both differing amounts of compensation in income and differing degrees of prestige in society.

Occupational prestige is often determined by the requirements for the job and by the characteristics of the job. The requirements for an occupation with prestige usually include more education and training. Job characteristics that add to the prestige of an occupation are rooted in the division between mental and manual labor. When the prestige of an occupation is high, fewer people gain entry into that occupation. When the prestige of an occupation is low, employees are allotted less security and income, and accessibility to that occupation is greater. Occupations with the highest prestige generally have the highest salaries.

Education

The best predictor of occupational prestige is the amount of education one acquires. Financial compensation is usually greater for occupations that require more years of education. For example, medical doctors and lawyers remain in school for several years beyond the bachelor's degree program. Many professionals and other white-collar workers have completed at least an undergraduate program at a college or university. Craft workers often earn more money than many white-collar workers, but their positions require specialized training that often takes as long to complete as a college degree.

A great discrepancy exists among the incomes of persons who have less than a high school education and those who have completed professional training after college. In 1997, the average income of a male who had not completed the ninth grade was $22,746; if he had completed four years of college or more, it was $66,393. The differential for a female was $14,957 and $41,626 (U.S. Bureau of the Census, 1999).

Education is rightfully viewed as a way to enhance one's economic status. However, impressive educational credentials are more likely to be achieved as a result of family background, rather than other factors. The higher the socioeconomic level of students' families, the greater the students' chances of finishing high school and college. College participation rates immediately after high school range "from 51.5 percent of those from families with incomes of less than $10,000 per year, to 88.3 percent of those from families with incomes of more than $75,000 per year" (Higher Educational Opportunity, 2000).

The conditions under which low-income students live often make it difficult for them to go to school instead of going to work. They often begin by attending community colleges. The greater the income of families, the greater the chances that their children will have books, magazines, and newspapers available in the home; that they will have attended plays or concerts; and that they will have traveled beyond the region in which they live. Even the colleges that students attend are influenced more by the SES of the family than by the academic ability of the

VIDEO INSIGHT

Looking for a Chance In Appalachia

Most Appalachian counties have unemployment and poverty rates well above the national average. These once-vibrant communities are now shrinking because many people can simply not find work in their hometowns. In this video segment you will see that there are a number of factors contributing to this problem, but one of the biggest is education.

The coal mining industry that brought so many jobs to Appalachia has changed over the years. Many coal mines have been shut down, while others have replaced loyal, hard workers with new, efficient technologies. But, because only half of the people in this region have a high school diploma, other big business and industries are hesitant to enter the area.

Things are appearing to change, however. Federal programs are helping to educate workers, giving them the opportunity to get their diploma and receive job training in different vocations. After watching this video segment, in what ways do you think these programs can make a difference in an area like this? What else can be done to reduce poverty in the Appalachian region?

student. Many students simply cannot afford to attend private colleges and instead choose state colleges and universities or community colleges. Thus, a student's socioeconomic origins have a substantial influence on the amount and type of schooling received and, in turn, the type of job obtained.

Education is one of the main ways families pass on class position to their children. One's class position determines, in great part, the material conditions that affect one's lifestyle and the types of jobs one seeks. Thus, educational level is a strong determinant of the future occupation and income of a family's children.

Power

Individuals and families who are at the upper SES levels exert more power than those at any other level. These individuals are more likely to sit on boards that determine state and local policies, on boards of colleges and universities, and on boards of corporations. They determine who receives benefits and rewards in governmental, occupational, and community affairs.

Groups and individuals with power control resources that influence their lives and the lives of others. Groups or individuals with little power do not have the means to get what they need or the access to others who could influence their interests. Powerless groups continually obtain fewer of the good things in life because they lack accessibility to sources of power.

VIDEO INSIGHT

Smart Kid, Tough School

In recent years, more and more attention has been given to the deteriorating condition of many of the nation's schools. Surely, students who are educated in such surroundings do not receive an education equal to the education given to students who attend schools with greater financial and community resources. Cedric Jennings, a star student from a high school in the poorest section of Washington, DC, saw this confirmed when he enrolled in a summer program for gifted minority students, only to find that the students from higher-income neighborhoods were better prepared academically. Yet, when scholarship offers to attend expensive prep schools came his way, Cedric refused and returned to his old high school for his senior year. Why do you think Cedric decided to return to Ballou High School?

Imagine you were a teacher at an inner-city school like the high school profiled in the video segment. How would you try to instill a sense of the value of an education in students in a world where being smart is "a badge of shame"? How would your own class background affect your ability to relate to the students? What could you do in your classroom on a day-to-day basis to help eradicate the crippling effects of class differences?

The sphere of education is not exempt from the exercise of power. Power relationships between teachers and students are manifested in schools. Teachers and administrators wield power over students by controlling the knowledge dispensed (predominantly grounded in a Western European worldview) and the acceptable behaviors, thoughts, and values for experiencing success in schools. Fewer teachers today are totally authoritarian; a growing number of teachers use cooperative learning rather than lecture and competitive strategies. Nevertheless, the curriculum is controlled by teachers, school boards, and national standards. Family and students have little input into what is taught.

CLASS DIFFERENCES

Many Americans identify themselves as middle class. It is an amorphous category that often includes everyone who works steadily and who is not accepted as a member of the upper class. It ranges from well-paid professionals to service workers. Most white-collar workers, no matter what their salary, see themselves as middle class. Manual workers, in contrast, may view themselves as working class, rather than as middle class; however, for the most part their incomes and cultural values are similar to those of many white-collar workers.

LINK TO THE CLASSROOM

Power Limits Detracking

Power plays an important role in school decisions. For example, the teachers and administrators in some racially and SES-mixed schools decided to detrack their classrooms. They made this decisioin, in part, because researchers have found that students placed in low-ability tracks "fall further and further behind their peers and become increasingly bored with school" (Wells & Serna, 1996, p. 93). When students are integrated into high-ability classrooms, the academic performance of the students labeled "slow" increases and the "fast" students continue to achieve at the same level.

Detracking a system that has given privilege to a group of students was not easy for these educators. Many parents whose children were most likely to be in the high-ability or gifted tracks fought the integration of their children with others. It soon became clear that students in the high-ability tracks were the children of elite and powerful families in the communities. Many parents believed that their achievements should be passed on to their children by ensuring that they receive the highest-quality education possible. To prevent detracking, these parents employed strategies to hold on to the privilege that their children had been extended in schools. They threatened to remove their children from public schools, used their power to change the minds of school administrators, held out for other special privileges for their children, and co-opted parents from the middle class to support their stand.

Why and how were parents wielding their power in this situation to ensure that their children received a better education than children of color and from low-income families? Would you argue on the side of the elite, powerful parents or on the side of providing a high-quality education for all students? What is the rationale for your stance? Why were the educators in this school trying to eliminate the tracking of students?

Source: Wells, A. S., & Serna, I. (1996, Spring). The politics of culture: Understanding local political resistance to detracking in racially mixed schools. *Harvard Educational Review,* 66(1), 93–118.

Despite the popular myth, most people in the United States are not affluent. A medium budget representing a reasonably comfortable life for a family in the United States would require about $40,000. The family would be buying a home, but would not be able to accumulate any significant savings. This compares to the $13,314 set as the federal government's poverty line for a family of three (Rose, 2000). Just over 13% of the population lives in poverty by federal standards, but 40.7% of households earned less than $35,000 in 1997 (U.S. Bureau of the Census, 1999). Many of these individuals identify themselves as middle class but are unable to obtain the material goods and necessities to live comfortably. The so-called middle class is certainly not homogeneous. The differences in education, occupation, prestige, income, and ability to accumulate wealth vary widely among persons who identify themselves in this group.

This chapter section provides a broad sketch of classes that are often used to describe people and families: the underclass, the working class, the middle class, the upper middle class, and the upper class.

The Underclass

845,000 homeless children

The term *underclass* is sometimes used as the label for the portion of the population who suffers the most from the lack of a stable income or other economic resources. It usually does not include those individuals who are temporarily in poverty because of a job loss or family illness; it does include the long-term poor. Of the individuals classified as living in poverty, "only 2.2 percent were persistently poor (that is, lived in poverty for at least eight out of the last ten years)" (Rose, 2000, p. 26).

The underclass includes the hard-core unemployed—those who have seldom, if ever, worked and who lack the skills to find and maintain a job. It also includes many discouraged workers who have given up looking for work and are no longer included in the federal government's report of the unemployed. Disproportionately, these families are headed by single mothers, who are more likely than married women to be in poverty for more than two years. The number of people included in this group is not found in the census data. Researchers suggest that it varies from two to eighteen million (Auletta, 1999).

Members of the underclass have become socially isolated from the dominant society. They usually are not integrated into, or wanted in, the communities of the other classes. Recommendations to build low-income housing, homeless shelters, or halfway houses in middle- or working-class communities often result in vocal outrage from the residents of these communities. Some analysts think the lack of integration has exacerbated the differences in behavior between members of the underclass and those of other classes.

During the past decade, the number of homeless persons and families has increased dramatically. Children and families beg on the streets of our cities. It is difficult to report accurately the number of homeless people. Because almost all cities report more homeless people than shelter space, the number who are housed nightly in shelters would undercount the actual number of homeless people. The National Law Center on Homelessness and Poverty (1999) projects more than 700,000 per night and up to two million who have experienced homelessness during a year. The Urban Institute (2000) estimates that 3.5 million persons will be homeless at least once in any given year. As many as 12 million U.S. adults have probably experienced homelessness at least once during their lifetime (National Coalition for the Homeless, 1999a). Many of the homeless work, but at such low wages they are unable to afford housing. Half of the homeless have graduated from high school, and approximately one fourth have attended college (Urban Institute, 2000).

Why are people homeless? Poverty and the lack of affordable housing are the primary reasons for homelessness. The federal definition of affordable housing is rent equal to 30% of one's income. A person earning minimum wage would have to work 87 hours weekly to afford a two-bedroom apartment in most parts of the country (National Low Income Housing Coalition, 1998). The supply of affordable housing for low-income families is more than four million units short of what is needed (Daskal, 1998). Domestic violence is another cause of homelessness, because women who are escaping violent relationships do not always have another place to go.

Forty percent of the homeless are now families, and one third of the residents of homeless shelters are children (Shinn & Weitzman, 1996). Some teenagers leave home because of family problems, economic problems, or residential instability, often ending up homeless on city streets (National Coalition for the Homeless, 1999b). The Urban Institute (2000) found the following characteristics among homeless families:

- Families headed by single mothers predominate.
- Homeless families have, on the average, two children, but they are not all with the homeless parent during the period of homelessness.
- Most homeless students are in school and regularly attending classes.

The U.S. Department of Education reported 845,000 homeless children from prekindergarten through high school age during the 1993 school year. "There is no

An increasing number of homeless adults, families, and children are found in communities around the country.

population of students more at risk of school failure, if not outright school exclusion, than the homeless" (Stronge, 1995, p. 130). Some homeless students do not attend school for extended periods of time, and homeless children are not as healthy as other children. Many have not received immunizations that are expected in childhood. In New York City, they disproportionately suffer from asthma and middle ear infections (Redlener and Johnson, 1999). They suffer from hypothermia and are often hungry. Further, they are more likely to be abused or neglected by parents and other adults.

Members of the underclass suffer from economic insecurity and from social, political, and economic deprivation. When they hold full-time jobs, they are of the lowest prestige and income levels. The jobs are often eliminated when economic conditions tighten or jobs move to the suburbs, resulting in the underclass members being unemployed again. The work for which they are hired is often the dirty work—not only physically dirty but also dangerous, menial, undignified, and degrading. The jobs are the least desirable ones in society, and they are performed by persons with no other options if they are to work.

Too often, this group is blamed for its own condition. The members are generally unnoticed when they remain isolated from the majority and work sporadically. In many cities they are isolated from others. Homeless citizens and others hanging on corners are moved to areas where they will not be visible to tourists. Members on welfare are subjected to the pejorative and inaccurate opinions of many other Americans. They are often thought of as dishonest and having loose morals. They are stereotyped as lazy and unwilling to work. Economic and political reasons for landing in this class are given little credence by those in power.

Many stereotypical notions about the underclass need to be overcome for teachers to effectively serve students who come from this background. Such students should not be blamed if they show acceptance, resignation, and even accommodation to their poverty as they learn to live with their economic disabilities. Should they be blamed for lethargy when their diets are inadequate to sustain vigor, for family instability when they are under torturing financial stress, for low standardized test scores when their education has been sporadic and of low quality, or for loose workforce attachments when they are in dead-end jobs that cannot lift them out of poverty anyway?

Anthropologists and sociologists have studied the relationship between cultural values and poverty status. Some have proposed a thesis called culture of poverty; it asserts that the poor have a unique way of life that developed as a reaction to their impoverished environment. This thesis suggests that people in poverty have a different value system and lifestyle that is perpetuated and transmitted to other generations.

Critics of the culture of poverty thesis believe that the cultural values of this group are much like those of the rest of the population but have been modified in practice because of situational stresses. In a classic study of street-corner men, Liebow (1967) suggested the following about a poor person's behavior: "Behavior appears not so much as a way of realizing the distinctive goals and values of his own microculture, or of conforming to its models, but rather as his way of trying to achieve many of the goals and values of the larger society, of failing to do this, and of concealing his failure from others and from himself as best he can" (p. 222). This explanation suggests that the differences in values and lifestyles of the underclass are not passed from one generation to the next, but rather are the adaptations by them to the experience of living in poverty.

The Working Class

The occupations pursued by the working class are those that require manual work for which income varies widely, depending on the skill required in the specific job. The factor that is most important in the description of the working class is the subordination of members to the capitalist control of production. These workers do not have control of their work. They do not give orders; they take orders from others. Included in the working class are craft and precision workers (11% of all workers) and operators, fabricators, and laborers (10.6%). This latter group has been hurt the most because of job losses resulting from technological advances and the movement of jobs to other countries. When farm laborers and service workers are added to this group, the working class comprises 38.4% of the employed population (U.S. Bureau of the Census, 1999).

Blue-collar workers are engaged primarily in manual work that is routine and mechanical. Service workers participate in nonmechanical and less routine work. They include employees in private households, protective services (police and firefighters), food services, health services, cleaning services, and personal services (hairdressers and early childhood assistants).

In 1998, the median income of these workers varied from $11,440 for female private household workers and $24,544 for male machine operators to $31,148 for male mechanics and repairers. The median income of female and male workers in farming, forestry, and fishing was $14,144 and $15,964 respectively (U.S. Bureau of the Census, 1999). Although the income of the working class is equal to and sometimes higher than that of nonprofessional white-collar workers, the working class has less job security. Work is more sporadic, and unemployment is unpredictably affected by the economy. Jobs are uncertain because of displacement as a result of technology and more stringent educational requirements. Fringe benefits available to these workers are often not as good as those offered to other workers. Vacation time is usually shorter, health insurance is available less often, and working conditions are more dangerous.

The education required for most blue-collar jobs is not as high as for white-collar jobs. The better-paying, skilled jobs, however, require specialized training and apprenticeships. Without additional training, it becomes difficult to move into a higher-level position. Many factory workers earn little more after 20 years on the job than a beginner does, and within a few years the new worker is earning the same pay as the worker with seniority.

Except for the skilled jobs and some service and farm jobs that allow autonomy to the worker, most jobs at this level are routine and are often perceived as not very meaningful or satisfying to the worker. Some studies report that blue-collar workers are more likely to separate work and social activities than workers at other levels. They tend not to socialize with coworkers to the same degree as other workers but maintain strong kinship ties with parents and siblings for social life.

Blue-collar workers generally perceive themselves as hardworking and honest, and as performing decent and important work for society. They want to be successful and often hope that their children will not have to spend their lives in a factory. Mistakenly, they are often perceived by others as authoritarian and intolerant of civil rights. This image, however, has not proved accurate; blue-collar workers are no more intolerant or prejudiced than members of other classes.

The Middle Class

In the past, the myth of middle-class Americans was a married couple with two or three children in a suburban house with a double garage, a television set, and the latest household gadgets. The father was almost always the primary breadwinner. In reality, the male-breadwinner family no longer provides the central experience for the vast majority of children, but it has not been replaced by any new modal category. Most Americans move in and out of a variety of family types over the course of their lives—families headed by a divorced parent, couples raising children out of wedlock, two-earner families, same-sex couples, families with no spouse in the labor force, blended families, and empty-nest families (Furstenberg, 1999).

The incomes of Americans who are popularly considered middle class vary greatly. Families generally are classified as middle class if their annual incomes fall between $30,000 and $80,000—about 38% of those submitting tax returns (Rose, 2000). Although some members of this supposed middle class have comfortable incomes, they have virtually no wealth. Many live from paycheck to paycheck, with little cushion against the loss of earning power through catastrophe, recession, layoffs, wage cuts, or old age. At various periods in the life cycle, some members fall into poverty for brief periods of time. Many families have found it necessary for both husband and wife to work to make ends meet. For discussion purposes, the middle class is divided into two distinct groups: white-collar workers and professionals/managers.

Professionals, managers, and administrators are accorded higher prestige in society than other white-collar workers. A major difference between these two groups is the amount of control they have over their work and the work of others. White-collar clerical workers, technicians, and salespersons are usually supervised by the professionals, managers, or administrators.

The jobs held by the middle class differ greatly, especially in income compensation. Overall, middle-class workers earn a median income above that of most blue-collar workers, except for skilled workers and many operatives. The median income of sales workers was $26,492 in 1998; workers who provide administrative support, including clerical work, earned less, with a median income of $22,966. The median income for the technical and related support occupations was $31,567 (U.S. Bureau of the Census, 1999). As a group, these workers have greater job security and better fringe benefits than many blue-collar workers. Whereas the formal education required for these jobs varies, more formal education is usually expected than for blue-collar jobs.

As white-collar jobs expanded during the past five decades, many people believed that such jobs were more meaningful and satisfying than jobs in blue-collar occupations. How meaningful and satisfying a job is, however, depends on the particular job. Certainly, many are as routine and boring as many blue-collar jobs; others are highly interesting and challenging. Still others are extremely alienating in that employees cannot control their environments. Some employees perceive their work as meaningless, are socially isolated from coworkers, and develop low levels of self-esteem. The type of job and the environment in which it is performed vary greatly for workers with white-collar jobs.

Members of this class appear to believe strongly in the Protestant work ethic. They see themselves as respectable and as adhering to a specific set of beliefs and values that are inherent in the good life. Although they are only slightly better off economically than their blue-collar counterparts, they live or try to live a more affluent lifestyle.

PAUSE TO REFLECT

Perceptions of others develop early in life and are corrected or reinforced on the basis of one's experiences throughout life. What images do you conjure up when you think of the underclass, the working class, and the middle class? Which characteristics are positive, and which are negative? Why are your perceptions value laden? What must you watch for in your own perceptions to ensure that you do not discriminate against students from one of these groups?

To answer these questions online, go to the Pause to Reflect module for this chapter of the Companion Website.

The Upper Middle Class

Professionals, managers, and administrators are the elite of the middle class. They represent the status that many who are concerned with upward mobility are trying to reach. Their income level allows them to lead lives that are, in many cases, quite different from those of white-collar and blue-collar workers. They are the group that seems to have benefited most from the nation's economic growth since the 1940s. Although at a level far below the upper class, they are the affluent middle class. They reflect the middle-class myth more accurately than any of the other groups described.

The professionals who best fit this category include those who must receive professional or advanced degrees and credentials to practice their professions. Judges, lawyers, physicians, college professors, teachers, and scientists are the professionals. Excluding teachers, most professionals earn far more than the median income of $40,688 reported for this category. They may be classified as members of the upper middle class, many earning more than $50,000 annually, especially when the family has two wage earners. They usually own a home and a new car and are able to take vacations to other parts of the country and abroad (Rose, 2000).

This group also includes managers and administrators, who make up 14.5% of the employed population. They are the successful executives and businesspeople, who are very diverse and include the chief executive officers of major corporations, presidents of colleges, and owners and administrators of local nursing homes. Those who are the most affluent make up the middle and upper management in financing, marketing, and production. The gap between men's and women's earnings is greater for administrators than for professionals. Men's median salary is $47,580, as compared with women's, which is $32,552 or 68% of that of male administrators. The administrators of large corporations earn salaries far above this level; their salaries and fringe benefits place them in the upper class instead of the middle class.

Educational credentials are more important for the professionals and managers at this level than at any other class level. The prospect of gaining the necessary qualifications to enter this level is severely restricted, because children of parents with college degrees are much more likely to attend and graduate from college than are children of parents who did not attend college. Thus, a position in this status level most often becomes a part of one's inheritance as a result of the advantages that prestige and income bring to members of the upper middle class.

The incomes and opportunities to accumulate wealth are high for this group compared with the bulk of the population. Members of this class play an active role in civic and voluntary organizations. Their occupations and incomes give them access to policy-making roles within these organizations. They are active participants in political processes and thus are major recipients of public benefits. Of all the groups studied so far, this one holds the greatest power.

The occupations of the people in this group play a central role in their lives, often determining their friends as well as their business and professional associates. Their jobs allow more autonomy than jobs at any other level previously discussed. For the most part, they are allowed a great amount of self-direction. Members of this group tend to view their affluence, advantages, and comforts as universal, rather than as unique. They believe that their class includes almost everyone (Rose, 2000). They believe in the American dream of success because they have achieved it.

The Upper Class

Whereas the number of studies about the working and middle classes in the United States is abundant, the number about the upper class is meager. High income and wealth are necessary characteristics for entering the upper class, as well as for being accepted by those persons who are already members. Within the upper class, however, are great variations in the wealth of individual families.

The upper class is comprised of two groups. One group includes the individuals and families who control great inherited wealth; the other group includes top-level administrators and professionals. Prestige positions, rather than great wealth, allow some families to enter or maintain their status at this level. The upper class includes persons with top-level and highly paid positions in large banks, entertainment corporations, and industrial corporations. It also includes those who serve as primary advisors to these positions and government leaders—for example, corporate lawyers.

The disparity between the income and wealth of members of this class and members of other classes is astounding. In 1970, for example, chief executive officers (CEOs) earned about 79 times as much as the average worker. In 1990, their pay reached 85 times the average worker's earnings. By 1999, the ratio had increased to 475 (Anderson et al., 2000). The number of people reporting incomes of more than a half-million dollars has grown dramatically since the 1980s. This increase in the size of the upper class has occurred, in part, because of the income received from increased rent, dividends, and interest payments available to the holders of financial assets, including property and stock.

A study of elite boarding schools attended by the upper class identified characteristics that confirm the differences between this and the other classes. In 1985, nearly half of the students were from families with an annual income of more than $100,000 (this figure represents income only and does not include earnings from wealth). The wealthiest students were from Jewish, Presbyterian, Episcopalian, and Roman Catholic backgrounds; 50% of their fathers were professionals, and 40% were managers; and more than three fourths of their parents had finished college. "Nearly two-thirds of the fathers have attended graduate or professional school, compared to less than one-tenth of the fathers of high school seniors nationally. One-third of boarding school mothers had attended graduate or professional schools, while nationally less than one in twenty mothers of high school students have attended graduate school" (Cookson & Persell, 1985, p. 59). Families traveled with their children; 69% of students had traveled abroad. Books abounded in the home; 51% had more than 500 books at home. Graduates of these schools attended elite colleges and universities at a higher rate than other students (Cookson & Persell, 1985).

Wealth and income ensure power. The extremely small portion of the population that holds a vastly disproportionate share of the wealth also benefits disproportionately when resources are distributed. The power of these people allows them to protect their wealth. The only progressive tax in this country is the federal income tax, in which a greater percentage of the income is taxed as the income increases. Loopholes in the tax laws provide benefits to those whose unearned income is based on assets. What does this mean in terms of advantage to the rich? "Differences in tax laws between 1977 and 1998 lowered the federal tax payments of the top 1% of families by an average of $36,710 (or 14.2% of their average initial tax liability). Over the same period, the bottom four-fifths of families saw their average tax payments fall by just $335 (or 6.9%)" (Mishel, Bernstein, & Schmitt, 1999). Thus, tax relief has been more beneficial to the rich than to those with the lowest incomes.

Although families with inherited wealth do not represent a completely closed status group, they do have an overrepresentation of Anglo, Protestant members who were born in the United States. They tend to intermarry with other members of the upper class. They are well-educated, although a college degree is not essential. The educational mark of prestige is attendance at the elite private prep schools.

For example, less than 10% of U.S. high school students attend private schools. Less than 1% of the high school population attends the elite prep schools, and these students are overwhelmingly the children of the upper class. Cookson and Persell (1985) found that "where a person goes to school may have little to do with his and her technical abilities, but it may have a lot to do with social abilities. . . . Where individuals go to school determines with whom they associate" (p. 16).

The upper class probably represents the most distinct and closed microcultural group of all of those studied. Cookson and Persell (1985) report the following:

> The founding of boarding schools in the United States was part of an upper-class "enclosure movement" that took place in the late nineteenth century. In order to insulate themselves from the rest of society, the American upper class established their own neighborhoods, churches, suburban and rural recreational retreats, and a number of social and sporting clubs. It was during this period that the Social Register was first published and, in lavish displays of conspicuous consumption, the social season was highlighted by debutante balls and charity benefits. (p. 23)

Greater assimilation of lifestyles and values has occurred within this class than in any other. Although diversity exists within the group, members of the upper class may be the most homogeneous group, and they are likely to remain so as long as their cross-cultural and cross-class interactions are limited.

INTERACTION OF CLASS WITH RACE AND ETHNICITY, GENDER, AND AGE

Poverty is most likely to be a condition of the young, persons of color, women, full-time workers in the lowest-paying jobs, and the illiterate. In 1997, the federal government set the poverty level at $8,183 for a one-person family and $16,400 for a four-person family. On the basis of this poverty threshold, 35.6 million persons are in poverty, or 13.3% of the total population; many of these individuals are members of the 7.3 million low-income families that make up 10.3% of all families (U.S. Bureau of the Census, 1999). Low-income persons include members of the following groups:

Group	Number	Percentage
White	24.4 million	11.0 of all whites
Black	9.1 million	26.5 of all blacks
Latino	8.3 million	27.1 of all Latinos
Older than 65 years	3.4 million	10.5 of all such persons
Younger than 18 years	14.1 million	19.9 of all such persons
Female-headed households	13.5 million	35.1 of all such families

Many low-income people do have full-time, year-round jobs but are not paid wages high enough to move their families out of poverty. Nearly 2.5 million people work full-time, year-round but live in poverty, and another 5.7 million poor individuals work full-time for part of the year or part-time (Mishel et al., 1999). The working poor can be found in all occupational groups, but they are disproportionately located in service and retail trade occupations. Experts report that it is difficult for the working poor to rise above poverty when the minimum wage is low and part-time jobs are often all that is available. A growing economy should lead to a decrease in poverty, but "the character of American income inequality has been increasing real incomes at the top of the income scale and lowering them at the bottom, and this pattern of income growth has meant higher poverty rates for those at the low end of the income scale" (Mishel et al., 1999, p. 303).

Although the ceiling for poverty level is supposed to indicate an income level necessary to maintain an adequate, not comfortable, living, it is misleading to assume that any family near this level can live adequately or comfortably. Many families who have incomes just above this level find it difficult to pay even for essential food, housing, and clothing, let alone live comfortably by the American standard. Thus, they are economically poor even though they technically earn an income above the poverty level.

The poor are a very heterogeneous group. They do not all have the same values or lifestyles. They cannot be expected to react alike to the conditions of poverty. To many, their ethnicity or religion is the most important determinant of the way they live within the economic constraints of poverty. To others, the devastating impact of limited resources is the greatest influence in determining their values and lifestyles. No matter what aspects of the various microcultures have the greatest impact on the lives of individuals or families, lifestyles are limited severely by the economic constraints that keep people in poverty. Individual choice is more limited for people with low incomes than for any other microcultural group studied in this book.

Data projections on occupational patterns, earnings, and levels of education show that it will be necessary for the numbers of minorities and women in critical occupations to increase during the next 50 years. Murdock (1995) foresees the future in this regard as follows:

> The potential problem is not, of course, the growth of women and minorities in the workforce. Rather, it is the levels of occupational involvement, compensation, and education that are accessible to, and acquired by, women and minorities. Patterns of discrimination, limited access to social and economic opportunities, and cultural differences have all played a role in the development of such differences. It is apparent, however, that the level of involvement in the labor force of both women and minorities must be enhanced, through improved access to all occupations and to higher levels of education. Unless this is done, the United States may find itself with a labor force that is declining in competitiveness at a time when the world's labor market has become larger and more competitive. (p. 87)

Race and Ethnic Inequality

African Americans, Mexican Americans, Puerto Ricans, and American Indians experience the severest economic deprivation of all ethnic groups in this country. Although the census data on consumer income are not broken down for American

Indians, Eskimos, and Aleuts, these groups probably suffer more from economic inequity than any other group.

In 1997, the median income of white families was $46,754; of black families, $28,602; of Latino families, $18,142; and of Asian American and Pacific Islander families, $51,850. Therefore, black families had a median income that was 61% of the median income of whites; Latinos earned 60% of the median income of whites; and Asian Americans and Pacific Islanders earned 111% of the median income (U.S. Bureau of the Census, 1999). A study released in 1993 by UNESCO, which compared the standards of living of different nations, clearly showed the difference in the way most whites live as compared with blacks and Latinos in this country. The United States was ranked sixth of the nations in the study. If the data had included only whites, the United States would have ranked first. Blacks would have ranked thirty-first—at the same level as an underdeveloped country (Spencer, 1993).

When families with married couples are compared, the gap between groups becomes smaller. Black married couples earn 87% and Latinos 66% of the median income of whites (U.S. Bureau of the Census, 1999). Therefore, when age, education, experience, and other factors are equal to those of white men, the earnings of minorities and whites become more similar, but the income ratios between the groups still favor whites.

People of color make up a disproportionately high percentage of people in poverty. Of the white population, 11% fall below the poverty level, compared with 27% of the black and Latino populations (U.S. Bureau of the Census, 1999). Within the Latino population, Puerto Ricans suffer the most (34%) from poverty and Cuban Americans the least (20%). "For whites, poverty tends to be viewed as atypical or accidental. Among blacks, it comes close to being seen as a natural outgrowth of their history and culture" (Hacker, 1992, p. 100).

Persons of color are more likely to be concentrated in low-paying jobs. Figure 2–2 shows the occupational levels of different groups. The percentage of blacks in the higher-paying and higher-status jobs is much lower than that of whites. Although both absolute and relative gains in the occupational status of blacks have been made during the past 40 years, blacks and Latinos are still heavily overrepresented in the semiskilled and unskilled positions.

This inequitable condition is perpetuated by several factors. Historically, students of color dropped out of school in greater proportions than white students, limiting their income potential. Although the gap has been greatly reduced over time, it still exists. Seven percent of white 25 to 34 year olds had dropped out of high school in 1997 as compared to 9% of Asian Americans and 12% of blacks and Latinos (U.S. Department of Education, 2000). Dropout rates are related to family income, especially for 18 to 24 year olds. High school graduation rates range "from 48.2 percent for those from families with less than $10,000 per year in family income, to 92.7 percent for those from families with more than $75,000" (Higher Educational Opportunity, 2000).

Unemployment for people of color is higher than for whites; 3.9% of the white population was unemployed in 1998, compared with 8.9% of the black population

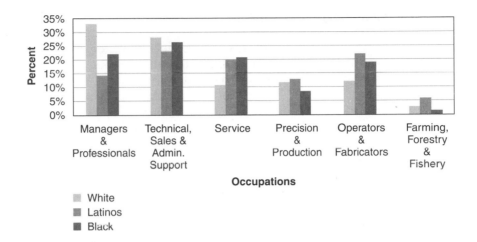

Figure 2–2

Participation of Blacks, Hispanics, and others in different occupations in 1998.

Source: U.S. Census Bureau. (1999). *Statistical abstract of the United States* (119th edition). Washington, DC: U.S. Government Printing Office.

and 7.2% of the Latino population. For 16 to 19 year olds, the differences were even greater, with 12.6% of whites, 27.6% of blacks, and 21.3% of Latinos unemployed (U.S. Bureau of the Census, 1999). Discrimination against blacks and Latinos is still widespread, contributing to unemployment and lack of participation in the labor market.

The historical experiences of ethnic groups have had a great impact on their gains in SES. For example, the absolute class position (income, occupation, rate of employment) of African Americans improved as a result of their migration to America's large cities during the first half of the twentieth century, and especially during the 1940s. Their educational attainments have narrowed the formerly enormous gap between blacks and whites with regard to completion of high school; median number of school years completed; and, to a lesser degree, standardized test scores and prevalence of college attendance. Since the 1960s, the number of African American families that have entered the middle class has increased significantly. Even so, the jobs that are available and the salaries earned are not equal to those of whites, particularly white males.

Other oppressed groups with a disproportionately low SES have had different historical experiences than blacks but suffer similarly from discrimination. Mexican Americans are highly overrepresented as farm laborers, one of the lowest-status occupations. Many American Indians have been isolated on reservations, away from most occupations except those lowest in prestige, and the numbers of such positions are limited. Asian Americans, who as a group have a high educational level and a relatively high SES, often reach middle-management positions but may then face a class ceiling that prevents them from moving into upper management.

Gender Inequality

As a group, women earn less and are more likely to suffer from poverty than any other group, with women of color suffering the greatest oppression. The reasons for such inequality, however, have very different origins from inequality based on race and ethnicity. Institutional discrimination based on gender is based on a patriarchal society in which women were assigned to traditional roles of mother and wife and, if they had to work outside the home, to jobs in which subordination was expected. This status has limited their job opportunities and has kept their wages low. Overt discrimination against women has resulted in the use of gender to determine wages, hiring, and promotion of individuals by using mechanisms similar to those that promote inequality for members of other oppressed groups.

The number of women in the workforce has increased dramatically during the past three decades. Seventy-three percent of women between the ages of 25 and 64 were working in the civilian workforce in 1998, as compared with 88% of the men (U.S. Bureau of the Census, 1999). Black women and white women participate in the labor force at about the same rate today; 61% of all women over 16 years of age have jobs. Latino women are somewhat less likely to work outside the home; 54% were working in 1998.

To maintain an adequate or desirable standard of living today, in many families both husband and wife must work. The difference that two incomes make on the family income is obvious. Although the percentages in the workforce of women who are single, widowed, divorced, or separated have increased during the past 30 years, the percentages of married women and white women in the workforce have increased dramatically since 1940. In 1940, only 16.7% of all married women worked outside the home; by 1998, 61.2% did. Seventy-one percent of married women with children under 18 years of age worked outside the home. These figures reveal the stagnation of groups most likely to suffer poverty (unmarried persons and persons of color), with the increases concentrated in those groups least susceptible to poverty (married white women).

Historically, the sexual division of labor has been fairly rigid. The roles of women were limited to reproduction, childrearing, and homemaking. When they did work outside the home, their jobs were often similar to roles in the home—that is, caring for children or the sick. Jobs were stereotyped by gender. As recently as 1998, women comprised more than 90% and less than 10% of the workforce in the occupations shown in Table 2–1.

The jobs in which women predominate are accompanied by neither high prestige nor high income. People in the category of professional (teachers and nurses) do not compete in income or prestige with architects and engineers. Women continue to be overrepresented as clerical and service workers and underrepresented as managers and skilled workers. Even within these occupation groups, salaries between women and men differ. Table 2–2 compares the salaries for selected jobs.

Below graduate and professional school levels, the percentages of graduates at the various levels of education are similar for men and women, matching closely their percentages of the population. College enrollment is 56% female and 44% male.

Table 2–1

Occupations in which women are most likely and least likely to participate.

Women's Occupations	Percent Participation	Men's Occupations	Percent Participation
Dental hygienists	99.1	Carpenters	1.2
Secretaries	98.4	Extractive occupations	1.4
Dental assistants	98.1	Firefighting	2.3
Prekindergarten & kindergarten teachers	97.8	Airplane pilots & navigators	3.4
Family child care providers	97.1	Mechanics & repairers	4.0
Child care workers	96.5	Transportation occupations, except motor vehicles	4.1
Early childhood teacher assistants	95.9	Truck drivers	5.3
Receptionists	95.5	Material moving equipment operators	6.2
Cleaners & servants	94.3	Forestry & logging	6.7
Typists	94.3	Mechanical engineering	7.0
Billing, posting, & calculating machine operators	94.1	Aerospace engineering	8.4
Bookkeepers, accounting, & auditing clerks	93.0	Electrical & electronic engineering	9.0
Teacher aides	93.0	Protective service supervisors	9.3
Speech therapists	92.6		
Registered nurses	92.5		
Hairdressers & cosmetologists	90.8		

Source: U.S. Census Bureau. (1999). *Statistical abstract of the United States* (119th edition). Washington, DC: U.S. Government Printing Office.

Table 2–2

Comparison of selected jobs by salaries of women and men.

Job Category	Women's Annual Salary	Men's Annual Salary	Women's Salaries as Percentage of Men's
Construction trades	$21,216	$28,340	75%
Farming, forestry, & fishing	$14,144	$15,964	89%
Mechanics & repairers	$26,988	$31,148	87%
Professional specialty	$35,464	$46,540	76%
Protective services	$25,012	$31,876	78%
Sales	$19,344	$32,344	60%
Technical & related support	$26,572	$36,452	73%

Source: U.S. Census Bureau. (1999). *Statistical abstract of the United States* (119th edition). Washington, DC: U.S. Government Printing Office.

In 1996, women received 43.5% of all law degrees, 40.9% of all medical degrees, and 16.1% of all engineering degrees (U.S. Bureau of the Census, 1999). Compared with the earnings of men with the same education, however, women still earn less.

PAUSE TO REFLECT

Throughout the next week, systematically record the types of jobs that men and women hold in your community. You might use a table such as this:

Type of Job	Number of Women	Number of Men

To answer these questions online, go to the Pause to Reflect module for this chapter of the Companion Website.

At the end of the week, analyze the data to determine whether men and women hold the same or similar jobs. What are the differences? What are the economic implications for the women and men in your study?

Women, especially those who are the heads of households, are more likely than men to fall below the poverty level. Thirty-five percent of families maintained by women with no husband present earn an income below the official poverty level. The large number of families in this group is a result of a combination of low-paying jobs and an increase in divorces, separations, and out-of-wedlock births. When compared with male households where the wife is absent, women without husbands earn only 64% of what men earn.

Women as individuals are assigned a lower status than men in the stratification system of this country. The occupations most open to women are the low-status and low-paying ones, compounding the women's chances of being in poverty and being dependent on men for their well-being.

Age Inequality

The highest incidence of poverty occurs at both ends of the life span. Society has determined that adults over 65 years of age and children are in nonworking periods of their lives. The poverty rate for children, which is much greater than for all other ages, is shown in Figure 2–3.

Both women and men earn their maximum income between the ages of 45 and 54. The median income of persons who are 14 to 19 years old is lower than for any other group, primarily because most of these persons are just beginning to enter the workforce at the end of this period and some may not enter for several more

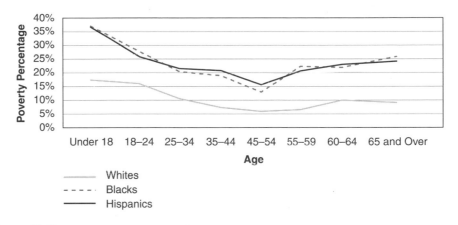

Figure 2–3

Persons in poverty by age and ethnicity in 1997.

Source: U.S. Census Bureau. (1999). *Statistical abstract of the United States* (119th edition). Washington, DC: U.S. Government Printing Office.

years, especially if they attend college. Income then increases steadily for most people until after they reach 55 years of age. The income of women remains fairly constant throughout much of their working lives, whereas the income for a large percentage of men increases dramatically during their lifetimes.

"Although 20 percent of American children live in poverty this year, it is estimated that 45 percent of white children and 85 percent of black children will experience poverty while growing up" (Rose, 2000, p. 26). Children's class status depends on their families, and they have little or no control over their destiny during their early years. Children born in low-income families will be disadvantaged in developing their adult earning power by inferior schooling, an oppressive financial environment, and poor health. Once they enter the adult world, they may be able to earn an adequate income to keep themselves and their children out of poverty.

To prevent poverty after age 65, individuals must plan throughout their working lives to defer or save income that can be used for support once they stop earning regular incomes. Social Security benefits provide some support to the elderly, and often these benefits are the only support available. Some workers participate in pension plans that provide an income after a lifetime of work, but many employees, especially blue-collar and low-level white-collar workers, still do not have the opportunity to participate in such programs. Nearly 13% of all persons older than age 65 have an income under the poverty level (U.S. Bureau of the Census, 1999).

In a society in which high ranking is given to individuals who either control wealth or are productive in the labor force, persons who do not contribute to this production are assigned a low status. Many elderly persons receive financial and medical support from the government, making them nonproductive drawers on the nation's wealth. Often, they are accorded little deference and instead face impatience, patronization, and neglect by people still in the workforce.

EDUCATIONAL IMPLICATIONS

Many social reformers, educators, and parents view education as a powerful device for achieving social change and the reduction of poverty. From the beginning of the public school movement in the early nineteenth century, low incomes were believed to result from inadequate education. Discrimination in employment and housing was blamed on the lack of education in other segments of the population. This view was still pervasive in the 1960s as the federal government attempted to eliminate poverty through the establishment of Head Start, Title I (compensatory education), Upward Bound, Job Corps, Neighborhood Youth Corps, and other educational programs. Test scores of students from low-income groups have not appeared to improve as much as expected, however, and racial/ethnic segregation between and within schools has increased.

This lack of progress in overcoming the effects of poverty on students should not suggest that educational reforms are not worthwhile. Some changes make schooling more attractive to students and even increase the achievement of many individual students; educational resources also become more equitably distributed. Nevertheless, the intended goal of increasing income equity and eliminating poverty has not been realized. Different social-historical interpretations of education explain the role of schools in society and the degree to which this goal and others are met. Two views are prevalent. One view sees schools as an agent of social reform that can improve the chances of economic success for its graduates. The second view concludes that schools exist as agents of the larger social, economic, and political context, with the goal of inculcating the values necessary to maintain the current socioeconomic and political systems.

Supporters of the first view are much more benign in their description of the role of schools in helping students become socially mobile. They are optimistic that social reform can be achieved by providing low-income students with more effective schools. The others see schools as preparing students to work efficiently at appropriate levels in corporate organizations. The needs of business and industry are met "by developing lower-class children to be better workers and middle-class ones to be better managers in the corporate economy and by reproducing the social relations of production in the schools to inculcate children with values and norms supportive of capitalist work organizations" (Carnoy & Levin, 1976, p. 10).

Students are tracked in courses for either college or vocational preparation. The curriculum sorts and selects students so that children of blue-collar or unemployed workers and children of the elite will be socialized for jobs they later will hold. In a study of five schools whose students represented different class levels, Anyon (1996) found that students were being prepared for their future roles. In the working-class school, students began to develop skills and abilities for resisting authority, usually carried out by not doing assignments and skipping classes. Middle-class students were rewarded for knowing the answers, where to find the answers, and the correct form and procedures to use. Affluent schools provided students with "the opportunity to develop skills of linguistic, artistic, and scientific expression and creative elaboration of ideas into concrete form" (p. 201). In the executive elite schools, students were "given the opportunity to learn and to utilize the intellectually and socially prestigious grammatical, mathematical, and other vocabularies and rules by which elements are arranged" (p. 202).

Rather than provide equal educational opportunity, many schools perpetuate existing social and economic inequities in society. In this section, we examine three areas that influence the inequities that exist in schools not serving low-income and many working- and middle-class students well.

Teacher Expectations and Tracking

Students in most classrooms will be heterogeneous in terms of ethnicity, gender, religion, and ability. Too often, a teacher assigns academic expectations to students on the basis of their membership in class, race, ethnic, and gender groups. Students not classified as middle class are often viewed as academically inferior. Most of these students are greatly harmed by such expectations. In contrast, students from the upper middle class usually benefit from a teacher's judgments because they are expected to perform better in school, are treated more favorably, and perform at a higher level in most cases.

Differences in mathematics and science achievement based on class and race are found by age nine, but are clearly in place by age thirteen. In junior high school, students from low-income families typically take fewer courses in mathematics

Some inner-city schools are squeezed between office buildings and housing units, leaving small playgrounds that differ greatly from those in suburban and rural areas.

and science, which contributes to later differences in college enrollments and vocational choices. In many schools with large numbers of low-income populations, advanced courses in these subjects are often not even offered. Thus, even those students who are achieving at a level equal to students from the dominant group are further stifled in their attempts to achieve equitably. It is no wonder that they score less well on standardized assessments. They have not had the opportunity to take the same high-level courses as their middle-class peers.

In an early ethnographic study of an inner-city school, Rist (1970) documented how students are classified, segregated, and taught differently, starting with their first days in school. Most teachers can identify the personal characteristics of students that will lead to academic success. They then develop instruction and interactions with their students that ensure that the students will, in fact, behave as the teachers expect—a phenomenon called the self-fulfilling prophecy. Rist found that a kindergarten teacher was able to divide a class into three reading and mathematics groups as early as the eighth day of school. Although such groupings may be helpful in providing the most effective instruction to students who enter the classroom with different skills, the researcher found that the groups were organized by nonacademic factors. Students in the highest group were all dressed in clean clothes that were relatively new and well pressed; they interacted well with the teacher and other students; they were quite verbal and used standard English; and they came from "better families." Students in the lower two groupings were poorly dressed and often in dirty clothes; they frequently carried the odor of urine; they used black dialect; and their families were less stable than those of students in the highest group. Throughout the year, the teacher interacted more with students in the highest group than with those in either of the other groups. This division of students, and teachers' involvement with the three groups continued through the second grade, at which time the study ended. Students in the highest group continually performed better academically and behaved in a more acceptable manner than students in the other two groups. As the kindergarten teacher had projected, these students were more successful in school than students from lower socioeconomic levels.

When teachers make such judgments about students, they are taking the first step in preventing students from having an equal opportunity for academic achievement. Rather than ensure that students have access to an egalitarian system, such classification and subsequent treatment of students ensures the maintenance of an inequitable system. This action is not congruent with the democratic belief that all students can learn and should be provided equal educational opportunities.

Educational researchers continue to find that simply being in the low-ability group diminishes students' achievement. Such students are provided with fewer and less effective opportunities to learn than other students. Critical thinking tasks are reserved for the high-ability groups. Oral recitation and structured written work are common in low-ability groups. Students are exposed to low-status knowledge at a slower pace than their peers in higher-ability groups, helping them fall further behind in subjects like mathematics, foreign languages, and sciences.

Teachers in low-ability classrooms spend more time on administration and discipline and less time actually teaching. As one might expect, student behavior in low tracks is more disruptive than in higher-level groups. However, this probably happens, in part, because students and teachers have developed behavioral standards that are more tolerant of inattention, and not because of students' individual abilities. To compound the problem, the more experienced and more successful teachers are disproportionately assigned to the higher-ability groups. Unfortunately, teachers generally view high-track students positively and low-track students negatively.

Disproportionately large numbers of students from lower socioeconomic levels are assigned to low-ability groups beginning very early in their school careers. The long-term effects are similar to those that Rist (1970) found in the 1960s. Even more tragic is the fact that the number of students from low-income families who are classified as being mentally challenged is disproportionately high. This inequitable classification places students of color in double jeopardy because they also disproportionately suffer from poverty.

How can the development of negative and harmful expectations for students be prevented? Teachers, counselors, and administrators can unconsciously fall into such behavior because they have learned that poverty is the fault of the individual. As a result, students are blamed for circumstances beyond their control. Instead, educators should see as a challenge the opportunity to provide these students with the knowledge and skills to overcome poverty. Educators should select approaches they would use for the most gifted students. The goal should be to *level up* the educational experiences for students who previously would have been tracked into the low-ability classes.

Equality in the achievement of students could be increased "by raising the caliber of both instructional content and instructional discourse in general and remedial courses [if students continue to be tracked in them]" (Gamoran, Nystrand, Berends, & LePore, 1995, p. 708). Researchers are finding that achievement is improved when teachers help students interact with the academic content through discussion and authenticity—relating the content to students' prior experiences and real-world applications. These strategies work for all students, not just those in the advanced placement and honors courses.

In helping to overcome the stigma of being poor, educators must consciously review their expectations for students. Some homeless students often do not go to school because they are so embarrassed by their inability to shower daily or to dress appropriately. Teachers should figure out strategies to ensure that they do not further exacerbate students' feelings of low esteem. Seeing students as individuals, rather than as members of a specific socioeconomic group, may also assist the educator in overcoming class biases that may exist in the school and the community. Information about a student's family background can be used in understanding the power of environment on a student's expression of self; it must not be used to rationalize stereotypes and label students. Educators must be aware of any prejudices they themselves hold against members of lower socioeconomic groups. Otherwise, discriminatory practices will surface in the classroom in the form of self-fulfilling prophecies that harm students and perpetuate societal inequities.

In inner-city schools, educators face many low-income and working-class students whose environment outside the school is very different from that of students in most suburban schools. Isolated rural areas require that families respond to their nonschool environment much differently than families in other areas. Educators should not expect to be able to teach every student effectively in the same way. Equity does not mean that the same instructional strategies must be used to teach all students. Although it is essential to ensure that all students learn academics, how the educator teaches these skills may vary, depending on the environment in which students live—a factor greatly dependent on the family's SES.

Curriculum for Equality

The discussion so far has focused on teachers' expectations for students on the basis of SES. The curriculum should also reflect accurately the class structure and inequities that exist in the United States. Too often, the existence of nearly half the population is not validated in the curriculum.

The curriculum and the textbooks usually focus on the values and experiences of a middle-class society. They highlight the heroes of our capitalist system and emphasize the importance of developing the skills to earn an income that will enable students to soon own the home, car, furniture, and appliances that have become the symbols of middle-class living. They usually ignore the history and heroes of the labor struggle in this country, in which laborers resisted and endured under great odds to improve their conditions (Zandy, 1996). They do not discuss the role of the working class in the development of the nation. The inequities based on the income and wealth of one's family are usually neither described nor discussed. In classrooms, students should learn of the existence of these discrepancies. They should understand that the majority of the population does not live the upper-middle-class reality.

Often overlooked are the experiences that students bring to the classroom. School is not the only place where students learn about life. Differences in school behavior and knowledge among students from dissimilar socioeconomic levels are strongly dependent on the knowledge and skills needed to survive appropriately in their community environments. Most low-income students, especially those in urban areas, have learned how to live in a world that is not imaginable to most middle-class students or teachers. Yet, the knowledge and skills they bring to school are not valued by teachers in a system with a middle-class orientation. Educators should recognize the value of the community's informal education in sustaining its own culture and realize that formal education is often viewed as undermining that culture.

Students need to see some of their own cultural experiences reflected in the curriculum. They need to see ordinary working people as valued members of society. These students and their families need to be helped to see themselves as desirable and integral members of the school community, rather than as second-class citizens who must learn the ways of the more economically advantaged to even succeed in school. "Students' motivation is enhanced in schools in which they feel cared for, supported, valued, and influential—schools that they experience as communities" (Battistich, Solomon, Kim, Watson, & Schaps, 1995, p. 652).

Educators should become cognizant of the materials, films, and books used in class. If students never see their communities in these instructional materials, their motivation and acceptance are likely to be limited. All students should be encouraged to read novels and short stories about people from different socioeconomic levels. When studying historical or current events, they should examine the events from the perspective of the working class and those in poverty, as well as from the perspective of the country's leaders. Teaching can be enhanced by drawing examples from experiences with which students are familiar, especially when the experiences are different from the teacher's own.

Instruction should show that not all persons share equally in material things in the United States, but that all persons have potential to be developed. All students, no matter what their SES, should be helped to develop strong and positive self-concepts. Many students do not realize the diversity that exists in this country, let alone understand the reasons for the diversity and the resulting discrimination against some groups. Most middle-class children, especially those from white-collar and professional levels, believe that most persons are as affluent as they are. Educators are expected to expand their students' knowledge of the world, not to hide from them the realities that exist because of class differences.

In a classroom in which democracy and equity are important, social justice should inform the curriculum. Low-income students should receive priority time from teachers and have access to the necessary resources to become academically competitive with middle-class students.

Finally, all students should be encouraged to be critical of what they read, see, and hear in textbooks; through the mass media; and from their parents and friends. The curriculum should encourage the development of critical thinking and problem-solving skills. Unfortunately, schools traditionally have talked about the democratic vision but have been unwilling to model it. Students and teachers who become involved through the curriculum in asking why the inequities in society exist are beginning to practice democracy.

Financial Support for Schools

Inequities are greatly exacerbated by the fact that the current system for funding schools mirrors these inequities. Education is supported by local property taxes, which supply 40% to 50% of all school funds. State support averages about 47%, and federal support is less than 7% (Karp, 1995). "What this means is that a few American students (who just happen to live in rich communities within generous states) are now attending public schools that are funded at $15,000 or more per student per year, whereas other American students (who are stuck in poor communities within niggardly states) must make do with $3,000 or less per year in funding for their schools" (Payne & Biddle, 1999). Students in rich schools and poor schools experience very different kinds of education and environments in which learning is to occur. It is little wonder that the gap in academic achievement in such different schools is so great. Through the schools, wealthy and upper-middle-class parents are able to pass on their economic advantages.

Researchers and policymakers disagree as to whether money matters in schools, especially in the improvement of achievement. In a reanalysis of data from studies on this relationship, University of Chicago researchers concluded that higher per-pupil expenditures, better teacher salaries, more educated and experienced teachers, and smaller class and school sizes are strongly related to improved student learning (Greenwald, Hedges, & Laine, 1996). If we agree that more money would help reduce the inequities across groups in schools and that greater resources are needed in low-wealth school districts, what areas would provide the greatest payoff for improved student achievement? Slavin (1995) recommends smaller class sizes, prekindergarten programs for four-year-olds, tutoring for students having difficulty, cooperative learning, family support systems, and extensive staff and teacher development for delivering effective programs.

Many schools, such as the one that Tomas Juarez entered at the beginning of this chapter, no longer serve students well. Is there any compelling reason for students not to attend comfortable, clean, and attractive schools? Why shouldn't low-income students have teachers who are qualified to teach and who have high academic expectations for them? More equitable funding of schools would provide low-income students with at least some of the basic opportunities that many middle-class students currently enjoy.

Summary

Socioeconomic status (SES) is a composite of the economic status of a family or unrelated individuals, based on income, wealth, occupation, educational attainment, and power. It is a means of measuring inequalities based on economic differences and the way families live as a result of their economic well-being. Families' SESs range from the indigent poor to the very rich. Where a family falls along this continuum affects the way its members live, how they think and act, and the way others react to them. Persons who share the same class form a microculture. Although a family may actively participate in other microcultural groups centered around ethnicity, religion, gender, exceptionality, language, or age, the class to which a family belongs is probably the strongest factor in determining differences among groups.

Social stratification is possible because consistent and recurring relationships exist between people who occupy different levels of the social structure. Persons of color, women, the young, the elderly, and individuals with disabilities are disproportionately represented at the low end of the social stratification system.

The United States can be divided into classes based on income and occupation. In this chapter, the following classes were described: underclass, working class, middle class, upper middle class, and upper class. The income and wealth that keep families at one of these levels vary greatly. Individual choice is most limited for those persons who are in poverty and who often can barely meet essential needs. Whereas ethnic and religious diversity exists at all levels, the upper class is the most homogeneous. Persons of color and women who head families are overly represented in the underclass, working class, and middle class. Class consciousness is strongest among the upper classes, whose members know the value of solidarity in the protection and maintenance of their power and privilege.

Disproportionately large numbers of students from lower levels of SES are assigned to low-ability groups in their early school years. Educators must consciously review their expectations for students and their behavior toward students from different levels of SES to ensure that they are not discriminating. Instructional methods and teaching strategies may vary greatly, depending on the environment in which students live. It is essential that all students be provided with a quality education.

Educators also need to pay attention to the curriculum. Too often, low-income students are placed in remedial programs because of discriminatory testing and placement. In addition, the curriculum does not serve students well if it reflects only the perspective of middle-class America. Students need to see some of their own cultural values reflected in the curriculum, in addition to learning about the cultural values of others.

Financial support for more equitable funding of schools, no matter where they are located or which students attend them, is likely to reduce the achievement gap between groups of students. The current property tax system for supporting schools gives the advantage to families with high incomes.

Questions for Review

To answer these questions online, go to the Chapter Questions module for this chapter of the Companion Website.

1. What is social stratification? How does it differentially affect microcultural groups in society?
2. Why is social mobility unreal for many members of society?
3. What is the mythical middle class? Why does it not match reality?
4. Which workers are included under the classification of working and middle class?
5. What socioeconomic factors make it difficult for members of the underclass to improve their conditions?
6. Why are the professional and managerial workers, who comprise the upper middle class, gaining more power in society?
7. Why have schools not been able to eliminate poverty in this country?
8. What is the self-fulfilling prophecy, and how is it affected by the class of families?
9. How might the tracking of students perpetuate inequalities in schools and society?
10. How can teachers ensure that students from low-income and working class families are able to achieve academically at the same level as other students?

References

Anderson, S., Cavanagh, J., Collins, C., Hartman, C., & Yeskel, F. (2000). *Executive excess 2000: Seventh annual CEO compensation survey.* Washington, DC: Institute for Policy Studies.

Anyon, J. (1996). Social class and the hidden curriculum of work. In E. R. Hollins (Ed.), *Transforming curriculum for a culturally diverse society* (pp. 179–203). Mahwah, NJ: Erlbaum.

Auletta, K. (1999). *The underclass.* New York: Random House.

Battistich, V., Solomon, D., Kim, D., Watson, M., & Schaps, E. (1995, Fall). Schools as communities, poverty levels of student populations, and students' attitudes, motives, and performance: A multilevel analysis. *American Educational Research Journal, 32*(3), 627–658.

Carnoy, M., & Levin, H. M. (1976). *The limits of educational reform.* New York: McKay.

Cookson, P. W., & Persell, C. H. (1985). *Preparing for power: America's elite boarding schools.* New York: Basic Books.

Daskal, J. (1998). *In search of shelter: The growing shortage of affordable rental housing.* Washington, DC: Center on Budget and Policy Priorities.

Furstenberg, F. F., Jr. (1999). Family change and family diversity. In N. J. Smelser, & J. C. Alexander, (Eds.). *Diversity and its discontents: Cultural conflict and common ground in contemporary American society.* Princeton, NJ: Princeton University Press.

Gamoran, A., Nystrand, M., Berends, M., & LePore, P. C. (1995, Winter). An organizational analysis of the effects of ability grouping. *American Educational Research Journal, 32*(4), 687–715.

Greenwald, R., Hedges, L. V., & Laine, R. D. (1996, Fall). The effect of school resources on student achievement. *Review of Educational Research, 66*(3), 361–396.

Hacker, A. (1992). *Two nations: Black and white, separate, hostile, unequal.* New York: Ballantine.

Higher educational opportunity by family income: 1998. (2000, April). *Postsecondary Education Opportunity,* No. 94.

Karp, S. (1995, Summer). Equity suits clog the courts. *Rethinking Schools, 9*(4), 3, 18–19.

Lasch, C. (1995). *The revolt of the elites and the betrayal of democracy.* New York: Norton.

Liebow, E. (1967). *Tally's corner: A study of Negro street corner men.* Boston: Little, Brown.

Mishel, L., Bernstein, J., & Schmitt, J. (1999). *The state of working America: 1996–97.* Armonk, NY: Economic Policy Institute.

Murdock, S. H. (1995). *An America challenged: Population change and the future of the United States.* Boulder, CO: Westview Press.

National Coalition for the Homeless. (1999a). *How many people experience homelessness?* (NCH Fact Sheet #2). Washington, DC: Author.

National Coalition for the Homeless. (1999b). *Homeless Youth.* (NCH Fact Sheet #11). Washington, DC: Author.

National Law Center on Homelessness and Poverty. (1999). *Out of sight—out of mind? A report on anti-homeless laws, litigation, and alternatives in 50 United States cities.* Washington, DC: Author.

National Low Income Housing Coalition. (1998). *Out of reach: Rental housing at what cost?* Washington, DC: Author.

Payne, K. J., & Biddle, B. J. (1999, August–September). Poor school funding, child poverty, and mathematics achievement. *Educational Researcher, 28*(6), 4–13.

Redlener, I., & Johnson, D. (1999). *Still in crisis: The health status of New York's homeless children.* New York: The Children's Health Fund.

Rist, R. C. (1970). Student social class and teacher expectations: The self-fulfilling prophecy in ghetto education. *Harvard Educational Review, 40*(3), 70–110.

Rose, S. J. (2000). *Social stratification in the United States.* New York: New Press.

Shinn, M., & Weitzman, B. (1996). Homeless families are different. In National Coalition for the Homeless, *Homelessness in America.* Washington, DC: National Coalition for the Homeless.

Slavin, R. (1995, Summer). Making money make a difference. *Rethinking Schools, 9*(4), 10, 23.

Smith, Dan. (2000). *The state of the world atlas.* New York: Penguin.

Spencer, R. (1993, May 18). U.S. ranks 6th in quality of life; Japan is 1st. *The Washington Post,* p. A7.

Stronge, J. H. (1995, April). Educating homeless students: How can we help? *Journal for a Just and Caring Education, 1*(2), 128–141.

U.S. Census Bureau. (1999). *Statistical abstract of the United States, 1999* (119th ed.). Washington, DC: U.S. Government Printing Office.

U.S. Department of Education, National Center for Education Statistics (2000, June). *High school dropouts, by race-ethnicity and recency of migration* (NCES2000-009). Washington, DC: Author.

Urban Institute. (2000). *America's homeless II: Populations and services.* Washington, DC: Author.

Zandy, J. (1996). Decloaking class: Why class identity and consciousness count. *Race, Gender, and Class, 4*(1), 7–23.

Suggested Readings

Galinsky, E. (1999). *Ask the children: What America's children really think about working parents.* New York: William Morrow.
This report of the findings of a comprehensive study on children's perspectives on work and family life today contradicts the popular belief that working mothers do irreconcilable damage to their children.

Kozol, J. (1988). *Rachel and her children: Homeless families in America.* New York: Crown.
This chronicle of the lives of homeless families headed by women provides descriptions of life in emergency shelters and welfare hotels and the humiliation felt by these women and their children.

Kozol, J. (1991). *Savage inequalities: Children in America's schools.* New York: Crown.
These descriptions of rich and poor schools are a powerful statement on the class and racial inequities that exist in the United States. Interwoven with the stories of students and educators is an analysis of the inadequacy of the current funding of schools.

Mishel, L., Bernstein, J., & Schmitt, J. (1999). *The state of working America: 1998–99.* Ithaca, NY: ILR Press.
Data on family incomes, taxes, wages, unemployment, wealth, and poverty are compiled biennially by the Economic Policy Institute to provide an analysis of the impact of the economy on the living standards of U.S. citizens.

Rose, S. J. (2000). *Social stratification in the United States.* New York: New Press.
This booklet compiles and analyzes data on income, wealth, race, and marital and occupational status. The accompanying poster and its discussion provide a vivid description of the U.S. social structure.

Tilly, C. (1999). *Durable inequality.* Berkeley, CA: University of California Press.
This exploration of the reasons for continuing equality provides a theoretical framework for examining the existing inequalities.

CRITICAL INCIDENTS IN TEACHING

Differences in Socioeconomic Status

The middle school in a rural community of 9000 residents has four school-sponsored dances each year. At the Valentine's dance, a coat-and-tie affair, six eighth-grade boys showed up in rented tuxedos. They had planned this together, and their parents, among the more affluent in the community, thought it would be "cute" and paid for the rentals. The final dance of the year is scheduled for May, and it, too, is a coat-and-tie dance. This time, rumors are circulating around school that "everyone" is renting a tux and that the girls are getting new formal dresses. The parents of three boys are, according to the grapevine, renting a limousine for their sons and their dates. These behaviors and dress standards are far in excess of anything previously observed at the middle school.

Several students, particularly those from lower socioeconomic backgrounds, have said they will boycott the dance. They cannot afford the expensive attire, and they claim that the ones behind the dress-up movement have said that only the nerds or geeks would show up in anything less than a tux or a formal gown.

Questions for Discussion

To answer these questions online, go to the Critical Incidents module for this chapter of the Companion Website.

1. Should the school administration intervene?
2. Should the limo-renting parents be contacted?
3. Should the matter be discussed in the homerooms? In a school assembly?
4. Should the May dance be canceled?
5. Should limits be set on how dressed up students can be? Could the school legally enforce limits?
6. Can and should an issue be made of the hiring of limousine services for middle school students?

Chapter 3

Ethnicity and Race

Nobody recognizes I am Vietnamese because when they look at me they think I am Chinese. They cannot recognize who I am.

My Lien Nguyen, 1996

Denise Williams had become increasingly aware of the racial tension in the high school in which she teaches, but she did not expect the hostility that erupted between some black and white students that Friday. In the week that followed, the faculty decided they had to do more to develop positive interethnic and interracial relations among students. They established a committee to identify consultants and other resources to guide them in this effort.

Ms. Williams, however, thought that neither she nor her students could wait for months to receive a report from the committee. She was ready to introduce the civil rights movement in her social studies class. It seemed a perfect time to promote better cross-cultural communications. She decided that she would let students talk about their feelings.

She soon learned that this topic was not an easy one to handle. African American students expressed their anger at the discriminatory practices in the school and the community. Most white students did not believe that *there was any discrimination. They believed that there were no valid reasons for the anger and that if other students just followed the rules and worked harder, they would not have these problems. She thought the class was getting nowhere. In fact, sometimes the anger on both sides was so intense that she worried a physical fight would erupt. She was frustrated that the class discussions and activities were not helping students correct their stereotypes and prejudices. At times, she thought students were just becoming more entrenched in them. She wondered whether she could do anything in her class to improve understanding, empathy, and communications across groups.*

What factors contribute to racial and ethnic conflict in some schools? What racial groups are most likely to see themselves in the school curriculum and activities? How can a classroom reflect the diversity of its students so that they all feel valued and respected? What were the positive and negative outcomes of the steps taken by Ms. Williams? What would you have done to improve cross-cultural relations among class members?

ETHNIC AND RACIAL DIVERSITY

The United States is an ethnically and racially diverse nation comprised of at least 276 ethnic groups, including 170 Native American groups. Today, the indigenous first Americans make up less than 1% of the total U.S. population. Therefore, the majority of the population or their ancestors immigrated during the past 500 years.

The reasons for immigration have varied greatly. Most Africans originally were imported involuntarily to this country to provide labor for an expanding Southern agricultural economy. Most European immigrants came voluntarily to escape oppressive political, religious, or economic conditions. Chinese were recruited to help build railroads in the mid-nineteenth century. Southern and Eastern Europeans were recruited to meet the expanding labor needs of a developing industrial nation at the end of the nineteenth and beginning of the twentieth centuries. Some of today's immigrants come to join family members who have already settled here. Others are fleeing oppressive conditions in their native countries; still others are seeking the perceived advantages of U.S. citizenship.

Many people forget that the United States was already populated by the time Europeans arrived on its shores. As more and more foreigners arrived, American Indians were not treated as equal citizens in the formation of the new nation. Eventually, most first Americans were forcibly segregated from the dominant group and, in many cases, forced to move from their geographic homeland to reservations in other parts of the country. This separation led to a pattern of isolation and inequities that still exists today. The atrocities and near genocide that resulted from the treatment of American Indians have been ignored in most historical accounts of U.S. history. Not until 2000 did an official of the U.S. government apologize for the Bureau of Indian Affairs' "legacy of racism and inhumanity that included massacres, forced relocations of tribes and attempts to wipe out Indian languages and cultures" (Kelley, 2000, p. 1).

Although most of the first European settlers were English, the French, Dutch, and Spanish also established early settlements. After the consolidation and development of the United States as an independent nation, successive waves of Western Europeans joined the earlier settlers. Irish, Swedish, and German immigrants often came to escape economic impoverishment or political repression in the countries of origin. These early European settlers brought with them the political institutions that provided the framework for our government. The melding of their cultures over time became the dominant culture to which other immigrant groups strived or were forced to assimilate.

People of African descent have been a part of the American experience from the early days of colonization. The thousands of Africans who were kidnapped and

VIDEO INSIGHT

Denying School to Children of Illegal Immigrants

In 1996, between 300,000 to 500,000 illegal aliens were enrolled in California's public schools. The cost to the state and its taxpayers to educate these children? About 1.8 billion dollars. As California's public school rankings drop to among the lowest in the nation, some citizens and lawmakers blame the diminishing quality of education in the state on the enormous expense of educating the children of illegal immigrants, and have tried to pass laws denying public education to these children. Supporters of such initiatives say that legal, tax-paying citizens are suffering as a result of unenforced immigration laws; detractors assert that denying these children education will only lead to more gang and criminal activity, and an uneducated workforce.

Consider the racism, prejudice, and discrimination that this country's citizens—most of them immigrants at one time or another—have both suffered through and participated in during our nation's short history. What do you think of our country's current efforts to regulate immigration? As a citizen, do you believe it is our country's responsibility to educate all children, or only those whose parents are tax-paying American citizens? As a teacher, do you believe it is your responsibility to educate all children, or only those whose parents are tax-paying American citizens?

sold into bondage underwent a process quite different from that of immigrants who voluntarily emigrated. Separated from their families and homelands, robbed of their freedom and cultures, Africans developed a new culture out of their different African, European, and Native American heritages and their unique experiences in this country. Initially, the majority of African Americans lived in the South; they remain the majority population in many counties across the Southern states. In the first half of the twentieth century, however, many African Americans migrated to Northern, Eastern, and Western cities. This migration was generally fueled by the same factors that brought Eastern and Southern Europeans to the United States—the need for labor in industrial jobs.

Another factor that contributed to this migration was the racism and political terror that existed in much of the South at that time. Even today, a racial ideology is implicit in the policies and practices of institutions. It continues to block significant assimilation of many African Americans into the dominant society. Although the civil rights movement of the 1960s reduced the barriers that prevented most African Americans from enjoying the advantages of the middle class, the number of African Americans who remain in poverty is disproportionately high. At the same time, the number of families and individuals who have been able to join the ranks of the middle class has increased dramatically since the 1960s.

Mexican Americans also occupy a unique role in the formation of the United States. Spain was the first European country to colonize Mexico and the Western and Southwestern United States. In 1848, the U.S. government annexed the northern sections of the Mexican Territory, including the current areas of Texas, Arizona, New Mexico, and southern California. The Mexican population and Native American people living within that territory became an oppressed minority—in the area in which they had previously been the dominant population. Dominant supremacy theories based on color and language also were used against these ethnic groups in a way that, even today, prevents many of them from assimilating fully into the dominant culture.

The industrial opening of the West signaled the need for labor that could be met through immigration from Asia. Chinese worked the plantations in Hawaii. Chinese, Japanese, and Phillipinos (Filipinos) were recruited to provide the labor needed on the West Coast for mining gold and building railroads. Later immigrants came from the relatively more impoverished Eastern and Southern European countries to work primarily in Midwestern and Eastern cities. At the end of the nineteenth and beginning of the twentieth centuries, many immigrants arrived from nations such as Poland, Hungary, Italy, Russia, and Greece. The reasons for their immigration were the same as for earlier immigrants: devastating economic and political hardship in the homeland and demand for labor in the United States. Many immigrants came to the United States with the hope of sharing the better wages and living conditions they thought existed here. But many found conditions here much worse than they had expected. Most were forced to live in substandard housing near the business and manufacturing districts where they worked, in urban ghettos that grew into ethnic enclaves in which others from the same country continued to use the native language. To support their social and welfare needs, ethnic institutions often were established.

The same dominant racist policies that had been used against African Americans, Mexican Americans, and Native Americans earlier came to be used against the new immigrants. At various times, the U.S. Congress has prohibited the immigration of different national or ethnic groups on the basis of the racial superiority of the older, established immigrant groups that had colonized the nation. As early as 1729, immigration was being discouraged. In that year, Pennsylvania passed a statute that increased the head tax on foreigners in that colony. Later that century, Congress passed the Alien and Sedition Acts, which lengthened the time required to become a citizen from five years to fourteen years. In the nineteenth century, native-born Americans again began to worry about their majority and superiority status over entering immigrant groups. This movement, *nativism,* was designed to restrict immigration and to protect the interests of native-born Americans. It was an extreme form of nationalism and ethnocentrism.

In 1881, Congress passed the Chinese Exclusion Act, which halted all immigration from China. The Dillingham Commission reported in 1917 that all immigrants should be able to pass a literacy test. The nativists received further support for their views when Congress passed the Johnson-Reed Act in 1924, which discriminated against Southern and Eastern Europeans and nonwhite nationals, and stopped all immigration from Japan. The act established annual immigration quotas to disproportionately favor immigrants from Western European countries.

The Johnson-Reed Act was not abolished until 1965, when a new quota system was established that dramatically increased the number of immigrants annually allowed from the Eastern Hemisphere and reduced the number from the Western Hemisphere. As shown in Figure 3–1, the change in the immigration law has allowed the influx of immigrants from nations that formerly were restricted or excluded. In 1960, the nations contributing the most legal immigrants were Mexico,

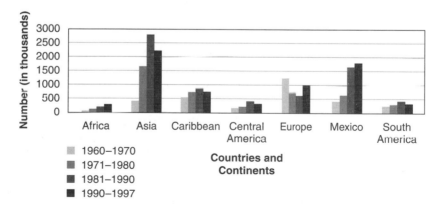

Figure 3–1

Immigration patterns to the United States from selected countries and continents have changed over the past four decades.

Source: U.S. Census Bureau. (1999). *Statistical Abstract of the United States* (119th ed.). Washington, DC: U.S. Government Printing Office.

Germany, Canada, the United Kingdom, and Italy. In 1997, the five leading countries were Mexico, the Philippines, China, Vietnam, and India. Russia and Ukraine contributed the largest number of European immigrants. The immigration rate during the past decade has been nearly 1 million per year. Immigration is not just a U.S. phenomenon, however; it is worldwide. "More that 100 million people live in countries of which they are not citizens" (Clawson, 1995, p. ix).

Refugees are sometimes admitted under special acts of Congress. Favoritism has been granted to refugees fleeing countries not supported by the U.S. government. From 1991 to 1996, almost three-quarters of a million immigrants were admitted as refugees; the largest number came from Vietnam, followed by Cuba, Ukraine, Russia, Yugoslavia, Uzbekistan, Belarus, and Iraq. Refugees from some countries, like Haiti, are refused entry as refugees, no matter how oppressive the government may be. As a result of governmental immigration and refugee policies, the U.S. population from various national and ethnic groups has been controlled, but has become increasingly diverse.

The Immigration and Naturalization Services (INS) estimates that 5 million undocumented immigrants reside in the United States. About 80% of the illegal immigrants are from Mexico and other countries in the Western Hemisphere. California is home to the largest number, with 40% of the undocumented population. The majority of undocumented immigrants settle in the same states as most legal immigrants—California, Texas, New York, Florida, Illinois, New Jersey, and Arizona.

In *Plyer v. Doe*, the U.S. Supreme Court ruled in 1982 that undocumented children have the right to seek a public education. Educators are not INS officials who enforce immigration laws. In fact, they cannot require students or parents to declare their immigration status, and they cannot make inquiries that might expose such status. For example, parents cannot be forced to provide social security numbers to school districts. Educators should take all possible action to encourage undocumented students to attend school.

The border between Mexico and the United States is an ever-present reality in the Southwestern states, having an impact on politics and economics in the region. Border patrols search for illegal immigrants. Latinos from all walks of life are regularly stopped and searched by police. Power struggles are common among powerful and oppressed groups, landowners and migrant workers, and potential industries and the owners of water rights.

Forty-five percent of today's immigrants live in New York City, Los Angeles/Long Beach, Chicago, Miami, the Washington, DC area, San Francisco, Orange County (CA), Oakland (CA), Houston, and the Boston area (Olson, 2000). Others have settled in rural and suburban areas. Immigration to these areas is often dependent on job availability and perceived quality of life. Some refugee families (e.g., from the Hmong population) have been sponsored by church and community groups in these areas (Schnalberg, 1996). Thus, schools in Arkansas, Iowa, Nebraska, Montana, and Wisconsin include students from different cultures and with languages other than English.

As people from all over the world joined Native Americans in populating this nation, they brought with them cultural experiences from their native countries.

The conditions they encountered, the reasons they came, and their expectations about life in this country differed greatly, causing each ethnic group to view itself as distinct from other ethnic groups. Just because individuals have the same national origins does not mean that they have the same history and experiences as other individuals in that group. The time of immigration, the place in which groups settled, the reasons for emigrating, and the degree to which they are affected by racism and discrimination interact with other factors to form a new American group that differs from those who came before and will come afterward.

ETHNIC AND RACIAL GROUPS

The uniqueness of an individual, a family, and sometimes a neighborhood can be identified as ethnic by an outsider. Children become aware of gender, race, ethnicity, and disabilities between the ages of two and five. At the same time, they become sensitive to the positive and negative biases associated with those groups (Derman-Sparks & A.B.C. Task Force, 1989). Often, this distinction is made because of the physical characteristics of individuals or the distinct language and shops in a neighborhood. Other times, the distinction may be based on observed behaviors that suggest a particular ethnic background. This uniqueness is most often based almost solely on skin color and other distinctive physical characteristics.

Ethnic Groups

Many definitions have been proposed for the term *ethnic group* during the past four decades. Gordon (1964) wrote that the ethnic identity of an American is based on national origin, religion, and race. Some writers have expanded the definition to include gender, religion, class, and lifestyle. Many authors identify Jewish Americans as an ethnic group, in part, because many members of the Jewish faith emphasize their Judaism, rather than their national origin, as the most meaningful basis of their identity. Jews from Germany, Spain, and India may share more commonalities because of religion than they share with non-Jewish Germans, Spaniards, or Indians. In this text, however, religious differences are examined separately from ethnicity, and *ethnic group* is defined only as an individual's national origin or origins.

A *nation* is a historically constituted, stable community of people formed on the basis of a common language, territory, economic life, and psychological makeup or culture. Of course, nations change over time because of boundaries being moved (or removed) as a result of political negotiations. New boundaries do not always translate into new national identities; it may take generations for such a conversion.

Ethnic identity is determined by living in a nation or maintaining ancestral ties even after having emigrated from a country. The strongest support for the country of origin is usually based on continuing family ties in that country. In many families, ties in the country of origin weaken after several generations. Without extensive tracing of the family lineage, most members of ethnic groups who have been in this country for several generations probably could not identify relatives in their country of origin. Yet, support for the country of origin often continues. For example, in the aftermath of natural disasters, ethnic groups across the United States organize to collect money for relief. When Congressional cuts are being proposed in foreign aid or conflicts develop between groups in other countries, ethnic groups sometimes lobby on behalf of their country of origin.

Many members of ethnic groups in the United States maintain some of the cultural uniqueness of their national origin. A common bond is developed through family, friends, and neighbors with whom the same intimate characteristics of living are shared. These are the people invited to baptisms, marriages, funerals, and family reunions. They are the people with whom we feel the most comfortable. They know the meaning of our behavior; they share the same language and nonverbal patterns, traditions, and customs. Endogamy, segregated residential areas, and restriction of activities with the dominant group help preserve ethnic cohesiveness across generations.

The ethnic group allows for the maintenance of group cohesiveness. It helps sustain and enhance the ethnic identity of its members. It establishes the social networks and communicative patterns that are important for the group's optimization of its position in society. As a result, members are inherently ethnocentric.

The character of an ethnic group changes over time from its existence in the country of origin. Members within ethnic groups have different attitudes and behaviors based on their experiences in the United States and the conditions in the country of origin at the time of emigration. Recent immigrants may have little in common with other members of their ethnic group whose ancestors immigrated a century, or even 20 years, before. Ethnic communities undergo constant change in population characteristics, locations, occupations, educational levels, and political and economic struggles. All of these aspects affect the nature of the group and its members.

A person does not have to live in the same community with other members of the ethnic group to continue to identify with the group. Boundaries are maintained by ascription from within the group, as well as from external sources that place persons in a specific group because of the way they look, the color of their skin, the location of their homes, or their names. Although many individuals are several generations removed from an immigrant status, some continue to consciously emphasize their ethnicity as a meaningful basis of their identity. In this case, the maintenance of one's identity with an ethnic group becomes a choice and is no longer ascriptive. It is characterized by a nostalgic allegiance to the culture of one's ancestral homeland. As the dominant society allows members of an ethnic group to assimilate, it views that particular ethnic group as less distinct. Ethnicity then becomes more voluntary for group members—a process much more likely to occur for those with European backgrounds and others who look white.

Group identity is reinforced by the political and economic barriers established by the dominant society to prevent the assimilation of oppressed groups. Ethnicity is strongest within groups that develop group solidarity through similar lifestyles, common social and economic interests, and a high degree of interpersonal connections. Historically, oppressed groups have often been segregated from the dominant group and have developed enclaves in cities and suburbs that help members maintain a strong ethnic identity.

Members of oppressed groups sometimes coalesce to fight against the harsh economic and political realities and injustices imposed on them. Thus, movements for democratic rights and economic justice develop among different ethnic groups. These movements invariably entail a rise in the concern of the community with its original or indigenous culture, as this aspect of their lives also may have been suppressed and excluded by the dominant majority.

This reaction was seen in the United States in the civil rights movement of the 1960s when African Americans challenged their oppressed status in society. The call for "Black Power" followed years of civil rights struggle that led to the passage of the 1964 Civil Rights Act and the 1965 Voting Rights Act. Yet, changes did not necessarily follow. Although legislation guaranteed equality, many European Americans continued to fight against desegregation of schools and other public facilities. Frustrations with the majority group led members of oppressed groups to identify strongly with other members of their ethnic group and to fight discrimination and inequality with a unified voice. These struggles continue today not only in this country, but throughout the world.

Racial Groups

Are racial groups also ethnic groups? In the United States, many people use the two terms interchangeably. *Race* is a concept that was developed by physical anthropologists to describe the physical characteristics of people in the world more than a century ago—a practice that has now been discredited. Racial groups include many ethnic groups, and ethnic groups may include members of one or more racial groups. How has such mixed usage of the terms developed in this country?

Throughout U.S. history, racial identification has been used by policymakers and much of the population to classify groups of people as inferior or superior to other racial groups. Some theorists suggest that *race*, as used in the United States, is equivalent to *caste* in other countries. Both are distinctions imposed at birth on a group of people to justify the inequitable social distribution of power and privilege.

Many persons with Northern and Western European ancestry view themselves as the superior racial and ethnic group in the United States and the world. Until 1952, immigrants had to be white to be eligible for naturalized citizenship. At one time, slaves and American Indians were perceived as so inferior to the dominant group that each individual was counted by the government as only a fraction of a person. This phenomenon of racial consciousness in the United States was repeated on the West Coast in the late nineteenth century when Chinese immigrants were charged an additional tax. Even the large influx of Southern and Eastern Europeans in the late nineteenth and early twentieth centuries were viewed as members of an inferior race. However, these Europeans were eligible for citizenship because they were white; persons from most other continents were not eligible. Arab American immigrants, for example, argued in courts that they were white so that they could become citizens.

In 1916, *The Passing of the Great Race* by Madison Grant detailed the U.S. racist ideology. Northern and Western Europeans of the Nordic race were considered by the powerful to be the political and military geniuses of the world. Protecting the purity of the Nordic race became such an emotional and popular issue for the majority of U.S. citizens that laws were passed to severely limit immigration from any region except Northern European countries. Miscegenation laws in many states legally prevented the marriage of whites to members of other races until the U.S. Supreme Court declared the laws unconstitutional in 1967. The immigration quota system passed by Congress in 1921 remained in effect until it was repealed in 1965. Nativism reappeared in the 1990s in resolutions, referenda, and legislation that denied education to illegal immigrants, restricted communication to the English language, and limited available prenatal care and preschool service to low-income families who are disproportionately of color.

Once race identification became codified in this country, it was acceptable, even necessary at times, to identify oneself by race. Federal forms and reports classify the population on the basis of a mixture of racial and pan-ethnic categorizations as shown in Figure 3–2.

The problem with identifying the U.S. population by such characteristics is that it tells little about the people in these groups. Although whites are numerically dominant, this classification includes many different ethnic groups. Neither the ethnic identification nor the actual racial heritage of African Americans is recognized. The Hispanic grouping includes different racial groups and mixtures of racial groups, as well as distinct ethnic groups whose members identify themselves as Mexican Americans, Puerto Ricans, Spanish Americans, and Cuban Americans. This category also includes persons with roots in numerous Central and South American countries.

Figure 3–2

In 2000, the U.S. population was comprised of five pan-ethnic and racial groups.

Source: U.S. Census Bureau. (1999). *Statistical Abstract of the United States* (119th ed.). Washington, DC: U.S. Government Printing Office.

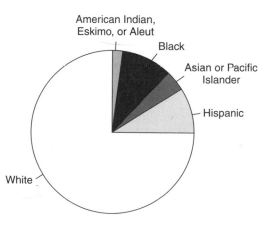

The pan-ethnic classification of Asian and Pacific Islander Americans includes both individuals whose families have been here for more than a generation and those who are first-generation citizens. Many do not have much more in common than that their countries of origin are on the same continent. They are "Bangladeshi, Bhutanese, Bornean, Burmese, Cambodian, Celbesian, Cernan, Chamorro, Chinese, East Indian, Filipino, Hawaiian, Hmong, Indonesian, Japanese, Korean, Laotian, Okinawan, Samoan, Sikkimese, Singaporean, Sri Lankan, and Vietnamese" (Young & Pang, 1995, p. 5). Further, whether Asian Americans are American born or immigrants has significance in how they identify themselves. These pan-ethnic classifications often have imposed boundaries and do not always reflect how group members see themselves.

Although ideas about racial superiority have found no support within the scientific community, many people continue to believe in the inferiority of races other than white. This belief can be observed in cases of mixed racial heritage. Individuals of black and white parentage are usually classified as black, not white; those of Japanese and white heritage usually are classified as nonwhite. However, the number of persons with multiracial backgrounds is growing. Although multiracial individuals made up only 2% of the population in 1995, the number of interracial couples has increased nearly tenfold since 1960 (Tafoya, 2000). Half of the children of Asian immigrants marry non-Asians, and 35% of the children of Latino immigrants marry members of other groups (Diversity Data, 2000).

Race is no longer a function of biological or genetic differences among groups. It is not a stable category for organizing and differentiating people. Instead, it is a social-historical concept dependent on society's perception that differences exist and that these differences are important. The cultural distinctions between racial groups become the rationale for an inferior status, discrimination, and inequality.

African Americans range in skin color along a continuum from black to white. Thus, it is not the color of their skin that defines them. Their identification is based, in part, on sharing a common origin that can be traced to numerous African tribes and European and Native American nations. They have become a single ethnic group because they share a common history, language, economic life, and culture that have developed over centuries of living in the United States. Members of a group become cohesive, in part, as a response to the way they are treated by others. For example, all African Americans continue to face discrimination in racial profiling by police, segregated schools and housing, and treatment in shopping centers and on the job.

Because individuals appear to be African American is not an indication that they always identify themselves as African Americans. Some identify themselves as blacks; others with a specific ethnic group—for example, Puerto Rican or Somalian American or West Indian. Africans who are recent immigrants generally identify themselves ethnically by nation or tribe of origin.

Many whites see themselves as raceless. They are the norm against which everyone else is *other*. To many, race has been equated with European ethnicity in which the social system is viewed as open and individuals can attain success with hard work. This view allows ethnicity to disappear as a determinant of life chances after a group has been in the country for a while. Many whites have their own stories or narratives of the mobility they or their families have experienced. Because they believe that their mobility was based totally on individual achievement, they cannot understand why members of other groups have not experienced the same success. They deny that racial inequality has any impact on their ability to achieve. They seldom acknowledge that white oppression of people of color around the world has contributed to the subordinate status of these groups. Most whites are unable to acknowledge that they are privileged in our social, political, and economic systems. Just as gender studies should not focus solely on girls and women, the study of race should not be limited to persons of color. Whiteness and privilege should also be addressed to expose the privilege and power it bestows on its members in the maintenance of an inequitable system.

An understanding of race and how we have been advantaged or disadvantaged because of our race is important in working with both white students and students of color. It is natural for white students to become defensive as they learn their own role in racism and begin to understand the privilege that has historically accompanied whiteness. Studying race "often generates emotional responses in students that range from guilt and shame to anger and despair. The discomfort associated with these emotions can lead students to resist the learning process" (Tatum, 1992, p. 1). Unless one becomes comfortable with confronting one's own race, as well as those of others, it will be difficult to be an effective teacher in a community and school where members are from racial groups unlike one's own.

The issue of race may become even more contentious as whites lose their majority status. More than one-third of the nation is African American, Latino, Asian American, and American Indian. These groups will comprise more than 40% of the population by 2020, and 50% of the population by 2040. This pattern is not unique to the United States. "Of the 5.7 billion people in the world, only 17% are white, a figure that is expected to drop to 9% by 2010" (Diversity Data, 2000).

There are two variables that contribute to the significant population growth of individuals of color. The U.S. population has been increasing at a rate of approximately 2 million annually. Of that number, close to 1 million of the increase can be attributed to immigration. Nearly 80% of the immigrants are nonwhite, and approximately 70% are from Latin America or Asia.

The second variable contributing to the changing face of America is the birth rate. To maintain the status quo, each woman must bear, on average, 2.1 children. One child will eventually take the place of the mother, and the other, the father; the .1 is for infant mortality. In the baby boom years of 1946 to 1964, the U.S. population grew dramatically, with a birth rate of 2.9 children per woman. Today the birth rate is approximately 2.1, the highest among industrialized nations (e.g., it is 1.4 in Europe). As we examine the various groups, we can see how the differential birth rate is contributing to differing growth patterns. White women in the United States are having an average of 1.8 children, Asian/Pacific average of 1.9, Indian/Aleut average of 2.1, African American average of 2.2, and Latinos average of 2.9.

Race has been important in this country only because racial identity singled out certain people as inferior to whites of Northern and Western Europe. Thus, people who looked different than whites were eligible for discriminatory treatment. As whites lose their majority status, will the power that some think is their natural right be reduced as well? Will egalitarianism across groups become a more achievable goal? Some white extremists believe that they must fight to maintain their supremacy. This movement could lead to greater conflict among groups if a large number of people actually believe that one group should be superior to all others. Or, the changing demographics could lead to a more equitable sharing of power and societal benefits across all groups.

PAUSE TO REFLECT

Although race has no scientific significance in describing people, it is a social construct that endures in the United States to classify groups. It is nearly impossible to be color-blind. What characteristics do you attribute to whites, blacks, Latinos, Asians, and American Indians? Do you view some groups more positively than others? What has influenced your perceptions of your own group and others? How will you overcome any negative stereotypes you hold to ensure that you do not discriminate against students in your classroom?

To answer these questions online, go to the Pause to Reflect module for this chapter of the Companion Website.

INTERGROUP RELATIONS

In a national survey by the National Conference for Community and Justice (2000) on the state of intergroup relations in the U.S., 42% of the African Americans reported incidents of discrimination in the past month, as compared with 13% of the whites, 16% of the Latinos, and 31% of the Asian Americans. Where the discrimination occurred during the past month differed by group, as shown in the following chart.

	While Shopping	At Work	In a Restaurant, Bar, or Theater	At Place of Worship	Other
Whites	4%	3%	4%	1%	3%
Blacks	20%	14%	12%	1%	9%
Latinos	8%	6%	3%	1%	3%
Asian Americans	14%	11%	8%	0%	10%

The National Conference survey found that only 29% of the respondents "are satisfied with 'how well different groups in society get along with each other' and when looking at the 'country as a whole,' 79% consider 'racial, religious, or ethnic tension' a very serious or somewhat serious problem." Intergroup tensions and conflicts are often the result of some groups receiving more rewards from society than others. Persons of color overwhelmingly perceive whites as having too much power. They also perceive whites as having greater opportunities for job advancement, equal pay, and fair and unbiased treatment by the police and media. Most whites do recognize that persons of color do not have the same opportunities as they do, but the percentage of whites who acknowledge these differences is smaller than in any other group.

Interethnic conflict is certainly not new in the United States, although the intensity of such conflicts has been mild compared to that in many other nations. Oppressed people in this country do have a history of resistance, however, as shown in revolts organized by slaves, riots after particularly egregious actions of police or others, and strikes by workers. American Indian and white conflicts were common in the European American attempt to subjugate the native peoples.

What are the reasons for continued interethnic conflict? Discriminatory practices have protected the superior status of the dominant group for centuries. When other ethnic groups try to share more equitably in the rewards and privileges of society, the dominant group must concede some of its advantages. Most recently, this concern about giving up some advantages of the dominant group has been reflected in reverse discrimination cases as a reaction to affirmative action programs. As long as one ethnic or racial group has an institutional advantage over others, some intergroup conflict will exist.

Competition for economic resources can also contribute to intergroup conflict. As economic conditions become tighter, fewer jobs are available. Discriminatory practices in the past have forced people of color into positions with the least seniority. As a result, when jobs are cut back, disproportionately high numbers are laid off. The tension between ethnic groups increases as members of specific groups determine that they disproportionately suffer the hardships resulting from economic depression. Conflict sometimes occurs between oppressed groups when they are forced to share limited societal resources, such as affordable housing and access to quality education programs. Conflict as a result of inequitable distribution of economic rewards is likely to continue as long as members of groups can observe and feel those inequities.

During the past 50 years, educational strategies have been developed to reduce and overcome intergroup conflicts. These strategies have focused on training teachers to be effective in intergroup or human relations; on attempting to change the prejudicial attitudes of teachers; on fighting institutional discrimination through affirmative action and civil rights legislation; on encouraging changes in textbooks and other resources to more accurately reflect the multiethnic nature of society; and on attempting to remove discriminatory behavior from classroom interactions and classroom practices. All of these strategies are important to combat prejudice and discrimination in the educational setting. Alone or in combination, however, the strategies are not enough, but that does not diminish the need for professional educators to further develop the strategies. It is not a sign of failure, but a recognition that prejudice, discrimination, and racism are diseases that infect all of society, not only the schools and many professional educators.

Prejudice and Discrimination

Prejudice and *discrimination* stem from a combination of several factors related to *us* and *them*. People generally lack an understanding of the history, experiences, values, and perceptions of ethnic groups other than their own. Members of other groups are stereotyped without consideration of individual differences within the group. Other groups are judged according to the standards and values of one's own group. Negative attributes are assigned to members of other ethnic groups. The qualities and experiences of other groups are believed to be inferior to one's own. In other words, prejudice and discrimination are forms of ethnocentrism.

Prejudice is a set of negative attitudes about a group of people. This aversion to members of certain ethnic groups manifests itself in feelings of anger, fear, hatred, and distrust about members of that group. These attitudes are often translated into fear of walking in the group's neighborhood, fear of being robbed or hurt by group members, distrust of a merchant from the group, anger at any advantages that group members may be perceived as receiving, and fear that housing prices will be deflated if someone from that group moves next door.

Prejudice is not limited to one ethnic or racial group. Some members of all groups express negative stereotypes of others. For example, the majority of African Americans and Latinos believe that whites are bigoted, bossy, and unwilling to share power (National Conference, 1994). In a 2-year study of teachers in a staff development project, Sleeter (1993) found that many white teachers "associated people of color—and particularly African Americans and Latinos—with dysfunctional families and communities, and lack of ability and motivation" (p. 162).

Although prejudice may not always directly hurt members of a group, it can be easily translated into behavior that does harm them. An ideology based on aversion to a group and perceived superiority undergirds the activities of the neo-Nazis, Ku Klux Klan, and other white racist groups that currently exist in our society.

VIDEO INSIGHT

America in Black and White

Society forms impressions of people everyday based solely on appearance. Many people make judgments about intelligence, happiness, and earning potential without any real information. Do you think our society in general continues to judge people based on skin tone, consciously or unconsciously?

The issue of colorism is as big an issue now as ever. In this video segment you will see people working in different industries, and they are all saying the same thing: it's easier to get a job if you are a lighter skinned African American than if you are a darker skinned African American. In addition, this segment shows the disparity between salaries of lighter versus darker skinned men and women and the judgments people make about them simply based on the color of their skin.

What do you think of the experiment Professor Midge Wilson of DePaul University conducted with her introductory psychology class? Do you think it is fair to say that most college students would respond in the same way as those chosen by Professor Wilson? How do you think college students on your campus would respond? What can you do as an individual to change this way of thinking?

Whereas prejudice focuses on attitudes, discrimination focuses on behavior. *Discrimination* is the arbitrary denial of the privileges and rewards of society to members of a group. Discrimination occurs at two levels: individual and institutional. *Individual discrimination* is attributed to, or influenced by, prejudice. Individuals discriminate against a member of a group for at least two reasons: (1) either they have strong prejudicial, or bigoted, feelings about the group, or (2) they believe that societal pressures demand that they discriminate even though they may not be prejudiced. Realtors, personnel managers, receptionists, and membership chairpersons all work directly with individuals. Their own personal attitudes about members of certain groups can influence whether a house is sold, a job is offered, a loan is granted, an appointment is made, a meal is served, or a membership is extended to a member of the group. The action of these individuals can prevent others from gaining the experiences and economic advantage that these activities offer.

An individual has less control in the other form of discrimination. *Institutional discrimination* cannot be attributed to prejudicial attitudes. It refers to the effects of inequalities that have been integrated into the system-wide operation of a society through legislation and practices that ensure benefits to some groups and not to others. Laws that disproportionately limit immigration to people from specific countries are one example. Other examples include practices that lead to a disproportionately large number of African Americans being incarcerated, single low-income mothers being denied adequate prenatal care, and children in low-income neighborhoods suffering disproportionately from asthma as a result of poor environmental conditions in their neighborhoods.

We all face a dilemma, because we have grown up in a society that has inherently discriminated against persons of color since the first European Americans arrived. Throughout our lives, we have participated in societal institutions, including schools, Social Security, transportation, welfare, and housing patterns. We often do not realize the extent to which members of different groups receive the benefits and privileges of these institutions. Because we believe that we have never been discriminated against, we should not assume that others do not suffer from discrimination.

Many individuals might argue that institutional discrimination no longer exists because today's laws require equal access to the benefits of society. Omi and Winant (1994) suggest the following:

> With the exception of some on the far right, the racial reaction which has developed in the last two decades claims to favor racial equality. Its vision is that of a "colorblind" society where racial considerations are never entertained in the selection of leaders, in hiring decisions, and the distribution of goods and services in general. As the right sees it, racial problems today center on the new forms of racial "injustice" which originated in the "great transformation." This new injustice confers group rights on racial minority groups, thus granting a new form of privilege—that of preferential treatment.
>
> The culprit behind this new form of "racism" is seen as the state itself. Advocates of this view believe that the state went too far in attempting to eliminate racial discrimination. It legitimated group rights, established affirmative action mandates, and

spent money on a range of social programs, which, according to the right, debilitated, rather than uplifted, its target populations. In this scenario, the victims of racial discrimination have dramatically shifted from racial minorities to whites, particularly white males. (p. 117)

Criteria for access are often applied arbitrarily and unfairly. A disproportionately high number of persons of color do not possess the qualifications for skilled jobs or college entrance or have the economic resources to purchase a home in the suburbs. As businesses and industries move from the city to the suburbs, access to employment by those who live in the inner city is limited. The crucial issue is not the equal treatment of those with equal qualifications, but the accessibility to the qualifications and jobs themselves.

The consequences are the same in individual and institutional discrimination. Members of some groups do not receive the same benefits from society as the dominant group. Individuals are harmed by circumstances beyond their control because of their membership in a specific group. The role of teachers and other professional educators requires that they not discriminate against any student because of his or her ethnic or racial background. This consideration must be paramount in assigning students to special education and gifted classes and in giving and interpreting standardized tests. Classroom interactions, classroom resources, extracurricular activities, and counseling practices must be evaluated to ensure that discrimination against students from various ethnic groups does not occur.

Racism

Racism is "the belief in the inherent superiority of one race over all others and thereby the right to dominance" (Lorde, 1995, p. 192). In this sense, racism is an extreme form of prejudice. Often, this prejudice is transferred by individuals and government policy into discrimination against groups in immigration policies, the availability of housing and jobs, legal matters, and so forth.

Many members of the dominant group do not acknowledge the existence of external impingements and disabilities that make it much more difficult for people of color to shed their minority status than it was for their own European ancestors. They ignore the fact that some people of color have adopted the cultural values and standards of the dominant group to a greater degree than many white ethnic groups. Yet, discriminatory policies and practices prevent them from sharing equally in society's benefits with whites. In addition, the opportunities to gain qualifications with which people of color could compete equally with whites have been severely restricted throughout most of U.S. history.

The most crucial fact in understanding racism is that the dominant group has power over an oppressed group. This power has been used to prevent people of color from securing the prestige, power, and privilege held by whites. Professional educators should prevent such practices from occurring in their classrooms and schools.

A first step for educators is the recognition that racism exists and that, if they are white, they have benefited from it. This is not an easy process. People often resist discussion of these issues because they must eventually confront their own feelings. In predominantly white college classrooms, Tatum (1992) found three sources of resistance:

1. Race is considered a taboo topic for discussion, especially in racially mixed settings.
2. Many students, regardless of racial group membership, have been socialized to think of the United States as a just society.
3. Many students, particularly white students, initially deny any personal prejudice, recognizing the impact of racism on other people's lives but failing to acknowledge its impact on their own.

The challenge is to confront these issues seriously before entering a classroom. We experience stages of racial identity as we learn to accept the existence of racism and to feel comfortable with our own racial identities. The developmental stages differ for members of oppressed and dominant groups because of their own lived encounters with racism and oppression (Cross, 1991). It is important that educators seek opportunities to confront these issues in their own lives. Once in the classroom, they will be in the position to help students grapple with these topics and their own feelings. The goal should be to attack racism and oppression in daily life, rather than reinforce it in the classroom.

LINK TO THE CLASSROOM

Is it Discrimination?

Your principal has asked you to serve on the Equity Committee for the school district. At the committee's first meeting, a community advocate seeks figures on the diversity of students who are enrolled in advanced math and science classes, admitted to postsecondary education, and suspended. The committee soon learns that few girls and students of color are enrolled in advanced courses; students of color—usually males—are suspended at a much higher rate than white students; and nearly 80% of the white students—versus just 30% of students of color—in last year's graduating class were admitted to postsecondary programs. Why do these differences exist? What questions must you ask to determine if school policies and practices discriminate against one or more groups of students? What additional data might you request to help clarify issues related to discrimination and equity in the school district?

Hate Groups

Since World War II, overt acts of prejudice have decreased dramatically. In the early 1940s, the majority of whites supported segregation of and discrimination against, blacks. Today, most whites support policies against racial discrimination and prejudice. Intolerance of other groups and violence against their members, however, continue to exist. During the 1980s, it became more acceptable to openly express one's prejudice, as evidenced by cross burnings and racist themes at fraternity parties on some college campuses. The Southern Poverty Law Center documented 108 bias-motivated murders between 1990 and 1993 (Carnes, 1995). Motivations for attacks on blacks, whites, gays, lesbians, Latinos, Asians, American Indians, Jews, and Arabs are of three distinct types (Levin & McDevitt, 1993). The most common hate crime is done for the thrill or "fun of it." A second is to protect the neighborhood, workplace, or campus from outsiders. The rarest but most serious is carried out by those who are committed to prejudice and bigotry and are likely to belong to one of the 500 or so hate groups that exist in the United States.

The increasing number of individuals of color in the United States, television programming to accommodate new language groups, and new temples and mosques, has forever changed the U.S. landscape. These visible symbols of growth and change have become threatening to some individuals, whose comfort level does not extend beyond white Anglo-Saxon control or Judeo-Christian religious traditions. Eck (2000) discusses the case of a member of a state board of education who verbally attacked Buddhists and Muslims and who referred to Islam as a cult—worshipers of Lucifer. This is an individual entrusted with the responsibility of formulating public educational policy in his state.

Because of the increasing adversarial relationship that developed between fundamentalist Muslims in Iran and the United States, and the Persian Gulf War, American Muslims have been the targets of vicious attacks. In 1991, during the Gulf War, a Massachusetts mosque sustained a half million dollars in arson damages. A mosque in Yuba City, California was burned to the ground in 1994. Arsonists also victimized a South Carolina mosque in 1995.

After the devastating bombing of the Federal Building in Oklahoma City in 1994, many Americans were quick to conclude that Muslim terrorists were responsible for this heinous deed. Even the news media played into the hysteria, reporting that Muslims were suspected. While it is undeniable that Muslim terrorists have been responsible for some terrorist attacks, the overwhelming majority of American Muslims vigorously condemn terrorism and are model citizens. Nevertheless, they are routinely wrongly accused of being terrorists or sympathizers. Muslims have not been the only victims of religious intolerance. In 1999, as in the past, arsonists victimized Jewish synagogues around the country. Black churches had been the targets of arson earlier in the 1990s. In 1999, a gunman in Los Angeles attacked young children at a Jewish day care center. That same year, a member of a hate group went on a rampage in Illinois and Indiana and did not stop until he had shot at several individuals, and had killed an African American basketball coach and a Korean graduate student. There is no evidence that the gunman knew his victims. He was just out to kill individuals of color.

Hate has also become commonplace on college campuses. The FBI reported about 250 hate crimes on campuses in 1998 (Hate on Campus, 2000). The Southern Poverty Law Center described a few of the incidents:

At SUNY Maritime College in the Bronx, 21 Arab students flee after a series of assaults and incidents of racist harassment. At Brown University in Rhode Island, a black senior is beaten by three white students who tell her she is a "quota" who doesn't belong. At the State University of New York at Binghamton, three students are charged in a racially motivated assault that left an Asian American student with a fractured skull. A Harvard resident tutor quits after being subjected to homophobic vandalism. E-mail threats and slurs are sent to 30,000 students and faculty at Stanford University, along with others at many other schools. Holocaust deniers publish their screed in campus newspapers and, in a few cases, are backed up ideologically by professors (Hate on Campus, 2000, p. 8).

Estimates suggest that there are now more than 500 hate groups in the United States (Southern Poverty Law Center, 2000). While freedom of speech, guaranteed by the First Amendment, is one of the most cherished values in the country, it is also one of the variables that contributes to the proliferation of hate groups. Each individual's freedom of speech is guaranteed, and this includes those who express messages of hate in their speeches, writings, and now the Internet.

The Turner Diaries, written by William Pierce under the pseudonym Andrew McDonald (1978), provides a blueprint for terrorism, and is believed to have given Timothy McVeigh his inspiration for the Oklahoma City Federal Building bombing. It is readily available from bookstores and can be accessed on the Internet. It continues to influence terrorists and is legally available to anyone.

Recruitment efforts often focus on areas that have experienced economic and racial change, such as a factory layoff or increased diversity in a school as a result of desegregation. A student contact in a school can provide information about the mood and anger of students that might make the school a potential candidate for recruitment (Youth and Hate, 1999).

Many hate groups attract individuals with their appearance of religious affiliation. Leaders are sometimes referred to as pastor. Some use "Church" in their name. Many use Biblical scriptures in their websites. Some use the name of "Jesus" and refer to their efforts as "His work" and themselves as "His People."

Other recruits are angry about economic conditions that have led to the loss of jobs in their communities. Rather than blaming corporations that are economizing and moving jobs to sources of cheaper labor, they blame African Americans, women, Arabs, Jews, or the government. Hate group organizers convince new recruits that it is these other groups that are taking their jobs and being pandered to by government programs. Members of the white extremist groups believe that whites are the superior race and that the government and others are emasculating their power and privilege.

Many of the hate groups have developed sophisticated websites and are active in the business of recruitment. Some hate groups have links on their websites that are developed primarily for school age youngsters. Some contain cartoons, others crossword puzzles for children. All contain a message of hate. Because so many children have become proficient in the use of computers and in surfing the web, it has become imperative for parents and educators to be able to recognize online hate and to be able to minimize the risks to their children and students. Software that will block or filter hate group websites is available through Internet providers and through software dealers.

RACIAL AND ETHNIC IDENTITY

Students in a classroom are likely to come from several different racial and ethnic groups, although physical differences are not always identifiable. Two white students who appear to be from similar backgrounds may actually identify strongly with their Irish or Polish backgrounds. The two families may live next door to each other in similar homes, but the insides of the homes may be furnished or decorated differently. The churches they attend may differ, as well as their ideas about raising children and maintaining the family. Their political ideologies may differ markedly. Yet, students often are viewed as coming from the same cultural background if they have similar racial characteristics, even though their families may be Vietnamese, Hmong, Korean, Cambodian, or Indian American. The educator should not assume that all students who look alike come from the same ethnic

Many individuals and families in the United States maintain ties with their national origin or ethnic group by participating in family and cultural traditions.

background. Factors other than physical characteristics must be used to determine a student's ethnicity. Many intragroup differences exist that may have a great influence on student behavior in the classroom.

Degree of Ethnic and Racial Identity

The degree of ethnic identity differs greatly from student to student, family to family, and community to community. Some Americans grow up in ethnic enclaves and not in multiethnic communities. Chinatown, Little Italy, Harlem, and Little Saigon are examples of ethnic enclaves in the nation's cities. The suburbs also include pockets of families from the same ethnic backgrounds. Throughout the country are small towns and surrounding farmland where the population comes from the same ethnic background, all the residents being African American, German American, Danish American, Anglo American, or Mexican American. These individuals may be culturally encapsulated, so that most of their primary relationships, and many of their secondary relationships, are with members of their own ethnic group. They may not have the opportunity to interact with members of other ethnic groups or to recognize or share the richness of a second culture that exists in another setting. They may never learn how to live with people who speak a different language or dialect, eat different foods, and value things that their own ethnic group does not value. They often learn to fear or denigrate individuals from other ethnic groups primarily because the ways of others seem strange and are thus perceived as wrong or bad.

With few exceptions, however, the ethnic enclave does not increase in size. Families move away because of job opportunities and economic rewards that are available outside the community. Children who move away to attend college often do not return. Yet, some families continue to maintain a strong identity with the ethnic group even after they have moved away. Children are less likely to maintain such a strong identity because many of their primary relationships are with members of other ethnic groups.

Many European Americans participate in ethnic activities, although their acceptance and practice of the ethnic ethos may decrease significantly as they move geographically and emotionally away from the ethnic community. Second- and third-generation ethnics living in the suburbs often rediscover their ethnic ties and identities. Although their primary relationships may not be restricted totally to other members of the ethnic group, they may organize or join ethnic social clubs and organizations to revitalize their identification with their national origin.

Many people have mixed ancestry, allowing them to identify with two or more national origins. They may identify with one ethnic group more than others, or they may view their ethnicity as just American. The racial and pan-ethnic classifications used for the census and by many schools do not make allowances for persons of mixed racial heritage, such as black and white, or Japanese and Hawaiian, or black and Vietnamese. They are forced to choose one group over the other to be counted. A growing number of students are refusing to classify themselves on forms that request this information, often because they belong to more than one of the groups or because they resist the racial categories forced on them. At the same time, teachers and others with whom students interact may continue to respond to them primarily on the basis of their identifiable race or ethnicity.

Unlike their white counterparts, most people of color are forced out of their ethnic encapsulation to achieve social and economic mobility. Many secondary relationships are with members of other ethnic groups because they often work with or for members of the dominant group. Members of the dominant group, however, rarely take the opportunity to develop even secondary relationships with African, Asian, Latino, or Native Americans. Dominant group members could spend their lives not knowing or participating in the culture of another ethnic group.

An individual's degree of ethnic identity is influenced early in that person's life by whether or not the family members recognize or promote ethnicity as an important part of their identity. Sometimes, the choice about how ethnic one should be is imposed; this is particularly true for members of oppressed ethnic minority groups. When the ethnic group believes that strong and loyal ethnic identity is necessary to maintain group solidarity, the pressure of other members of the group makes it difficult to withdraw from the group. For many members of the group, this ethnic identity provides them with the security of belonging and knowing who they are. The ethnic identity becomes the primary source of identification, and they feel no need to identify themselves differently. In fact, they may find it emotionally very difficult to sever their primary identification with the group. Some families fight the assimilative aspects of schooling that draw children into adopting the dress, language, music, and values of their peers from the dominant culture. These are usually immigrant families, families with origins other than Europe, and families who are either conservative Christians or not Christians. They are trying to maintain the values, beliefs, and codes of behavior that are important in their cultures.

Because of prejudice and discrimination against members of oppressed groups, an individual is likely to face the discriminatory practices used against most members of the group. Many individuals from oppressed groups have been acculturated and share cultural characteristics with dominant group individuals. Denied full access into the economic, political, and social spheres of the dominant group, however, they cannot assimilate. In the process of acculturation, some individuals reject the traditional culture of the ethnic group and are in a transitional stage between the ethnic minority group and the assimilated majority. The majority of these individuals probably function biculturally, participating as appropriate in either the oppressed group or the dominant group. Others reject the culture of the ethnic group and assimilate into the culture of the dominant group. If the dominant group denies assimilation, some individuals become marginalized, being suspended between two cultural groups, belonging to neither and sometimes not able to establish an ethnic identity with which they are comfortable.

The degree of ethnic identity varies greatly among individuals whom we classify as members of an ethnic or racial group. Members of the same ethnic group differ in their own historical experiences gathered from the old country, as well as from their new country. For example, families who emigrated from Vietnam in the early 1970s were predominantly from the wealthy and the professional middle classes. They differ greatly in their social and economic backgrounds from Vietnamese who emigrated from peasant and rural backgrounds later. To expect the same cultural patterns for individuals from both groups might lead to ineffective instructional planning for them. Knowing what students and their families expect within an ethnic context can be very helpful in developing effective instructional strategies.

Identifying the degree of students' assimilation into the majority culture may be helpful in determining appropriate instructional strategies. Such information can help the educator understand students' values, particularly the students' and their families' expectations for school. It also allows the teacher to more accurately determine the learning styles of students so that the teaching style can be effectively adapted to individual differences. The only way to know the importance of ethnicity in the lives of students is to listen to them. Familiarity and participation with the community from which students come also helps the educator know the importance of ethnicity to students and their families.

People's racial identities of themselves and others are based on their own, often limited experiences that are influenced by their families and by reflections in newspapers, on television, and in movies. How racial groups are defined influences the interactions between members of the groups. If one group is seen as aggressive and violent, the reaction of the second group may be fear and protection. The construct of whiteness by many students of color may be based on distrust of whites that has grown out of their own or their communities' lived experiences. Unlike most whites, persons of color see the privilege of whiteness and, in many cases, have suffered the consequences of the lack of privilege and power in society.

Educators must remember that students from oppressed groups face societal constraints and restrictions that seldom affect dominant students. Such recognition is essential in the development of instructional programs and schools to effectively serve diverse populations that as yet do not share equally in the benefits that education offers.

Oppositional Identity

Researchers have found that groups without power "usually react to their subordination and exploitation by forming ambivalent or oppositional identities as well as oppositional cultural frames of reference" (Ogbu, 1988, p. 176). These groups do not view the attitudes and behaviors of the dominant group as appropriate for them. Many members develop attitudes and behaviors that are clearly opposed to those of the dominant group. Group members who cross the boundaries into the dominant group "may experience both internal opposition or identity crisis and external opposition or peer and community pressures" (Ogbu, 1988, p. 176).

This opposition becomes very important in schooling because members of some groups (especially African Americans, Mexican Americans, and Native Americans) equate schooling with accepting the culture of the dominant group and giving up their own cultural identity. They believe "that in order for a minority person to succeed, academically, in school, he or she must learn to think and act white" (Ogbu, 1988, p. 177). In many cases, minority students resist assimilation by developing strategies of resistance, including poor academic achievement (Fordham, 1988; Gibson, 1988; Ogbu, 1988).

Students are not always inactive participants in the stratification that occurs in schools. Researchers are finding that many working-class boys and students of color develop resistance or oppositional patterns to handle their subordination within schools (Ogbu, 1988; Solomon, 1988; Willis, 1977). These patterns often take the form of breaking school rules and norms, belittling academic achievement, and valuing manual over mental work. These students equate schooling with accepting the culture of the dominant group and thinking and acting white or middle class—characteristics that could have them expelled from the minority or class peer group. In many cases, "black youths accepted academic work and schooling, but behaved in ways that ensured that they would not, and did not, succeed" (Weis, quoted in Ogbu, 1994, p. 284). Although middle-class African American students perform academically better than their working-class peers, they do not do as well as white students, in part, because of this oppositional process.

Not all minority students adopt an oppositional form, and not all minority groups are equally affected. Asian American students have high achievement records in mathematics and science and attend college at rates disproportionately higher than other groups. One explanation is that Asian American adults are over-represented in professional occupations, which should indicate an income above that of most other minority groups. Oakes (1988) attributes their high levels of achievement and participation in mathematics and science to the economic advantages in the home backgrounds of many of these students. Generally, the cultural group values mathematics and science skills, and families provide experiences that encourage their development.

At the same time, it is unfair to expect that all Asian American students have the characteristics that are congruent with the school culture. Many families do not trust white institutions, and not all students assimilate well in the school setting. The model minority is a stereotype that has led many teachers and employers to view Asians as intelligent and hard-working. Although it has opened some opportunities, it has also been harmful. "Asian Americans can find their diversity as individuals denied: many feel forced into the 'model minority' mold and want more freedom to be their individual selves, to be 'extravagant'" (Takaki, 1989, p. 477).

Recent immigrants also appear not to develop the oppositional forms of the long-established minority groups. They are more willing to accept school norms and succeed academically, in part because they compare the conditions of living in the United States with those in the country they just left (Gibson, 1988). At the same time, many families are not willing to surrender their ethnic culture totally to become assimilated. In her study of Sikh immigrants in a California high school, Gibson (1988) found that families developed a strategy of accommodation and acculturation without assimilation. A high degree of academic success has also been found for Cuban, Central American, and Vietnamese refugees.

Educators cannot expect that the cultural experiences of all immigrant students will be congruent with the norms of school. An important contributing factor is the status of the immigrant. Are the families legal immigrants, refugees, migrant workers, or undocumented workers without legal papers (Gibson, 1992/1993)? School achievement is dependent on many factors: how long the family has been in the country, the student's age on arrival, the parents' education and economic status in the country of origin, exposure to Western and urban lifestyles, languages spoken in the family, quality of educational experiences before immigrating, and others. It will be important for educators to interact with immigrant families to determine the most effective instructional strategies for ensuring academic achievement. Studies indicate that "many first and second generation immigrant children are successful not because they relinquish their traditional ways but because they draw strength from their home cultures and a positive sense of their ethnic identity" (Gibson, 1992/1993, p. 7).

EDUCATIONAL IMPLICATIONS

Because immigrants today are younger than in the past and birth rates are higher among some groups, the diversity of the student population is increasing at a faster rate than the total population. These demographics are obviously having a profound impact on schools throughout the United States. The changing diversity of school-aged children is shown in Figure 3–3. At the beginning of the twenty-first century, Latinos replaced African Americans as the largest non-European group. The West has the largest concentration of students of color; the Midwest the least. California, Hawaii, New Mexico, and the District of Columbia have student populations that are less than 40% white. Texas, New York, and Mississippi are less than 50% white, while students of color comprise more than 40% of the student population in Arizona, Georgia, Louisiana, Maryland, and South Carolina. The highest concentration (28%) of African American students is in the South; Latinos make up 30% of the students in the West. The majority of population in many urban schools consisits of students of color.

Schools are the recipients of today's young immigrants. *Education Week* reports, for example, "Broward County, Fla.—the nation's fifth-largest district, with nearly 242,000 students—young people come from at least 52 different countries and speak 52 different languages, ranging from Spanish and Haitian-Creole to Tagalog. The number of children identified as having limited fluency in English has nearly doubled since 1993–94, from 12,039 to 23,459" (Olson, 2000, p. 38). In the mid-1990s, 4.4% of all U.S. school-age children were born outside the United States. Many more students were born into first-generation families. Although racial and ethnic diversity has long existed in the country, the next 40 years will be characterized by either greater conflict among groups or more effective sharing of resources and power. As teachers, you can help influence this direction.

At least two theories have been developed for educators to consider in developing strategies to better serve ethnically and racially diverse students. The *cultural discontinuity theory* attributes the differences in outcomes between students of oppressed groups and students of dominant groups to the differences between the

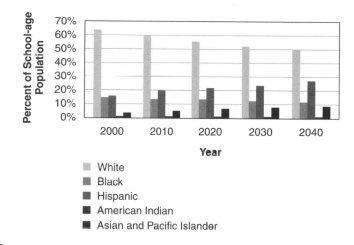

Figure 3–3

The changing diversity of the school-age population.

Source: U.S. Census Bureau. (1999). *Statistical Abstract of the United States* (199th ed.). Washington, DC: U.S. Government Printing Office.

culture and language of the school and those of the students. The school reflects the culture and values of the dominant society and usually ignores or denigrates the cultures and values of the ethnic groups from which students come. For example, many schools have set aside the month of February to celebrate black history. This in itself may be a helpful strategy for learning about a specific ethnic group. However, it often substitutes for integrating the contributions and experiences of African Americans throughout the curriculum during the whole school year. Often, other groups are studied only by students' participation in a traditional ethnic event or in tasting ethnic foods. The advantage in these cases goes to the students of the dominant group. The curriculum almost always is centered on their culture, and their behavior requires little or no adjusting because it matches the prevalent culture of the school.

The *structural inequalities theory* "emphasizes the status of a particular minority or social class group within the socioeconomic structure of the host society and the group's relationship with the dominant majority" (Gibson, 1988, p. 30). The low achievement in schools of students of color reflects the social stratification system that operates in society, and most schools are designed to maintain that status quo. Thus, students from oppressed groups are tracked into low-ability classes and vocational programs in which low achievement is expected. On entry into junior and senior high school, disproportionately few are guided into advanced, more rigorous academic classes. Participation in computer science, mathematics, and science courses varies considerably by race, class, and gender, leading to unequal outcomes in achievement.

Ethnicity and race play an important role in the lives of many students and communities. Membership in oppressed groups has a significant impact on students' perceptions of themselves, unlike whites who usually don't think of themselves as belonging to a racial group. It is also significant for educators because their cultural background and experiences are often incongruent with the cultural experiences of the students. This incongruence may lead to students dropping out of school. Eight percent of white youth between the ages of 16 and 24 have dropped out of school and not completed high school; 13% of African American and 25% of Latino young people have dropped out (U.S. Department of Education, 2000).

In responding equitably to ethnic differences, educators should do the following:

- Encourage students to build and maintain a positive self-concept
- Build on the cultural backgrounds and experiences of students to teach effectively
- Help students face and overcome their prejudices
- Assist students in improving their intergroup skills
- Expand the knowledge and appreciation of the historical, economic, political, and social experiences of ethnic and racial groups
- Assist students in understanding that the world's knowledge and culture have been, and continue to be, created from the contributions of all ethnic groups and nations

Acknowledging Ethnic Differences

Teachers often declare that they are color-blind, that they do not see a student's color and treat all students equally regardless of race. Issues of race in schools and classrooms are usually not confronted directly by faculty, in part because race is not supposed to matter. The discomfort becomes intertwined with teachers' own uncertainties about race and their possible complicity in maintaining racial inequities. Teachers should understand the ethnic backgrounds of their students and the community. Rather than pretending that race and ethnicity do not exist, teachers should acknowledge the differences and be aware of ways race and ethnicity can influence learning. Equity does not mean sameness; students can be treated differently, as long as the treatment is fair and appropriate, to accomplish the goal of student learning.

The ethnic communities to which students belong provide the real-life examples on which teachers can draw as they teach. Knowing students' ethnic and cultural experiences and how subject matter interacts with students' reality are important in designing effective strategies to help students learn.

In her study of successful teachers of African American students, Ladson-Billings (1994) learned that parents wanted their teachers "to help their children succeed at traditional academic tasks (reading, writing, mathematics, and so on), but at the same time they wanted them to provide an education that would not alienate their children from their homes, their community, and their culture" (p. 27). Successful teachers are able to help students learn academics and skills that will help them compete effectively in the dominant workplace. At the same time, they acknowledge and value the ethnicity of their students and the community in

LINK TO THE CLASSROOM

Ethnic and Racial Groups

Many students who feel alienated from school because of their ethnicity or the low-income status of their families are apathetic about their classes. To engage them requires teachers who can relate content to the lived experiences of the students—not an easy task in a class with students from diverse ethnic, language, and economic backgrounds.

With a loud, unruly, and almost out-of-control class, an English teacher was trying to find what would connect students to the novel Thousand Pieces of Gold, *by Ruthann Lum McCunn, which they had been assigned to read but weren't reading. She found the connection in the violence that surrounded their lives. The teacher reported:*

> *In an attempt to get them involved in the novel, I read aloud an evocative passage about the unemployed peasants sweeping through the Chinese countryside, pillaging, raping, and grabbing what was denied them through legal employment. Suddenly students saw their own lives reflected back at them through Chen, whose anger at losing his job and ultimately his family led him to become an outlaw. Chen created a new family with this group of bandits. Students could relate: Chen was a gang member. I had stumbled on a way to interest my class. The violence created a contact point between the literature and the students' lives.*
>
> *This connection, this reverberation across cultures, time, and gender, challenged the students' previous notion that reading and talking about novels didn't have relevance for them. They could empathize with the Chinese but also explore those issues in their own lives.*
>
> *This connection also created space to unpack the assumption that all gangs are bad. . . . The discussion of gangs broke the barrier and students began writing about violence in their own lives and their neighborhoods. (Christensen, 1994, p. 14)*

Why did the teacher decide that she needed to find a way to connect the novel to the lives of her students? Why did the topic of violence work in her classroom? What topics might have engaged rural or suburban students with the novel?

which the school is located. "They help students make connections between their local, national, racial, cultural, and global identities" (Ladson-Billings, 1994, p. 25).

Curriculum Approaches

Schools need to provide environments in which students can learn to participate in the dominant society while maintaining connections to their distinct ethnicities if they choose. Respect for and support of ethnic differences will be essential in this effort. Students know when a teacher or counselor does not respect or value students' ethnic backgrounds. As educators, we cannot afford to reject or neglect students because their ethnic backgrounds are different from our own. We are responsible for making sure all students learn to think, read, write, and compute so that they can function effectively in society. We can help accomplish this goal by accurately reflecting ethnicity in the curriculum and positively using it to teach and interact with students.

Traditionally, the curriculum of most schools has been centered in the dominant culture, with information on, and perspectives of, other groups sometimes added as a unit during a school year. Some schools have replaced this traditional curriculum with one based on the culture of students and communities. Multicultural education, on the other hand, encourages a culturally responsive curriculum in which diversity is integrated throughout the courses, activities, and interactions in the classroom.

Dominant Culture as Center.   The curriculum in most schools is based on the knowledge and perspective of the West (Northern and Western Europe). The inherent bias of the curriculum does not encourage candid admissions of racism and oppression within society. In fact, it supports the superiority of Western thought over all others and provides minimal or no introduction to the non-Western cultures of Asia, Africa, and South and Central America.

Ethnic studies courses are sometimes offered to introduce students to the history and contemporary conditions of one or more ethnic groups. Many universities have ethnic studies programs, such as African American, Asian American, American Indian, or Latino Studies, in which students can major. These courses and programs allow for in-depth exposure to the social, economic, and political history of a specific group. They are designed to correct the distortions and omissions that prevail in society about a specific ethnic group. Events that have been neglected in textbooks are addressed, myths are dispelled, and history is viewed from the perspective of the ethnic group, as well as the dominant group. Prospective teachers and other professional school personnel who have not been exposed to an examination of an ethnic group different from their own should take such a course or undertake individual study.

Traditionally, ethnic studies have been offered as separate courses that students elect from many offerings in the curriculum. Seldom have ethnic studies been required courses for all students. The majority of students who choose these courses are students from the ethnic group or groups being studied. Although the information and experiences offered in these courses are important to these students, they are also important for students from other ethnic groups.

Ethnocentric Curriculum.   Historically, some immigrant groups have established their own schools, with classes often held in the evenings or on Saturdays, to reinforce cultural values, traditions, and the native language. This pattern is being expanded to the regular school by some ethnic groups. For example, some Native American tribes have established their own tribal-controlled public schools in which the traditional culture serves as the social and intellectual starting point. Although most of these schools are located in rural Native American communities, some urban areas have also established magnet American Indian schools with similar goals.

Some school systems and schools in urban areas have adopted an Afrocentric curriculum to challenge Eurocentrism and confront racism and oppression. At the core of this approach is an African perspective of the world and historical events. It has been initiated most often in urban schools with large African American student populations to improve students' self-esteem, academic skills, values, and positive identity with their ethnic group.

Afrocentric public schools are now found in Atlanta, Cleveland, Detroit, Kansas City, Milwaukee, Oakland, and Washington, DC. Some schools "were created because local communities demanded a curriculum that told the 'truth' about black history. Others came about because educators and administrators saw the Afrocentric approach as a good strategy for boosting black students' self-esteem and keeping them in school" (Viadero, 1996, p. 28).

Another development is the establishment of public school programs for African American male students. These programs are designed to prepare African American youth to overcome the harsh realities they face—unemployment, drugs, violence, and poverty. Programs provide a strong gender and cultural identity to assist young men in becoming successful in their academic, occupational, and community achievements. The programs use strong, positive role models as teachers and focus on an Afrocentric curriculum. The goals are laudable. Such programs may play a role in protecting young African American males against forces that lead to their being murdered, arrested, or unemployed in disproportionate numbers.

Some parents, educators, and community activists who believed that the public schools were not effectively serving their children have established urban, ethnocentric, and grassroots charter schools. Many of these schools have placed the ethnic culture of the enrolled students at the center of the curriculum; they are Afrocentric, Chicano-centric, or American Indian-centric, emphasizing what is known, valued, and respected from their own cultural roots. Although a number of these schools have been established within the public system, the schools do not have the financial support that charter school parents in the suburbs are able to generate. They face the same inequities of other public schools in their communities.

Integrating Ethnic Diversity Throughout the Curriculum.   A multiethnic curriculum permeates all subject areas at all levels of education, from preschool through adult education. All courses reflect accurate and positive references to ethnic diversity. The amount of specific content about ethnic groups varies according to the course taught, but an awareness and a recognition of the multiethnic nature of the nation is reflected in all classroom experiences. No matter how assimilated students in a classroom are, it is the teacher's responsibility to expose them to the ethnic diversity of this nation and the world.

Bulletin boards, resource books, and films that show ethnic diversity should constantly reinforce these realities, although teachers should not depend entirely on these resources for instructional content about groups. Too often, persons of color are studied only during a unit on African American history or Native Americans. Too often, they are not included on reading lists or in the study of biographies, labor unions, or the environment. Too often, students finish school without reading or seeing anything written or produced by females and males of color. If ethnic groups are included only during a unit or a week focusing on a particular group, students do not learn to view them as an integral part of society. They are viewed as separate, distinct, and inferior to the dominant group. A multiethnic curriculum prevents the distortion of history and contemporary conditions. Without it, the perspective of the dominant group becomes the only valid and correct curriculum to which students are exposed.

It is the educator's responsibility to ensure that ethnic groups become an integral part of the total curriculum. This mandate does not require the teacher to discuss every ethnic group. It does require that the classroom resources and instruction not focus completely on the dominant group. It requires that perspectives of ethnic groups and the dominant group be examined in discussions of historical and current events. For example, one should consider the perspectives of Mexican and Native Americans as well as the dominant group in a presentation and discussion of the westward movement of European Americans in the eighteenth and nineteenth centuries. It requires students to read literature by authors from different ethnic backgrounds. It expects that mathematics and science be explored from an American Indian as well as a Western perspective. The contributions of different ethnic groups are reflected in the books that are used by students, in the movies that they view, and in the activities in which they participate.

Multiethnic education should include learning experiences to help students examine their own stereotypes about and prejudice against ethnic groups. These are not easy topics to address but should be a part of the curriculum beginning in preschool. At all levels, but particularly in junior high and secondary classrooms, students may resist discussion of these issues. Teachers can create a safe classroom climate by establishing clear guidelines for such discussions. When students use derogatory terms for ethnic group members or tell ethnic jokes, teachers should use the opportunity to discuss attitudes about those groups. Students should not be allowed to express their hostility to other group members in any classroom.

Development of a multiethnic curriculum requires the educator to evaluate textbooks and classroom resources for ethnic content and biases. Although advances have been made in eliminating ethnic biases and adding information about ethnic groups in newer textbooks, many older textbooks are still used in classrooms across the nation. With many textbook revisions, ethnic content has been added to what already existed, rather than being carefully integrated throughout the text. Biased books should not prevent the teacher from providing multiethnic instruction. Supplementary materials can fill the gap in this area. The biases and omissions in the texts can be used for discussions of the experiences of ethnic groups. None of these instructional activities will occur, however, unless the teacher is aware of and values ethnic differences and their importance in the curriculum.

Student Achievement and Assessment

Schools conduct widespread testing of students for entrance into programs for the gifted, advanced courses, special education programs, colleges and universities, and professional schools. In a number of states, students must perform at specified levels to be promoted to the next class or to graduate from high school. These standardized tests have limited the access of many students from low-income and oppressed ethnic groups to more rigorous study at all educational levels and may prevent students from entering professional schools. They are also used to assign disproportionately large numbers of these students to special education programs for the mentally retarded, learning disabled, and emotionally disturbed.

Tests are trumpeted as measures of competence to move from one grade to another, graduate from high school, enter upper-division college courses, earn a baccalaureate, and become licensed to teach. Some proponents of testing suggest that the tests alone can determine whether students know and perform at levels acceptable by society. Tests are promoted by politicians as measures of quality in the nation's schools. Overwhelmingly, promoters suggest that anyone who cannot pass the appropriate test certainly cannot be qualified to move on to further study. In fact, such testing limits the access of many individuals to practice the career of their choice.

Between 1970 and 1990, students had been improving their performance on national tests, with the largest gains being made by students of color (Grissmer, Kirby, Berends, & Williamson, 1994). The progress came to a halt in the 1990s, and the achievement gap between whites and most students of color remains wide. Why do students from oppressed groups score lower than dominant group members on standardized tests? It is not, as the authors of *The Bell Curve* (Hernstein & Murray, 1994) claim, due to genetic differences of intelligence between the races. *Education Watch: The 1996 Education Trust State and National Data Book* reports the following disparities between the groups:

- Low-income and minority students are less likely than their more advantaged peers to be in classes taught by teachers who majored in their fields.
- In schools where more than 30% of students are poor, 59% of teachers report that they lack sufficient books and other reading resources, as compared with 16% of teachers in more affluent schools.
- Low-income and minority students are more likely to be taught a low-level curriculum with low standards for performance.

- About 55 out of every 100 white and Asian American students complete Algebra II and geometry. Only 35% of African American and Native American seniors take these courses.
- Only 60% of Latino students nationally earn a high school diploma.
- African American and Latino high school graduates are much less likely than whites to go to college (The Education Trust, 1996).

Should it be a surprise that many students of color do not perform as well as white students when they have not taken advanced mathematics and science courses or had teachers who majored in those subjects? In urban schools in which students of color are overrepresented, teachers are less likely to be licensed than in schools with middle class white students. Advanced courses in mathematics and science are not even available to students in many of these schools. Students must have access to such courses and qualified teachers to study the content on which they will be tested.

As educators, we must be careful not to label low-income students and students of color intellectually inferior because their standardized test scores are low. These scores too often influence a teacher's expectations for the academic performance of students in the classroom. It is essential that we maintain high expectations for all students, regardless of test scores. Standardized test scores can help in determining how assimilated into the majority culture and how affluent one's family may be, but they provide little evidence of how intelligent a person is. Many other factors can be used to provide information about intelligence—for example, the ability to think and respond appropriately in different situations.

In developing tests and using the results of standardized tests, educators should recognize the inherent cultural bias that favors dominant students. Few tests have been developed from the bias of African Americans, American Indians, or Latinos. Test bias is a serious educational issue with devastating results for many students of color.

Educators should be aware that these cultural biases exist and continually remind themselves not to rely on test scores as the only indication of students' intelligence and academic potential. There are many examples of good teachers who have helped students with low scores achieve at advanced levels. African American and Latino students have performed at the same level as other students in mathematics and other subjects after teachers raised their expectations and changed their teaching strategies. Project SEED, the Algebra Project, and the work of Jamie Escalante in Los Angeles and Philip Uri Treisman at Berkeley are examples of successful programs.

What should the purposes of assessments be? Rather than use tests to sort students on the basis of income, ethnicity, and family characteristics, could assessments be used to help us understand what students know so that curriculum and activities can be designed to increase their knowledge and skills? They should provide us with information that will help improve student learning. The traditional multiple-choice tests are beginning to be replaced by performance assessments. These assessments use observations, portfolios, projects, and essays for students to demonstrate what they know in many different ways. They should promote complex and engaged learning.

Performance assessments are also being used to assess the knowledge, skills, and dispositions of teacher candidates like yourself. Some states have developed assessment activities and portfolio requirements. These expectations are based on a set of standards that define effective teaching of a subject or subjects. Some experienced teachers are also seeking recognition for outstanding teaching by pursuing national certification from the National Board for Professional Teaching Standards. In this process, they prepare portfolios that include lesson plans and videotapes of actual teaching. During the year or more that it takes to prepare for national board certification, these teachers—even those who are not successful—report that it is the best professional activity in which they have ever participated. The assessments require that they explain why they chose one teaching strategy over another and how students' cultural backgrounds and the content of the lesson influenced their selections. The process encouraged them to reflect on their practice and improve their teaching, with the goal of promoting student learning.

Educators are capable of making valid decisions about ability on the basis of numerous objective and subjective factors about students. If decisions about the capabilities of students of color match exactly the standardized scores, the educator should reevaluate his or her own responses and interactions with these students. This is an area that none of us can afford to neglect; testing results today are making differences in the life chances for many students.

Desegregation and Intergroup Relations

In its 1954 decision in *Brown v. Board of Education*, the U.S. Supreme Court declared that separate but equal schooling was not equal. It took more than a decade, however, for schools to begin serious desegregation. The early focus of these efforts was on the placement of black and white students in the same schools.

Although it has been almost 50 years since the *Brown* decision, current desegregation is similar to that in 1972 (Schofield, 1991). In fact, the number of students attending racially or ethnically isolated schools has increased (Bates, 1990). Rather than schools desegregating, it appears that they are being resegregated. Bates reports that the "outlook for achieving meaningful desegregation when the minority enrollment in a school district is more than 50% is very discouraging" (p. 13). Residential segregation in school districts severely limits desegregation efforts. White students comprise less than 5% of the classmates of black students in Atlanta, Chicago, New Orleans, Newark, and Washington, DC (Rivkin, 1994).

Second-generation desegregation efforts have expanded beyond just ensuring that schools are racially/ethnically diverse. The focus has been on the inequities within schools with ethnic- and gender-diverse populations (Bates, 1990). Researchers have found unequal access to advanced mathematics and science classes and gifted programs. Low-income students and students of color are

When students of different ethnic groups have the opportunity to develop interpersonal relationships, racial and ethnic relations are likely to be improved.

disproportionately represented in nonacademic and special education classes. Rates of school suspension and dropping out of school vary for different ethnic groups.

No longer does segregation affect primarily black and white students, although most urban schools in the South, the East, and the Midwest have student bodies that are predominantly African American. Latino students are now the most highly segregated group in schools (Valencia, 1991). Bilingual classes are very segregated. Some researchers believe that native language instruction should be integrated throughout the curriculum, rather than treated as a segregated, pull-out program that separates Latino students and others for academic study (Donato, Menchaca, & Valencia, 1991; Meier & Stewart, 1991).

The goal of desegregation has changed from the physical integration of students within a school building to the achievement of equal learning opportunities and outcomes for all students (Bates, 1990). It is recognized that effective interpersonal skills are important in achieving this goal. "The ability to work effectively with out-group members is an important skill for both majority and minority group members in a pluralistic society striving to overcome a long history of discrimination in education and employment" (Schofield, 1991, p. 340).

Small-group teams and cooperative learning should promote both learning and interracial friendships. Educators should be engaging parents in school activities and decision making to decrease the dissonance between school and home. Students from different groups should have equal access to the curriculum, advanced courses, qualified teachers, and activities to develop high-order thinking skills. They should see themselves in the curriculum and in textbooks. Practices such as tracking and pull-out programs are barriers to providing equal access and improving intergroup relations. Multicultural education is a critical component in the continued effort to desegregate schools and improve intergroup relations.

Summary

Almost from the beginning of European settlement, the population of the United States has been multiethnic, with individuals representing many American Indian and European nations, later to be joined by Africans, Latinos, and Asians. Primary reasons for immigration were internal economic impoverishment and political repression in the countries of origin and the demands of a vigorous U.S. economy that required a large labor force. The conditions encountered by different ethnic groups, the reasons they came, and their expectations about life here differed greatly and have led ethnic groups to view themselves as distinct from each other.

Ethnicity is a sense of peoplehood based on national origin. Although no longer useful in describing groups of people, the term race continues to be used in this country to classify groups of people as inferior or superior. Its popular usage is based on society's perception that racial differences are important—a belief not upheld by scientific study. Members of oppressed groups experience discriminatory treatment and often are relegated to relatively low-status positions in society.

Prejudice is a set of negative attitudes toward a group of people. Discrimination focuses on behavior that treats individuals differently because of their membership in a specific group. When discrimination is institutionalized, inequalities are inherent in policies and practices that benefit dominant group members while appearing to be neutral in their effect on other groups.

In a classroom, students are likely to come from different ethnic groups, although physical differences are not always identifiable. Not all people view their ethnic origins as important in understanding who they are. Their membership in other microcultures may have a greater impact on their identity than the nations from which their ancestors came. Educators must be careful of stereotyping all persons from the same ethnic group; many differences exist within the same group

The school curriculum has traditionally represented the dominant culture as the focus of study. Since the 1970s, ethnic studies have been added to curricula as an extension or special segment that focuses on the in-depth study of the history and contemporary conditions of one or more ethnic groups. Some ethnic groups have established schools, or programs in traditional schools, that centers the curriculum on their ethnicity. Afrocentric and Native American schools are examples of ethnocentric curriculum approaches. Multiethnic education is broader in scope in that it requires ethnic content to permeate the total curriculum; thus, all courses taught reflect the multiethnic nature of society. Understanding ethnicity is an advantage in developing effective teaching strategies for individual students.

Educators should examine how they are administering and using standardized tests in the classroom. Too often, testing programs have been used for the purpose of identifying native intelligence and thus sorting people for education and jobs. If disproportionately large numbers of students of color are scoring poorly on such tests and being placed in special classes as a result, the program must be reviewed. Many factors can be used to provide information about intelligence and ability—for example, the ability to think and respond appropriately in different situations.

Desegregation is a process for decreasing racial/ethnic isolation in schools. Although early desegregation efforts focused on ensuring that black and white students attended the same schools, increasing numbers of students attend predominantly minority schools. The emphasis is on ensuring the academic achievement of all students and eliminating the inequities in educational opportunities.

Questions for Review

To answer these questions online, go to the Chapter Questions module for this chapter of the Companion Website.

1. Why is membership in an ethnic group more important to some individuals than to others?
2. Describe factors that cause members of oppressed groups to view ethnicity differently from dominant group members.
3. Describe differences and similarities in the immigration patterns of Africans, Asians, Central Americans, Europeans, and South Americans during the past four centuries.
4. Distinguish between prejudice and discrimination, and describe their impact on groups in the United States.
5. Why does race remain such an important factor in the social, political, and economic patterns of the United States?
6. What characteristics might an educator look for to determine a student's ethnic background and the importance it plays in that student's life?
7. List ways in which an educator should be able to use ethnicity in the classroom.
8. Contrast ethnic studies, ethnocentric education, and multiethnic education, and list the advantages of each.
9. If you are working in a desegregated school setting, what skills and instructional strategies should you develop to help you be an effective teacher?
10. Why is the use of standardized tests so controversial? What are the dangers of depending too heavily on the results of standardized tests?

Web Resources

To link to the following websites, go to the Web Resources module for this chapter of the Companion Website.

The Anti-Defamation League fights anti-Semitism, bigotry and extremism. Its website includes information on religious freedom, civil rights, and the holocaust, as well as resources for teachers on fighting hate.

The website of the Bureau of Indian Affairs includes information on the bureau's projects.

The League of United Latin American Citizens advances the economic condition, educational attainment, political influence, health, and civil rights of the Hispanic population of the United States.

The website of the National Association for the Advancement of Colored People addresses issues of school desegregation, fair housing, employment, and voter registration, as well as elections, health, and equal economic opportunity.

The National Congress of American Indians works to inform the public and Congress on the governmental rights of American Indians and Alaska Natives. The website includes a directory of tribes in the United States.

The National Urban League has sought to emphasize greater reliance on the unique resources and strengths of the African American community to find solutions to its own problems. It has strong roots in the community that are focused on the social and educational development of youth, economic self-sufficiency, and racial inclusion.

The Southern Poverty Law Center combats hate, intolerance and discrimination through education and litigation against hate groups. It publishes *Teaching Tolerance,* which is available at no cost to teachers, and numerous other teaching resources.

References

Bates, P. (1990). Desegregation: Can we get there from here? *Phi Delta Kappan, 72*(1), 8–17.

Brown v. Board of Education, 349 U.S. 294, at 300 (1955).

Carnes, J. (1995). *Us and them.* Montgomery, AL: Southern Poverty Law Center.

Christensen, L. (1994, Autumn). Building community from chaos. *Rethinking Schools, 9*(1), 1, 14, 15, 17.

Clawson, D. (1995, July). From the editor's desk. *Contemporary Sociology: A Journal of Reviews, 24*(4), ix.

Cross, W. E., Jr. (1991). *Shades of black: Diversity in African American identity.* Philadelphia: Temple University Press.

Derman-Sparks, L., & A.B.C. Task Force. (1989). *Anti-bias curriculum: Tools for empowering young children.* Washington, DC: National Association for the Education of Young Children.

Diversity data. (2000). *Principal, 79*(5), 18.

Donato, R., Menchaca, M., & Valencia, R. R. (1991). Segregation, desegregation, and integration of Chicano students: Problems and prospects. In R. R. Valencia (Ed.), *Chicano school failure and success: Research and policy agendas for the 1990s* (pp. 27–63). London: Falmer Press.

Eck, D. L. (2000). Religious pluralism in America in the year 2000. In E. W. Linder (Ed.), *Yearbook of American and Canadian churches 2000.* Nashville, TN: Abingdon Press.

The Education Trust. (1996). *Education watch: The 1996 education trust state and national data book.* Washington, DC: Author.

Fordham, S. (1988). Racelessness as a factor in black students' school success: Pragmatic strategy or pyrrhic victory? *Harvard Educational Review, 58*(1), 54–84.

Gibson, M. A. (1988). *Accommodation without assimilation: Sikh immigrants in an American high school.* Ithaca, NY: Cornell University Press.

Gibson, M. A. (1992/1993, Winter). Variability in immigrant students' school performance: The U.S. case. In *The Social Context of Education.* Washington, DC: American Educational Research Association—Division G.

Gordon, M. M. (1964). *Assimilation in American life: The role of race, religion, and national origins.* New York: Oxford University Press.

Grissmer, D. W., Kirby, S. N., Berends, M., & Williamson, S. (1994). *Student achievement and the changing American family.* Santa Monica, CA: RAND.

Hate on campus. (2000, Spring). *Intelligence Report* (Southern Poverty Law Center), *98,* 6–15.

Hernstein, R. J., & Murray, C. (1994). *The bell curve: Intelligence and class structure in American life.* New York: Free Press.

Kelley, M. (2000, September 8). Indian affairs head makes apology. Associated Press.

Ladson-Billings, G. (1994). *The dreamkeepers: Successful teachers of African American children.* San Francisco: Jossey-Bass.

Levin, J., & McDevitt, J. (1993). *Hate crimes: The rising tide of bigotry and bloodshed.* New York: Plenum.

Lorde, A. (1995). Age, race, class, and sex: Women redefining difference. In J. Arthur & A. Shapiro (Eds.), *Campus wars: Multiculturalism and the politics of difference* (pp. 191–198). Boulder, CO: Westview Press.

McDonald, Andrew. (1978). *The Turner Diaries.* Author.

Meier, K. J., & Stewart, J., Jr. (1991). *The politics of Hispanic education.* Albany: State University of New York Press.

National Conference for Community and Justice. (1994). *Taking America's pulse: A summary report of the National Conference Survey on intergroup relations.* New York: Author.

National Conference for Community and Justice. (2000). *Taking America's pulse II: A survey of intergroup relations.* New York: Author.

Nguyen, M. L. (1996, Fall). In our own words: Asian American students give voice to the challenges of living in two cultures. *Teaching Tolerance, 5*(2), 48–59.

Oakes, J. (1988). Tracking in mathematics and science education: A structural contribution to unequal schooling. In L. Weis (Ed.), *Class, race, and gender in American education* (pp. 106–125). Albany: State University of New York Press.

Ogbu, J. (1988). Class stratification, racial stratification, and schooling. In L. Weis (Ed.), *Class, race, and gender in American education* (pp. 163–183). Albany: State University of New York Press.

Ogbu, J. (1994, Winter). Racial stratification and education in the United States: Shy inequality persists. *Teachers College Record, 96*(2), 264–298.

Olson, L. (2000, September 27). Mixed needs of immigrants pose challenges for schools. *Education Week, XX*(4): 38–39.

Omi, M., & Winant, H. (1994). *Racial formation in the United States: From the 1960s to the 1990s* (2nd ed.). New York: Routledge.

Plyer v. Doe, 457 U.S. 202 (1982).

Rivkin, S. G. (1994). Residential segregation and school integration. *Sociology of Education, 67*(4), 279–292.

Schnalberg, L. (1996). Immigration plays key supporting role in record-enrollment drama. *Education Week, XVI*(2), 14–15.

Schofield, J. W. (1991). School desegregation and intergroup relations: A review of the literature. In G. Grant (Ed.), *Review of research in education* (Volume 17, pp. 335–409). Washington, DC: American Educational Research Association.

Sleeter, C. E. (1993). How white teachers construct race. In C. McCarthy & W. Crichlow (Eds.), *Race, identity, and representation in education* (pp. 157–171). New York: Routledge.

Solomon, R. P. (1988). Black cultural forms in schools: A cross-national comparison. In L. Weis (Ed.), *Class, race, and gender in American education* (pp. 249–265). Albany: State University of New York Press.

Southern Poverty Law Center. (2000, Summer). *Intelligence Report.* Montgomery, AL: Author.

Tafoya, S. M. (2000, January). Check one or more . . . Mixed race and ethnicity in California, *California Counts, 1*(2), 1–9.

Takaki, R. (1989). *Strangers from a different shore.* Boston: Little, Brown.

Tatum, B. D. (1992). Talking about race, learning about racism: The application of racial identity development theory in the classroom. *Harvard Educational Review, 62*(1), 1–24.

U.S. Census Bureau. (1999). *Statistical abstract of the United States* (119th ed.). Washington, DC: U.S. Government Printing Office.

U.S. Department of Education, National Center for Education Statistics. (2000, June). High school dropouts, by race-ethnicity and recency of migration (NCES 2000–009). Washington, DC: Author.

Valencia, R. R. (1991). The plight of Chicano students: An overview of schooling conditions and outcomes. In R. R. Valencia (Ed.), *Chicano school failure and success: Research and policy agendas for the 1990s.* London: Falmer Press.

Viadero, D. (1996, October 16). A school of their own. *Education Week, XVI*(7), 27–31.

Willis, P. E. (1977). *Learning to labor: How working-class kids get working-class jobs.* Farnborough, UK: Saxon House.

Young, R. L., & Pang, V. O. (1995, Winter). Asian Pacific American students: A rainbow of dreams. *Multicultural Education, 3*(2), 4–7.

Youth and Hate. (1999, Fall). *Intelligence Report* (Southern Poverty Law Center), *96,* 24–27.

Suggested Readings

Bigelow, B., & Peterson, B. (Eds.). (1998). *Rethinking Columbus: The next 500 years.* Milwaukee WI: Rethinking Schools.

This book calls for a replacement of the murky legends of Columbus with a more honest sense of who we are and why we are here. It also discusses the courageous struggles and lasting wisdom of indigenous peoples.

Derman-Sparks, L., Gutierrez, M., & Phillips, C. B. (n.d.). *Teaching young children to resist bias: What parents can do.* Washington, DC: National Association for the Education of Young Children.

This pamphlet provides recommendations for helping primary-age students and their parents understand ethnic, race, gender, and disability biases.

Ladson-Billings, G. (1994). *The dreamkeepers: Successful teachers of African American children.* San Francisco: Jossey Bass.

Eight exemplary teachers of African American students and their approaches to teaching are portrayed. The teachers differ in racial background, personal styles, and methods but affirm and strengthen cultural diversity in their classrooms.

Lee, E., Menkart, D., & Okazawa-Rey, M. (Eds.). (1998). *Beyond heroes and holidays: A practical guide to K–12 anti-racist, multicultural education and staff development.* Washington, DC: Network of Educators on the Americas.

This interdisciplinary guide for educators, students, and parents includes lessons and readings on racism, transforming the curriculum, tracking, parent/school relations, and language policies.

Nakanishi, D. T., & Nishida, T. Y. (Eds.). (1995). *The Asian American educational experience: A source book for teachers and students.* New York: Routledge.

This volume explores Asian American educational experiences from the perspectives of ethnic studies, education, psychology, sociology, urban studies, and Asian American studies.

Olmos, E. J., Ybarra, L., & Monterrey, M. (1999). *Americanos: Latino Life in the United States.* Boston: Little, Brown.
This pictorial presentation of Latino life in the United States is accompanied by bilingual essays, poetry, and commentaries on Cuban, Panamanian, Puerto Rican, Mexican, Argentinean, and other Latino cultures.

Reddy, M. T. (Ed.). (1996). *Everyday acts against racism: Raising children in a multiracial world.* Seattle: Seal Press.
Mothers and teachers draw on their own experiences to describe the effects of racism on children and communities. Practical suggestions are offered.

Slapin, B., & Seale, D. (Eds.). (1998). *Through Indian eyes: The Native experience in books for children.* Los Angeles: American Indian Studies Center, University of California.
This compilation of work by Native parents, educators, poets, and writers is an excellent resource for educators interested in nonbiased material about indigenous people.

Stern-LaRosa, C., & Bettmann, E. H. (2000). *Close the book on hate.* New York: Anti-Defamation League.
This book provides an understanding of the richness and beauty of our multicultural society. It encourages parents and children to discuss the value of diversity and the hurtfulness of hate.

Suleiman, M. W. (Ed.). (1999). *Arabs in America: Building a new future.* Philadelphia: Temple University Press.
The articles in this volume range from the career of an Arab American singer, dancer, and storyteller to the historical examination of Arab Americans and Zionism.

Takaki, R. (1993). *A different mirror: A history of multicultural America.* Boston: Little, Brown.
The history of America is retold from the voices of Native Americans, African Americans, Jews, Irish Americans, Asian Americans, Latinos, and others. It covers the period from the colonization of the New World to the 1992 Los Angeles riots.

Teaching Tolerance. (Published by the Southern Poverty Law Center, 400 Washington Ave., Montgomery, AL 36104)
This semiannual magazine provides teachers with resources and ideas to promote harmony in the classroom. Articles are written from the perspectives of multiple ethnic groups. It is available at no cost to teachers.

Teaching Tolerance. (1999). Responding to hate at school: A guide for teachers, counselors and administrators. Montgomery, AL: Southern Poverty Law Center.
These guidelines should help educators in responding promptly and effectively to incidents of bias in schools.

CRITICAL INCIDENTS IN TEACHING

Enthnicity

Racism

Just seconds before the school bell is to ring to start the school day, Jimmy Schultz runs into the classroom and exclaims, "And did you see Antonio Gomez's father on TV? The cops busted him yesterday in a bank robbery. It was on the news last night and again this morning. I saw it. They gave his name and everything. My Dad said that you could expect that when they let them Mexicans into the country. We got too many of them wetbacks here already, and most of them are crooks or on welfare."

"That's not true," says Antonio meekly. "That wasn't my father. There are a lot of people in this town named Gomez. That guy wasn't my father."

"Yes it was, Tony. I recognized him. Same beard. I'd know your father anywhere," says Jimmy.

"No it isn't, damn you," responds Antonio. "Shut up or I'll beat the crap out of you."

At this point, Vivian Correa, the teacher, indicates that this is enough discussion on the matter and that she will hear nothing more of it. She notices, however, that the students are still whispering about the incident and that there are tears in Antonio's eyes.

Questions for Discussion

To answer these questions online, go to the Critical Incidents module for this chapter of the Companion Website.

1. Should Ms. Correa have stopped the discussion?
2. Should she have taken the opportunity to clear the air and get closure on the matter?
3. Should she say anything to Tony?
4. Should she contact Mrs. Gomez?
5. Should the matter be brought up again to settle it once and for all?

Student Conflict Between Family and Peer Values

Wing Tek Lau is a sixth-grade student in a predominantly white and African American Southern community. He and his parents emigrated from Hong Kong 4 years ago. His uncle, an engineer at a local high-tech company, had encouraged Wing Tek's father to immigrate to this country and open a Chinese restaurant. The restaurant is the only Chinese restaurant in the community, and it was an instant success. Mr. Lau and his family have enjoyed considerable acceptance in both his business and his neighborhood. Wing Tek and his younger sister have also enjoyed academic success at school and appear to be well liked by the other students.

One day when Mrs. Baca, Wing Tek's teacher, calls him by name, he announces before the class, "My American name is Kevin. Please, everybody call me Kevin from now on." Mrs. Baca and Wing Tek's classmates honor this request, and Wing Tek is "Kevin" from then on.

Three weeks later, Mr. and Mrs. Lau make an appointment to see Mrs. Baca. When the teacher makes reference to "Kevin," Mrs. Lau says, "Who are you talking about? Who is Kevin? We came here to talk about our son, Wing Tek."

"But I thought his American name was Kevin. That's what he asked us to call him from now on," Mrs. Baca replies.

"That child," Mrs. Lau says in disgust, "is a disgrace to our family."

"We have heard his sister call him by that name, but she said it was just a joke," Mr. Lau adds. "We came to see you because we are having problems with him in our home. Wing Tek refuses to speak Chinese to us. He argues with us about going to his Chinese lessons on Saturday with the other Chinese students in the community. He says he does not want to eat Chinese food anymore. He says that he is an American now and wants pizza, hamburgers, and tacos. What are you people teaching these children in school? Is there no respect for family, no respect for our culture?"

Mrs. Baca, an acculturated Mexican American who was raised in East Los Angeles, begins to put things together. Wing Tek, in his attempt to ensure his acceptance by his classmates, has chosen to acculturate to an extreme, to the point of rejecting his family heritage. He want to be as "American" as anyone else in the class, perhaps more so. Like Wing Tek, Mrs. Baca had acculturated linguistically and in other ways, but she had never given up her Hispanic values. She knows the internal turmoil Wing Tek is experiencing.

Questions for Discussion

1. Is Wing Tek wrong in his desire to acculturate?
2. Are Mr. and Mrs. Lau wrong in wanting their son to maintain their traditional family values?
3. What can Mrs. Baca do to bring about a compromise?
4. What can Mrs. Baca do in the classroom to resolve the problem or at least to lessen the problem?

To answer these questions online, go to the Critical Incidents module for this chapter of the Companion Website.

Racial Identification

Roosevelt High School annually celebrates Black History Month in February. The month-long study includes a convocation to celebrate African American heritage. For 10 years, students have organized and conducted this convocation in which the whole student body participates.

The students who have organized the event this year begin the convocation with the black national anthem. The African American students, a few other students, and some faculty members stand for the singing of the anthem. Many of the African American students become very angry with what they perceive to be a lack of respect by the students and faculty who do not stand.

In discussions that follow the convocation, some students and faculty who did not stand for the anthem argue that the only national anthem to which they should be expected to respond is their own national anthem. They say it is unfair to be required to attend a convocation celebrating the heritage of one racial group when there is no convocation to celebrate their own racial or ethnic heritage.

Questions for Discussion

To answer these questions online, go to the Critical Incidents module for this chapter of the Companion Website.

1. What may have been happening in the school that led to the tensions that surfaced during this convocation?
2. How may the African American students perceive the refusal to stand by some of the students and faculty?
3. Do you think the reasons for not standing during the anthem are valid? Why or why not?
4. If you are meeting with a class immediately after the convocation, how will you handle the tension between students?
5. What activities might be initiated within the school to reduce the interracial tensions that have developed?

One Person, One Vote

Flint Ridge is a small K–12 private school in a suburb of a major city. The senior class has 47 members. Of that number, three are Asian American, two are Latino, eleven are African American, and the remainder are white. It is February, and plans are being made for the prom. The site has already been selected, and many details must now be determined. One of the most important decisions is who the disc jockey will be for the prom. Suggestions have been made about which DJ is to be hired. Opinions are strong and tend to be drawn along ethnic lines. The African American students want a popular African American DJ who plays music popular to that ethnic group. The white students want a white DJ who plays the type of music they prefer.

The chair of the DJ Committee calls for a vote. Not surprisingly, all African American students vote for the black DJ. One Latino student votes with them. The other Latino student and the three Asian American students, however, vote with the white students for the white DJ.

"Twelve to thirty-five," announces the chair. "It's Jerry Smith who will be our DJ for the prom."

"That's not fair," says Tyson Edwards, the captain of the basketball team. "You guys always get your way because there are more of you than us."

"Not fair? What are you talking about?" says Keith Van Fleet, president of the senior class. "How much fairer can you get? It's a democratic election. Everything in this school is done democratically. Every person gets a vote. Jerry Smith got the most votes, and everyone voted and every vote counted."

"You think you can ram everything down our throats just because you outnumber us," says Tyson. "We don't have to listen to you. I'm leaving." As Tyson leaves, so do the other African American students.

The next day, Tyson asks to speak with Shelly Brooks, the senior class advisor. "I don't mean any disrespect, Miss Brooks, but we don't get any respect with the things that matter to black students. Everything is one person and one vote. We never have enough votes to get anything that we want as African Americans. We've decided to boycott the senior prom. We are going to have our own prom. We can't really afford it, but our parents said that we are right, and they will help us hire a DJ who will play our kind of music. This is our last dance at this school, and for just once, we want to hear and dance to our kind of music."

To answer these questions online, go to the Critical Incidents module for this chapter of the Companion Website.

Questions for Discussion

1. Is "one person, one vote" always the most democratic way of deciding issues?
2. Are the white students wrong in holding to the vote outcome?
3. Are the black students wrong in protesting so vehemently?
4. Are there similar parallel situations in the rest of society?
5. What compromises could be made that might be acceptable to both groups?

Ethnic/Cultural Values

Returning from their spring break, the students in Kristin Franco's homeroom were anxious to share their vacation experiences. Amber O' Quinn said she had been to Mexico, but had had a "disgusting experience." Mexican men were rude and lecherous, she said. She said that while walking from her hotel to the beach, the Mexican men stopped their cars, honked their horns, and yelled at her. She experienced much of the same behavior on the beach. She had never been so humiliated in her life. "Latino men are crude and a bunch of perverts. They don't know the meaning of decency," she said. Maria Elena, who had emigrated from Central America, responded that Amber had brought this on herself. "Wearing a skimpy string bikini on the streets is provocative. When you do that, you can expect that sort of reaction from the local men. Visitors need to respect local mores. The way they dress and carry on in the States is inappropriate in many other countries," Maria Elena said. Amber countered by exclaiming that it was a resort town, and that the locals live off our tourist dollars. She said they should be grateful that we spend our money there and should expect tourists to dress the way they do at home. The heated argument continued, with several other students entering and taking sides.

To answer these questions online, go to the Critical Incidents module for this chapter of the Companion Website.

Questions for Discussion

1. Is Amber right? Should women expect a minimum amount of respect from men, no matter what country they are in?
2. Is Maria Elena right? Should visitors be expected to conform to local mores?
3. How should Ms. Franco handle this situation? Can she turn this argument into a learning situation?
4. Should Ms. Franco stop the discussion, which is turning into a heated argument?

Chapter 4

Gender

In the schoolroom more than any other place, does the difference of sex, if there is any, need to be forgotten.

Susan B. Anthony, 1856

Abdul Rashid planned to introduce ecology to his science class to-day. Since school began 7 months ago, he has not been able to in-terest most of the girls in the science content.

Most of his female students are capable of understanding and using sci-ence, but they show no interest. Sometimes he thinks they just do not want to upstage the boys in the class. He knows that some of them should be in an advanced science class because they score extremely well on the written tests, but they show no interest in class discussions and experiments.

For the ecology orientation, he decided to take a different approach. Per-haps he could relate the subject to something meaningful in their real lives maybe even their families' or their own social activities. He wanted to find examples they would care about. He decided to focus on the toxic chemicals found in the creek that runs behind many of their homes. Premature births in that area are being blamed on the chemical dumping that has been going on for more than 20 years.

Why do most of the females in Mr. Rashid's class appear to be uninterested in science? What are the participation rates of females in advanced mathe-matics and science courses? What are the reasons for the lack of participation *by girls and young women? What do you think of Mr. Rashid's approach to introducing ecology? What would you do to increase the interest and participation of females in science and mathematics?*

GENDER AND SOCIETY

Although there are few differences between males and females, the popular, and sometimes "scientific," beliefs about differences between the genders have not always matched reality. At the beginning of the twentieth century, some scientists and many lay persons thought that men, particularly those with ancestors from Northern and Western Europe, were intellectually superior to women and therefore generally more capable of most professional and administrative work. It was believed that women's nature made it imperative that men give orders and women take orders in the workplace. Because their physical strength was not comparable to that of men, women were also unable to obtain many manual or working-class jobs, except for the most menial and the lowest paid. Well-adjusted women were expected to be married homemakers, performing services for the family without remuneration.

Even though there is now clear evidence that women and men do not differ in intelligence, the percentage of men in the best-paying and most demanding professional jobs is disproportionately higher than the percentage of women in those jobs. Because of technological advances, brute strength is usually no longer a requirement for most manual jobs, but the percentage of women in those jobs still falls far behind that of men. Many men and women still believe that biological differences prevent gender equality in the home and the workplace.

In response to the patriarchal arrangements that have kept women subordinate to men in the home and in our capitalist system, strong women's movements have developed at different periods in history. Some of the women and men in the antislavery movements prior to the Civil War raised concerns about women's issues, including divorce, property rights, the right to speak in public, abuse by husbands, work with little or no pay, and suffrage. At the Seneca Falls Convention in 1848, women organized to fight against their oppression. This effort involved some male supporters, including Frederick Douglass and white abolitionists who were fighting against slavery and for human and civil rights for all. At the same time, many women did not view their conditions as oppressive and were not supportive of the movement for equality.

During the last half of the nineteenth century, protective legislation for women and children was enacted. This legislation made some manual jobs inaccessible to women because of the danger involved and limited the number of hours women could work and the time at which they could work. Such legislation did little, however, to extend equal rights to women. Unfortunately, during this period, feminists segregated their fight for equal rights from the struggles of other oppressed groups and refused to take a stand against Jim Crow laws and other violations of the civil rights of African and Asian Americans. Women's groups, which were predominantly white, also pitted themselves against African American men in the fight for the right to vote.

The most significant advances in the status of women were initiated in the 1960s, when feminists were able to gain the support of more women and men than at any previous time in history. As in the previous century, this movement developed out of the struggle for civil rights by African Americans. In an attempt to defeat the Civil Rights Bill in Congress, a Southern congressman added the words "or sex" to Title VII, declaring that discrimination based on "race, color, national origin, or sex" was prohibited. This legislation, which was approved in 1964, was the first time that equal rights had been extended to women. By 1983, Congress was no longer disposed to extend full equal rights to women. It refused to adopt the one-sentence Equal Rights Amendment (ERA)—*Equality of rights under the law shall not be denied or abridged by the United States or by any state on account of sex*—even though two-thirds of the U.S. population supported it.

The women's movements that were initiated in the nineteenth century were dominated by middle-class white women. The struggle at that time was limited to women's issues, rather than to broader civil rights for all oppressed groups. This focus prevented the widespread involvement in the movement of both men and women who are African Americans, Asian Americans, Latinos, and Native Americans. Support from the working class has also been limited. The 1990s ushered in a change toward broader support for civil rights for all groups and greater inclusion of men and women from diverse ethnic groups in the feminist movement. As an example, the nation's largest feminist organization, the National Organization for Women (NOW), has added to its agenda fighting racism and supporting welfare reform, immigrant rights, and affirmative action (Zia, 1996). A growing number of articles and books on equity by feminists, sociologists, and critical theorists address the interaction of race, gender, and class in the struggle for equity for all groups.

Increasing numbers of men also support the equity agenda, including women's issues. Some men have established their own male liberation groups to promote choices beyond traditional male roles. Unlike the women's movement, which became a social action, male liberation usually remains a personal, not a political, matter.

Why do equal rights for women, gays, and lesbians continue to be contested? People hold different views about the equality of the sexes. Feminists fight for equality in jobs, pay, schooling, responsibilities in the home, and the nation's laws. They believe that women and men should have a choice about working in the home or outside the home, having children, and acknowledging their sexual orientation. They believe that women should not have to be subordinate to men at home, in the workplace, or in society. They fight to eliminate the physical and mental violence that has resulted from such subordination by providing support groups and shelters for abused women and children, as well as by pushing the judicial system to outlaw such violence. In addition, they promote shared male and female responsibilities in the home and the availability of child care to all families.

Some feminists think that there are few differences between males and females and that those differences are not linked to psychological traits or social roles. Differences are socially constructed. Others think that women's psyches and values do differ from those of men—that there are distinct female and male cultures. They believe that the world would be better served if traditional female values, rather than equality, guided society. They focus on the special qualities of being a woman and do not accept the adoption of male characteristics and values to succeed.

A vocal group of antifeminists that includes both men and women have fought against the Equal Rights Amendment and other equality issues. This group is led by political conservatives who believe that the primary responsibilities of a woman are to be a good wife and mother. Employment outside the home is viewed as interfering with these roles. Homemaking is in itself a viable career that should be pursued. The male is to be the primary breadwinner in the family, and a woman's dependency on the husband or father is expected. They believe that feminism and equal rights will lead to the disintegration of the nuclear family unit. Homosexuality and abortion are rejected. The men and women who support these positions have effectively organized themselves politically to defeat the ERA, promote positions against gays and lesbians, and curtail dissemination of information on sexuality.

GENDER AND BIOLOGY

Do biological differences prevent male- and female-assigned roles from being interchanged? Because women alone can bear offspring, does that also mean only they can rear children? Do biological differences suggest that males and females do different types of work?

People do not choose to be born female or male. Biological sex is determined before birth and is one of the first characteristics reported to others. Ethnicity, religion, and class status are automatically the same as one's parents. The baby's gender, however, elicits different responses from both society and the family.

Although newborns are described by their sex, they have few observable differences in physical characteristics other than reproductive organs. Boys tend to be slightly longer and heavier than girls. Girls have a lower percentage of total body weight in muscle, and their lungs and hearts are proportionally smaller. Nevertheless, parents describe girls and boys differently. Girls are more likely to be described as little, beautiful, pretty, and cute, whereas boys are described as big, strong, and hardy.

Most of us can easily identify physical differences between men and women by appearance alone. Girls tend to have lighter skeletons and different shoulder and pelvic proportions. Although the proportion of different hormones in the body differs by gender, boys and girls have similar hormonal levels and similar physical development during the first 8 years of life. The onset of puberty marks the difference in hormonal levels that control the physical development of the two sexes.

VIDEO INSIGHT

The Secret Life of Boys

Boys will be boys. This is a belief espoused by many—in schools, in homes, in the media, by society as a whole—but does it ring true? Do boys and girls act differently because of genetics, or are their behaviors learned from society?

In this video segment you will see that boys have a more difficult time showing emotion and feelings. By the age of 5 it's often difficult to tell if something is bothering a little boy, because he has already learned to mask his feelings. In addition, while boys are conditioned to keep their feelings and emotions inside, girls are supported and expected to share and discuss their feelings with others. Does this difference have an outward effect? Some researchers say yes; this emotional repression leads to boys acting out more in school and being labeled with learning disorders and behavior problems more often than girls.

After watching the video segment, where do you stand on this discussion? Do you notice little boys being treated differently than girls? Give some examples. How do you interact with children? How will you monitor yourself more closely as you interact with children?

At this time, the proportion of fat to total body weight increases in girls and decreases in boys. The differences in physical structure contribute to a female's diminished strength, lower endurance for heavy labor, greater difficulty in running or overarm throwing, and better ability to float in water. Of course, environment and culture greatly influence the extent of these physical differences for both males and females. Thus, the feminine characteristics listed here can be altered with good nutrition, physical activity, practice, and different behavioral expectations.

There are other reported physical differences between males and females. Because of different expectations and behaviors of males and females in the past, it is hard to determine how many of these differences are actually biological. Some may result from different cultural expectations and lived experiences, rather than from different biological makeup. For example, gender differences in the incidence of cardiovascular disease may decrease as more women enter jobs associated with stress.

Prior to the twentieth century, intelligence was equated with the size of the brain. Because men's heads were larger than women's, the conclusion was that women were not as intelligent as men, and thus, inferior to them. Today we know that brain size is related to body size, not to intelligence. When Alfred Binet developed the first intelligence test at the beginning of the twentieth century, no differences were found in the general intelligence between the sexes. Many studies done during the past half century have found some gender differences in mathematical, verbal, and spatial skills. Some researchers have attributed these differences to biological determinism, especially hormones affecting hemispheric specialization in the brain. They argue that the right hemisphere of the cerebral cortex controls spatial relations and the left hemisphere controls language and other sequential skills. Because males perform better on tests of spatial visualization, these researchers conclude that males have greater right-hemisphere specialization and thus achieve better in mathematics and science. Other researchers attribute the gender differences in these areas to socialization patterns in childrearing and schooling, rather than to biological factors.

Using more sophisticated methods for compiling the findings of the numerous studies conducted in this area, other researchers have concluded that the differences in mathematics skills, verbal skills, and spatial skills are almost nonexistent. These changes in gender differences over a short period of time speak against a heavy reliance on biological arguments. These researchers (Hyde, 1996) found the following:

- *On mathematical abilities:* The difference in mathematical performance moderately favors boys. However, the magnitude of differences in performance in both mathematics and science has declined since 1974.
- *On spatial abilities:* When males and females are tested on distinct types of spatial skills, moderate, high, and no differences are found. The largest difference is in the area of mental rotation—the ability to select correct matches when a three-dimensional figure shown in two dimensions on paper is rotated.
- *On verbal abilities:* Although past research found that adolescent females had greater verbal ability, data today show no gender difference in verbal abilities.

GENDER AND CULTURE

"*Sex* refers to the biological differences between men and women; *gender* relates to the normative expectations attached to each sex" (Walsh, 1997, p. 7). Gender focuses on characteristics of femininity and masculinity that are determined by culture, not biology. Gender traits most often differentiate between females and males.

The factor that complicates discussions about gender differences is the tendency to equate women with nature and men with culture, which controls and transcends nature (Ortner, 1996). In this view, women were traditionally associated with childbearing, childrearing, and nurturing, which kept them near the home. Men had the freedom to move beyond the home to hunt and seek resources for supporting the family. These male and female patterns have evolved into the current cultural patterns in which women are the predominant workers in the nurturing professions of teaching and health care, whereas men are over-represented as corporate leaders, engineers, and construction workers. However, no research shows that women cannot do men's work and that men cannot be successful nurturers. Both men and women are active participants in the culture, but the acceptable range of roles and behaviors is more extensive for men than for women, from sexual activity and available jobs to roles assigned by their religious group. Recent research analyses of gender differences provide little support for a biological explanation. A society's image of the two sexes and their appropriate roles and behaviors are determined almost totally by culture, not biology.

Although few differences separate men and women, and they participate in the same or similar everyday activities, the two are often symbolically segregated. Students are sometimes segregated by sex in schools or school activities. Women and men often congregate separately at social gatherings. They dress and groom differently. They participate in gender-specific leisure activities. Most members of each sex have stereotypical perceptions about themselves and the other sex. Men and women disproportionately enter different occupations and have different activities and opportunities in the economic world. Even when women and men do the same thing, different terminology is used. Males are chefs, females are cooks. There are poets and poetesses, waiters and waitresses, stewards and stewardesses, and so on. The male incarnation of the same role is almost always of higher prestige and receives higher remuneration than the female version.

"Many gender differences in social behavior may be attributed to differences in the status of men and women" (Walsh, 1997, p. 92). The status and characteristics of males are assigned higher value in society than those of women in all cultures, even though some cultures are more egalitarian than others (Ortner, 1996). The superior status is reflected in the inequities that exist in the prestige of different jobs held by men and women, the difference in wages earned by men and women, and the economic rewards for housework and childrearing compared

Often, culture determines the appropriate activities in which boys and girls participate.

with nonhousehold work. Of course, the range of social and economic differences within one gender is as great as it is between the genders. There is no doubt that some women are economically and socially better off than many men. The differences that we perceive between the sexes more likely "result from differences in power and social roles held by men and women. Research shows that men and women act quite similarly when we place them in identical roles and give them equal access to power" (Walsh, 1997, p. 93).

Men are also affected by society's view of gender. The masculine characteristics that are rewarded in our society are independence, assertiveness, leadership ability, self-reliance, and emotional stability. Male identity has undergone serious study over the past decade. Three perspectives pervade the work in this area (Walsh, 1997). Some researchers report that the traditional male role is harmful to men as well as to women. Others investigate the discrimination against men, especially in divorce courts and child-custody battles. The third set of research focuses on the loss of masculinity in a society that diminishes the differences between men and women.

GENDER IDENTITY

Most people take their gender identity for granted and do not question it because it agrees with their biological identity. One's recognition of the appropriate gender identity occurs unconsciously early in life. It becomes a basic anchor in the personality and forms a core part of one's self-identity. By the age of 2 years, children realize that they are either boys or girls and begin to learn their expected behaviors. By the time they enter school, children have clear ideas about gender. Most know that girls and boys behave differently based on behaviors and language reinforced at home. Many are prepared to strive for conformity with these gender-stereotyped roles.

Gender identity begins with the assignment of gender at birth, followed by differential treatment by doctors, nurses, parents, family, and friends. Appropriate gender behavior is reinforced in magazines, on television, in play with peers, and with gender-specific toys. In this socialization process, children develop social skills and a sense of self in accordance with socially prescribed roles and expectations. Appropriate gender behavior is reinforced throughout the life cycle by social processes of approval and disapproval, reward and punishment.

Socialization does not end with parents and relatives. When a child enters school, the socialization process continues. Generally, schools convey the same standards for gender roles as the dominant culture. How many times have you heard the voice on the intercom in an elementary school say "boys and girls. . ."? "By frequently using gender labels when they interact with kids, adults make being a girl or a boy central to self-definition, and to the ongoing life of schools" (Thorne, 1997, p. 35). The attitudes and values about appropriate gender roles are embedded in the curriculum of schools. Elementary schools appear to imitate the mothering role, with a predominance of female teachers and an emphasis on obedience and conformity. In classrooms, males and females receive different feedback and encouragement for their work, but the patterns are similar to those used at home.

Children are also active participants in the socialization process (Thorne, 1997). They don't always follow the socially acceptable ways of their sex. Not all boys participate in large group activities and are aggressive; it is usually the most popular boys who participate in these gender-specific activities. The forgotten boys whose voices have been silenced and marginalized may follow behavior patterns generally associated with girls. The same is true for girls; many do not follow the gender-specific behaviors expected of their sex. Nevertheless, most girls and boys do choose to be engaged in separate activities as youngsters. They develop a sense of gender as a dichotomy and opposition when they divide themselves into academic and athletic competitions that pit boys against girls. When they work cooperatively on projects in classrooms, "they actively undermine a sense of gender as opposition" (Thorne, 1997, p. 4).

The socialization of boys has been oriented toward achievement and self-reliance, that of girls toward nurturance and responsibility. The knowledge required to carry out the traditional roles associated with being female has not been as highly valued by society as the knowledge required to achieve manhood. School playgrounds reflect the importance placed on male as compared to female activities. The space required to play baseball, soccer, basketball, and kickball is much greater than that for girl's jump rope, foursquare, and bar tricks. Some girls may play the boys' sports with them, but almost no boys join the girls' games. When boys do engage in girls' games like jump rope, it is usually to disrupt the game, not to be an equal participant (Thorne, 1997).

During socialization, we internalize the social norms considered appropriate for our gender, including gender-appropriate behavior, personality characteristics, emotional responses, attitudes, and beliefs. These characteristics become so much a part of our self-identification that we forget they are learned and are not innate characteristics. Socialization is a lifelong process, and sex-role socialization can be changed as a result of personal experiences or planned interventions during adulthood.

In our society, women are supposed to be feminine and men masculine, with society tolerating little crossover. Some men and women prefer to behave like the opposite gender, sometimes in overt ways such as cross-dressing. Generally, females are allowed more flexibility in their gender identification than males. Even young girls receive positive attributes from acting like boys by being physically active, participating in sports, and rejecting feminine stereotypical behavior. On the other hand, boys are often ostracized by other boys, girls, and adults when they join in girl's games, act effeminate, and don't engage in the same sports as the popular males. Unlike girls who have crossed gender lines, boys suffer loss of prestige.

Gender can no longer be viewed in the traditional bipolar fashion as if masculine and feminine traits never coexist in an individual. We are both male and female, exhibiting the traits of one or the other as appropriate in a specific situation or setting. The dilemma is that not all of us, especially males, are encouraged to be ourselves when our behavior is counter to society's norms of gender identity.

Impact of Perceived Differences

Anthropologists have found some universal practices related to gender roles. First, in all societies, men have clear control of political and military apparatus. Second, no society fosters achievement and self-reliance in females more than in males. Third, boys tend to seek dominance more than girls do and are significantly more physically and verbally aggressive. No clear evidence suggests, however, that these characteristics are universal gender-role characteristics, rather than a function of a near-universal cultural practice. The fact that these universal practices exist is the result of historical development, rather than the superiority of the male (de Beauvoir, 1974).

In many families today, both wife and husband work. Although a growing number of men assist with childrearing and household chores, working mothers often have the primary responsibility for these activities in addition to their paid employment. Almost half of the nation's workforce is female, and more than 90% of all women will work outside the home at some time. A growing number of women are divorced, widowed, or otherwise alone. Unable to depend on a male wage earner, they are economically forced to fulfill that role alone. Although both men and women now work in a variety of careers and share many roles and activities that were formerly gender-typed, many adults retain their traditional gender roles.

Gender role expectations are also reflected in schools. Girls and young women are expected to be well-behaved and make good grades. Males are expected to be less well-behaved and to not achieve academically as well as females prior to puberty. Many working-class males develop patterns of resistance to school and its authority figures because it is considered feminine and emphasizes mental rather than manual work (Willis, 1977).

Stereotyping of Gender Roles

Although gender roles are gradually changing, they continue to be projected stereotypically in the socialization process. Stereotyping defines the male and female roles narrowly and as quite distinct from one another. It leads children to generalize that all persons within a group behave in the same way. Men and women become automatically associated with the characteristics and roles with which they are constantly endowed by the mass media and by classroom materials. Careers are not the only areas in which stereotyping occurs. Female and male intellectual abilities, personality characteristics, physical appearance, social status, and domestic roles have also been stereotyped. Persons who differ from the stereotype of their group, especially gays and lesbians, are often ostracized by the dominant group. Such role stereotyping denies individuals the wide range of human potential that is possible.

Television is one of the perpetuators of gender stereotyping. Studies show that by 3 years of age, children have already developed tastes in television programs related to age, gender, and race. By the time of high school graduation, the average child will have spent 11,000 hours in the classroom and 15,000 hours in front of the television. Few children are exempt from this practice because most homes in this country have one or more television sets. The ideals and ideas of dominant America are incorporated into program development as symbolic representations of American society. They are not literal portrayals, yet these representations announce to viewers what is valued and approved in society.

On television, beauty counts for more than intelligence. Adult working women are portrayed, but both they and adolescent women are predominantly rich or middle class. Strong, intelligent, working-class women are generally invisible. Female heroines are not social workers, teachers, or secretaries. The 2000 Olympics began to project different roles for women: female athletes competed in the same sports as men, but in most cases, except in equestrian events, against other women. More than 40% of the athletes in these competitions were women—the highest level of participation of women in the history of the Olympics.

A number of men's and women's magazines continue to portray the two sexes stereotypically. Most newspapers have women's pages that include articles on fashion, food, and social events—pages specifically written for what is believed to be the interests of women. Women's magazines often send contradictory messages by indicating that women should both be successful in their chosen professions and exhibit all of the positive feminine attributes of beauty, caring, and housekeeping. Working mothers are supposed to be supermoms who not only work, but are devoted mothers who meet the needs of their children like stay-at-home mothers do. The men's pages of newspapers are the sports and business sections, in which competition and winning are stressed. The athletic performances of women seldom make the front page of those sections.

Whereas adults read newspapers, magazines, and books, children spend much of their reading time with school textbooks. How do the genders fare in the resources used in classrooms across the nation? Studies show that great improvements have been made over the past 25 years. Textbooks are not as racist and sexist as in the past, and perspectives are better balanced. However, teachers still need to be cognizant of the gender and ethnicity of the authors being read by students. Are they exposing them to the perspectives of women, girls, and diverse ethnic and religious groups?

In contemporary society, the male and female traditional roles are practiced interchangeably in a growing number of families. Both men and women work in nontraditional careers and share many of the formerly gender-typical roles. Even the portrayal of the woman who stays at home is stereotypical; the reality and difficulty of juggling the care of children and a husband, cleaning, cooking, shopping, doing laundry, repairing a leaky faucet, entertaining, and keeping books are seldom presented.

Consciousness-raising activities to help men and women understand and evaluate the stereotypical roles for which they have been socialized have been helpful in opening options for both groups. In many communities, one no longer has to have rigid feminine or masculine characteristics, behavior, or job options; it is becoming easier to have both. More couples are sharing the role of wage earner—a traditionally gender-typical role for men. It is possible that, in the future, a growing number of men will share more equally in the responsibilities of childrearing and homemaking. Optimistically, both men and women will be able to choose roles with which they are comfortable, rather than have to accept a gender role determined by society.

We are living in an era of changing norms in which old, unequal roles are being rejected by many. These changes are resulting in many new uncertainties in which the norms of the appropriate gender role are no longer so distinct. As new norms develop, more flexible roles, personalities, and behaviors are evolving for both females and males.

SEXISM AND GENDER DISCRIMINATION

Only a century ago, most women could not attend college, had no control of either their property or their children, could not initiate a divorce, and were forbidden to smoke or drink. Because these inequities no longer exist and laws now protect the rights of women, many people believe that men and women are treated equally in society. Society continues to hold deep-rooted assumptions, however, about how

Women still work disproportionately in traditionally female jobs. For example, they make up more than 98% of the preschool and kindergarten teachers in the United States.

men and women should think, look, and behave. These societal expectations lead to discriminatory behavior based on gender alone.

When physical strength determined who performed certain tasks, men conducted the hunt for food, which required them to leave the home, whereas women raised food close to the home. With industrialization, this pattern of men working away from home and women working close to home was translated into labor market activity for men and nonlabor market activity for women. Men began to work specific hours and to receive pay for that work. By contrast, women worked irregular and unspecified working periods in the home and received no wages for their work. The value of a woman's work was never rewarded by money paid directly to her. It certainly was not as valued as the work of men, who contributed in labor market production. In our society, individuals who provide services for which they are paid have a higher status than those who are not paid for their work, such as homemakers.

"Sexism is the belief in the inherent superiority of one sex over all others and thereby the right to dominance" (Lorde, 1995, p. 192). Often, sex discrimination is practiced by individuals in personal situations of marriage and family life, as well as in their occupational roles as manager, realtor, secretary, or legislator. Socialization patterns within the family may limit the potential of children when they are taught gender-differentiated behaviors. For example, girls are sometimes taught to be more obedient, neat, passive, and dependent, whereas boys are allowed to be more disobedient, aggressive, independent, exploring, and creative. These gender-differentiated behaviors prepare each for gender-specific jobs and roles. Aggressive and independent individuals (usually men) are likely to manage those who are obedient and dependent (usually women).

Many of us discriminate on the basis of gender without realizing it. Because we were raised in a sexist society, we think our behavior is natural and acceptable, even when it is discriminatory. Women often do not realize the extent to which they do not participate equally in society, nor men the privilege that maleness bestows on them—a sign that the distinct roles have been internalized well during the socialization process. Most parents do not directly plan to harm their daughters by teaching them feminine roles. They do not realize that such characteristics may prevent their daughters from achieving societal benefits comparable with those of men. Too often, young women are encouraged to gain such societal rewards through marriage, rather than by their own achievement and independence.

Many individuals outside the family also practice gender discrimination. The kindergarten teacher who scolds the boy for playing in the girls' corner is discriminating. The personnel director who hires only women for secretarial positions and only men as managers is overtly discriminating on the basis of gender. Educators have the opportunity to help all students break out of group stereotypes and provide opportunities to explore and pursue a wide variety of options in fulfilling their potential as individuals.

Gender discrimination not only is practiced by individuals but also has been institutionalized in policies, laws, rules, and precedents in society. These institutional arrangements benefit one gender over the other.

Jobs and Wages

Regardless of their education, men are expected to work; but women sometimes have a choice about working. The amount of education obtained by women does little to close the gap between the earnings of men and women. The more education received, the greater the expected earnings for both genders. However, women with bachelor's degrees earn less than men with some college, but no degree. Women with bachelor's degrees or beyond have median incomes that are only 63% of the income earned by males with the same degree.

The difference in income between men and women generally increases with age. The difference shown in Figure 4–1 is not affected by women who do not work for wages. It reflects the income of male and female full-time workers. Why do these differences exist and continue to increase throughout life?

Discrepancies in income are, in part, a result of the types of jobs held by the two groups. The stereotypes about the capabilities and roles of women in the domestic setting have been transferred to the labor market. Women first entered the labor market in jobs that were similar to those performed in the home, such as sewing, teaching, nursing, and doing household services. Women workers continue to be heavily concentrated in a few occupations that are accompanied by neither high prestige nor high income. Women continue to be underrepresented as managers and skilled workers. Figure 4–2 shows that women are overly represented in sales, administrative support, and service occupations.

It has been difficult for women to enter administrative and skilled jobs. These jobs have fewer entry-level positions than the less prestigious ones. The available openings are often for jobs that have short or nonexistent promotion ladders, few opportunities for training, low wages, few chances for stability, and poor working conditions. Clerical and sales positions are examples of such jobs, but even professions such as teaching and nursing offer little opportunity for career advancement.

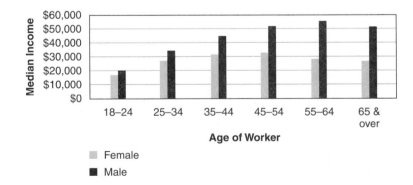

Figure 4–1
Median annual income of year-round, full-time workers by age and gender in 1997.

Source: U.S. Census Bureau, 1999. *Statistical Abstract of the United States: 1999* (119th ed.). Washington, DC: U.S. Government Printing Office.

To earn the comfortable living that is the *American Dream* requires women to seek either a traditionally male job or a husband with a *good* job. Unfortunately, society does not currently value traditional female jobs, which are essential to society, enough to afford them the prestige and salaries they deserve.

When men enter traditionally female fields, they often do not hold the same positions as women in the field. In 1998, men comprised less than 2% of all prekindergarten and kindergarten teachers and less than 17% of all elementary teachers. However, nearly half of the high school teachers, and 55% of the principals and assistant principals were men (U.S. Bureau of the Census, 1999). Male social workers are more often community organizers, rather than group workers or caseworkers. Although the percentage of men participating in traditionally female jobs has increased over the years, they have become overrepresented in the higher status, administrative levels of these occupations. For example, 71% of all preschool through grade 12 teachers are women as compared with 36% of the college and university faculty (U.S. Bureau of the Census, 1999).

Gender segregation and wage discrimination also affect women in blue-collar and white-collar jobs. The majority of women enter the labor force at the lowest level of these categories, with unstable employment opportunities and low wages. Much of the discrimination against women in the labor force results from decisions of employers concerning promotions and wage increases. In addition, many of the occupations in which women are concentrated have not been organized by unions that might help change poor working conditions and low wages.

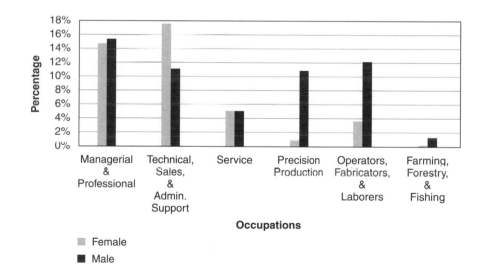

Figure 4–2

Percentage of workers in different occupations by gender in 1998.

Source: U.S. Census Bureau, 1999. *Statistical Abstract of the United States: 1999* (119th ed.). Washington, DC: U.S. Government Printing Office.

VIDEO INSIGHT

The Fairer Sex?

Although those fighting for women's rights have made great strides in the past several decades, women still earn only 74 cents for every dollar that men make, and they often pay more for things like consumer goods and medical care. In the video segment, a man and a woman decide to see for themselves whether men and women are treated differently in otherwise identical situations, such as buying a car, getting clothes dry cleaned, setting a tee time at a golf course, and interviewing for a job. Using hidden cameras, they document that women often suffer from a subtle and insidious kind of discrimination, the kind of discrimination that is difficult to quantify and even more difficult to prove.

Have you ever felt as though you suffered from gender bias? Share with a group of male and female peers your own stories about how you believe your gender has affected your opportunities and life decisions. Note not only the differences in how men and women respond but also the differences in the way men and women in your group react to those differences. What do the stories and responses that you've shared tell you about how entrenched cultural stereotypes about gender are? What gendered behaviors do you think are developed through stereotyping, and what might be innate to each sex?

Gradually, more women are entering traditionally male occupations as barriers against their entry are broken. In 1950, only 6.5% of all physicians were women; by 1998, 16% were women. The percentage of lawyers and judges has increased from 4% to 16%, but only 6% of all engineers and 13% of architects are women (U.S. Bureau of the Census, 1999). The number of women in these professional jobs should rise over time since the percentage receiving degrees in these fields has increased dramatically over the past 2 decades. Women are earning more than 40% of the professional degrees being granted in medicine and law. Although women are earning nearly 40% of the architecture degrees, they receive only 16% of the engineering degrees and 28% of the computer science degrees. Even in education, the percentage of female principals has increased from 20% in 1982 to 45% in 1996.

Although more women are entering the traditionally male-dominated fields, they continue to face discrimination in wages earned. In 1970, women working full-time earned 59 cents for every dollar earned by men; by 1997, they were earning only 74 cents for every dollar earned by men. This disparity is, in part, a result of the lower-status jobs held by many women but is also a result of lower salaries for women holding positions comparable to men's. Such discrimination greatly affects the quality of life for women, particularly those who are single heads of households, and their children.

Sexual Orientation

Heterosexuality is the valued sexual orientation promoted by the dominant group in the United States. It is so highly valued that laws and social practices try to prevent homosexuality. Until recently, laws in most states forbade sexual liaisons between members of the same sex; some states still have laws against sodomy. In many areas of the country where overt discrimination against homosexuals remains, gays and lesbians may not be able to find housing or jobs. Often, they are not admitted to "straight" clubs and are vulnerable to attacks on city streets. The National Gay and Lesbian Task Force collects data on reports of harassment and violence against gays and reports that such incidents continue to increase.

Many people have little knowledge about homosexuality, but they know many myths about it. As a result, they often develop an irrational fear of homosexuals, which is manifested in feelings of disgust, anxiety, and anger. Individuals who harbor these negative feelings usually have had little or no personal contact with gays and lesbians; have participated in little or no homosexual behavior themselves; hold a conservative religious ideology; and/or have little knowledge about the social, medical, and legal issues related to homosexuality (Sears, 1992). In the past, many people viewed homosexuality as a sin, a sickness, or a crime.

In 1948, Alfred Charles Kinsey, the American sexologist, estimated that 10% of the population is exclusively homosexual. Other studies suggest that the number is less than 5%. Although experts disagree on the number, they agree that sexual orientation is established early in life, rather than being learned from others in adolescence and adulthood. Many gay and lesbian adults report having attractions to same-sex peers when they were children, but these remembered experiences may be no different for heterosexuals than for homosexuals. Young people usually become aware that they have different sexual attractions around age 12 (Mondimore, 1996; Anderson, 1995).

Prior to the 1970s, most lesbians and gays hid their homosexuality from their families, landlords, and coworkers because of the fear of rejection and retaliation. Following the 1969 Stonewall Inn riot in Greenwich Village, in which gays fought back against police, it became somewhat easier to openly admit their homosexuality. However, many still cannot be open because of community hostility and discrimination. They, like other oppressed groups, have extended the fight for civil rights to include gays and lesbians. As a result, most states have repealed sodomy laws, the Democratic Party platform supports gay rights, a growing number of companies and governments are extending insurance benefits to homosexual partners, non-discrimination policies have been extended to include sexual orientation, and public support for gay rights is higher.

Nevertheless, discrimination and prejudice against gays and lesbians remain, as evidenced by policies to prevent them from organizing clubs on some college campuses or to openly declare their homosexuality in the armed services. Derogatory terms are used by many adults and students in schools. Much work is still required to overcome prejudices and discrimination against those who are not heterosexual.

To answer these
questions online,
go to the Pause to
Reflect module for
this chapter of the
Companion
Website.

PAUSE TO REFLECT

Imagine you are teaching a high school class. You are leading a discussion about current events, and today's topic is AIDS. After several minutes of give-and-take discussion among students in the class, the following dialogue occurs:

Mary: I think it's too bad that all these people are so sick and are going to die. I just think . . .

Paul (interrupting): Those fags get what they deserve. What makes me mad is that we're spending money trying to find a cure. If we just let God and nature take its course, I won't have to worry about any queer bothering me.

Mary: I never thought about it that way before.

Mary then faces you and asks, "What do you think about Paul's comments?" Briefly state how you would respond.

Source: Sears, J. T. (1992). Educators, homosexuality, and homosexual students: Are personal feelings related to professional beliefs? In K. M. Harbeck (Ed.), *Coming out of the classroom closet: Gay and lesbian students, teachers, and curricula.* Binghamton, NY: Harrington Park Press, pp. 62–64.

Even though a growing number of gays and lesbians are open about their sexual orientation, many of them still fear reprisal. In many areas of the country and in many classrooms, they are harassed and abused if they openly acknowledge their sexual orientation. Unfortunately, it is not just other students who reject gay and lesbian students. A number of families, religious leaders, and teachers not only reject them, but label them as immoral and deviant. Unlike persons whose race can be easily identified by others, gays and lesbians can hide their identities from a hostile society. As a result, they suffer loneliness and alienation by not acknowledging it.

Gay and lesbian educators are often forced to separate their personal and professional lives for fear of losing their jobs. Because they are silent about their homosexuality, these teachers neither serve as role models for gay and lesbian students nor provide the support needed by a group of students who are not recognized by school officials. Heterosexual teachers who are willing to support gay and lesbian students also may face discriminatory retaliation by others.

High school is a difficult time for many adolescents, but it is particularly stressful for gays and lesbians as they struggle with the knowledge that they are members of one of the most despised groups in society. They have few, if any, support systems in their schools or communities. They are alone in making decisions about acknowledging their sexual orientation and facing the attacks by others. This period is described by Gerald Unks (1995):

In virtually every way, lesbian, gay, and bisexual adolescents are *worse off* than their adult counterparts. While forces in the larger adult society might hint at political correctness, acceptance, and accommodation, the high school—the center of most adolescent life and culture—stands staunchly aloof and rigidly resistant to even a suggestion that any of its faculty or student body might be homosexual or that homosexuals deserve anything but derision and scorn within its walls. High schools may be the most homophobic institutions in American society, and woe be to anyone who would challenge the heterosexist premises on which they operate (p. 5).

Professional educators have the responsibility to eliminate sexism and homophobia in the classroom and school. Their role requires that they not limit the potential of any student because of sexual orientation. Teachers and administrators should confront colleagues and students who engage in name calling and harassment. Classroom interactions, resources, extracurricular activities, and counseling practices must be evaluated to ensure that students are not being discriminated against because of their sexual orientation.

Sexual Harassment

Sexual harassment of women has long been reported in the workplace. Sometimes the perpetuator is in a position of power over another and uses that power to secure favors or to make sexual advances. In other cases, it is a coworker who makes unwanted advances. As in other areas related to gender socialization, schools mirror society in its perpetuation of sexual harassment. In fact, students in high schools probably fare much worse than adults in other settings: 83% of girls and 60% of boys report receiving unwanted sexual attention in schools, and more than half of these students have been both the harassed and the harasser (Lee, Croninger, Linn, & Chen, 1996).

A 1993 study by the American Association of University Women, *Hostile Hallways*, found not only that sexual harassment was pervasive in high schools but that it occurred in public places. Students reported that the harassment was unwelcome and problematic and that their calls for help from school officials were generally ignored. "Sizable proportions of students (especially girls) are harassed by school officials: principals, teachers, and staff" (Lee et al., 1996, p. 408).

Male students are particularly confused by accusations of sexual harassment, in part because the behavior has long been viewed as typical for adolescents. Educators and parents alike explain behavior such as snapping bras and calling girls *whores* and *bitches* as "boys will be boys" and attribute the pushing of other students to the perennial school bullies. It is not only girls who are harassed. "Boys get chastised and into trouble when they sexually harass girls, but when boys are targets of sexual harassment, the events are overlooked, excused as a rite of passage or regarded as an honor" (Stein, 1996, p. 67). Many principals and teachers either don't know that harassment is occurring in schools or ignore it. Surveys of young people provide a different picture of school behavior. More than 90% of the gay, lesbian, bisexual, and transgender students responding to a 1999 survey reported that they regularly heard homophobic comments (Gay, Lesbian, and Straight Education Network, 1999). Nearly 70% had experienced verbal harassment and 24% suffered physical harassment.

Harassment and sex discrimination are social justice issues and are included under civil rights laws. Therefore, females, gays, and others who have suffered from such harassment are beginning to fight back through the courts. They argue that even though the harassment has been reported to teachers, counselors, or administrators, no action has been taken to stop it. In a 1999 survey of gay students, 39% reported that no one intervened when homophobic remarks were made in school (Gay, Lesbian, & Straight Education Network, 1999).

School officials are no longer allowed to ignore the sexual harassment and abuse of students and may face the payment of damage awards. Teachers, administrators, and staff need to become more alert to sexual harassment among students. In addition, they should monitor their own behaviors to ensure that they are not using their power as an authority figure to harass students. Policies and practices within schools may need to be revised, but discussions should involve the broader community of students and parents.

INTERACTION OF GENDER WITH ETHNICITY, CLASS, AND RELIGION

The degree to which a student adheres to a traditional gender identity is influenced by the family's ethnicity, class, and religion. It is impossible to isolate gender from one's ethnic background. For many women who are not members of the dominant group, ethnic identity takes precedence over gender identity. In some religions, gender identity and relations are strictly controlled by church doctrine. Thus, gender inequality takes on different forms among different ethnic, class, and religious groups.

Middle-class women are more likely to attend college immediately after high school than are women from working-class families. Young women, especially working-class ones, may not be clear about their future work lives. Most young women, however, take for granted that they will work outside the home as adults.

Many working-class women, both black and white, value commonsense knowledge that they have gained through their lived experiences. Their ways of knowing are embedded in their culture, community, and family and cannot be judged by dominant academic standards. Although these women believe that both men and women have common sense, more value is placed on that of men. Working-class men gain their knowledge collectively in the workplace, whereas the women learn theirs individually as mothers and homemakers. Individuals with accumulated academic knowledge are sometimes viewed by the working-class as not having the common sense that is required for working-class life. Still, many working-class women pursue additional education, most often in community colleges, to increase their ability to find better employment. After this, education is usually not sought until the women are older and have children. Such academic achievement, however, puts a strain on the working-class family, where men's knowledge has traditionally been more valued.

Ethnic group membership also influences the socialization patterns of males and females. The degree to which traditional gender roles are accepted depends, in large part, on the degree to which the family maintains the traditional patterns and on the particular experiences of the ethnic group in this country. Puerto Rican, Mexican American, Appalachian, and Native American families that adhere to traditional religious and cultural patterns are more likely to encourage adherence to rigid gender roles than families that have adopted bicultural patterns.

Women in African American families have developed a different pattern. Historically, they have worked outside the home and are less likely to hold strict traditional views about their roles. They have learned to be both homemakers and wage earners. They are more likely than African American men to complete high school and college. At the same time, African American women who have low incomes and are working class attain less schooling than most other ethnic groups. Unlike many middle-class white women, middle-class black women do not necessarily perceive marriage as a route to upward mobility or a way out of poverty.

African American, Latino, and American Indian women of all classes have current and historical experiences of discrimination based on their race and ethnicity. Feminists and gays from these groups may feel forced to choose between a racial and a gender identity, which has led to the lack of attention to the divisions of class, gender, and sexual orientation within their communities. The relationship of memberships in multiple groups varies over time and with experience. Identification with one group may be prevalent in one setting, but not another. It is often a struggle to develop an identity that incorporates one's gender, ethnic identity, sexual orientation, class, and religion into a whole with which one feels comfortable and self-assured.

It is dangerous to assume that students will hold certain views or behave in gender-typical ways because of their ethnicity or class level. Individual families within those two microcultures vary greatly in their support of gender-typical roles for men and women and their subsequent behavior along a continuum of gender identity. Religions, however, generally recognize and include masculine and feminine principles as part of their doctrines. Regardless of the specific religion, rituals usually reflect and reinforce systems of male dominance. When a religious dogma declares that homosexuality is wrong, it is very difficult for its members to recognize homosexuality as normal and of equal status to heterosexuality. Awareness of the community and cultures within which schools are located will be essential as teachers ensure that they don't discriminate, that they support students as appropriate, and that they help all students know their possibilities and develop their potential to reach them.

Gay men share with heterosexual men a dominant position in relation to women but are subordinate in relation to heterosexual men. As a result of the isolation and discrimination forces on homosexuals, gay cultural forms have developed. These include gay newspapers, magazines, churches, health clinics, and social clubs. Equality has yet to be extended to many females and males who openly define their sexual orientation against the national norm.

The more fundamentalist religious groups support a strict adherence to gender-differentiated roles. Their influence extends into issues of sexuality, marriage, and reproductive rights. They sometimes have successfully organized politically to control state and federal policies on family and women's affairs. At the same time, the more liberal religious groups support gays and lesbians and the equality of the sexes.

The classroom teacher is likely to find students at different points along the gender identity continuum, both in their beliefs about female and male roles and in their actual behavior. Lesbian and gay adolescents are struggling with their sexual orientation and its meaning in a homophobic climate. Understanding the influence of students' microcultural memberships will be important as teachers try to open up the possibilities for all of them, regardless of their gender and sexual orientation.

EDUCATIONAL IMPLICATIONS

Education is a key to upward mobility and financial security in adulthood. Therefore, the occupational roles that individuals pursue will influence the way they are able to live in the future. One's chances to pursue postsecondary education are greatly influenced by one's education in elementary and secondary schools. By the time students reach the secondary level, they have chosen, or been helped to choose, a college preparatory program, a general education program, or a specific vocational training program. When college students select a major, disproportionate numbers of males select engineering and computer science, which provides the highest salary upon graduation. These early choices can make a great difference in later job satisfaction and rewards.

Tests and other assessments provide evidence of performance and learning throughout school. The assessments may assist teachers in knowing the gaps in student learning, allowing them to develop strategies that build on the prior experiences of students. Tests are also used to make high stakes decisions that may dramatically affect a student's future. They are used to determine promotion to the next grade, eligibility for a high school diploma, and admission into college and a profession. Although differences between the scores of females and males are narrowing, outcomes measured by national tests continue to favor males.

- At ages 9, 13, and 17, girls outperform males on assessments of reading and writing (U.S. Department of Education, 2000).
- The achievement scores of 9- and 13-year-old males slightly exceed females on mathematics and science assessment, but the differences increase in favor of males at age 17. However, differences in science achievement are narrowing by age 17 (U.S. Department of Education, 2000).
- With the exception of foreign language, males score higher on Advanced Placement Examinations than females (American Association of University Women, 1999).
- Males score higher than females on the SAT and ACT in all areas other than the ACT verbal section (American Association of University Women, 1999).
- Males score higher on admission tests for graduate and professional schools (the Graduate Record Examination [GRE], the MCATs for medical schools, the LSATs for law schools, and the GMATs for business schools) (Sadker, 1996).

The gender differences between achievement at different ages is not the same across ethnic groups. "In fourth grade, Hispanic girls score higher than Hispanic boys in reading and history; by the eighth grade, they score higher in mathematics and reading; and by the twelfth grade, they score higher than Hispanic boys in science as well as reading" (American Association of University Women, 1999, p. 43). African American girls perform better than, or equal to, African American boys on all assessments at every level. Achievement differences between white girls and boys are small at all assessment points; white girls score higher on reading at the fourth and twelfth grades and have a slight advantage in mathematics at the eighth grade.

Many people believe that if the experiences of boys and girls are changed in school, differences in academic achievement will be eliminated, and both will have a chance for more equitable lives as adults. There is not common agreement, however, on how to accomplish these goals. There is general agreement that "public education should be free of gender bias. The question is rather what is the best way to achieve this freedom from gender bias. Should we undertake to ignore gender or to obliterate gender differentiations, or should we in some way pay deliberate attention to gender?" (Houston, 1996, p. 51)

Programs designed to end gender stratification focus on changing the behavior of teachers and the content and interactions in classrooms. Teachers, counselors, teacher aides, coaches, and principals all have roles in eradicating the inequities that result from sexism. Schools have used two approaches in this process: women's studies and nonsexist or gender sensitive education. In addition, laws have been passed at the federal level that influence education in this area.

Women's Studies

Women's studies programs are similar to ethnic studies programs in their attempt to record and analyze the historical and contemporary experiences of a group that has usually been ignored in the curriculum. Courses in women's studies include concepts of consciousness-raising and views of women as a separate group with unique needs and disadvantages in schools and other institutions. They examine the culture, status, development, and achievement of women as a group.

Women's studies have evolved in secondary and higher education as units in history, sociology, and literature courses; as separate courses; and as programs from which students can choose a major or minor field of study. Similar to the ethnic studies programs, the experiences and contributions of women and related concepts have been the focus.

Women's studies provide a perspective that is foreign to most students. Historical, economic, and sociological events are viewed from the perspective of a group that has been in a position subordinate to men throughout history. Until students participate in such courses, they usually do not realize that 51% of the population has received so little coverage in most textbooks and courses. These programs allow students to increase both their awareness and their knowledge base about women's history and the contributions of women. Sometimes women are taught skills for competing successfully in a man's world or for managing a career and a family. In addition, many women's studies programs assist in developing a positive female self-image within a society that has viewed women as inferior to men. Psychological and career assistance to women is also a part of some programs.

Although the content of women's studies is desperately needed to fill the gaps of current educational programs, it usually is a program set aside from the general academic offerings. Instead of being required, it is usually an elective course. Thus, the majority of students may never integrate the information and concepts of women's studies into their academic work. The treatment of women as a separate entity also subtly suggests that the study of women is secondary to the important study of the world—a world that is reflected in textbooks and courses as one of males from a male perspective. All students need to learn about a world in which the contributions of both males and females are valued.

Gender-Sensitive Education

When women's studies programs are part of a gender sensitive education, they become an integral part of the total education program, rather than a separate luxury. Even with sexist materials, alert teachers can point out the discrepancies that exist between the genders, discuss how and why such inequities are portrayed, and supplement the materials with information that provides a more balanced view of the roles and contributions of both men and women. Required readings should include the writings of women, as well as those of men. At a minimum, nonstereotypical male and female examples can appear on bulletin boards and in teacher-prepared materials.

All students should be exposed to the contributions of women as well as men throughout history. History courses that focus primarily on wars and political power will almost totally focus on men; history courses that focus on the family and the arts will more equitably include both genders. Science courses that discuss all of the great scientists often forget to discuss the societal limitations that prevented women from being scientists. (Women scientists and writers of the past often had to use male names or give their work to men for publication.) Students are being cheated of a wealth of information about the majority of the world's population when women are not included as an integral part of the curriculum. Because teachers control the information and concepts taught to students, it is their responsibility to present a view of the world that includes women and men and their wide ranges of perspectives.

It is also the responsibility of the teacher to provide each student with the opportunity to reach his or her potential. If girls constantly see boys as more active, smarter, more aggressive, and exerting more control over their lives, they see themselves as the other with characteristics that are opposite those of males. Boys who are always expected to behave in stereotypically masculine ways also suffer. Students are bombarded by subtle influences in schools that reinforce the notion that boys are more important than girls. This unplanned, unofficial learning—the hidden curriculum—has an impact on how students feel about themselves and others. Sexism is often projected in the messages that children receive in the illustrations, language, and content of texts, films, and other instructional materials. Sexism should be eliminated in the interaction of school authorities with male and female students and in the participation of the two sexes in sports and extracurricular activities. A school that is gender-sensitive is staffed by influential female and male role models who are sensitive to the importance of gender in the classroom and who model nonsexist and nonhomophobic behavior.

One of the goals of nonsexist education is to allow girls and young women to be heard and to understand the legitimacy of their experiences as females. Young men should have the opportunity to explore their privileged role in our inequitable society. They should learn to speak on behalf of women. Teachers will not find this an easy task. Many females and males resist discussions of power relations and how they benefit or lose within those relations. However, the value to students and society is worth the discomfort that such discussions may cause to students, and perhaps to the teacher. The classroom may be the only place in which students can confront these issues and be helped to make sense of them.

An area over which all educators have control is their own interactions with students. Consistently, researchers find that educators react differently to boys and girls in the classroom, on the athletic field, in the hall, and in the counseling office. When asked whether they discriminate in the way they react to boys and girls in the classroom, most teachers say no. Once they critically examine their interactions, however, most find that they do respond differently. The most important factor in overcoming gender biases in the classroom is recognizing that subtle and unintentional biases exist. Once these are recognized, the teacher can begin to make changes in the classroom and in the lives of the students in that classroom.

One of the goals of a gender-sensitive education is to eliminate the power relationships based on gender in the classroom. Teachers should monitor the tasks and activities in which students participate in the classroom. Female and male students should share the leadership in classroom activities and discussions. Girls and young women may need to be encouraged to participate actively in hands-on activities, and boys may need encouragement in reading and writing activities. Research suggests that boys and girls provide leadership equally in middle school science activities, but girls begin to lose confidence in their science abilities. The problem observed in a number of science classes is that boys manipulate the equipment, usually delegating the girls in their group to note-taking and providing information (Jovanovic & King, 1998). Teachers need to intervene in these cases to ensure that girls are involved in all levels of the hands-on work.

If left alone, many female and male students choose to sit with members of the same sex and participate in group activities with members of the same sex. To ensure that boys and girls work together in classrooms, the teacher may have to assign seats and groups. Small, heterogeneous, cooperative work groups reduce the emphasis on power relationships that characterize competitive activities. These activities can be designed to provide all students, even those who are often marginalized in the classroom, with the opportunity to participate at a more equitable level.

LINK TO THE CLASSROOM

Most teachers are surprised to learn that they interact with female and male students differently. To check one's interactions requires the systematic recording of them. Observe teacher-student interactions in schools in which you are visiting or in one of the classrooms in which you are now a student. Use one of the following methods to record the interactions:

1. *Tally how many times the teacher calls on or responds to males and to females.*
2. *Draw a seating plan of the students in the classroom and place a check mark at the location of each student with whom the teacher interacts and for each time an interaction occurs.*

What did you learn from your observations? Did the teacher interact with one group more than the other? What differences did you notice in the types of interactions between the teacher and male and female students?

Gender-sensitive education does not ignore gender in the classroom. It does not require that boys and girls be treated the same in all cases. Gender may need to be emphasized at times to ensure equity. However, gender-sensitive education is reflected in the school setting when students are not sorted, grouped, or tracked by gender in any aspect of the school program, including special education. The teacher can develop a curriculum that does not give preferential treatment to boys over girls; that shows both genders in aggressive, nurturing, independent, exciting, and emotional roles; that encourages all students to explore traditional and nontraditional roles; and that assists them in developing positive self-images about their sexuality. One's actions and reactions to students can make a difference.

Educators also should incorporate factual information on homosexuality. The contributions of gays and lesbians to society should not be ignored. Homophobic name-calling by students could be used to provide facts and correct myths about homosexuality. If educators ignore homophobic remarks made by students or other adults, children and youth are quick to conclude that something is wrong with gays and that they can be treated disrespectfully.

In addition to helping all students correct the myths they have about gays and lesbians, educators should promote the healthy development of self-identified homosexual youngsters in the school setting. Key to this approach is breaking the silence that surrounds the discussion of homosexuality. The classroom and the school should provide a safe and supportive climate for adolescents to discuss their sexual orientation in a nonthreatening way. Finally, teachers and other school personnel need to develop a nonjudgmental posture on this topic.

Participation in Science, Mathematics, and Technology

As indicated at the beginning of this section, girls do not perform as well on mathematics and science assessments as boys. Although both groups use computers at home and at school at about the same rate, females are more likely to be involved in data entry and word processing while boys are more involved in programming and designing. The choices about courses taken in middle school and high school have an influence not only on achievement on standardized testing, but on one's future job options. For instance, technology jobs are among the fastest growing occupations at the beginning of the twenty-first century with some of the highest salaries. Women and African Americans, Latinos, and American Indians are not preparing for jobs in this field at the same rate as white and Asian American men.

These and other findings suggest that the participation of females in mathematics, science, and computer science in schools deserves special attention.

Although girls and boys use computers at about the same rate, girls are less likely to take courses in computer programming and design. As a result, they are less likely to select computer science as a college major.

Different approaches to schooling and teaching may increase the participation rates of diverse ethnic and racial groups, as well as females, in mathematics and science. Generally, researchers have found that the percentage of class time spent on mathematics does not differ, nor do the mathematics activities in which students participate. Teacher interactions with the two groups, however, sometimes differ. Teachers initiate more interactions with boys than with girls concerning classroom behavior. They more often work individually with boys on classroom management, directions, and procedures. More social interactions are initiated with boys than with girls. In response to low-level mathematics questions, more called-out responses are received and accepted from boys. Teachers engage boys in significantly more low-level and high-level interactions related directly to mathematics. At the same time, girls learn at a high cognitive level when teachers interact about mathematics at a high cognitive level.

Girls are more likely to learn in cooperative mathematics activities, and are influenced positively by the teacher's praise of a correct answer. Boys achieve better when the teacher corrects a wrong answer, but girls achieve better when the teacher prompts them for the correct answer. To help both girls and boys achieve well in mathematics requires different teaching strategies for boys than for girls as is sometimes required in a gender-sensitive curriculum.

Another difference in mathematics and science achievement is the result of courses taken. Females now participate in mathematics and science courses at about the same rate as males. However, males earn more credits in the most advanced mathematics courses. Matching their desire to attend college, females earn more credits in the basic college preparatory sequence. At the other end of the scale, males earn more credits in non-college preparatory courses. There are differences in course-taking patterns among ethnic groups as well. Asian Americans take more advanced mathematics courses than members of any other group. African Americans and Latino students are less likely to take either advanced or college preparatory courses in mathematics. African Americans and Latinos earn the same number of credits in mathematics, but they are in courses below the level of algebra, not courses needed for college (Davenport, Davison, Kuang, Ding, Kim, and Kwak, 1998).

The percentage of female high school students taking science courses has increased during the past decade. As with mathematics, the gender difference occurs with the courses taken. Girls are more likely to take biology and chemistry; boys are more likely to take physics (American Association of University Women, 1999). Although males participate at higher rates than females in advanced mathematics and science courses, not all males are engaged with these subjects at this level. African American, Latino, and American Indian boys and girls are overrepresented in remedial courses of all subjects.

Some research shows that girls are more likely to participate in advanced mathematics and science courses when they are in single-sex classes. They may feel less threatened when they are not competing with males in coeducational settings. Teachers are more likely to use strategies such as cooperative teaching, which are well suited to the learning styles of many girls. Opponents to single-sex classes argue that teachers should learn to teach both groups of students effectively and that girls should be encouraged throughout their schooling to enroll in advanced courses.

One of the most critical factors in mathematics and science achievement is placement in an academic track in high school. Girls sometimes think that they do not have the ability for these courses. Advanced Placement (AP) courses are not available to either girls or boys in a number of low-income schools, limiting their ability to compete with students from other schools. As educators, we may be able to improve minority and female participation in these areas by encouraging students, developing positive attitudes about these subjects, and counseling students into advanced mathematics and science courses as well as computer science classes.

Nondiscrimination and Title IX

Title IX of the 1972 Education Amendments addresses the differential, stereotypical, and discriminatory treatment of students on the basis of their gender. It states that "no person shall, on the basis of sex, be excluded from participation in, be denied the benefits of, or be subjected to discrimination under any education program or activity receiving federal financial assistance." It protects students and employees in virtually all 16,000 public school systems and 2,700 postsecondary institutions in the United States. The law prevents gender discrimination in: (1) the admission of students, particularly to postsecondary and vocational education institutions, (2) the treatment of students, and (3) the employment of all personnel.

What does Title IX require of teachers and other educators in kindergarten through twelfth-grade settings? The law clearly makes it illegal to treat students differently or separately on the basis of gender. It requires that all programs, activities, and opportunities offered by a school district be equally available to males and females. All courses must be open to all students. Boys must be allowed to enroll in family and consumer science classes, and girls allowed in technology and agriculture courses. Regarding the counseling of students, Title IX prohibits biased course or career guidance; the use of biased achievement, ability, or interest tests; and the use of college and career materials that are biased in content, language, or illustration. Schools cannot assist any business or individual in employing students if the request is for a student of a particular gender. There can be no discrimination in the type or amount of financial assistance or eligibility for such assistance. Health and insurance benefits available to students cannot be discriminated against or excluded from any educational program or activity.

Membership in clubs and other activities based on gender alone is prohibited in schools, with the exceptions of YWCA, YMCA, Girl Scouts, Boy Scouts, Boys' State, Girls' State, Key clubs, and other voluntary and tax-exempt youth service organizations that have been traditionally limited to members of one gender who are 19 years of age or younger. Rules of behavior and punishments for violation of those rules must be the same for all students. Honors and awards may not designate the gender of the student as a criterion for the award.

Probably the most controversial program covered by Title IX has been the area of athletics. Provisions for girls to participate in intramural, club, or interscholastic sports must be included in the school's athletic program. The sports offered by a school must be coeducational with two major exceptions: (1) when selection for teams is based on competitive skill and (2) when the activity is a contact sport. In these two situations, separate teams are permitted but are not required. Although the law does not require equal funding for girls' and boys' athletic programs, equal opportunity in athletics must be provided.

The law alone will not change the basic assumptions and attitudes that people hold about appropriate female and male roles, occupations, and behaviors, but it will equalize the rights, opportunities, and treatment of students within the school setting. Experience has shown that once discriminatory practices are eliminated and discriminatory behavior is altered, even unwillingly, changes in prejudiced attitudes often follow. Equal treatment of students from kindergarten through college will more adequately encourage all students to explore available career options.

Summary

Anthropologists have observed many cultural differences in sexual behavior and in the division of labor between males and females. Research indicates, however, that the biological differences between the sexes have little influence on behavior and roles in a culture. Instead, the differences within a society are primarily culturally determined, rather than biologically determined. Our culture determines, in large part, how parents and others treat boys and girls. Although girls and boys are members of all other microcultures, the culture at large has different expectations of them solely on the basis of their gender. Culture establishes the norms of acceptable gender-typical behavior.

Socialization is the process of learning to behave in accordance with socially prescribed roles and expectations. During this period, children learn to be male or female. These roles are usually defined as quite distinct from one another and are often portrayed stereotypically by the media and reinforced in many families. Consciousness-raising activities during the past decade have helped men and women understand and evaluate the stereotypical roles for which they have been socialized, thereby opening new options for both groups.

An individual has no choice about gender identity, but he or she can have either feminine or masculine characteristics or a combination of the two. The degree to which an individual adheres to a traditional gender identity varies as a result of past socialization patterns and is influenced by the family's ethnicity, socioeconomic level, or religion.

Gender discrimination has kept women in less prestigious and lower-paying jobs than men. Even the amount of education obtained by a woman does little to close the gap between the earnings of men and women—now at 74 cents earned by a woman for every dollar earned by a man. Such discrimination greatly affects the quality of life for families, single mothers, and children.

Women's studies and gender-sensitive education represent educational approaches to combating sexism in schools and society. Women's studies programs, on the one hand, attempt to record and analyze the historical and contemporary experiences of women and are usually offered as separate courses. Gender sensitive education, on the other hand, attempts to make the total school curriculum less sexist by incorporating content that reflects female as well as male perspectives. Gender sensitive education also incorporates positive and supportive interactions of teachers with students. Educators are asked to be aware of behavior that discriminates against one of the sexes in a way that prevents equitable benefits from schooling.

The federal government provides support for eliminating sexism in education through Title IX of the 1972 Education Amendments. This law protects against the differential, stereotypical, and discriminatory treatment of students on the basis of their sex.

Questions for Review

To answer these questions online, go to the Chapter Questions module for this chapter of the Companion Website.

1. In what ways are differences between the sexes culturally, rather than biologically, determined?
2. How does socialization into stereotypical roles harm females and males in our changing society?
3. Explain how gender discrimination has disproportionately affected women.
4. In what ways do men have power over women? Why is it difficult for men to see they have a privileged position in society?
5. Contrast women's studies and gender-sensitive education and explain the advantages of both.
6. How can teachers learn whether they are discriminating against students on the basis of gender?
7. How does homophobia manifest itself in schools? What can educators do toward eliminating the prejudice and discrimination that occur?
8. What are signs of sexual harassment in schools?
9. How can you as an educator help increase the participation of females and other underrepresented groups in computer science, mathematics, and science careers?
10. What impact has Title IX had on schooling during the past 20 years?

Web Resources

To link to the following websites, go to the Web Resources module for this chapter of the Companion Website.

The website of the American Association of University Women includes discussions of issues, government policies, and research related to education and equity for girls and women.

"Protecting Students from Harassment and Hate Crimes: A Guide for Schools" has been prepared by the U.S. Office of Civil Rights to assist schools in handling harassment in schools.

The website of the Women's Educational Equity Association provides information about Title IX and women's equity issues, including links to additional resources.

The website of the Gay, Lesbian, and Straight Education Network provides resources and updates for ending bias against gays in schools and society.

The National Organization for Women is a women's advocacy group that supports legislation for equity and candidates who support women's rights and equity. They actively fight against sexual discrimination and harassment.

References

American Association of University Women (AAUW). (1999). *Gender gaps: Where schools still fail our children.* Washington DC: Author.

Anderson, D. (1995). Lesbian and gay adolescents: Social and developmental considerations. In G. Unks (Ed.), *The gay teen: Educational practice and theory for lesbian, gay, and bisexual adolescents* (pp. 17–28). New York: Routledge.

Davenport, E. C., Davison, M. I., Kuang, H., Ding, S., Kim, S., & Kwak, N. (1998, Fall). High school mathematics course-taking by gender and ethnicity. *American Educational Research Journal, 35*(3), 497–514.

de Beauvoir, S. (1974). *The second sex.* New York: Vintage Books.

Gay, Lesbian, & Straight Education Network. (1999). *GLSEN's national school climate survey: Lesbian, gay, bisexual and transgender students and their experiences in school.* New York: Author.

Houston, B. (1996). Gender freedom and the subtleties of sexist education. In A. Diller, B. Houston, K. P. Morgan (Eds.) & M. Ayim. *The gender question in education: Theory, pedagogy, and Politics* (pp. 50–74). Boulder, CO: Westview Press.

Hyde, J. S. (1996). Meta-analysis and the psychology of gender differences. In B. Laslett, S. G. Kohlstedt, H. Longino, & E. Hammonds (Eds.), *Gender and scientific authority* (pp. 302–320). Chicago: The University of Chicago Press.

Jovanovic, J. & King, S. S. (1998, Fall). Boys and girls in the performance-based science classroom: Who's doing the performing? *American Educational Research Journal, 35*(3), 477–496.

Lee, V. E., Croninger, R. G., Linn, E., & Chen, X. (1996, Summer). The culture of sexual harassment in secondary schools. *American Educational Research Journal, 33*(2), 383–417.

Lorde, A. (1995). Age, race, class, and sex: Women redefining difference. In J. Arthur & A. Shapiro (Eds.), *Campus wars: Multiculturalism and the politics of difference* (pp. 191–198). Boulder, CO: Westview Press.

Mondimore, F. M. (1996). *A natural history of homosexuality.* Baltimore: The Johns Hopkins University Press.

Ortner, S. B. (1996). *Making gender: The politics and erotics of culture.* Boston: Beacon.

Sadker, D. (1996, September 4). Where the girls are: Confusing political arguments with educational research. *Education Week, XVI*(1), 49–50.

Sears, J. T. (1992). Educators, homosexuality, and homosexual students: Are personal feelings related to professional beliefs? In K. M. Harbeck (Ed.), *Coming out of the classroom closet: Gay and lesbian students, teachers, and curricula* (pp. 29–79). Binghamton, NY: Harrington Park Press.

Stein, N. (1996, May). Slippery justice. *Educational Leadership, 53*(8), 64–68.

Thorne, B. (1997). *Gender play: Girls and boys in school.* New Brunswick, NJ: Rutgers University Press.

U.S. Bureau of the Census. (1999). *Statistical abstract of the United States.* Washington, DC: Government Printing Office.

U.S. Department of Education, National Center for Education Statistics. (2000). *Trends in educational equity of girls and women.* Washington, DC: U.S. Government Printing Office.

Unks, G. (1995). Thinking about the gay teens. In G. Unks (Ed.), *The gay teen: Educational practice and theory for lesbian, gay, and bisexual adolescents* (pp. 3–12). New York: Routledge.

Walsh, M. R. (Ed.). (1997). *Women, men, and gender: Ongoing debates.* New Haven, CT: Yale University Press.

Willis, P. E. (1977). *Learning to labour: How working class kids get working class jobs.* Farnborough, UK: Saxon House.

Zia, H. (1996, July/August). *How NOW? Ms. Magazine, 7(1),* 49–57.

Suggested Readings

Kivel, P. (1999). *Boys will be men: Raising our sons for courage, caring and community.* Gabriola Island, British Columbia: New Society Publishers.

Written for parents and educators, this book grapples with the issues that boys face — racism, homophobia, pornography, drugs, class, consumerism, sex, and violence. It provides a vision for raising boys to think critically and become invested in promoting a multicultural and democratic society.

Kleinfeld, J. S., & Yerian, S. (1995). *Gender tales: Tension in the schools.* New York: St. Martin's Press.

Cases from classrooms and schools introduce gender-equity dilemmas faced by educators. They help readers think critically about their own work in classrooms toward designing alternative strategies for action.

Lesbian, gay, bisexual, and transgender people and education. (1996, Summer). *Harvard Educational Review, 66(2) [Special issue].*

This special issue of the *Harvard Educational Review* explores homosexuality and education through the voices of those who are lesbian, gay, bisexual, and transgendered. It includes articles by youth, as well as teachers and professors.

Rosen, R. (2000). *The world split open: How the modern women's movement changed America.* New York: Viking.

This history of the women's movement and resulting changes over the past 50 years provides insights into the movement from those who were involved.

Sullivan, A. (1996). *Virtually normal: An argument about homosexuality.* New York: Vintage.

The former editor of *The New Republic* describes the debates around homosexuality and proposes a political position that guarantees civil rights to gays and lesbians.

Thorne, B. (1997). *Gender play: Girls and boys in school.* New Brunswick, NJ: Rutgers University Press.

The author's analysis of her observations of the gender development of girls and boys in elementary schools challenges the popular theory that boys and girls have different cultures. The book contains suggestions for establishing gender-sensitive education.

Unks, G. (Ed.).(1995). *The gay teen: Educational practice and theory for lesbian, gay, and bisexual adolescents.* New York: Routledge.

Exploring adolescent homosexuality through theoretical and practical perspectives, these authors address problems faced by gay teens and make recommendations to educators on teaching strategies, providing safe environments, and reducing homophobia in schools.

CRITICAL INCIDENTS IN TEACHING

Gender

Gender Stereotyping

Jane Irwin is the director of the Model Learning Center at a regional university located in the Southwest. The center is a kindergarten laboratory school located on the university campus to provide observation and practicum opportunities for students in the teacher education program. The children at the center affectionately refer to Ms. Irwin as "Miss Janie." At the end of a lesson on health, Miss Janie dismisses the children for 30 minutes of free play in the classroom. Each child is free to select his or her activity of choice. The Model Learning Center is well equipped with a wide variety of play materials, and the children quickly move to their chosen activities. In the classroom are two undergraduate students in early childhood education who are visiting as part of their required practicum.

Some of the children choose puzzles; some a large playhouse; and others an indoor slide, airplanes, dolls, and various other activities. One of the boys, Tim, moves to an area where two girls are playing with dolls. Tim gently picks up a doll and begins combing its long blonde hair. Shocked by this behavior, one of the practicum students rushes over to Tim, helps him to his feet, takes the doll and comb out of his hands, places them on the floor, and says, "Come with me," as she leads him by the hand to an area where two boys are playing with a model airplane and a helicopter. She picks up an airplane, hands it to Tim, and says, "Here, you play with this. Boys like airplanes, not dolls."

Miss Janie has observed the entire sequence of events as she sits at her desk, watching her students and the university teacher education candidate.

To answer these questions online, go to the Critical Incidents module for this chapter of the Companion Website.

Questions for Discussion

1. What should Miss Janie do with regard to the child who is now obediently playing with the airplane?
2. What should she do with regard to the class because several children observed the incident?
3. What should she do with regard to the university student?

Sexual Orientation

Maureen Flynn is a third-grade teacher in a suburban public school. Each year, she looks forward to Parents' Night, when she can meet the parents of her students. As she inspects her room one final time, the door opens and two nicely dressed women appear. "Good evening," they say, almost in unison. "Good evening. Welcome to the third grade. I'm Maureen Flynn." "We're Amy Gentry and Kirsten Bowers. We're Allison Gentry-Bower's mothers." "Oh," says Ms. Flynn, trying not to show any surprise. "Let me show you some of Allison's artwork and where her desk is."

The rest of the evening is routine. Ms. Flynn introduces herself, welcomes the parents, and asks them to introduce themselves. As the parents exchange names and greetings, there are a few questioning looks as Allison's two mothers introduce themselves as her mothers. Ms. Flynn explains what the class is currently doing and what the goals and activities are for the remainder of the year. The parents and Ms. Flynn exchange pleasantries and then go home.

The next morning as class begins, Colleen Burke blurts out, "Miss Flynn, my mommy said that Allison has two mommies. How can that be? How can anyone have two mommies? Everyone is supposed to have a father and a mother." All of the students look to Ms. Flynn for her response.

To answer these questions online, go to the Critical Incidents module for this chapter of the Companion Website.

Questions for Discussion

1. What should Maureen Flynn's response be to Colleen's question?
2. Should she just evade the question?
3. Should she use the opportunity to discuss alternative family structures?

Sexual Harassment

Jenny Reid is a middle-school teacher in a suburb of Atlanta. Her sixth-grade students are primarily majority group students from middle-class backgrounds. The children in her class are good students, well motivated, and reasonably well behaved. Her only discipline problem is the excessive teasing that some of the boys in the class impose on the girls.

Near the end of recess, Amy Hotchkiss approaches Ms. Reid, obviously very upset. Amy is one of the more physically mature girls in the class. She is one of a half dozen in the class who has started wearing a bra. Angry and trying to control her temper, she whispers rather loudly that Eric, Darren, Kevin, and Myles have been teasing some of the girls, calling them names and making reference to their physical development. In addition, they have been running up to the girls wearing bras and pulling at the elastic in the back. "What are you going to do to them?" she asks.

To answer these questions online, go to the Critical Incidents module for this chapter of the Companion Website.

Questions for Discussion

1. Is this incident simply a schoolboy prank, or is this sexual harassment?
2. Should the boys involved be punished? If so, what should the punishment be?
3. Should this incident be limited to the class, or should the principal and parents be notified?
4. Should Ms. Reid turn the incident into a learning situation for the entire class? If she does so, how should she do it? What can the class learn from the incident?

Chapter 5

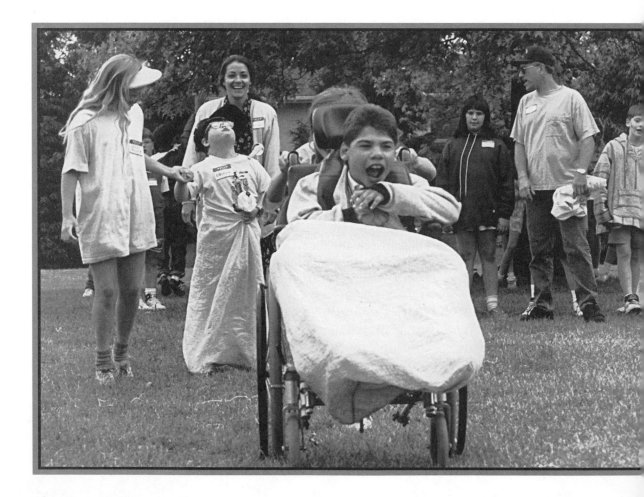

Exceptionality

"No otherwise qualified handicapped individual in the United States . . . shall, solely by reason of his [or her] handicap, be excluded from the participation in, be denied benefits of, or be subjected to discrimination under any program or activity receiving federal financial assistance."

Section 504, PL 93–112 (Vocational Rehabilitation Act, 1993)

Riley Behler, a third-grade teacher at the Martin Luther King Elementary School, has been asked to see the principal, Erin Wilkerson, after the students leave. Dr. Wilkerson explains that the district is implementing a full inclusion program in which children with severe disabilities will be fully integrated into general education classrooms. Because he had been a nominee for the district's teacher of the year award two years ago and singled out for his outstanding classroom skills, Behler had been recommended to be a part of the district's first attempt at full inclusion. "What this will involve, Riley, is two students with severe disabilities. One is a child with Down syndrome who has developmental disabilities. He has some severe learning problems. The other child has normal intelligence but is nonambulatory, with limited speech and severe cerebral palsy. If you are willing to be a part of this program, you will have a full-time aide with a special education background. Morgan Andersen, the inclusion specialist, will assist you with instructional plans and strategies. What is important is that you prepare the students in your class and the parents so that a smooth transition can be made when these students come into your class in January, in

161

just two and a half months. If you agree to do this, I'd like you and Morgan to map out a plan of action and give it to me in two weeks."

This scenario has been played out in schools across the country in recent years. What are Behler and Andersen's plan of action to include? What are some critical elements in a successful plan to move into full inclusion? When students with severe disabilities are integrated into general education classrooms, do they detract from the programming of nondisabled students? Are the students with disabilities potentially a disrupting influence in the classroom? Do general education teachers like Riley Behler have adequate training and background to accommodate students with disabilities in their classrooms? Should all children with disabilities be integrated into general education classes? Regardless of the type of disability? Regardless of the degree of disability?

STUDENTS WITH DISABILITIES AND THOSE WHO ARE GIFTED AND TALENTED

A significant segment of the population in the United States is made up of exceptional individuals. Twenty-five million or more individuals from every ethnic and socioeconomic group fall into one or more of the categories of exceptionality. Nearly every day, educators come into contact with exceptional children and adults. They may be students in our classes, our professional colleagues, our friends and neighbors, or people we meet in our everyday experiences.

Exceptional people include both individuals with disabilities and gifted individuals. Some, particularly persons with disabilities, have been rejected by society. Because of their unique social and personal needs and special interests, many exceptional people become part of a microculture composed of individuals with similar exceptionalities. For some, this cultural identity is by ascription; they have been labeled and forced into enclaves by virtue of the residential institutions where they live. Others live in the same communities by their own choosing. This chapter will examine the exceptional individual's relationship to society. It will address the struggle for equal rights and the ways the treatment of individuals with disabilities often parallels that of oppressed ethnic minorities.

Definitions for exceptional children vary slightly from one writer to another, but Heward's (2000) is typical of most:

> Exceptional children differ from the norm (either below or above) to such an extent that an individualized program of adapted specialized education is required to meet their needs. The term *exceptional children* includes children who experience difficulties in

VIDEO INSIGHT

Billy Golfus

Individuals with disabilities are more like nondisabled individuals than unlike them. Filmmaker Billy Golfus has made it his mission to communicate this message to others. Yet he acknowledges that nondisabled persons think that individuals with disabilities are "depressing," "lazy," or "too gimped out to work." Others, he says, fear individuals with disabilities. Examine your own attitudes toward persons with disabilities. How does interacting with an individual who has a disability make you feel?

Watch the video segment on filmmaker Billy Golfus, who suffered brain damage and partial paralysis as a result of a traffic accident, or talk with a person you know who functions with a disability to see how he or she would like to be treated by others. How will what this person says affect your own attitudes and behavior when, in the future, you teach students or work with colleagues who have disabilities?

learning and children whose performance is so superior that modifications in curriculum and instruction are necessary to help them fulfill their potential. Thus, exceptional children is an inclusive term that refers to children with learning and/or behavior problems, children with physical disabilities or sensory impairments, and children who are intellectually gifted or have a special talent (p. 4).

This definition is specific to school-age children who are usually referred, tested to determine eligibility, and then placed in special education programs. Included in the process is the labeling of the child. At one end of the continuum are the gifted and talented children. At the other end are children with disabilities (some of whom may also be gifted). Students with disabilities are categorized with labels such as having mental retardation, learning disabilities, speech impairment, visual impairment, hearing impairment, emotional disturbance (or behavioral disorders), or physical and health impairments.

LABELING

The categorizing and labeling process has its share of critics. Opponents characterize the practice as demeaning and stigmatizing to people with disabilities, with the effects often carried through adulthood. Earlier classifications and labels, such as moron, imbecile, and idiot, have become so derogatory that they are no longer used in a professional context. Some individuals, including many with learning disabilities and mild mental retardation (MMR), were never considered to have disabilities prior to entering school. The school setting, however, intensifies their academic and cognitive deficits. Many, when they return to their homes and communities, do not seem to function as individuals with disabilities. Instead, they participate in activities with their neighborhood peers until they return to school the following day, where they may attend special classes (sometimes segregated) and resume their role in the academic and social structure of the school as children with disabilities. The problem is so pervasive that it has led to the designation of "the 6-hour retarded child." These are children who spend 6 hours a day as children with mental retardation in our nation's schools. During the remaining 18 hours a day away from the school setting, they are not considered retarded by the people they interact with (President's Committee on Mental Retardation, 1969). Heward (2000) suggests that the demands of the school seem to "cause" the mental retardation.

The labels carry with them connotations and stigmas of varying degrees. Some disabilities are socially more acceptable than others. Visual impairment carries with it public empathy and sometimes sympathy. The public has for years given generously to causes for the blind, as evidenced by the financially well-endowed Seeing Eye Institute, which produces the well-known guide dogs. The blind are the only group with a disability who are permitted to claim an additional personal income tax deduction by reason of their disability. Yet, the general public looks on blindness as one of the worst afflictions imposed on humankind.

In contrast, mental retardation, and to some extent emotional disturbance, is often linked to lower socioeconomic status. Both labels are among the lowest socially acceptable disabilities and perhaps the most stigmatizing. This is, in part, because of the general public's lack of understanding of these two disabilities and the sometimes debilitating impact they can bring to the family structure.

Learning disabilities, one of the newest categories of exceptionality, is one of the more socially acceptable disability conditions. Whereas mental retardation is often identified with lower socioeconomic groups, those with learning disabilities often have middle-class backgrounds. Whether these perceptions are accurate or not, middle-class parents more readily accept learning disabilities than mental retardation as a cause of their child's learning deficits. What has been observed is a reclassification of many children from having mental retardation to being learning disabled. It has sometimes been said that one person's mental retardation is another's learning disability and still another's emotional disturbance. The sometimes fine line that distinguishes one of these disabilities from another is at times so difficult to distinguish that an individual could be identified as a student with mild emotional disturbance by one school psychologist and as a student with learning disabilities by another.

Although the labeling controversy persists, even its critics often concede its necessity. Federal funding for special education is predicated on the identification of individuals in specific disabling conditions. These funds, which total more than $1 billion each year, are so significant that many special education programs would all but collapse without them, leaving school districts in severe financial distress. Consequently, the labeling process continues, sometimes even into adulthood, where university students may have to be identified with a disability in order to receive necessary accommodations to their learning needs. Others are placed in jobs by vocational rehabilitation counselors, with labels more indicative of their learning problems than their work skills. This, in turn, tends to stigmatize, enhancing the likelihood of social isolation.

HISTORICAL ANTECEDENTS

The plight of persons with disabilities has, in many instances, closely paralleled that of oppressed ethnic groups. The history of the treatment of those with disabilities has not shown a society eager to meet its responsibilities. Prior to 1800, with a few exceptions, those with mental retardation, for example, were not considered a major social problem in any society. Those with more severe retardation were simply killed, or they died early of natural causes (Drew & Hardman, 2000).

The treatment and care of people with mental and physical disabilities have typically been a function of the socioeconomic conditions of the times. In addition to attitudes of fear and disgrace brought on by superstition, early nomadic tribes viewed individuals with disabilities as nonproductive and as a burden, draining available resources. As civilization progressed from a less nomadic existence, individuals with disabilities were still often viewed as nonproductive and expendable (Drew & Hardman, 2000).

They were frequently shunted away to institutions designated as hospitals, asylums, and colonies. Many institutions were deliberately built great distances from the population centers, where the residents could be segregated and more easily contained. For decades, American society did not have to deal with its conscience with respect to its citizens with severe disabilities. Society simply sent them far away and forgot about them. Most Americans did not know of the cruel and inhumane treatment that existed in many facilities, and they did not really want to know. Those individuals with mild disabilities were generally able to be absorbed into society, sometimes seeming to disappear, sometimes contributing meaningfully to an agrarian society, often not even being identified as having a disability.

As society became more industrialized and educational reforms required school attendance, the academic problems of students with disabilities became increasingly more visible. Special schools and special classes were designated to meet the needs of these children. Thus, society segregated these individuals, often in the guise of acting in their best interests.

Society's treatment of some groups with disabilities, such as those with mental retardation, has frequently been questionable with respect to their civil rights. Although many Americans find the old miscegenation laws prohibiting intermarriage between different ethnic groups abhorrent, few realize that as recently as 25 years ago, more than 20 states prohibited marriage between individuals with mental retardation.

The issue of marriage prohibitions and eugenic sterilization for persons with mental retardation raises serious social and ethical issues. The nondisabled segment of society, charged with the care and education of people with disabilities, apparently views as its right and responsibility those matters dealing with sexual behavior, marriage, and procreation. In a similar way, educators determine the means of communication for the blind individual, either an oral/aural approach or a manual/total communication approach. Such decisions have profound implications because they determine not only how these individuals will communicate but also, to a great extent, with whom they will be able to communicate. Too often, society seeks to dehumanize people with disabilities by ignoring their personal wishes, making critical decisions for them, and treating them as children throughout their lives.

DISPROPORTIONATE PLACEMENTS IN SPECIAL EDUCATION

The overrepresentation of students of color in special education classes has been one of the most problematic issues facing educators in recent years. Dunn (1968) reported that one third of the students in special education had been placed in classes for students with mild mental retardation. Dunn stated, "In my judgment, about 60 to 80 percent of the pupils taught by these teachers are children from low status backgrounds—including Afro-Americans, American Indians, Mexicans, and Puerto Rican Americans; those from nonstandard English speaking, broken, disorganized, and inadequate homes; and children from other non-middle class environments." Special education had become a dumping ground for poor children of color.

Dunn's findings were supported by Mercer (1973) who found that Mexican American students in Riverside, California, were placed in classes for students with mild mental retardation at a rate four times that of the general school population. African American students were placed in the same special education classes at a rate three times what should have been expected given their numbers in the general school population.

In 1968, the Office of Civil Rights (OCR) began their biannual survey of student placement in special education classes. The data also provided racial backgrounds of the students in the broad categories of white, black, Asian/Pacific American, American Indian, and Hispanic. While the actual percentages have varied from survey to survey, one fact has remained consistent. African American students, particularly males, have been greatly overrepresented in classes for students with mild mental retardation, moderate mental retardation, and serious emotional disturbance. In some states, Hispanic students are overrepresented in classes for students with mild mental retardation. Another consistent finding is that African American, American Indian, and Hispanic students are greatly underrepresented in classes for the gifted and talented.

There are two valid means of reporting data related to the placement of students of color in special education classes. The OCR reports special education enrollments by group. For example, in 1997, African American students comprised 16.95% of the total OCR sample. They comprised 27.51% of those in classes for students with serious emotional disturbance, 33.18% of those in classes for students with mental retardation, and only 7.29% of those individuals placed in classes for the gifted and talented (OCR, 1999).

A second way to present the data is to examine the percentage of the group in a special education program. In 1997, the percentage of African American students placed in classes for students with mental retardation was 2.54%. The percentage of African Americans placed in classes for students with serious emotional disturbance was 1.29% in 1997 (OCR, 1999). These percentages may appear to be small, but they are problematic when we realize that the percent of African Americans who are in classes of students with mental retardation is five times greater than that of Asian/Pacific American students and twice that of white students. Also important is the fact that one third of African American students are not mentally retarded, as one might mistakenly assume from the OCR data. Rather, a little less than one third of those in classes for students with mental retardation are African American. This is a very important concept for the reader to understand.

While the majority of students in special education have most likely been carefully diagnosed and placed, educators and child advocates have raised concerns that it is also highly likely that many children are inappropriately placed in special education. The misplacement of students in special education is problematic in that it is often stigmatizing to the individual and it can deny the student the high quality and life enhancing education to which he or she is entitled (Patton, 1998).

The variables that contribute to the disproportionate special education placement are multifaceted. Some of the problems that contribute to the placement of these students are rooted in the social structure of the country. Other problems may be related to medical and genetic causes, particularly moderate and severe forms of disability, and may be beyond the ability of educators to remediate.

Dunn's 1968 findings that large percentages of students in classes for individuals with mental retardation were from backgrounds of poverty persist to this day. Poverty contributes to a significant number of problems. Pregnant women in poverty are provided less than optimal care during the prenatal period, as well as the period during and after birth. Physicians who provide medical care through government clinics are often burdened with excessive case loads and are unable to provide the quality of care that women are afforded from private physicians and managed care medical facilities. Appropriate nutrition and dietary supplements may be less available both to expectant mothers and to their children. Poverty may necessitate working late into term, even if it would be advisable to stop working and rest.

Children born preterm (those under normal gestation and less than 5 lbs 8 oz [2,500 grams]) may be at risk to develop cognitive and sensory disabilities (Widerstrom, Mowder, & Sandall, 1991; Drew & Hardman, 2000). Though more closely aligned with socioeconomic factors, preterm births have been associated with ethnicity. Younger women having children are more likely to have preterm babies, crack babies, and fetal alcohol syndrome children (Drew & Hardman, 2000), and teen births are disproportionately higher among the poor. Gelfand, Jenson, and Drew (1988) report that 51 percent of nonwhite births have complications as opposed to 5 percent of white upper class births.

Many of the nation's poor live in older homes, and children living in older homes are at greater risk of lead poisoning. Children who suffer from lead poisoning typically have ingested the paint chips from older homes, which had used lead-based paints. Other factors that contribute to lead poisoning are believed to be pollution from auto and factory emissions. The U. S. Public Health Service estimates that one in six children may suffer from lead poisoning (Carolina Environment, Inc. 1999). Lead poisoning can create problems for children such as reading and learning disabilities, speech and language disabilities, lowered IQ, neurological deficits, behavior problems, mental retardation, kidney disease, heart disease, stroke, and death (Carolina Environment, Inc., 1999).

The individuals who are placed in classes for students with mild mental retardation and severe emotional disturbance are disproportionately male, African American, and from lower socioeconomic backgrounds. The first step in special education placement is referrals. Anyone (parents, doctors, educators) can make referrals. Most are made by teachers in the elementary school years. These teachers are overwhelmingly female, white, and middle class. There is often a lack of understanding between the two groups with respect to cultural values, acceptable behaviors in the school, and educational expectations. This may result in overreferrals to classes for students with disabilities and underreferrals to classes for the gifted and talented. Ysseldyke, Thurlow, Graden, Wesson, Algozzine, and Deno (1983) suggest that a very large percentage of students who are referred to special education are eventually placed in special education programs.

Assessment of students of color is also a major concern as a contributing variable to the overrepresentation of these students in special education classes. Litigation such as *Diana v. State Board of Education* (1970), involving language minority Latino students, and *Larry P. v. Riles* (1979), involving culturally diverse African American students, demonstrated the dangers of biased assessment instruments and procedures. It is clear that some students in special education have central nervous system damage and that others have visual, auditory, orthopedic, and speech disabilities. There is no dispute regarding the appropriateness of the special education placement of these individuals. However, the sometimes inappropriate placement of the students of color in the judgmental categories of mild mental retardation and severe emotional disturbance must be addressed if we are to have true equity in our educational system. The problem has persisted for decades and will not be easily ameliorated. It will take a concerted effort to eliminate all bias from the assessment process, a restructuring of teacher education curricula, and a commitment of the wealthiest nation to eliminate the insidious effects of poverty on our children.

Litigation and Legislation

Educational rights of individuals with disabilities were not easily gained. In many respects, the struggle for these rights paralleled the struggles of ethnic minorities for their rights to education. Some of the same court decisions, and many of the arguments that advanced the rights of African Americans and other oppressed groups, were used by the advocates of children with disabilities. However, in reality, the battles and the rights gained by the disability rights advocates followed years after similar rights were won by ethnic minority groups.

As was the case with African American students, the initial struggles for children with disabilities involved the right to, or the access to, a public education. The U.S. Constitution mandates that all citizens have a right to life, liberty, and property. They cannot be denied these without due process. *Brown v. Board of Education of Topeka* (1954) determined that education was a property right. Although there is no Constitutional guarantee of a free public education, in *Brown* the U.S. Supreme Court found that if a state undertakes the provision of free education for its citizenry, a property right of an education is established. *Brown* did not involve children with disabilities, but as the precedent was set to guarantee equal educational opportunity for ethnic minority children, it too, set a precedent in the argument of guaranteeing the rights of students with disabilities. Not only have the courts supported rights of students with disabilities to have a free education, but legislation has also sought to bring them the right to an appropriate education.

The *Brown* decision found "separate but equal" education to be unequal. Separate education denied African American students an equal education. It mandated a fully integrated education, free from the stigma of segregation. Chief Justice Warren stated that segregation "generates a feeling of inferiority as to their (children) status in the community that may affect their hearts and minds in a way unlikely ever to be undone."

Throughout the history of special education in the United States, children with disabilities have faced a continuous uphill struggle to gain their right to attend public schools. Eventually some programs were instituted, but until the mid-1970s some children, particularly those with moderate to severe disabilities, were routinely excluded from public education. One of the arguments to deny admission to children with moderate and severe mental retardation was that they could not learn to read, write, and do arithmetic. Learning these academic skills is education, it was argued. Since they were not educable, they did not belong in schools.

Parents and supporters of these children countered by arguing that learning self-help skills and other important life skills was indeed learning, and this was education. These children, along with children with severe physical disabilities could learn, particularly if support services were provided.

PARC v. the Commonwealth of Pennsylvania

In 1971, the Pennsylvania Association for Retarded Children (PARC) brought a class action suit against the Commonwealth of Pennsylvania for the failure to provide a public supported education to students with mental retardation. The attorneys for the plaintiffs argued the following:

- Education cannot be defined as only the provision of academic experiences for children.
- All students with mental retardation were capable of benefiting from programs of education and training.

- Having undertaken a free public education for the children of Pennsylvania, the state could not deny children with mental retardation the same opportunities.
- The earlier the students with mental retardation were provided education, the greater the amount of learning could be predicted.

The Federal District Court ruled in favor of the plaintiffs, and all children ages 6 to 21 were to be provided a free public education. The court stipulated that it was most desirable to educate children with mental retardation in programs most like those provided to their peers without disabilities (Yell, 1998)

Following the PARC decision, another class action suit, *Mills v. Board of Education,* was brought before the Federal District Court in the District of Columbia, on behalf of 18,000 out-of-school children with behavior problems, hyperactivity, epilepsy, mental retardation, and physical problems. The court again ruled in favor of the plaintiffs and mandated the District of Columbia schools to provide a public supported education to all children with disabilities. In addition, the court ordered the following:

- The district to provide procedural safeguards.
- Clearly outlined due process procedures for labeling, placement, and exclusion.
- Procedural safeguards to include right to appeal, right to access records, and written notice of all stages of the process.

While these two high-profile cases were being played out in their respective communities, other states were finding similar challenges. The PARC was a state chapter of the National Association for Retarded Children (NARC). The NARC and other national organizations, such as the Council for Exceptional Children, actively supported disability advocates throughout the country in preparing court briefs and in offering other means of support. Fresh with many court victories, disability advocates in the early 1970s were busy preparing for their next battleground, the U.S. Congress.

In 1973, Congress enacted Section 504 of Public Law 93-112 as part of the Vocational Rehabilitation Act. Section 504 was the counterpart of Title VI of the Civil Rights Act of 1964. The language was brief, but its implications are far reaching:

> No otherwise qualified handicapped individual in the United States . . . Shall, solely by reason of his (or her) handicap, be excluded from the participation in, be denied the benefits of, or be subjected to discrimination under any program or activity receiving federal financial assistance.

Section 504 prohibits the exclusion from programs solely on the basis of an individual's disability. A football coach, marching band director, or a university admissions officer cannot deny participation solely on the basis of a disability. However, if a learning disability prevents a student from learning marching band formations even with accommodations, if test scores are clearly below the university admissions standards and indicative of likely failure, and if mental retardation inhibits a student's ability to learn football rules and plays, then exclusion can be justified. If denial of participation is unjustified, the school or agency risks the loss of all federal funds even in other programs in the institution that are not involved in the discriminatory practice.

In 1975, Public Law 94-142, the Education for All Handicapped Children Act, was signed into law. This comprehensive legislation provided individuals, ages 3 to 21, with the following:

- A free and appropriate education for all children with disabilities
- Procedural safeguards to protect the rights of students and their parents
- Education in the least restrictive environment
- Individualized Educational Programs
- Parental involvement in educational decisions related to their children with disabilities
- Fair, accurate, and nonbiased evaluations

President George Bush signed Public Law 101-336, the Americans with Disabilities Act (ADA), into law on January 26, 1990. ADA was the most significant civil rights legislation in the United States since the Civil Rights Act of 1964. ADA was designed to end discrimination against individuals with disabilities in private-sector employment, public services, public accommodations, transportation, and telecommunications.

Among the many components of this legislation, the following are a sampling of the efforts to break down barriers for individuals with disabilities:

- Employers cannot discriminate against individuals with disabilities in hiring or promotion if they are otherwise qualified for the job.
- Employers must provide reasonable accommodations for individuals with disabilities, such as attaching an amplifier to the individual's telephone.
- New buses, bus and train stations, and rail systems must be accessible to persons with disabilities.
- Physical barriers in restaurants, hotels, retail stores, and stadiums must be removed; if not readily achievable, alternative means of offering services must be implemented.
- Companies offering telephone services to the general public must offer telephone relay services to those using telecommunication devices for the deaf.

Congress passed Public Law 101-476, the Individuals with Disabilities Education Act (IDEA), in 1990 as amendments to Public Law 94-142. Key components of this amendment act included the addition of students with autism and traumatic brain injury as a separate class entitled to services. A transition plan was an added requirement to be included on every student's IEP by age 16. A far-reaching change in the new legislation included the change in language to emphasize the person first and the disability second. The title of the legislation included "Individuals with Disabilities," and not "disabled individuals." In nearly all of the newer literature you will now see "children with mental retardation, students with learning disabilities, individuals with cerebral palsy, and people with hearing impairments." Individuals with disabilities are people or individuals first. Their disability is secondary and at times inconsequential in their ability to perform the tasks they undertake. Referring to a person as a spina bifida student calls immediate attention to his or her disability rather than the student's many assets or abilities.

In 1997, Congress passed Public Law 105-17, IDEA Amendments. The 1997 Amendments reauthorized and made improvements to the earlier law. It consolidated the law from eight to four parts and made significant additions, including the following:

- Strengthened the role of parents, ensured access to the general education curriculum, emphasized student progress by changing the IEP process
- Encouraged parents and educators to resolve their differences through non-adversarial mediation
- Gave school officials greater latitude in disciplining students by altering some procedural safeguards
- Set funding formulas

Even with 25 years of legislation, amendments, and refinements, there are aspects of special education law that are not always clear to the children, their parents and advocates, or the school district personnel. This at times is problematic. Up to this point, the federal government has not fully funded the programs that it has mandated. This creates serious fiscal issues for the school districts. In addition, there is an acute national shortage of fully qualified special education personnel and support staff. Even if the districts seek full compliance of the law, fiscal and staffing limitations may preclude the possibility of providing the quality educational services that the parents demand and the district wants to provide.

Since IDEA does not provide a substantive definition for a "free and appropriate education," the issue has often been resolved in the courts (e.g. *Hendrick Hudson School District v. Rowley*). Parents, as might be expected, often view an appropriate education as the best possible education for their child. As stated earlier, school district fiscal concerns may preclude giving the parents whatever they want. Court decisions have set the standard to be more than simple access to education but less than the best possible educational program (Yell, 1998). Consequently, when a school can demonstrate that a student is making satisfactory progress (this too is open for debate), the district's position tends to prevail. However, the courts have also ruled in favor of the child when parents have sought non-physician support services necessary to sustain the student's ability to function in school (e. g. *Irving Independent School District v. Tatro*).

ASK YOURSELF

During the next week, keep track of the buildings you enter, the streets you cross, and the activities in which you participate. How accessible are these to persons who are in wheelchairs, blind, or hearing impaired? What areas have not been made

To answer these questions online, go to the Ask Yourself module for this chapter of the Companion Website.

accessible to these individuals? How does accessibility limit their participation in the activities in which you regularly participate? How could these areas be made more accessible to individuals with disabilities?

More than ever, children and adults with disabilities are becoming an integral part of the nation's educational system and are finding their rightful place in society. Although the progress that has been made in recent years is indeed encouraging, society's attitudes toward individuals with disabilities have not always kept pace with their legal rights. As long as people are motivated more by fear of litigation than by a moral ethical response, we cannot consider our efforts in this arena a success.

EXCEPTIONALITY AND SOCIETY

Even in modern times, the treatment and understanding of any type of deviance has been limited. Society has begun to accept its basic responsibilities for people with disabilities by providing for their education and care, but social equality has yet to become a reality.

Society's view of people with disabilities can perhaps be illustrated by the way the media portray our population with disabilities. In general, when the media wish to emphasize persons with disabilities, they are portrayed as (a) children, usually with severe mental retardation with obvious physical stigmata, or (b) persons with crippling conditions either in a wheelchair or on crutches. Thus, society has a mindset about who the people with disabilities are. They are children or childlike, and they have severe disabilities mentally, physically, or both.

Because society often views those with disabilities as children, they are denied the right to feel and want like nondisabled individuals. Teachers and other professional workers can often be observed talking about individuals with disabilities in their presence, as if the individuals are unable to feel any embarrassment. Their desire to love and be loved is often ignored, and they are often viewed as asexual, without the right to the same sexual desires as the nondisabled. Gliedman and Roth (1980) make the following statement:

> The able-bodied person sees that handicapped people rarely hold good jobs, become culture heroes, or are visible members of the community and concludes that this is "proof" that they cannot hold their own in society. In fact, society systematically discriminates against many perfectly capable blind men and women, cripples, adults with reading disabilities, epileptics, and so on. In other instances—and again the parallel with white racism is exact—beliefs about the incompatibility of a handicap with adult roles may be not more than a vague notion that "anyone that bad off" cannot possibly lead an adult life, and not more respectable than the view that a handicapped person is mentally or spiritually inferior because he is physically different or that "people like that" have no business being out on the streets with "us regular folks." (pp. 22–23)

Gliedman and Roth suggest that, with respect to discrimination, individuals with disabilities are in some ways better off than African Americans in that there is no overt discrimination, no organized brutality, no lynch mob "justice," and no rallies by supremacist groups. In some ways, however, people with disabilities are worse off. African Americans and other groups have developed ethnic pride. It is unlikely that one has ever heard a "cerebral palsy is beautiful" cry. Society opposes racism with the view that blacks are not self-evidently inferior, but at the same time it takes for granted the self-evidently inferior status of those who have disabilities.

Stereotypes of individuals with disabilities deny them a place in society. The disability dominates our perception of the person's social value. It creates a mind-set, and all perceptions are clouded by our view of deviance. Individuals with disabilities are viewed as vocationally limited and socially inept.

Persons with disabilities are tolerated and even accepted as long as they maintain the roles ascribed to them. They are often denied basic rights and dignity as human beings. They are placed under the perpetual tutelage of those more knowledgeable and more capable than they. They are expected to subordinate their own interests and desires to the goals of a program decreed for them by the professionals who provide services to them.

The general public may be required by law to provide educational and other services for individuals with disabilities. The public is prohibited by law against certain aspects of discrimination against our citizens with disabilities. No one, however, can require the person on the street to like persons with disabilities and to accept them as social equals. Many do not accept a person with a disability. Just as racism leads to discrimination or prejudice against other races because of the belief in one's racial superiority, handicapism leads to stereotyping of, and discrimi-

VIDEO INSIGHT

My Child

One fourth of all states surveyed 2 decades ago reported prohibitions against marriage between individuals with retardation. Fifteen states had statutes authorizing compulsory sterilization of individuals with mental illness or retardation, 24 states permitted such sterilization, and only two states prohibited it. Why would any segment of society believe it has the right and responsibility to take charge of matters dealing with sexual behavior, procreation, and marriage for individuals with disabilities?

Many individuals with disabilities believe that they are being robbed of a right that nondisabled people take for granted: the right to get married and start a family. People with even mild disabilities, however, are willing to acknowledge just how challenging raising a child can be. That challenge is greater if a parent's disabilities make it impossible for him or her to bathe, change, or feed a child. Consider this question: Should states have a right to regulate the intimate and family lives of individuals with disabilities?

nation against, individuals with disabilities because of attitudes of superiority held by some nondisabled individuals.

EXCEPTIONAL MICROCULTURES

Because of insensitivity, apathy, or prejudice, many of those responsible for implementing and upholding the laws that protect individuals with disabilities fail to do so. The failure to provide adequate educational and vocational opportunities for individuals with disabilities may preclude the possibility of social and economic equality. These social and economic limitations are often translated into rejection by nondisabled peers and ultimately into social isolation.

Not unlike many ethnic minority groups who are rejected by mainstream society, individuals with disabilities often find comfort and security with each other, and in some instances they may form their own enclaves and social organizational structures. Throughout the country, one can find microcultures of groups of individuals, such as those who have visual or hearing impairments and those who have mental retardation. In some instances, they congregate in similar jobs, in the same neighborhoods, and at various social settings and activities. For example, near Frankfort Avenue in Louisville, Kentucky, three major institutions provide services for individuals who have visual impairments. The American Printing House for the Blind, the Kentucky School for the Blind, and the Kentucky Industries for the Blind are all within close proximity of each other. The American Printing House for the Blind, the leading publisher of materials for individuals with visual impairments, employs a number of individuals who are blind. The Kentucky School for the Blind is a residential school for students with visual impairments, and it also employs a small number of individuals with visual impairments, including teachers. Finally, the Kentucky Industries for the Blind operates as a sheltered workshop for individuals who are blind. With the relatively large number of persons who are blind employed by these three institutions, it is understandable that many individuals with visual impairments live in the surrounding residential area. Living in this area allows them to live close enough to their work to minimize the many transportation problems related to their visual limitations. It also provides a sense of emotional security for the many who, in earlier years, attended the Kentucky School for the Blind and lived on its campus and thus became part of the neighborhood. The neighborhood community can also provide social and emotional security and feelings of acceptance. A few years ago, a mailing was sent from the Kentucky School for the Blind to its alumni; 90% of the mailings had the same zip code as the school.

Individuals Who Are Gifted

The gifted and talented usually do not experience the same type of discrimination and social rejection that many individuals with disabilities experience. Yet, like individuals with disabilities, they may suffer isolation from mainstream society and seek others with equal abilities that may provide a feeling of acceptance as well as intellectual or emotional stimulation. Rejection of the gifted and talented may differ from that of individuals with disabilities because the roots may stem from a lack of understanding or jealousy, rather than from the stigma that may relate to certain disabilities.

Unfortunately, many gifted and talented students are not properly identified and, as a result, are not properly provided for in their educational programs. Unchallenged and bored with the routine of school, a few of these gifted children may resort to negative forms of behavior that jeopardize acceptance by classmates and teachers. This rejection may lead to social isolation that, in turn, may contribute to the development of alliances with other gifted and talented individuals who can provide understanding and acceptance and who have similar interests. Some gifted and talented individuals may not be rejected by others but nevertheless may seek others with similar talents and interests to provide the necessary or desired stimulation. The existence of Mensa, an organization whose only membership prerequisite is a high score on an intelligence test, attests to the apparent need of some gifted individuals to be with others of their own kind.

LINK TO THE CLASSROOM

Programs for the Gifted

It is estimated that 3% to 5% of the population is gifted as determined by intelligence tests. To serve the gifted population, many school districts have established special programs and sometimes schools. These programs are usually more challenging and stimulating than general education offerings. Students are more engaged in their own learning, and instruction is designed to develop critical and higher-order thinking skills. The students accepted for gifted programs, however, are primarily from the dominant group. Parents from the professional and managerial classes often plan educational experiences to ensure that their children are identified as gifted and can enroll in these enrichment programs.

Some parents and educators have begun to question the validity of special gifted and talented programs. They argue that the high-quality education offered in these programs should be available to all students. They are concerned that the least-qualified teachers are assigned to teach students of color and students from low-income families. They cite research studies that show that the tests used to select the gifted are biased against these groups of students.

Do you agree that gifted students deserve and need an education program that is different from that offered to the majority of students? Why? Why are low-income and minority students underrepresented in gifted programs? Why do upper-middle-class families often fight for their children to be labeled gifted? Why are some advocates for equality against special classes for gifted and talented students?

Individuals with Mental Retardation

It has been estimated that approximately 3% of the general population has mental retardation. Translating this percentage into actual numbers suggests that 6.5 million or more individuals with mental retardation live in the United States (Drew & Hardman, 2000).

Many of the individuals with mild retardation live independently or in community-based and community-supported group homes. The group homes provide a family-like atmosphere, and house parents supervise the homes. Most of the individuals with moderate retardation who do not live in institutions tend to live at home. Many individuals with severe and profound retardation, and some with moderate retardation, are institutionalized and are thus forced into their own cultural group or enclave, isolated from the rest of society.

Because of their intellectual limitations, frequent poverty, and minority status, individuals with mental retardation are often discriminated against and rejected. Because of their alienation from society, those individuals may develop a cultural identity centered around their disability.

Persons with disabilities sometimes live in the same communities, share social activities and support systems, and develop their own microculture with characteristics that are not familiar to others.

Individuals with Visual or Hearing Impairments

Deaf or blind communities may exist when individuals who are sensory impaired live in the same neighborhood, work and socialize together, and marry one another. In other cases, the microcultural group of persons who are sensory impaired may consist of individuals from different communities. Because they do not feel like part of the mainstream society; because they share many commonalities such as forms of communication (sign language or Braille); and because they may have similar interests, these individuals with disabilities find comfort, satisfaction, and security in one another.

Of those with various disabling conditions, individuals with visual impairments and hearing impairments are among the most likely to form their own cultural groups. Both have overriding factors that contribute to the need for individuals in these groups to seek out one another and to form cultural groups. The blind have limited mobility. Living in cultural enclaves allows them easier access to one another. They share the same forms of communication—oral language, braille, and talking books. Social and cultural interests created partly by their physical limitations can often be shared. The hearing impaired may have communication limitations within the hearing world. Their unique means of communication provides them with an emotional as well as a functional bond. Religious programs and churches for individuals with hearing impairments have been formed to provide services in total communication and social activities.

Many students who are hearing impaired communicate with others by using sign English and/or American Sign Language (ASL).

Individuals with Physical and Health Impairments

Individuals with physical and health impairments often have conditions that interfere with their mobility. These limitations may affect school, work, and social interactions.

On one hand, advances in biomedical science have, in some instances, eliminated or reduced problems associated with these conditions. On the other hand, advances in medical science have also contributed to the existence of these conditions. Infants and children who previously would not have survived the physical trauma resulting from severe disease or accidents are often spared the loss of life through advanced medical techniques. They are, however, sometimes left with permanent physical impairments, such as cerebral palsy, or they may experience a life as a paraplegic with limited wheelchair mobility.

The range and variety of conditions related to physical and health impairment are numerous, and it would serve no useful purpose in this chapter to attempt to list them. It is important to note, however, the impact of physical disability on the individual, the family, and society. Contemporary American society places great emphasis on physical beauty and attractiveness. Individuals who deviate significantly from physical norms are subject to possible rejection, even if their physical deviations do not interfere with their day-to-day functioning.

Society tends to place behavioral expectations on both men and women. Males have specific masculine roles they are expected to fulfill. Boys are usually expected to be athletic. Physical impairments, however, may preclude athletic involvement. Unable to fulfill this role, the young paraplegic male may develop devalued feelings of self worth or a feeling that he is less than a man. Feminine roles are also assigned, and women with physical disabilities who are unable to assume these roles may suffer from feelings of inadequacy. With the increased participation of women

VIDEO INSIGHT

A Life without Limits

Often, you hear people say to children, "You can do anything you set your mind to—all you have to do is try." For Robin Tynan, these words became a reality. He's competed in swimming, shot-put, discus, and javelin, winning 18 gold medals and setting 14 world records. He is a doctor, an accomplished equestrian, and an internationally known singer. He is also a double amputee.

In this video segment you will see how one man has overcome his perceived disabilities. Through the support of family, friends, and a tremendous will, Robin has achieved what most people would deem impossible. With a group of your peers, discuss how this story has changed your perception of individuals with disabilities.

Individuals with disabilities have the same basic needs as nondisabled individuals, to belong, to love, and to be loved.

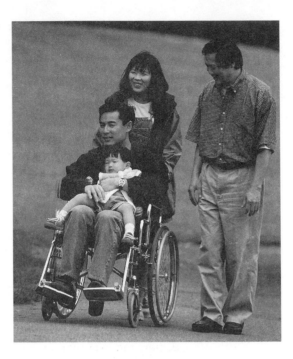

in athletics, some women may also suffer the frustration of being unable to compete in some athletic programs.

Individuals with physical disabilities may or may not become a part of a microcultural group related to the disability. Some function vocationally and socially as part of the mainstream society. With adequate cognitive functioning and adequate communication patterns, normal social interaction is possible. Socialization, however, may depend on the degree of impairment and the individual's emotional adjustment to the disability. Some individuals with physical disabilities may function in the mainstream world and also maintain social contacts with others with similar disabilities. Social clubs for individuals with physical disabilities have been formed to provide experiences commensurate with functional abilities, as well as a social climate that provides acceptance and security. Athletic leagues for competition in sports, such as wheelchair basketball and tennis, have been formed. Many racing events (e.g., the Boston marathon) now include competition for wheelchair entries.

Individuals with Emotional Disturbance and with Delinquent Behaviors

Emotional disturbance and delinquency significantly affect the adequate functioning of an individual's family as a unit, as well as social contacts beyond the family. The behavior exhibited by individuals with either emotional disturbance or delinquency is often negative and excessive, and the response to this behavior typically is rejection. Because the behavior may grossly affect the well-being of society, the individual and his or her family are often held accountable for the actions, even if the actions are, in reality, beyond their willful control.

It is clear that adverse environmental conditions contribute greatly to emotional disturbance. Where individuals are subjected to extreme stress, the likelihood of the development of emotional problems is greater. Extreme poverty, for example, may subject an individual to constant stress and the inability to cope with the stress may result in emotional disturbance. Problems with delinquency, particularly in childhood and adolescence, may be related to lower socioeconomic circumstances, including being on public welfare, living in low-rent housing, and being a member of a minority group that tends to be caught in the low-income poverty cycle. Extreme stress caused by environmental deprivation can contribute to delinquent behaviors. It would be wrong, however, to assume that children and adolescents faced with poverty-related stress are necessarily predisposed to delinquent behavior.

Although some emotional problems in children stem from early negative interactions between parents and children, no solid research findings would allow the blame for children's behavioral problems to be attributed primarily to their parents. It has become increasingly evident that influences are transactional and interactional, and that children affect their parents as much as their parents affect them.

It has been speculated that some delinquent children are rebelling against social standards that are different from those of their own minority or disadvantaged group. In other instances, the resentment and negative behaviors may be directed against their own social and economic system, such as the maladjustment problems observed among individuals in middle and higher socioeconomic groups.

Some individuals who have no viable means to attain their goals may develop social alienation and maladjustment. Individuals from low-income groups, for example, are often confronted with the problem of wanting the material comforts of the middle and upper classes but not having a legitimate means to obtain them. Frustrated and disillusioned with their attempts to achieve through socially acceptable means, they may begin to seek less legitimate means that seem to bring more satisfying results.

EDUCATIONAL IMPLICATIONS

The educational implications for working with exceptional individuals are numerous and entire chapters could be devoted to each exceptionality. Educators should remember that exceptional children, those with disabilities and those who are gifted, are more like than unlike normal children. Their basic needs are the same as all children's. Abraham Maslow's theory on self-actualization is familiar to most students in education. To be self-actualized or to meet one's full potential, Maslow (1954) theorized, one's basic needs must be fulfilled: That is, to reach self-actualization, one's physiological needs, safety needs, belongingness or love needs, and esteem needs must first be met. Although many individuals with disabilities may never match the accomplishments of their nondisabled peers, they can become proficient at whatever they are capable of doing. Educators can assist them by helping to ensure that their basic needs are met, allowing them to strive toward self-actualization.

Teachers must be constantly cognizant of the unique needs of their exceptional children. The exceptional adult may choose, or may be forced by society, to become part of a microcultural group. The interactions between educators and the exceptional child may not change what will eventually take place. Even if exceptional adults are part of a microcultural group, they also will interact with the mainstream society on a regular basis. Efforts on the part of the educator to meet the needs of the child may ultimately affect the exceptional adult's interaction with society.

Teachers of children with physical and other health impairments may find it advantageous to check the student records carefully to determine potential problem situations with these students in the classroom. If a child has particular health problems that may surface in the classroom, the child's teachers need to be prepared so that they will know precisely what to do should the child have, for example, an epileptic seizure. The parents will most likely be able to provide precise instructions, and the school nurse could also provide additional recommendations. If the children are old enough to understand, they too can be a valuable source of information. Ask them what kinds of adaptations, special equipment, or teaching procedures work best for them. Teachers should not be afraid of their own uncertainties. They should feel free to ask the students when they won't or don't want help. Teachers should treat their students with disabilities as normally as feasible, neither overprotecting them nor giving or doing more for them than is needed or deserved. Allowing them to assume responsibility for themselves will do much to facilitate their personal growth.

Many variables affect the learning, cognition, and adjustment of individuals with disabilities. This is particularly evident for culturally and linguistically diverse learners who must cope with issues of language, culture, and values. Harry, Kalyanpur, & Day (1999) implore professionals who work with students with disabilities to take special note of the cultural values that may be embedded in their interpretation of a particular student's difficulties. They suggest that developing a sense of cultural self-awareness is crucial to effective interactions with students and families and that it will enable them to make appropriate decisions regarding services.

The range and variety of experiences imposed on, or withheld from, persons with disabilities may result in undue limitations. Too often, parents and teachers assume that a child's visual limitation precludes the ability to appreciate the typical everyday experiences of sighted children. Children who are blind may not be able to see the animals in a zoo, but they can smell and hear them. They may not be able to enjoy the scenes along a bus route, but they can feel the stop-and-go movements, hear the traffic and people, and smell their fellow travelers. The child who is deaf may not be able to hear the sounds at the symphony or the crowd's roar at a football game. Both events, however, offer the possibility of extraordinary sensory experiences to which the child needs exposure. The child with cerebral palsy needs experiences such as going to restaurants, even if there is difficulty using eating utensils in a socially acceptable manner.

Well-adjusted individuals with a sensory disability usually attain a balance of control with their environment. Individuals who depend completely on other members of the family and on friends may develop an attitude of helplessness and a loss of self-identity. Individuals with disabilities who completely dominate and control their environment with unreasonable demands sometimes fail to make an acceptable adjustment and could become selfish and self-centered.

It is critical to remember that children who are exceptional are, first and foremost, children. Their exceptionality, though influencing their lives, is secondary to their needs as children. They are more like than unlike nondisabled children. They therefore have the same basic needs as those children. Chinn, Winn, & Walters (1978) identify three of those needs: communication, acceptance, and the freedom to grow.

Communication Needs

Exceptional children are far more perceptive than many adults give them credit for being. They are sensitive to nonverbal communication and hidden messages that may be concealed in half-truths. They, more than anyone else, need to deal with their exceptionality, whether it is a disability or giftedness. They need to know what their exceptionality is all about so that they can deal with it. They need to know how it will affect their lives in order to adjust appropriately, to make the best of their lives, and to reach their full potential. They need straight, honest communication tempered with sensitivity.

Acceptance Needs

The society in which we live often fails to provide the exceptional child with a positive and receptive environment. Even the educational setting can be hostile and lacking in acceptance. The teacher can facilitate the acceptance of a child in a classroom by exhibiting an open and positive attitude. Students tend to reflect the attitude of the teacher. If the teacher is hostile, the students will quickly pick up these cues. If the attitude is positive, the students are likely to respond and provide a receptive environment for their classmates with disabilities.

Jeff, a first-grade student who suffered from a hearing loss, was fitted with a hearing aid. When he came to school with the hearing aid, the students in the class immediately began whispering about the "thing" Jeff had in his ear. After observing the class behavior, the teacher assisted Jeff in a "show and tell" preparation for the next day. With the teacher's assistance and assurances, Jeff proudly demonstrated his hearing aid to the class. By the end of the demonstration, Jeff was the envy of the class, and any further discussion of the hearing aid was of a positive nature.

Freedom to Grow

Students with disabilities need acceptance and understanding. Acceptance implies a freedom for the exceptional child to grow. At times, it may seem easier to do things for a child, rather than to take the time to teach the child.

> Sarah was a nine-year-old girl who was blind and who had an orthopedic disability. She attended a state residential school for the blind. She wore leg braces but had a reasonable amount of mobility with crutches. To save time and effort, fellow students or staff members transported her between the cottage where she lived and the classroom building in a wagon. One day her teacher decided she needed to be more independent in her travel to and from her cottage. To Sarah's surprise, the teacher informed her after school that she would not ride back in the wagon but that he was walking her back. Angered, she denounced him as cruel and hateful in front of the entire class. She complained bitterly the full thirty minutes of their walk back to the cottage. After a few days the complaining subsided and the travel time was curtailed. Within a few weeks Sarah was traveling on her own in ten minutes or less with newfound self-respect (Chinn et al., 1978, p. 36).

At other times, it may be tempting for teachers and parents to make extra concessions for the exceptional child. Often, these exceptions preclude the emotional growth of the child and may later cause serious interpersonal problems.

> Jimmy was a seven-year-old boy who was blind at the same state institution attended by Sarah. He was a favorite of the staff members because of his pleasant personality and overall adjustment. On a Sunday afternoon in the fall, he was assisting a staff member in making block prints for Christmas. The conversation turned to Christmas and Jimmy's wish for a transistor radio. This incident took place in 1960 when transistor radios were new on the market and very expensive. Since Jimmy had already made his request to his parents, the staff member was confident that the parents would not deny this child his wish. To the surprise of the staff, Jimmy returned after the holidays without a radio. He very philosophically explained to the staff that the radios were so expensive that had his parents granted his wish it would be at the expense of the other children in the family. Weeks later, when Jimmy returned from his birthday weekend at home, he entered his cottage with a transistor radio in hand, but in tears. He informed the staff that he and his younger brother Ralph had been fighting in the car on the way to the school and both had received a spanking. When a staff member went out to greet Jimmy's parents, his younger brother Ralph was also crying from the insult to his rear end (Chinn et al., 1978, p. 36).

Jimmy's father was a laborer with a modest income. Although their child's disability created adjustment problems for everyone, they had resolved to treat him as an equal in the family. As such, he shared all of the family privileges. He also suffered the same consequences for inappropriate behavior. This attitude on the part of the parents was probably a primary factor in Jimmy's excellent adjustment to his disability.

NORMALIZATION AND MAINSTREAMING

Much effort is directed today toward the concept of normalization. **Normalization** means "making available to all persons with disabilities or other handicaps, patterns of life and conditions of everyday living which are as close as possible to or indeed the same as the regular circumstances and ways of life of society" (Nirje, 1985, p. 67). Normalization was expanded and advocated in the United States by Wolfensberger (1972). He has subsequently suggested a rethinking of the term *normalization* and introduced the concept of "social role valorization"—giving value to individuals with mental retardation. He suggests that the "most explicit and highest goal of normalization must be the creation, support, and defense of valued social roles for people who are at risk of social devaluation" (Wolfensberger, 1983, p. 234).

Drew and Hardman (2000) suggest that normalization and social valorization have brought about an emphasis on deinstitutionalization, whereby individuals from large residential facilities for people with retardation are returned to the community and home environments. They add that the concept is not limited to movement away from institutions to a less restrictive environment; it also pertains to those individuals living in the community for whom a more "normal" lifestyle may be an appropriate goal.

The principles of normalization as they were first introduced were developed with individuals with mental retardation as the target group. In more recent years, the concept has broadened so that all categories of individuals with disabilities are now targeted. Mainstreaming seemed to undergo a natural evolutionary process from the concept of normalization. Although IDEA mandates educating children with disabilities in the "least restrictive environment" (LRE), nowhere in the statute is the word *mainstream* used. "Least restrictive environment," however, means that children with disabilities are to be educated with nondisabled children whenever possible, in as normal an environment as possible. Although the concept of LRE does not necessarily mean integration into general education classes, the term **mainstreaming,** through common usage, refers to the practice of integrating children with disabilities into general education classes for all or a portion of the day. A goal in special education, therefore, is to mainstream as many children with disabilities as is feasible.

Initially, mainstreaming was intended for students with mild disabilities. A more current movement seeks to provide children with moderate to severe disabilities with similar opportunities. Although resistance to mainstreaming students with mild retardation is far less intense than it once was, resistance from some educators toward those with more severe disabilities is often still intense. The arguments against integrating children with severe disabilities have often been centered on the presumed inability of nondisabled children to accept their peers with disabilities. In reality, some of the reservations may be more a reflection of educators who themselves are unable or unwilling to accept the dignity and worth of individuals with severe disabilities.

Opponents of integration use many of the same arguments that segregationists used more than 40 years ago. Perhaps some of their arguments are valid, perhaps not. As educators, we must be cognizant of the fact that our fear of change and our fear of the unknown have often prevented us from making changes for the better.

The passage, implementation, and reauthorization of the IDEA provided a major impetus for the concept of inclusion. Although often used interchangeably with mainstreaming, inclusion claims as its imperative the individualization of the education system for ALL students, and attempts to develop a far more holistic approach to education in general (Salend, 2001). Although it focuses primarily on individuals with disabilities, inclusion is designed to benefit all students, teachers, families, and support personnel. It attempts to ensure that students with special learning needs have the opportunity to receive all or part of their instruction in regular education classes. Ysseldyke, Algozzine, and Thurlow (2000) suggest that it primarily reflects the view that the educational experiences of students with disabilities should mirror as much as possible those of their fellow students without disabilities.

Tiegerman-Farber and Radziewicz define inclusion as the "integration of children with and without disabilities" (1998, p. 13) and further assert that in its "purest" form it means that students with disabilities have a right to be integrated into general education classes regardless of their ability to meet "traditional" academic standards. Salend (2001) suggests that inclusion is a "principled philosophy" and that the four major principles are diversity, individual needs, reflective practices, and collaboration. Many supporters believe that merging special and general education and eliminating their separateness is crucial to the success of effective inclusion. The current emphasis on inclusion has been driven primarily by parents and educators who are impatient with the slow implementation of IDEA (Turnbull &Turnbull, 2001). Special educators themselves are seldom in complete agreement as to the appropriate classroom placement for students with disabilities. Most special educators support some degree of inclusion for those students who they believe would benefit from a general classroom setting. Most support a full continuum of services from residential schools and self-contained classrooms to itinerant teachers, resource rooms, and general education classrooms. Another point of view supports full inclusion of all children with disabilities regardless of the type or degree of disability. Full inclusionists represent a very vocal and committed segment of special educators. Full inclusion for these people is primarily a moral and ethical issue, rather than an efficacy issue. The issues are complex and difficult to resolve without examining individual situations.

Because it involves students, teachers, families, administrative support, resources, and communities, inclusion is admittedly a very complex undertaking and the research on the impact on educational outcomes for students with disabilities remains inconclusive (Salend, 2001). Disagreements abound regarding when and how inclusion should be provided within the regular classroom and whether inclusion is appropriate for all children with disabilities (Tiegerman-Farber & Radziewicz, 1998). Turnbull and Turnbull (2001) admit that serious concerns continue to be raised by many special educators. While inclusion does often result in positive social outcomes, some studies suggest that students with disabilities do not always receive the appropriate instructional modifications necessary to benefit from inclusion (Salend, 2001). Some traditionalists argue that many students require special education and that their teachers must possess special education skills. They express concern that efforts toward full inclusion may deplete the often-meager resources available for students with moderate and severe disabilities (Ysseldyke, Algozzine, & Thurlow, 2000). Other studies indicate that students without disabilities also benefit socially and do not appear to be academically harmed by an inclusive education (Salend, 2001).

To answer these questions online, go to the Pause to Reflect module for this chapter of the Companion Website.

PAUSE TO REFLECT

Students with disabilities are sometimes forced into segregated settings for reasons beyond their control. For example, Kevin was a student who lived with his family on the side of a mountain in Appalachia. Kevin was blind, with no travel vision. It was a three-quarter-mile hike down the side of the mountain to the school bus stop. Kevin had good mobility skills and could negotiate the trail to and from the bus stop when weather conditions were good. The school was able to provide appropriate special education and general education services for him. During the winter, however, when snow covered the ground for the entire season, he could not get his bearings with his long cane and could not negotiate the trail. There was no one who could help him get to and from the bus stop, so during the winter he stopped going to school. The only school that could apparently meet his needs was the state school for the blind, which could provide him with residential services. The state residential school, however, is the most extreme form of a segregated setting for students with disabilities. Is segregating Kevin from his nondisabled peers inappropriate? Immoral? Unethical?

Is the issue of full inclusion for students with disabilities similar to the issue of desegregation for all students of color into integrated classroom settings? When educators say they want a full continuum of services for students with disabilities that would permit inclusion for some and segregated classrooms for others or even institutionalization, is this a moral and ethical way to educate America's students? Is this an excuse for educators to discriminate against some?

It is important for us as educators to see the parallels and differences that exist between the current debate regarding this group of students and the issues that *Brown* addressed more than 40 years ago. The two situations have similarities, but the groups are different. It is important that, as educators, we maintain an open mind so that perhaps we ourselves can be educated.

The legal mandates do not eliminate special schools or classes, but they do offer a new philosophical view. Instead of the physical isolation of individuals with disabilities, an effort to enable students with disabilities to assume a more appropriate place in the educational setting is being promoted. Still, many children with disabilities apparently may not benefit appreciably from an inclusive setting and may be better educated in a special setting. As attitudes become more congruent with the laws, people with disabilities may have more options in the decision to be a part of the mainstream or to segregate themselves into their own cultural groups.

Summary

The concerns related to the disproportionate placement of ethnic minorities, males, and students from low-income families in special education programs have been addressed to focus on a long-standing educational problem. The issues raised are not intended to negate the fact that there are students with retardation, serious emotional disturbance, and other disabilities in both majority and minority groups. Rather, they are raised to call attention to problems in referral and assessment, as well as to the problems associated with poverty.

Adults with disabilities often become part of a microculture for individuals with disabilities by ascription or by individual choice. They do not choose to have a disability, and their situation often precludes full acceptance or integration into the world of those who are perceived to be physically, socially, or mentally normal. Their adjustment to their environment may be, in part, a function of the way they are perceived, treated, and accepted by educators. Consequently, teachers and other educators may have a greater influence on children with disabilities than they realize.

The Education for All Handicapped Children Act (EHA; PL 94–142), the Individuals with Disabilities Education Act (IDEA; PL 101–476), Section 504 of the Vocational Rehabilitation Act Amendments of 1973 (PL 93–112), and the Americans with Disabilities Act (ADA; PL 101–336) guarantee all exceptional children the right to a free and appropriate education and freedom from discrimination resulting from their disability. Despite these mandates, equality still eludes millions of individuals with disabilities in this country. Insensitivity, apathy, and prejudice contribute to the problems of those with disabilities. Because of prejudice, institutionalization, or a desire to meet their own needs, some exceptional individuals form their own microcultures and some their own enclaves, where they live and socialize with one another. The laws can force services for individuals with disabilities, but only time and effort can change public attitudes.

Questions for Review

To answer these questions online, go to the Chapter Questions module for this chapter of the Companion Website.

1. What are some of the objections to labeling children with disabilities?
2. In what ways has the treatment of individuals with disabilities paralleled that of oppressed minorities?
3. In what ways have ethnic minority children been disproportionately placed in special classes for students with disabilities and students who are gifted?
4. What are some of the variables contributing to the disproportionate placement of minorities in special education?

5. What are the major implications of PL 94–142, IDEA, Section 504 of PL 93–112, and the Americans with Disabilities Act?
6. Explain the difference between the terms *inclusion* and *full inclusion*. Which do you support and why?
7. Explain the concepts of normalization, social role valorization, and main-streaming.
8. What are some of the negative ways that individuals with disabilities are portrayed by the media and viewed by some members of society?
9. What are some ways in which exceptional individuals form their own micro-cultures?
10. What are some of the needs of exceptional children?

References

Berger, K. S. (1983). *The developing person through the life span.* New York: Worth.

Board of Education of the Hendrick Hudson School District v. Rowley, 458 U.S. 176 (1982).

Brown v. Board of Education of Topeka, 347 U.S. 483, 74 S. Ct. 686, 91, L. Ed. 873 (1954).

Carolina Environment, Inc. (1999). *How lead affects your child's health.* Available. http:// www.knowlead.com/affect.htm

Chinn, P. C., Winn, J., & Walters, R. H. (1978). *Two-way talking with parents of exceptional children: A process of positive communication.* St. Louis: Mosby.

Diana v. State Board of Education, Civil Action No. C–7037RFP (N.D. Cal. Jan. 7, 1970 & June 18, 1973).

Drew, C. J. & Hardman, M. L. (2000). *Mental retardation: A life cycle approach* (7th ed.). Upper Saddle River, NJ: Prentice Hall.

Dunn, L. (1968). Special education for the mildly retarded: Is much of it justifiable? *Exceptional Children, 7,* 5–24.

Education for All Handicapped Children's Act of 1975, 20 U.S.C. 1401 *et seq (P.L. 94–142).*

Gelfand, D. M., Jenson, W. R., & Drew, C. J. (1988). *Understanding child behavior disorders* (2nd ed.). New York: Holt, Rinehart and Winston.

Gliedman, J. & Roth, W. (1980). *The unexpected minority.* New York: Harcourt Brace Jovanovich.

Harry, B., Kalyanpur, M., & Day, M. (1999). *Building cultural reciprocity with families: Case studies in special education.* Baltimore: Paul H. Brookes Publishing Co.

Heward, W. L., (2000). *Exceptional children* (5th ed.). Upper Saddle River, NJ: Prentice Hall.

High, M. H. & Udall, A. I. (1983). Teacher ratings of students in relation to ethnicity of students and school ethnic balance. *Journal of Education and the Gifted, 6,* 154–166.

Individuals with Disabilities Education Act of 1990, 20 U.S.C. 1400 *et seq.*

Individuals with Disabilities Education Act Regulations, 34 C.F. R. 300. 1 *et seq.*

Irving Independent School District v. Tatro, 468 U. S. 883 (1984).

Larry P. v. Riles, C-71-2270, FRP. Dis. Ct (1979).

Maslow, A. (1954). *Motivation and personality.* New York: Harper.

Mercer, J. (1973). *Labeling the mentally retarded.* Los Angeles: University of California Press.

Mills v. Board of Education, 348 F. Supp. 866 (D.D.C 1972).

Nirje, B. (1985). The basis and logic of the normalization principle. *Australia and New Zealand Journal of Developmental Disabilities, 11,* 65–68.

Patton, J. M. (1998). The disproportionate representation of African Americans in special education: Looking behind the curtain for understanding and solutions. *The Journal of Special Education, 32*(1), 25–31.

Pennsylvania Association for Retarded Citizens v. Commonwealth of Pennsylvania, 343 F. Supp. 279 (E.D. Pa. 1972).

President's Committee on Mental Retardation. (1969). *The six-hour retarded child.* Washington, DC: U.S. Department of Health, Education & Welfare.

Salend, S. (2001). *Creating inclusive classrooms: Effective and reflective practices.* NJ: Prentice Hall.

Tiegerman-Farber, E. & Radziewicz, C. (1998). *Collaborative decision making: The pathway to inclusion.* NJ: Prentice Hall.

Turnbull, A. & Turnbull, R. (2001). *Families, professionals, and exceptionality: Collaborating for empowerment.* NJ: Prentice Hall.

U.S. Office of Civil Rights (OCR). (1988). *1986 Elementary and Secondary Schools Civil Rights Survey.* Washington, DC: U.S. Department of Education.

U.S. Office of Civil Rights (OCR). (1990). *1988 Elementary and Secondary Schools Civil Rights Survey.* Washington, DC: U.S. Department of Education.

U.S. Office of Civil Rights (OCR). (1999). *1997 Elementary and Secondary Schools Civil Rights Survey.* Washington, DC: U.S. Department of Education.

Widerstrom, A. H., Mowder, B. A., & Sandall, S. R. (1991). *At-risk and handicapped newborns and infants.* Englewood Cliffs, NJ: Prentice Hall.

Wolfensberger, W. (1972). *Normalization: The principle of normalization in human services.* Toronto: National Institute on Mental Retardation.

Wolfensberger, W. (1983). Social role valorization: Proposed new form for the principle of normalization. *Mental Retardation, 21*(6), 234–239.

Yell, M. L. (1998). *The law and special education.* Upper Saddle River, NJ: Prentice Hall

Ysseldyke, J. E., Algozzine, B., & Thurlow, M. L. (2000). *Critical issues in special education.* Boston: Houghton Mifflin.

Ysseldyke, J.E., Thurlow, M., Graden, J., Wesson, C., Algozzine, B., and Deno, S. (1983). Generalizations from five years of research on assessment and decision-making: The University of Minnesota Institute, *Exceptional Education Quarterly, 4,* 75–93.

Suggested Readings

Drew, C. J. & Hardman, M. L. (2000). *Mental retardation: A life cycle approach* (7th ed.). Upper Saddle River, NJ: Prentice Hall.
This is an excellent developmental approach to mental retardation. It includes a sensitive view of mental retardation and its impact on the family. It examines some of the early treatments of individuals with mental retardation. A chapter on legislative and legal issues related to individuals with mental retardation is also included.

Gliedman, J. & Roth, W. (1980). *The unexpected minority.* New York: Harcourt Brace Jovanovich.
This book examines how social, rather than biological, aspects of disability doom children and adults with disabilities to stunted and useless lives. It demonstrates how discrimination against the disabled is the result of stereotypes and misconceptions that distort the attitudes of both professionals and society at large.

Heward, W. L. (2000). *Exceptional children* (6th ed.). Upper Saddle River, NJ: Prentice Hall. This survey text is an overview of all exceptionalities that will provide a good basic understanding of the gifted and talented, as well as the various disabling conditions. It includes a chapter on culturally diverse exceptional students.

Yell, M. L. (1998). *The law and special education.* Upper Saddle River, NJ: Prentice Hall This text provides an excellent overview of litigation and legislation in special education. It provides excellent insights into how litigation is developed and how it influences legislation. Provides an explanation of legal terminology.

Ysseldyke, J. F., Algozzine, B., & Thurlow, M. L. (2000). *Critical issues in special education.* Boston: Houghton Mifflin. This text examines the major contemporary issues in special education including, but not limited to, issues in assessment, inclusion, early intervention, transition, and school reform.

CRITICAL INCIDENTS IN TEACHING

Exceptionality

Placement of a Child with Epilepsy

Max Laird is a sixth-grade teacher in a middle-class suburban school. After school, Mr. Laird finds a note in his in-box, indicating that the principal and the special education resource room teacher want to meet with him the next day before the students arrive.

At the meeting the next day, his principal, Dr. Gattelaro, explains to him that a new student, Chris Erickson, will be placed in his class the following Monday morning. He is informed that Chris is slightly above average in academics and a personable young man. However, Dr. Gattelaro wants Mr. Laird to know that Chris has epilepsy and occasionally has grand mal seizures. Although the seizures are generally under control through medication, there is a good possibility that sometime during the school year Chris will have a seizure in the classroom.

At this time, Ms. Chong, the resource room teacher, describes grand mal seizures. She explains that they are the most evident and serious type of epileptic seizure. They can be disturbing and frightening to anyone who has never seen one. Chris would have little or no warning that a seizure was about to occur. During a seizure, Chris' muscles will stiffen, and he will lose consciousness and fall to the floor. His whole body will shake violently, as his muscles alternately contract and relax. Saliva may be forced from his mouth, his legs and arms may jerk, and his bladder and bowels may empty. After a few minutes, the contractions will diminish, and Chris will either go to sleep or regain consciousness in a confused and drowsy state (Heward, 1996).

Stunned at this information, Mr. Laird sits in silence as Ms. Chong briefs him about the procedures to take if a seizure occurs in the classroom. She also explains to him that he should inform the other students that the seizure is painless to Chris and that it is not contagious.

Max Laird is aware that he has no option as to whether Chris will be in his class. He is determined to do the right thing and to make Chris' transition into his class as smooth as possible. He is also determined that he will help his class adjust and prepare for the likely seizure. Mr. Laird begins to map out a plan of action.

Questions for Discussion

To answer these questions online, go to the Critical Incidents module for this chapter of the Companion Website.

1. What can Mr. Laird do with regard to his class?
2. Should he talk to his class about Chris?
3. Should he explain what epilepsy is?
4. What should he say to Chris? What other actions can he take?

Student with a Health Problem

Michelle Adams is a third-grade teacher in a cattle and farming community of 40,000 in Colorado. Some residents in the community and some students in the school come from lower socioeconomic backgrounds; others come from middle-

and upper-class backgrounds. The students are primarily white and several are descendants of early German settlers in the region. A few students are Latino and some are children of migrant workers who work in the sugar beet fields. A handful of students are of Asian ancestry, mostly third- and fourth-generation Japanese Americans.

On the day after Christmas vacation, Ms. Adams notes that one student, Terry, is constantly touching his teeth with his index finger. Walking over to his desk, she asks him what his problem is. "My teeth hurt," he replies.

Asking him to open his mouth, she is shocked to see one of his teeth visibly eaten away with decay. "Do your parents know about this?" she asks the student.

"Sure they do," he responds.

"Then why don't you go to a dentist to have it taken care of?" she asks.

"Cause we ain't got no money," he replies

To answer these questions online, go to the Critical Incidents module for this chapter of the Companion Website.

Questions for Discussion

1. Should Ms. Adams have pursued the questioning in front of the class?
2. What could she have done to minimize any embarrassment to Terry in front of his classmates?
3. Are the health and dental needs of a child the responsibility or concern of the teacher?
4. Should she contact Terry's parents? The principal? The school nurse?

Inclusion

Larry Gladden is a junior high school social studies teacher and the head football coach for the eighth-grade team. With a poor turnout for his initial recruitment effort, Gladden has received permission from Principal W. O. Smith to make another recruitment pitch over the school's public address system. Making a strong appeal for all interested able-bodied boys to come out, Coach Gladden sets a meeting time immediately after school. As the new prospects arrive, the coach is shocked to see Massey Brunson walk into the room. Recognizing Massey from the special education classroom adjacent to his own, the coach knows that Massey is a student with mild mental retardation. The others in the room know this, too. "Hi, Coach," says Massey. "You said you need strong, healthy players. That's me! I work out every day at the Nautilus Fitness Center, and I'm in great shape."

Massey is indeed a great physical specimen. He is among the tallest of the new recruits and very muscular. When the coach saw the other team prospects shaking their heads as Massey entered, he had serious doubts about how Massey might fit on the team. Would he be accepted by his teammates? Could he learn the plays and follow instructions?

To answer these questions online, go to the Critical Incidents module for this chapter of the Companion Website.

Questions for Discussion

1. Is the coach obligated to allow Massey to try out?
2. Should he discourage Massey from trying to play?

3. Should he treat Massey differently from other players?
4. Should he make special allowances for Massey?
5. If Massey is good enough to play, how should the coach foster his acceptance by other team members?

Placement of a Student with a Contagious Disease

At a special education student placement meeting, the first case involves a three-year-old male with a history of medical problems. The child is developmentally delayed and is not ambulatory. Further, the child is not toilet trained. He also lacks oral muscle control and drools constantly.

The medical report indicates that the student tests positive for cytomegalovirus (CMV). This is a herpes-like virus that is excreted in urine and saliva. CMV may result in mental retardation, severe hearing loss, microcephaly, and chronic liver disease when transmitted to newborns. A woman may have contracted CMV several years previously and been asymptomatic but may transmit the virus in utero, during delivery, or via breast-feeding. Eighty percent of persons over age 35 show serologic evidence of previous infection. The majority of these infections are asymptomatic.

The placement committee checks the school district's special education policy concerning CMV and no justification is discovered for excluding children who are known shedders of this virus. According to the "least restrictive environment" clause of PL 94–142, a special day class in a special school is the most appropriate placement.

Because the child is only three years old, he qualifies for only one of the seven preschool classes. The preschool program is run by an innovative instructional team consisting of five young female instructors (of childbearing age), one older female, one male teacher, and fourteen female assistants (of childbearing age). Three of the teachers are pregnant. The preschool staff members are a very strong, informal group. Further, four of the teachers have leadership roles on the school's steering committee.

The student placement meeting is concluded, and the parent is told that the child will be placed in one preschool class and that transportation will begin in two weeks. Word leaks out that a child with CMV is about to enter the preschool program. A panic begins in the preschool department, and two teachers threaten to transfer if the child is put into their classrooms.

To answer these questions online, go to the Critical Incidents module for this chapter of the Companion Website.

Questions for Discussion

1. How should the administrator proceed?
2. How would you, as a teacher, react?
3. Where should the child be placed?
4. What would you do if the child were in your class?

Learning Disabilities

Campbell Andersen, a first grader, has just moved to a small Colorado town from New York. She is bright but has some reading problems. Her parents have noticed that she doesn't like to read because she says that "the words jump around too much."

During a writing session, each of the children was asked to come to the chalkboard and spell the word that Jorge Romero, the teacher, gave them. When Campbell came to the board to write her word, she wrote the word out backwards as if the word were reflected in a mirror. The rest of the class began to laugh and Mr. Romero stood there, stunned. Campbell walked to the back of the classroom and sat down with tears coming to her eyes. She thought that she had spelled the word right and didn't realize that there was anything wrong.

To Answer these questions online, go to the Critical Incidents module for this chapter of the Companion Website.

Questions for Discussion

1. How should Mr. Romero respond to Campbell?
2. How does Mr. Romero respond to the class?
3. What action should Mr. Romero take for Campbell in the future?

Chapter 6

Religion

"Congress shall make no law respecting an establishment of religion, or prohibiting the free exercise thereof; or abridging the freedom of speech, or of the press; or the right of the people peaceably to assemble, and to petition the Government for a redress of grievances."

First Amendment to the United States Constitution, 1791

I n a suburb of San Francisco, the teachers and administrators of the Edison Onizuka middle school have put the finishing touches on their plans for the school's honors convocation. The principal, Dr. Kendra Rose, had suggested that the event should recognize the school's high academic achievers in each grade. This effort to stimulate and reinforce student academic efforts was enthusiastically endorsed by the faculty. Maria Gutierrez and Lawrence Komar were tied with the highest grades in the eighth grade and were to be recognized and asked to make a 7- to 10-minute speech on the value of an education. Because the faculty and Dr. Rose wanted the district superintendent to be part of the ceremony, they had agreed to schedule the event at 3:00 P.M. on the fourth Saturday in May. This was the superintendent's only available time because she was participating in high school commencement ceremonies at all the other times that were proposed.

Dr. Rose called the Gutierrez and Komar families to inform them of their children's selection as convocation speakers. As expected, both sets of parents were delighted at the news of their daughter and their son's accomplishments and selection. Mr. Komar indicated, however, that Saturday was

197

quite impossible because it was the Sabbath for their family, who were Orthodox Jews. The event had to be rescheduled to any other day but the Sabbath. It was impossible, Dr. Rose pleaded. All the plans were made, and no satisfactory alternate dates were available. "Would you plan the event on a Sunday?" Mr. Komar exclaimed. "I would not ask you to. Then why do you schedule it on our Sabbath? You must change the day." At an impasse, Dr. Rose knew she had to come up with a Plan B in a hurry.

Is Mr. Komar being unreasonable? What if the event in question took place in a homogenous community that was primarily Christian and the Komar family was one of only two Jewish families in the community? In a democracy, does the majority always rule? What if you are a Christian living in a non-Christian community, and a major event that you were expected to attend was scheduled on Christmas Day? Are the situations comparable? Do the rights of every individual have to be considered?

RELIGION AND CULTURE

In the United States, 190 million people claim affiliation with a religious group. In an average week, 40% of adults attend a church, synagogue, mosque, or temple. Religion is clearly an important aspect of the lives of many people. Although it may have little impact on the lives of some people, it influences the way many other people think, perceive, and behave. The forces of religious groups are far from dormant. They can influence the election of school board members as well as the curriculum and textbooks used in schools. Principals, teachers, and superintendents have been hired and fired through the influence of religious groups. This chapter provides an overview of religion in the United States and its influence in the educational system.

The pluralistic nature of the school in which one teaches will be determined, in great part, by the geographic region of the United States. Because of various immigration and migration patterns throughout history, different ethnic and religious groups have settled in different parts of the country. Although few areas remain totally homogeneous, families that strongly identify with a particular ethnic group may dominate a school community. More often, families identify strongly with the religious orientation of one or more denominations in the community. The perspective of a particular religious doctrine often influences what a family expects from the school and therefore from the teacher. In an area where the religious perspectives and school expectations differ greatly, educators face numerous challenges. A look at the religious composition of schools in various sections of the country will provide a sense of the diversity one might face throughout a career in education.

A consolidated rural high school in the South may be made up primarily of students whose families are conservative Southern Baptist, Church of Christ, or Pentecostal. The United Methodist students are somewhat less conservative than the others. The church serves as the center of most community activities, and many families spend several nights a week at church or serving the church. Sex education is not allowed in the public school curriculum. Teachers may face harsh criticism if they teach about evolution or lifestyles that conflict with those acceptable in that community. Textbooks and assigned readings are often scrutinized to ensure that the content does not stray far from the beliefs of this conservative community.

At a middle school in northeastern Indiana, most students are from the same European background, but they dress and behave differently. Some students are from a local Old Order Amish community with strict codes for the behavior and dress of its members, whereas the majority of other students are Mennonites. The former are very respectful and well behaved, but some are ridiculed by non-Amish students. After completing the eighth grade, the Amish students are no longer part of the school system because their families withdraw them to work full-time on their farms. There is no electricity and there are no motorized vehicles on their farms.

Students from Catholic, Jewish, Protestant, Muslim, Hindu, Sikh, and Buddhist families attend a suburban school on the West Coast. Some students are from families with no religious affiliation. Although the religious backgrounds of the students differ, they seem to share many of the same values. The school projects a generally liberal curriculum that includes sex education, ethnic studies, and religion courses. Except for the students' celebration of various religious holidays, religion seems to have little impact on the students or the school.

At an inner-city school in an East Coast city, the religious backgrounds of students vary greatly. Some students attend Catholic services; others attend Baptist churches or storefront Pentecostal churches; some belong to a New Age group that has organized in the community; and others have no religious affiliation. Some students are involved in religious activities during their nonschool time. The school reflects little of these diverse religious perspectives in the curriculum or school environment.

In Utah, the educator will find a school in a moderate-size community dominated by members of the Church of Jesus Christ of Latter-Day Saints (LDS, or Mormons). Many Mormon families serve their ward several nights every week and socialize almost exclusively with other Mormon families. LDS beliefs do not permit smoking or the drinking of alcohol, coffee, or tea. In that Utah community, this religious group controls most major institutions and businesses. Religion itself is not taught as part of the school curriculum, but the perspective of the dominant religious group in this community is reflected in school and curriculum practices. Many students leave during school hours to receive religious instruction at a Mormon seminary adjacent to the school. Many will leave home following high school or shortly after to serve on a church mission for two years. Most of the elected officials are members of the Mormon Church; therefore state and local laws affecting education reflect a Mormon influence.

People differ greatly in their beliefs about the role that religious perspective should play in determining school curriculum and environment. Like all other institutions in the United States, schools have a historical background of rural, white, Protestant domination. Such influence has determined the holidays, usually Christian holidays, that are celebrated by schools. Moreover, the Protestant majority has determined the moral teachings that have been integrated into the public schools.

Although the First Amendment affirms the principle of separation of church and state, it is one of the most controversial parts of the Constitution because various individuals and groups tend to interpret it to meet their own needs and interests. For some people, religious emphasis is appropriate in the public schools as long as it is congruent with their own religious persuasion. These same people, however, may be quick to cite the constitutional safeguards for separation of church and state if other groups attempt the infusion of their religious dogmas. Equity and propriety are often in the eye of the beholder, and one's religious orientation may strongly influence one's perception of what constitutes objectivity, fairness, and legality.

Since the removal of prayer from the schools by a 1963 Supreme Court decision, parent groups have continued to fight (sometimes successfully) to restore prayer in the schools through state and federal legislation. Parent groups have fought on religious grounds to prevent the teaching of sex education and evolution. Coming from different religious backgrounds, parents have fought verbally and physically over what books their children should read in literature courses and what curriculum should be used in social studies and science classes. Members of more liberal Protestant, Catholic, and Jewish denominations often argue that they want their children exposed to the perspectives of different religious and ethnic groups. Members of the more conservative, especially fundamentalist, groups argue that they do not want their children exposed to what they consider immoral perspectives and language inherent in such instructional materials.

Community resistance to cultural pluralism and multicultural education has, at times, been led by some individuals associated with conservative religious groups. Because cultural pluralism inevitably involves religious diversity, multicultural education is sometimes viewed as an impediment to efforts to maintain the status quo or to return to the religious values of the past.

Sometimes maligned as a bedfellow of the secular humanist movement, multicultural education is erroneously accused of supporting movements that detract from basic moral values. Multicultural education, however, provides a basis for understanding and appreciating diversity and minimizes the problems inherent in people being different from one another.

Of all the microcultures examined in this book, religion may be the most problematic for educators. In one school, the religious beliefs of students appear to have little influence on what is taught in a classroom; in fact, the teacher is expected to expose students to many different perspectives. In another school, the teacher may be attacked for asking students to read *The Catcher in the Rye.*

Educators themselves vary in their beliefs about the role of religious perspective in education. If one shares the same religion or religious perspectives as the community, there will probably be little conflict between one's own beliefs and the beliefs reflected in the school. If the educator is from a religious background that is different from that prevalent in the community or has a perspective about the role of religion that differs from that of the community, misunderstanding and conflicts may arise that prevent effective instruction. If an educator does not understand the role of religion in the lives of students, it may be difficult to develop appropriate instructional strategies. In some cases, it would be difficult to retain one's job.

In this chapter, we examine religion and its impact on a student's life, some of the religions existing in the United States, the degree to which individuals identify with a particular religious doctrine, and the educational implications of religion.

RELIGION AS A WAY OF LIFE

Although the separation of church and state is an integral part of our heritage, the two usually support each other. In many churches, the American flag stands next to the church flag, and patriotism is an important part of religious loyalty. God has been mentioned in all presidential inaugural addresses except Washington's second address, and it is not uncommon for politicians and preachers to refer to the United States as the "promised land." The secular ideas of the American dream also pervade many religions in this country. In fact, many religions reflect the dominant values of our society.

Many Western religions emphasize individual control over life—an emphasis that prompts believers to blame the disadvantaged for their disadvantage. Many religions are particularistic in that members believe that their own religion is uniquely true and legitimate and all others are false. Some religious groups accept the validity of various religions that have grown out of different historical experiences. The values and lifestyles of families are affected by their religious beliefs.

Nine out of ten Americans regard their religious beliefs as very, or at least fairly, important to them. Two out of three adults indicate that religion provides all or most of the answers to today's problems (Gallup & Lindsay, 1999). Although less than half of the population attends church weekly, most people identify with a religious perspective that is reflected in their daily living (Bezilla, 1993). Religion appears to influence patterns of sex roles, marriage, divorce, birthrates, child training, sexual activity, friendships, and political attitudes. It may affect one's dress, social activities, and dietary habits, including alcohol consumption and smoking.

If the religious group is tightly knit, a member may have little chance to interact on a personal level with anyone other than another member of the same religion, especially if attendance at a religious school is involved. Tight control over criteria for membership in the group and little contact with those who are not group members are often key factors in maintaining the integrity of religious sects. The Hutterites and, to a great extent, the Amish have been able to survive in this way. Mormons, a much larger group, were able to grow with little outside interference once they were established in Salt Lake City. Even in suburban areas, friendship patterns are largely based on religious preference.

Churches and their religious programs serve as a strong socialization mechanism in the transmission of values from one generation to another. Rituals, parables, and stories reinforce these values, and Sunday schools serve as primary agents for transmitting these values. Religious institutions are also responsible for reinterpreting social failure in spiritual terms, compensating for the lack of value realization, and functioning as an agent of social control by reward and punishment.

Children become aware of their religious identity as Protestant, Catholic, or Jew by 5 years of age, although they tend to equate religion with national and racial identities. By 9 years of age, they are able to distinguish between religion and irreligion, and they can identify denominations by their practices. As one might expect, children of religious parents are more likely to be religious than children of nonreligious parents (Greeley, 1982).

Among teens, 51% indicated they were Protestant, 26% Roman Catholic, 3% Mormon, 2% Jewish, 1% Orthodox, and 8% other. Nine percent indicated no affiliation or preference (Gallup, 1999). Forty-nine percent of teens indicated they attended religious services regularly. Church attendance by African American, Latino, and other nonwhite teens was slightly higher than that of their white counterparts (Gallup, 1999). Forty-six percent of older (16–17 yrs.) teens indicated that they prayed regularly as compared to their younger (13–15 yrs.) counterparts (39%) (Gallup, 1999).

Today's teens tend to be religiously tolerant, and 64% agree very much or somewhat that all religions are equally good. Eighty-seven percent approve of interfaith marriages. Ninety-two percent of teens believed that schools should be involved in the battle against bigotry and should teach about other races, ethnicities, and cultural beliefs. Eighty-five percent indicated the need for schools to teach about religious groups to help them become more accepting. Female teens (97%) were more supportive of tolerance instruction than males (88%) (Gallup, 1999).

In the United States, 40% of adults attend church or synagogue as regularly as did their counterparts in 1950 (39%). Although not equal to the all-time high of 49% in 1955 and 1958, attendance from 1967 to 1998 deviated a maximum of 3 percentage points throughout that period (Gallup & Lindsay, 1999). Religious attendance patterns are listed in Table 6–1.

Table 6–1
Average weekly attendance at worship services among U.S. adults.

Year	Attendance	Note
1998	40%	
1995	43%	
1990	40%	
1985	42%	
1980	40%	
1975	40%	
1970	42%	
1965	44%	
1960	47%	
1955	49% (a)	a. High point tied with 1958 with 49%
1950	39%	
1940	37% (b)	b. Low point

Gallup, G., Jr., and Lindsay, D. M. (1999). *Surveying the Religious Landscape*. Harrisburg, P.A.: Morehouse Publishing.

Weekly attendance at a place of worship is apparently a function of one's microculture. In 1998, more women (42%) attended weekly services than men (37%). Latinos (48%) and African Americans (55%) attended more regularly than whites (39%). Southerners (48%) had a 16% higher attendance rate than Westerners (32%). The elderly ages 65 to 74 (52%) and 75 plus (43%) attended more regularly than the young ages 18 to 29 (33%). Catholics (46%) attended more regularly than Protestants (42%) or Jews (27%) (Gallup and Lindsay, 1999).

Religious behavior is learned as a normal part of the socialization pattern. Religion and religious differences are important in our study of this pluralistic nation because it is a way of life for many people.

RELIGIOUS PLURALISM IN THE UNITED STATES

Four decades ago, few Americans would have envisioned their country led by a Catholic president or foreseen an African American minister being elected as the majority whip in the U.S. House of Representatives. In 1988, Pat Robertson, a popular televangelist, was a serious candidate for the Republican Party's presidential nomination and received strong support financially and otherwise. In recent years, Jesse Jackson, an African American minister, has twice made a strong and serious bid for the Democratic Party's presidential nomination.

Thousands of young people, many white, have been led by a Korean minister and leader of the Unification church. African Americans have left traditional African American Protestant churches and joined the ranks of the Black Muslims. Tens of thousands of Latinos have left the Roman Catholic Church for Pentecostal churches, and college students have embraced Zen Buddhism.

Today, televangelism reaches the homes of millions of Americans, influences their lives and their voting patterns, and has helped elect or defeat politicians that will change the face of America for years to come.

Americans tend to identify not only with major groups, such as Protestants, Catholics, or Jews, but also with smaller groups or denominations within these major religious microcultures. For example, former President Jimmy Carter, a Southern Baptist, identifies himself as a "born again" Christian. Others may identify themselves as charismatic Catholics. It is important to note that within each major group is considerable heterogeneity.

Of the U.S. population, 90% identify themselves as belonging to one of the major faiths—Protestant, Catholic, Jewish, Islam, Eastern Orthodox, or Latter Day Saints (see Table 6–2). Until early in the twentieth century, however, Protestantism was by far the dominant religious force in the country. Most U.S. institutions continue to bear the mark of the white Protestants who established them. After the great immigrations from Southern and Eastern Europe, Catholic Ireland, and Asia, however, pluralism described the religious diversity of the nation. Protestants as a group are still in the majority, with 59% of the population; 27% of the population identify themselves as Catholic (Gallup and Lindsay, 1999), 2% as Muslim (Corduan, 1998), 1% as Jewish, 1% as Latter Day Saints (Mormon), and 1% as Orthodox. Less than 1%

Table 6–2

Religious preference among Americans 1998.

	Protestant	Catholic	Orthodox	Mormon	Jewish	Muslim	Hindu	None
National	59%	27%	1%	1%	1%	*	*	6%
Male	56%	27%	2%	1%	1%	*	*	7%
Female	60%	27%	1%	1%	1%	*	*	4%
White	57%	29%	1%	1%	2%	*	*	5%
Non-White	70%	14%	2%	*	1%	1%	*	6%
Black	81%	9%	3%	*	1%	*	*	2%
Latino	33%	50%	3%	2%	—	*	*	5%
East	46%	40%	1%	1%	2%	*	*	6%
Midwest	57%	29%	1%	*	1%	*	*	5%
South	72%	17%	1%	1%	1%	*	*	4%
West	53%	24%	2%	2%	2%	*	*	9%
PostGrad	55%	24%	2%	*	4%	1%	*	8%
College	54%	29%	1%	*	2%	*	*	7%
No College	64%	24%	1%	1%	1%	*	*	4%
								* = Less than 1%

Gallup, G., Jr., and Lindsay, D. M. (1998). *Surveying the Religious Landscape.* Harrisburg, PA: Morehouse Publishing.
Source: 1998 Gallup Poll

claim Buddhist or Hindu affiliation. Six percent claim no religious affiliation (Gallup & Lindsay, 1999). While Islam, in recent years, has grown rapidly in the United States, and may by now have become the third largest religious group, much of the literature still lists Judaism as one of the three major religious groups. This is likely due to the fact that Judaism has been a driving force in the country for such a long period of U. S. history, and because Jewish individuals have provided so much leadership in the cultural, economic, and political landscape of the country.

The fact that most Americans place themselves in one of the major faiths (Catholic, Protestant, Jewish, or Muslim) is misleading in understanding the great diversity of religious beliefs in this country. The first three categories describe three historical religious groups that share the same Old Testament heritage, but they do not attest to the diversity of beliefs and interpretations of the Bible.

Some denominational differences have their origin in ethnic differences. The English established the Anglican (Episcopalian) and Puritan (later Congregational) churches here; the Germans established some of the Lutheran, Anabaptist, and Evangelical churches; the Dutch, the Reformed churches; the Spanish, French, Italians, Poles, and others, the Roman Catholic churches; and the Ukrainians, Armenians, Greeks, and others, the Eastern Orthodox churches. Over time, many of these separate ethnic denominations have united or expanded their membership to include other ethnic groups, although they may still be dominated by the original ethnic group (see Table 6–3). A different pattern has developed for African Americans, however, because they often were not included in the expansion of membership.

Table 6–3

Estimates of U.S. membership by religious group.

Religion	1997 Estimates	
Christian	241,147,000	
Judaism	3,137,000	(4,300,000)
Islam	3,332,000	(5,100,000)
Hindu	1,285,000	(910,000)
Buddhism	565,000	(780,000)
Chinese Folk Religionists	123,000	(124,000)
New Age	1,439,000	
American Indian Tribal Religionist	47,000	(47,000)
Sikhs	257,000	(490,000)
Shamanism	1,000	
Confucians	26,000	
Baha'i	370,000	(300,000)
Jains	4,000	(4,000)
Shinto	1,000	(1,000)
Others	491,000	

Lindner, E. W. (1998) *The 1998 Yearbook of American and Canadian Churches.* Nashville, TN: Abingdon Press.

Figures in parentheses ( ) are estimates from Corduan, W. (1998). *Neighboring Faiths.* Downers Grove, IL: InterVarsity Press.

Many of the religious groups in the United States are extremely diverse without single headquarters. The U. S. Census Bureau does not compile data on religious preference or membership. Therefore, precise and consistent reporting are estimates at best.

Most denominations have remained in their traditional regional strongholds, with Catholics in the Northeast, liberal and moderate Protestants in the Northeast and Midwest, and conservative Protestants in the South. Some groups, however, have expanded their base considerably. Episcopalians, Presbyterians, and members of the United Church of Christ are no longer as concentrated in the Northeast as they once were; some numerical base shifts have been made into the Sun Belt. Conservative Protestants, such as the Southern Baptists, are growing in all regions, including the Northeast and the West. Mormons have extended their influence far beyond the borders of Utah, Idaho, and Nevada. Their presence is felt in every state, as well as in many other countries. The Jewish population tends to be located in metropolitan areas throughout the country, with the largest concentration in the mid-Atlantic region (Bezilla, 1993).

Although religious pluralism has fostered the rapid accommodation of many American religious movements toward a mainstream of acceptability and respectability by society, groups such as Jehovah's Witnesses and Seventh-Day Adventists have maintained their independence. The smaller groups that maintain their distinctiveness have historically been victims of harassment by members of mainstream religious groups. Christian Scientists, Jehovah's Witnesses, Children of God, and the Unification Church are minority groups that have been subjected to such treatment. Conflict among the three major faiths has also been intense at different periods in history. Anti-Semitic, anti-Muslim, and anti-Catholic sentiments are still perpetuated in some households and institutions. Although religious pluralism in our past has often led to conflict, the hope of the future is that it will lead to a better understanding and respect for religious differences. In this section, we examine in greater detail the three major faiths and selected others that the educator may find in various communities.

PROTESTANTISM

Many sects that separated from the Catholic Church after the Reformation are now recognized as established Protestant denominations. The Western Europeans who immigrated into this country in large numbers brought with them their various forms of Protestantism. Still claiming 59% of the population (Gallup & Lindsay, 1999), Protestants in the United States are not quite as dominant as they once were.

Similarities among Diversity

As one visits various Protestant services and listens to the different doctrines espoused by members, one may wonder how such a diverse conglomeration can be classified into one faith. No one doctrine or one church is representative of Protestantism. Traditionally, Protestantism has stressed individualism, activism, and pragmatism for its members. Other similarities have little to do with religious doctrine but are based instead on a shared American experience and its accompanying values.

To understand the differences that exist in Protestantism and that are often reflected in the classroom, the faith can be divided into two broad categories—liberal and conservative. Liberal Protestants attempt to rethink Christianity in forms that are meaningful for a world dominated by science and rapid change. They stress the right of individuals to determine for themselves what is true in religion. They believe in the authority of Christian experience and religious life, rather than in dogmatic church pronouncements of the Bible. They are likely to support and participate in social action programs because of their belief that what individuals become depends greatly on an environment over which they have little control. The mainline, traditional denominations are included in this group. The United Church of Christ and Episcopalian churches are examples, although the degree of liberalism depends on the individual congregation. Methodists and Disciples of Christ represent more moderate denominations within this category.

Conservative Protestants generally believe that the Bible is inerrant, that the supernatural is distinct from the natural, that salvation is essential, and that Jesus will return in bodily form during the Second Coming. They emphasize personal morality, rather than social ethics. The conservative branch can be divided further into the Fundamentalists, who are literalistic and inflexible, and the Evangelicals, who are less so. Billy Graham's ministry, for example, would fit more appropriately into the second category.

Conservative churches include the Church of Christ, Southern Baptist, Assembly of God, other Pentecostal groups, and Church of the Nazarene. Some sects of the more liberal denominations have reacted to liberalism and established themselves as conservative groups, such as Wesleyan Methodist and Orthodox Presbyterian (Roof & McKinney, 1985).

Although the Fundamentalist groups strictly and literally interpret the Bible, the different groups do not necessarily interpret it or practice their faith in the same way. The various sects and denominations are unrelenting in their belief that they are the one true church. Some groups, such as the Pentecostals, charismatic Catholics, and charismatic Episcopalians believe that their lives have been dramatically changed by infusion of the Holy Spirit in a spiritual baptism that results in the individual being able to speak in other tongues.

Some Fundamentalist groups, such as the Mormons and Jehovah's Witnesses, do not classify themselves as Protestants, although they are classified as such by some nonmembers. These two groups and the Seventh-Day Adventists stand out from many other groups because the practice of their religion thoroughly pervades their way of life. Members of these groups proselytize as a part of their commitment to their beliefs. Jehovah's Witnesses distribute the publication *Watchtower* widely in communities, and Mormon missionaries often work door-to-door. Members are unrelenting in their beliefs and in their commitment to prepare themselves for future fulfillment in the establishment of a latter-day sainthood and a life in heaven (Mormons), in life after the Armageddon (Jehovah's Witnesses), or in the millennium after Christ's Second Coming (Adventists).

Differences in beliefs among Protestants themselves have resulted in many court cases to determine what can or cannot be taught to or asked of students in the public schools. Fundamentalism versus liberalism came to the forefront in the 1925 Scopes trial, in which a biology teacher was convicted for teaching Darwin's theory of evolution. Although the teacher's conviction was later reversed, the argument continues today as Fundamentalists push for state legislation instituting the teaching of creationism. Jehovah's Witnesses have been taken to court because their children have refused to salute the flag. The Amish have fought in courts to remove their children from public schools after they have completed the eighth grade. Some religious groups continue to fight against the 1963 Supreme Court decision that disallowed prayer in school.

Political Influence

The political leadership in the country often reflects the influence of various religious groups. Table 6–4 shows the trends in the U. S. Senate, while Table 6–5 shows the religious representation in the U.S. House of Representatives by denomination. In 1999, as in the past, Protestants led in Congress with 47.96%, as compared to the 59% of the general population which indicated they were Protestants that year. Roman Catholics followed with 28.14%, which is slightly higher than the Gallup findings of 27% for the general population. Jewish congressional members made up 5.74% of congressional seats, which is considerably higher than their percentage of

Table 6–4

1999 religious affiliation of members of the U.S. Senate in 1999 (100 members).

	Democrats	Republicans
Catholic	14	11
Jewish	9	1
Protestant		2
Presbyterian	1	6
Baptist	1	8
Methodist	5	7
Episcopalian	4	8
Lutheran	3	2
Mormon	1	4
Christian		1
Muslim		
Buddhist		
Other	6	3
None	1	2

Source: Data extracted from Birkholz, E. L. (2000, Winter). *Congressional Yellow Book: Who's Who in Congress, 25*(4). New York: Leadership Directories, Inc.

Table 6–5

Religious affiliation of members of the U.S. House of Representatives in 1999 (440 members).

	Democrats	Republicans
Catholic	79	48
Jewish	21	1
Protestant	8	17
Presbyterian	14	26
Baptist	33	25
Methodist	16	36
Episcopalian	10	20
Lutheran	9	8
Mormon	2	11
Christian	6	16
Muslim		
Buddhist		
Other	7	10
None	12	5

Source: Data extracted from Birkholz, E. L. (2000, Winter). *Congressional Yellow Book: Who's Who in Congress, 25*(4). New York: Leadership Directories, Inc.

the general population. Those with no affiliation held 3.7% of the seats. Mormon presence in Congress was 2.59% (Birkholz, 2000).

Members of more liberal churches (e.g., Episcopalians, Presbyterians) and Jews may be disproportionately overrepresented because, historically, they have felt a responsibility for public issues. Another factor is probably related to the social class of members of these various denominations. Because running for and holding political office can be quite costly, religious groups whose members are typically upper middle class are overrepresented in political offices. For example, a survey by the Princeton Religion Research Center (1995) revealed that the income and education level of Presbyterians (who have high political representation) was significantly higher than that of Baptists, Methodists, and Lutherans.

Protestantism maintains not only the major religious influence on society but also on political leadership. Because Protestants continue to represent the majority of the population, such influence is to be expected. Pluralism increasingly forces the sharing of power and resources, however, among diverse groups of people in society.

CATHOLICISM

Although the doctrine and pattern of worship within the Catholic Church are uniform, individual parishes continue to differ to some extent according to the race, ethnic background, and social class of their members. Individual dioceses also may differ with the more conservative or liberal (progressive) views of the presiding bishop. Unlike the Protestant faith, however, which includes denominational pluralism, the Catholic faith is one denomination under papal authority.

In 1930, the United States had 20 million Roman Catholics. With approximately 27% of the U.S. population identifying with the Roman Catholic Church (Gallup & Lindsay, 1999), one could estimate the number of Catholics to be around 74 million at the beginning of the new millennium.

Today, the Catholic Church in the United States is the wealthiest national church in the Roman Catholic world and contributes approximately half of its income to the Church in Rome. The increasing number of American cardinals and American priests appointed to important posts in Rome attests to the growing importance of the Catholic Church in the U.S. (Hudson & Corrigan, 1992).

In addition to its phenomenal numerical growth, the Roman Catholic Church in the United States has developed the largest private educational system in the world. With thousands of elementary and secondary schools from Vermont to Hawaii and such internationally recognized universities as Notre Dame, Roman Catholic schools and universities have educated millions of Americans and greatly influenced the culture of the country.

The movement toward conservatism has not been limited to Protestants. Some Catholics have objected to changes in liturgy and other areas of modernization instituted by Vatican II. In many instances, conservative Catholics have joined forces with conservative Protestants on such issues as abortion and sexual morality. Some Catholics have even abandoned their traditional support of the Democratic Party to support conservative Republican candidates such as Ronald Reagan, George Bush, and Robert Dole. On the other end of the continuum, some Catholics have protested the conservative position of their church regarding the limited participation of women in leadership roles and some support the pro-choice movement. In the 1960s, Roman Catholics, including some priests, engaged in political activism and joined radical elements in opposing the Vietnam War.

By becoming a uniquely American church, members of the Catholic Church have not rejected the belief that they belong to the one universal church. Instead, they have accepted the fact that U.S. society is intrinsically pluralistic and that their religion is one of the three major faiths that exists side by side with Protestantism and Judaism.

JUDAISM

Judaism is one of the oldest religions known to humanity and provides the historical roots of both Catholicism and Protestantism. Primarily as a result of Jews from many countries amalgamating under the identification of Jewish American, Judaism has become one of the major faiths in this country. While Judaism represents only about 2% of the population, the contributions of Jewish Americans to the fields of medicine, science, academia, business, economics, entertainment, and politics in the United States has been profound.

In the nineteenth century, large numbers of Jews emigrated from Germany and many began moving from Jewish enclaves along the east coast to other parts of the country. By the 1920s, Eastern Europeans were immigrating in larger numbers, increasing the Jewish population to more than 2.5 million.

Later generations changed the entire picture of American Jewry and Judaism in America; ethnic and an American religious identity emerged. The lifestyle evolved into a microculture of the American middle class. Education, including higher education, played an important role in the Jewish community by advancing young people from the working class into white-collar and professional positions. Religious practices and patterns were modified in ways that made them characteristically American. While some Jewish families have maintained their ties to Orthodox and Conservative Judaism, the majority of American Jews affiliated with Reformed Synagogues.

Compared with the Protestant and Catholic populations, the Jewish population has declined, partly as a result of intermarriage and low birthrates. Yet, as a group, they remain a distinctive, identifiable religious minority whose social standing and influence are disproportionate to their numbers.

Jews in the United States and throughout the world have been the targets of prejudice and discrimination, sometimes leading to attempted annihilation of the population. During World War II, the Jewish Holocaust, which resulted in the brutal deaths of millions of European Jews, was systematically conducted by one of the most economically and technically advanced nations of the period. The civilized world cannot ignore the fact that despite overwhelming evidence of what was being done by the Nazis, nothing was done to stop one of the greatest atrocities ever committed against humankind. As the twenty-first century begins, other attempts at genocide persist. It is the responsibility of educators to help their students understand that, even today, other holocausts have taken place in places such as Europe and Africa.

Anti-Semitism is rooted in Jewish-Gentile conflicts that have existed for centuries. In the United States, Jews and Catholics were also targets of the Ku Klux

A thirteen-year-old Jewish female observes her Bat Mitzvah by reading from the Torah in Hebrew. The event marks her entry into religious adulthood. In a Los Angeles area church a fifteen-year-old Mexican American female observes mass in celebrating her entry into womanhood.

Klan in the 1920s (Williams, 1990). Discrimination has occurred in both occupational and social life. Jews have often been denied high-level corporate management positions and have been barred from membership in social clubs. The form and degree of anti-Semitism vary with world and national events; when non-Jews believe that events are the result of Jewish action, prejudices resurface in work and deed. Events in the Middle East that involve Israel often initiate these reactions. In the late 1990s anti-Semitic hate crimes persisted with the burning of synagogues and the 1999 attack on a Jewish day care center in Los Angeles.

Although most Jews strongly identify with their religion, the Jewish practice of religion is relatively low regarding synagogue attendance and home religious observance. Nevertheless, the U.S. synagogue is the strongest agency in the Jewish community. Although they may not attend services as regularly as their Catholic and Protestant counterparts, a large percentage of Jews retain some affiliation with a synagogue. Some believe that Jewish identity does not require regular attendance at the synagogue. Attending religious services and studying Jewish texts hold little interest for much of the Jewish population. Attendance on High Holidays such as Rosh Hashanah, Yom Kippur, and Passover, however, is always high. The synagogue in the United States serves not only as a place of religious worship but also as a primary base for Jewish identity and survival.

ISLAM

Islam is one of the major religions of the world, with a billion or more adherents worldwide. As a religious term, *Islam* means to surrender to the will or law of God. Those who practice Islam are Muslims. Islam is both a belief system and a way of life for individuals and entire societies. Islam is based on the holy writings or the Qur'an (or Koran), which are based on the revelations of the prophet Muhammad (A.D. 570–632). Believers are of two major groups. Sunni Muslims, the largest group, believe that the rightful leadership began with Abu Bakr and that the succession has passed to *caliphs*, or military and political leaders. Shi'i or Shi'ite Muslims are a smaller but highly visible group. Shi'ite Muslims believe that Muhammad intended the succession of leadership to pass through the bloodline of his cousin and son-in-law, 'Ali. Shi'ite Muslims have attracted considerable world attention in recent years because of their insistence of adherence to Islamic law by their country's government (Oxtoby, 1996; Robinson, 1996; Williams, 1990).

A radical group of Shi'ite Muslims, followers of the Ayatollah Kohmeni, overthrew Shah Reza Pahlavi of Iran and later gained international attention by seizing

Educators will continue to see increasing numbers of religious minority group students in their classrooms reflecting the religious diversity of the United States.

American hostages. Many of the religious/political Shi'ite leaders view Western culture as antithetical to Islam and have strongly resisted U.S. and other Western influences on their countries. This has often led to fierce political battles between the two groups and has occasionally resulted in acts of terrorism against Western countries (Williams, 1990). This terrorism has sometimes led to the unfortunate negative reaction of groups of Americans to broad groups of individuals with Arab backgrounds, when in reality the extreme behaviors are that of a very small group of individuals.

Islam now has more than 5 million followers in the United States (Corduan, 1998). Many Muslims in this country are immigrants who have brought their religion with them. Some native-born Americans have either converted to Islam or have been born into the faith. One small but highly visible group is the Black Muslims who may represent as many as 40% of the Muslims in the United States (Kosmin & Lachman, 1993).

Black Muslims

Although a few black slaves may have been Muslims, the origins of the Black Muslims in the United States likely began with Timothy Drew (1886–1927), who taught that blacks were Asiatics and therefore Moors or Muslims. His teachings bore only loose similarities to traditional Islam and accepted the spiritual authority of Confucius, Buddha, and Jesus, who he taught was black (Williams, 1990).

In the early 1930s, W. D. Fard established a temple in Detroit with teachings, activities, and institutions linked to Islam and an antiwhite sentiment. Leadership of the Detroit temple was assumed in 1934 by Elijah Poole (1875–1975) who became known as Elijah Muhammad, leading the Nation of Islam into national visibility. In the early 1960s, Malcolm X (1925–1965) became the most articulate spokesperson for the Nation of Islam. Born Malcolm Little, he renounced his "slave" name *Little* and adopted *X*, which symbolized identity lost when his ancestors were forcibly taken from their homeland as slaves (Lincoln, 1994).

Malcolm X and other Black Muslims sought to use the Nation of Islam to engage African Americans in economic nationalism and to instill in them a sense of pride and achievement. This was accomplished through the rejection of white America and the encouragement of black entrepreneurism within the African American community. Adherents are very disciplined, participating in daily prayers and abstaining from alcohol (Kosmin & Lachman, 1993).

In 1964, following a rift with Elijah Muhammad, Malcolm X broke with the Nation of Islam and formed the Organization of Afro-American Unity (OAAU). In that same year, he made a pilgrimage to Mecca and embraced traditional Sunni Islam, which he believed offered a superior religious path based on inclusiveness, rather than divisiveness and antagonism (Lincoln, 1994). In 1965, Malcolm X was assassinated.

Wallace Deen Muhammad became the leader of the Nation of Islam after the death of his father, Elijah Muhammad, in 1975. Under his leadership, the Nation of

Islam embraced traditional Sunni Islam and changed its name to the American Muslim Mission. "During the 1970s and 1980s, W. D. Muhammad, as he is known, slowly dispensed with the racist rhetoric of his sect's past and led his followers toward orthodox Koranic Islam" (Kosmin & Lachman, 1993, p. 136). As a result, the group often supports conservative causes such as the free market. Hard work, personal responsibility, and family values are expected of members (Kosmin & Lachman, 1993).

The well-known leader of Black Muslims, Louis Farrakhan, led a splinter movement in the 1980s that resumed the use of the original name, Nation of Islam, and the black separatist position. He continues to receive considerable attention from the press and political leaders because of his appeal to many African Americans who are not Muslims. This influence was demonstrated in his ability to mobilize an interfaith coalition that drew nearly 1 million African American men together for the One Million Man March in Washington, DC, in 1996. Members have become role models in many inner cities as they establish businesses. They often serve as visible neighborhood protectors against crime (Kosmin & Lachman, 1993; Corduan, 1998).

BUDDHISM

Buddhism is one of the world's major religions with an estimated 323,894,000 members worldwide and 780,000 in the United States. The immigration of Asians each year from countries such as Sri Lanka, China, Taiwan, Korea, Thailand, Japan, and Tibet brings in thousands of additional Buddhists, changing the religious landscape of the country forever. With the Buddhists coming from so many regions of the world, there are invariably different forms of Buddhism practiced. Consequently there is tremendous diversity in both belief and in practice, just as there is diversity among the various Christian faiths. Buddhists are united in a twofold orientation toward existence. There is a fundamental negative attitude toward life. Corduan (1998) suggests that there is a pessimistic approach to ordinary existence by all the Buddhist schools. Buddhists view existence itself as the problem with life. As long as there is existence, there is suffering. The second common orientation of all Buddhists is that Buddha provides a solution to the frustrations of life. Each school of Buddhism provides a pathway to overcome the meaninglessness of life. Buddha is the solution to life's dilemma.

Buddha was believed to be a prince of India, Siddhartha Gautama. Born to a life of privilege, early prophecies by a sage and court astrologers predicted that Siddhartha would either be a great king or a great religious leader. On an outing, Siddhartha saw successively an old man on the verge of death, a diseased man, a funeral procession, and a holy monk. This experience led him to see his life of luxury leading him to an end of death and decay. With this, he left his wife and child, cut his hair, and sought spiritual enlightenment through austerity (Corduan, 1998).

After 7 years as an ascetic, he decided to let his experience end in enlightenment or death. In spite of temptations by Mara, the god of desire, Siddhartha prevailed and finally found enlightenment as he sat under a fig tree known now as the

The Fo Kuang Shan Hsi Lai Temple opened in Hacienda Heights, California, in 1988. This Los Angeles county temple is the largest Buddhist temple in the Western Hemisphere.

"bodhi tree." He had now become a Buddha, an "awakened one." Buddha then set forth on a life of teaching (Corduan, 1998).

Buddha's secret to enlightenment was neither through a life of luxury nor through self-deprivation, but through the middle way, away from the extremes. The key to salvation, he taught, was to let go of everything. Salvation and enlightenment occurs when one realizes his or her place of non-self in the world. Nonexistence is the reality and self-extinction is the reality. With enlightenment comes the state of nirvana, meaning "blown out" (Corduan, 1998).

Buddha taught four noble truths:

- To live is to suffer
- Suffering is caused by desire
- One can eliminate suffering by eliminating desire
- Desire is eliminated by an eightfold path

The eightfold path to eliminating desire consists of the following:

1. The right view (understanding the truths of existence)
2. The right intention (willing to achieve enlightenment)
3. The right speech
4. The right action
5. The right livelihood (being a monk)
6. The right effort
7. The right mindfulness (meditating properly)
8. The right concentration (Corduan, 1998)

To know that your student is from a Buddhist family may or may not tell you much about the family belief structure or religious practices. While one might expect belief in the four noble truths and practice of the eightfold path from a Buddhist priest or monk, the layperson may take bits and pieces of the religion into his or her everyday life. As previously indicated there are varying forms of Buddhism, so there is likely to be considerable differences between a Buddhist layperson from Taiwan and one from Tibet.

Other Denominations and Religious Groups

In addition to the major faiths in the United States, what other religions might an educator encounter in a community? They include Christian religions that do not fall into the discrete categories of Protestantism or Catholicism, Islam, Eastern religions, and religions based on current psychological thinking.

One Christian religion that does not fall into the two major groupings is the Eastern Orthodox Church. With 4 million members in the United States, Eastern Orthodoxy probably claims about one fourth of all Christians worldwide. One reason that the Eastern Orthodox Church is less well known in this country may be that its members, from Syria, Greece, Armenia, Russia, and the Ukraine, only immigrated during the last century. Although they split with the Roman Catholic Church in 1054 over theological, practical, jurisdictional, cultural, and political differences, to many outsiders they appear very similar to the pre-Vatican II Catholic church.

At least two other religions have a Christian heritage but seem to fall through the cracks of discrete categorization because of their precepts. The Christian Scientists are one of these groups, with probably fewer than a half million members. Like some Fundamentalist Protestant groups and others described in this section, their beliefs are so different from conventional religious beliefs that they attract public attention. They exist "to dispel illusion and bring people into harmony with mind, with God as All—away from what others call disease, sin, evil, matter, and death" (Marty, 1975, p. 205). Although they do not proselytize, they maintain reading rooms in business and shopping centers of many communities. Their newspaper, *Christian Science Monitor,* is a highly respected general newspaper (Hudson & Corrigan, 1992).

The second group that defies categorization is the Unitarian Universalists—a church that connotes liberalism to most people. Their membership has included several U.S. presidents (William Howard Taft, Thomas Jefferson, John Adams, and John Quincy Adams) and several New England writers (Henry Wadsworth Longfellow, James Russell Lowell, and William Cullen Bryant), helping make the church an influence beyond that expected of a relatively small group. Unitarians are often found in suburbs, small towns, and college communities; many members could be described as political liberals. Although many members have the highest respect for Jesus Christ, the church is "most open to the wisdom of non-Christian religions and may draw many of its readings from scriptures of Buddhism, Hinduism and religious philosophies" (Marty, 1975, p. 217). As an expression of this openness, Unitarianism houses both Christian and non-Christian wings. The denomination follows no imposing standards of dogma or membership. Thus, their worship services appear extremely simple and are often experimental (Hudson & Corrigan, 1992; Marty, 1975).

American Indian religions are among the most difficult to describe or characterize, as there are 314 federally recognized tribes or groups and each is likely to have its own distinctive views on religion. Corduan (1998) estimates that there are only about 47,000 practitioners of Native American religion. Many of these individuals are likely to live on reservations and some of the children attend Bureau of Indian Affairs schools. There are a few general characteristics that are universal or tend to transcend across tribal boundaries. Traditional Native American religions recognize three levels of spiritual beings—a supreme god, nature spirits, and ancestor spirits. Superior spirits with god-like characteristics also factor into the religious equation. Tribes differ in their emphasis of the different spirits. *Wakan* or orenda apply to the spiritual power found in all entities. They are found in grass, rocks, animals, and spiritual beings. Each plant, rock, or even body of water may be sacred. Some may even inform a deer of its impending fate before killing it in a hunt in order to maintain harmony with the natural world (Corduan, 1998).

Shamans are men and women who heal through their contact with spirits. Individuals become shamans through supernatural calling. Frequently this happens when one vows to become a shaman if they are healed from an illness (Corduan, 1998).

Among some tribes, much importance is placed on receiving and implementing visions. Visions are attained in different ways. Sometimes they may come after a tranquil moment or after great stress. Fasting, self-imposed exposure to climatic extremes, or injury may induce a vision. Individuals from some tribes may experience a vision where an animal enters the body. A person or a group of individuals may come to an individual in order to deliver a message. The recipient of a vision can anticipate success because of it (Corduan, 1998).

Jainism evolved out of India in the sixth century B.C.E. Vardhamana Jnatiputra (a.k.a. Nataputta Mahariva) was the founder of this religion and a contemporary of Buddha. Both Jainism and Buddhism grew out of Hindu traditions. Jains reject karma and rebirth, observing the "three jewels" of right faith, right knowledge, and right conduct. They emphasize peacefulness and moderation, and refuse to injure animals. Their philosophy of nonviolence had a profound influence on Gandhi. There are an estimated 4,000 Jains in North America (Corduan, 1998).

Sikhism was founded by Guru Nanak during the fifteenth or sixteenth century B.C.E. in India. Nanak, who lived in India, was influenced by Kahir, a Muslim. He drew from the elements of Hinduism and Islam, and stressed a universal single God. Union with God, he said, is accomplished through meditation and surrender to divine will. He believed in reincarnation, karma, and the destruction and rebuilding of the universe, but he rejected the Hindu belief in the caste system. Devoted to divine incarnations, priesthood, and idol worship, Nanak was the first of ten gurus or teachers. Male Sikhs are initiated into a religious brotherhood called the Khalsa, vowing to never cut their hair or beard, to wear special pants, an iron bangle, a steel dagger, and a comb. There are an estimated 490,000 Sikhs in North America (Corduan, 1998).

Baha'ism was founded in Persia (Iran) in the late nineteenth century by Mirzu Hussein Ali Nuri (aka Baha'ullah, glory to God in Arabic). Baha'ullah claimed to be the divine manifestation of God and the last of a line of divine figures including Zoroaster, Buddha, Christ, and Muhammad. His son Abd al-Baha spread his father's teaching to the West emphasizing the principles of equality of sexes, races, and religious adherence. Bahai believers advocate for peace, justice, racial unity, economic development, and education. There are an estimated 300,000 members in the United States (Corduan, 1998).

The **New Age** movement began around the early 1980s. New Age has roots in nineteenth-century spiritualism and in the counterculture movement of the 1960s, rejecting materialism and favoring spiritual experience to organized religion. The movement emphasizes, among many of it followers, reincarnation, biofeedback, shamanism, the occult, psychic healing, and extraterrestrial life. It is a movement that is difficult to define as evidenced by the multitude of the movement's publications on a wide range of topics, viewpoints, and paraphernalia, from crystals to tarot. Much of the emphasis of the various groups is on the paranormal or parapsychology. It involves such experiences as meditation, visualization, dream interpretation, self-improvement, extrasensory perception, telepathy, clairvoyance, divination, precognition, out-of-body experiences, channeling spirit guides, angels, regression analysis of past lives, and so forth. It has influences from Eastern religions such as Buddhism, Sufism, Taoism, and Hinduism (Chryssides, 1999).

The term *New Age* refers to the 2000 zodiacal period Age of Aquarius. Since the Age of Aquarius is the successor to the Age of Pisces represented by the 2,000-year period of Christianity, some New Agers believe Christianity to be a thing of the past.

New Agers tend to reject highly structured institutionalized religion, such as the organized Christian religious authority of the Roman Catholic Church. There is no formal institutional structure for the New Age movement, nor is there any agreed upon creed. There is no authoritative hierarchy, and it is unclear precisely what the New Age groups are and what they are not. They are treated with suspicion by some evangelical Christians who see them as a threat to Christianity with the claim of being post-Christian (Chryssides, 1999).

Some New Agers place a lot of emphasis on healing, which often takes unconventional routes such as homeopathic and herbal remedies. Spiritual healing is often emphasized and the practice of *Reiki*, which is a ritualistic laying on of hands with a Japanese origin, is widely practiced by some groups (Chryssides, 1999).

Cults and Other Groups

Young people in many communities practice religions based on an Eastern religious tradition. This grouping includes the Hare Krishna, the Divine Light Mission, and the Unification Church. Members of some of these groups are very visible to the public. The Hare Krishna can sometimes be seen dancing with tambourines on sidewalks in larger cities.

These various religions are practiced by a small minority of the population, but their presence in a community is often exaggerated beyond that warranted by their numbers. This notoriety often stems from the fact that their doctrine and practices are viewed as heretical by members of the major faiths, yet orthodox by the believers. In addition, members of the majority faiths, especially parents, fear the attraction of some of these groups, some of which are considered cults, because they allegedly practice some degree of mind control.

The term *cult* will generally evoke negative reactions that may range from fear, to contempt, to disgust on the part of many individuals. The term may kindle thoughts of brainwashing or that which is most feared by families, suicide. During the past 20 or so years, there have been a number of highly publicized mass suicides among the so-called "Suicide Cults." Among those most publicized involving Americans were the People's Temple, the Branch Davidians, and the Heaven's Gate groups.

Jim Jones was the charismatic leader of the **People's Temple** based in California. Moving the majority of his membership to his complex in Jonestown, Guyana, Jones led 919 individuals to mass suicide through poisoning in 1978. However, some believe that many of the victims were murdered (Chryssides, 1999).

The **Branch Davidians** and their leader, David Koresh, evolved from fundamentalist Seventh Day Adventist roots. Koresh and his Davidians settled in Waco, Texas, where he taught that all of the Davidian women belonged to him and only he was permitted to have children. Authorities were alerted to allegations of child abuse and statutory rape, as well as the storage of illegal weapons. In 1993, four Federal agents were killed while attempting to serve a search warrant and, after days in a standoff, 93 Davidians including children died in a fire. The cause of the fire is still debated to this day. The federal government stands firm in their claim that Koresh and his followers started the fire, while others believe that the government agents were responsible (Chryssides, 1999).

In spring 1997, 39 bodies of **Heaven's Gate** members were found in a suburb of San Diego, California, resulting from mass suicide. Led by Marshall Applewhite in a blend of Christianity and UFOlogy, members were taught that a spacecraft trailed the Hale-Bopp Comet. This spacecraft would take Heaven's Gate members beyond the human level, on to the next evolutionary level. However, they had to leave their earthly bodies behind, requiring their suicide (Chryssides, 1999).

The three suicide groups contained some components of Christianity. While these groups had substantial differences, there are two common elements that are found in all of the groups. All were isolated from the rest of the community, operating on their own, remote, and separated from others. All of these groups tended to believe in the impending end of the world or humanity. The belief structure of groups of this nature tends to tie the cataclysmic end of the world to the end of the millennium (Corduan, 1998).

RELIGION AND GENDER

In many of the more conservative religious bodies, the role of women is clearly defined and limited. There are no female priests in the Roman Catholic Church, no women can attain the priesthood in the Mormon Church, and very few fundamentalist churches or denominations have or are willing to ordain women ministers. The same can be said about many other religious groups. At the 2000 annual convention of the Southern Baptist Convention, the 16,000 delegates voted on an explicit ban on women pastors. This action follows an earlier action by the Baptists to support the submission of women to their husbands.

Although Gomes (1996) indicates that Lydia, Phoebe, and Priscilla were women mentioned in the New Testament as having prominent roles in the formative days of early Christianity, other biblical passages are used to delimit the participation of women in leadership roles in religious activity. In supporting the ban or limitations of female leadership and wifely submission, these groups cite the fact that Jesus did not call on women to serve as his disciples. Biblical verses (e.g., I Corinthians 14:34–35) admonish women to submit themselves to their husbands and indicate that the husband is the head of the wife. Van Leeuwen (1990) suggests that some biblical interpreters believe that God gave men, through Adam (Genesis 1:26–27), dominion over Eve and, therefore, over women. At the same time, some biblical scholars argue that such an interpretation is incorrect and that both Adam and Eve (man and woman) were given dominion over every other living thing. Groothuis (1997) indicates that in addition to the examples provided by Gomes (1996), there are numerous other Biblical examples of women who were leaders or prophets (e.g., Deborah, Judges 4–5). Groothuis indicates that Deborah was a prime example of a woman called to lead by God and questions how her female leadership could be considered a violation of moral principles if ordained by God. Traditionalists counter that Deborah was an extreme exception to the long-standing precedent of male authority. Other traditionalists counter that Deborah's position of leadership was less authoritative than that of male prophets. Limitations on participation of females in religious activities are by no means the sole province of Judeo-Christian groups. Islam and other religions either limit the participation of females or typically rest leadership in the hands of men.

Not only is religion used to define the parameters of religious participation of males and females, but religion may also be used to prescribe male and female roles outside the religious context. Such prescriptions may be done either directly or indirectly. In religious groups in which women are given a less prominent status, this may carry over into general family life and other aspects of society as a natural course. In other instances, the pronouncements may be more direct. Religious writings with great importance, such as the Bible, are continuously interpreted, studied, and analyzed. In the United States, the Bible (or at least the Old Testament) is viewed as very sacred by most of its citizens who claim church membership. Consequently, the Bible and other religious writings, such as the Koran, have a profound influence on many Americans.

RELIGION AND HOMOSEXUALITY

Homosexuality is one of the most controversial issues in religious institutions today. Attacks on homosexuality in the religious context are often justified through biblical interpretation or other religious writings. Some argue that the textual interpretation and, in some cases, translation of biblical passages regarding homosexuality are not clear and may be subject to misinterpretation and misguided beliefs. Others argue that the Bible is clear on the issue of homosexuality, as in the book of Genesis where God destroyed Sodom and Gomorrah because of the sinful behaviors, including homosexuality, of the inhabitants. The debate is serious, as are the consequences. Conservative Christians and other conservative religious groups tend to view homosexuality as a matter of choice, a sin, and an abomination. More liberal religious groups tend to believe that the only choice is in whether or not the individual engages is homosexual behavior. They contend that the individual is born homosexual or predisposed to that life.

Because some conservative Christians, as well as members of other religious bodies, view homosexuality as a sin, they believe the AIDS epidemic is God's retribution for the gay life. Other Christian groups have willingly accepted gays and lesbians into their congregations, and some have even been ordained into leadership positions. Some conservative religious groups have developed websites that attack homosexuality.

It is important to understand that ministers, priests, and other church and religious authorities have considerable influence on the people they lead. They, the writers and theologians who influence others, often get their inspiration or their justification for their positions through religious scriptures. These writings are then interpreted for lay persons and may be used to shape their perceptions of self and others. Children growing up in a religious environment may learn to condemn or to practice tolerance. They may learn that homosexuality is an abomination, or they may learn that homosexuality is an innate and natural sexual orientation for some. Hopefully they will learn to respect all individuals as valued members of society.

RELIGION AND RACE

As with gender issues, religion has had a profound impact on race and ethnic diversity issues. Gomes (1996) notes that Christians seek to establish the kingdom of God on the earth. In doing so, they seek guidance from the Bible on how to conduct themselves in society. When individuals misinterpret biblical scriptures or interpret them to justify aberrant behavior, the consequences can be severe. Gomes points out that at their 1995 meeting the Southern Baptist Convention, the country's largest Protestant denomination, in an unprecedented act of contrition, apologized for the role it had played in the justification of slavery and in the maintenance of a culture of racism in the United States.

Historically, Southern Baptists and many other religious groups had found justification for the practice of slavery in the Bible. The Bible does not condemn slavery, and its practice can be found throughout both the Old and New Testaments. Therefore, proponents of slavery believed that this institution was built on a solid biblical foundation.

Gomes suggests that the Catholic king of Spain and his ministers viewed it as their divine right and obligation to enslave and Christianize or slaughter the natives of Latin America. Both Cortés and Pizarro operated under papal and governmental authority as they enslaved and killed thousands of natives and justified their behavior by biblical texts.

Anti-Semitism can also find many of its historical roots in the Bible and other religious works. Gomes suggests that Bach's *Passion of St. John*, though musically beautiful and inspiring, is filled with strong anti-Semitic German lyrics. Biblical passages are often used to justify anti-Semitic behaviors (e.g., Matthew 27:25–26, Romans 3:1). It is ironic that those who justify their anti-Semitic behaviors through religious doctrines and sacred writings may have failed to recognize that Jesus and his earliest followers were themselves Jews.

The modern civil rights movement was centered in Southern African American churches. Many of the civil rights leaders were or are ministers or church leaders—Martin Luther King, Jr., Ralph Abernathy, Andrew Young, and Jesse Jackson, to name a few. From their pulpits, these religious leaders were able to direct boycotts and organize civil disobedience and nonviolent confrontations.

In earlier times, spirituals provided comfort, hope, or a promise of a better life after death. Today, many of these spirituals are still sung in the churches, but the people who sing them and the people who listen to them seek a more immediate response to the demands for equity. Clearly, African American churches deserve much credit for bringing about many of the civil rights gained in the last 3 or 4 decades. Alienated and disillusioned by mainstream politics, few African Americans registered to vote in the past. Recent data suggest that well over 90% of African American clergy nationwide advocate church involvement in social and political issues. In recent years, black churches have been extremely successful in registering well over a million voters and in becoming an important voice in the electoral process (Lincoln & Mamiya, 1990).

In some religious groups, African Americans were permitted membership but prohibited from attaining the higher positions of church leadership. These prohibitions were justified through biblical interpretations or through divine revelations received by church leaders. Although nearly all such racial limitations on membership and church leadership have been removed in recent years, the effects of these religious prohibitions remain to be seen. Many individuals who read or listened to leaders justifying segregation or bans against leadership positions cannot readily dismiss some of the attitudes developed through years of prolonged exposure to negative points of view.

Like the gender issues that have become a center of religious debate, racial issues have been debated for decades. As the courts and society as a whole have turned their backs on segregation and racially limiting practices, so too have most religious bodies taken an official position of openness. Although the official position and the actual positions may differ somewhat, at least in churches that express brotherly love the two may be moving to a higher level of congruence.

It is important to note that society in general often reflects the positions of religious institutions. We are still experiencing the lingering effects of the proslavery and prosegregationist view of religious groups. Women who are not permitted leadership roles in their churches find the same attitudes in other areas of society where few are encouraged to seek leadership roles in school, work, or politics. The influence of religious beliefs on the everyday behavior of individuals can be considerable. Religion has often inspired goodness and charity. Unfortunately, in some instances, some people have used it to justify inflicting pain and suffering on others.

BELIEFS: A FUNCTION OF CLASS AND EDUCATION

Surveys conducted by the Princeton Religion Research Center (Bezilla, 1993) strongly suggest that religious beliefs are related to one's education and socioeconomic class. For example, the higher a person's educational level, the less likely that person is to accept the Bible literally. Although 58% of non–high-school graduates accepted the Bible literally, only 14% of college graduates did. Likewise, 49% of those with household incomes below $20,000 accepted the Bible literally, whereas only 14% of those with household incomes above $50,000 did. College graduates relied more on self and on science and less on their clergy as believable authorities in matters of truth. For those with less education, however, greater authority was placed in religious writings and in their religious leaders and considerably less on self and science. It appears that the more education one receives, the greater the self-dependence and the reliance on scientific data for determining one's belief structures.

INDIVIDUAL RELIGIOUS IDENTITY

Most Americans are born into the religion of their parents, later joining that same body. Within the context of the religious freedom espoused in the United States, however, individuals are always free to change their religion or to choose no religion. The greatest pressure to retain membership in the religious group in which one was born usually comes from the family and from other members of that same religious group. Often, it is more difficult for individuals to break away from their religious origins than to make breaks from any of the other microcultures of which they are members.

Although a person's ethnicity, class, or gender may have a considerable influence on behavior or values, religion may well be the primary microculture with which many individuals identify. When ethnic identity is very important to an individual, it is often combined with a religious identification such as Irish Catholic, Russian Jew, or Norwegian Lutheran. Understanding the individual's relationship to both microcultures is important in understanding the individual.

The region of the United States in which one lives also affects the strength of identification with a specific religious group. In much of Alabama, many people will have the same or similar views; religious diversity may be limited. In contrast, religious diversity in New York is common. "At a party one is careful not to be critical of other religious groups, because the other partner to a conversation may be a member of one, an alumnus of another, and married to a member of a third"

(Marty, 1975, p. 88). In many areas of the country, any deviation from the common religious beliefs and practices is considered heretical, making it very difficult for the nonadherent to be accepted by most members of the community. In other areas, the traditionally religious individual may not be accepted as a part of a community that is religiously liberal. Educators, as well as students, are usually expected to believe and behave according to the mores of the community—mores that are often determined by the prevailing religious doctrine and the degree of religious diversity.

Most communities have some degree of religious diversity, although the degree of difference may vary greatly, depending on the community. Often, students whose beliefs are different from those of the majority in the community are ostracized in school and social settings. Jews, atheists, Jehovah's Witnesses, and Pentecostals are among those groups whose members are sometimes shunned and suffer discrimination for their beliefs. Educators must be careful that their own religious beliefs and memberships do not interfere with their ability to provide equal educational opportunity to all students, regardless of their religious identification.

INFLUENCE OF THE RELIGIOUS RIGHT

Court cases involving religion became very significant in the 1970s and 1980s. The numerous laws that reinforced Protestant morality were challenged, and some were repealed. Attempts to legislate the public's morality, however, date back several decades. In the 1920s, Prohibition laws were passed in an attempt to address the welfare of the American people. After 13 years, however, this law was repealed and the courts began to protect the rights of those outside the Protestant mainstream. Laws restricting behaviors on moral grounds such as divorce and sexual practices were repealed, and the courts began to reinforce the principle of separation of church and state. One dramatic example of the courts' new attitude was the decision rendered by the U.S. Supreme Court in *Roe v. Wade,* which protected a woman's right to an abortion in early stages of pregnancy (Hudson & Corrigan, 1992).

By the late 1970s, the ideologies of a conservative and increasingly influential group referred to as the Religious Right were clashing head-on with the ideologies of secular humanism. The battle was waged on two fronts: the family and the school. Controversies centered on the family; gender roles; and issues such as abortion, the Equal Rights Amendment, and gay rights. Conservatives supported a return to traditional roles for men and women and opposed equal opportunity for women and homosexuals, such as the hiring of gays and lesbians as public school educators (Roof & McKinney, 1985).

The New Christian Right, or the Religious Right, became a potent force in the 1970s and 1980s partly because of the effective television ministries of individuals such as Jerry Falwell and Pat Robertson. With their ability to reach millions in their own homes, these religious leaders encouraged political involvement and mounted efforts on issues such as school prayer, abortion, pornography, and national defense. The Religious Right has provided strong support or opposition for political candidates on the basis of their voting records or positions on issues (Roof

VIDEO INSIGHT

God and Evolution in Kansas Classrooms

Proponents of creationism say it should be taught in schools because it is a more scientifically valid theory than evolution. To these people, it is not an issue of religious fundamentalism versus science; it's an issue of science versus science.

This video segment shows how and why the State Board of Education in Kansas, decided in the late 1990s to side with creationists and not require the teaching of evolution in their schools. To the opponents of creationism, this seemed an irresponsible move in the education of Kansas' children. Will these students have the education necessary to compete? Will they be able to pass standardized tests?

Should teachers be allowed to teach the book of Genesis in a public school science class? Why or why not? Do you think the decision of the Kansas Board of Education infringed on the separation of church and state? Or, as its proponents argue, is creationism a valid scientific theory that should be taught in the schools? Defend your opinions.

& McKinney, 1985). In 1980 and 1984, they were a strong factor in the election of Ronald Reagan. It is interesting to note that, in 1960, John F. Kennedy assured the American electorate that he would not allow American politics to be influenced by his Catholic faith. In 1980 and again in 1984, Ronald Reagan experienced the exact opposite, assuring Fundamentalist groups that he was a creationist and that he would seek to bring prayer back into the public schools. In the 1992 and the 1996 elections, the influence of the conservative television ministries was diminished somewhat as the more conservative of the candidates, George Bush (in 1992) and Robert Dole (in 1996), lost to Bill Clinton.

In 1982, an Arkansas law specifying that "creation science" be taught in the schools along with evolution was struck down in a U.S. District Court. By the end of the 1980s, Ronald Reagan and George Bush had been successful in placing conservative judges on the federal benches and on the U.S. Supreme Court, and groups outside the mainstream began losing cases in which they sought support for exercising their religious beliefs (Hudson & Corrigan, 1992). A survey conducted by the Princeton Religion Research Center (1995) suggests that 18% of Americans identify with the Religious Right, 8% are unsure of their status, and 74% indicate they are not a part of the movement. However, 42% of Americans surveyed would describe themselves as "born again" or Evangelical Christians (Princeton Religion Research Center, 1995). Although perhaps not as intense in their political and religious agenda as those who identify with the Religious Right, it would be well for educators to recognize that a significant segment of U.S. society considers itself to be part of the conservative Christian movement.

The efforts of religious conservatives have altered the course of American history and will affect the judicial system in the United States for decades. In the late 1980s and early 1990s, as the remaining liberal U.S. Supreme Court justices were advancing in age, President Bush appointed conservative replacements for retirees to match his own agenda. However, with a more liberal president elected in 1992 and reelected in 1996, the balance of power in the Supreme Court was affected as new appointments were made.

Sixty-eight percent of Americans believe that religion is losing its influence on American life (Princeton Religion Research Center, 1995). This, along with increasing frustration with drugs in the schools, gang violence, and declining achievement scores, has religious conservatives placing considerable pressure on the U.S. educational system. They want schools to support the values of the conservative Right as they once did. They have allied themselves with political conservatives and have worked diligently to elect their members to school boards. In some communities, they have established their own private schools to ensure that their convictions and values are reflected in all aspects of schooling. Today's educators should recognize the influence of these groups that in some communities enjoy considerable support.

ASK YOURSELF

What are the religious affiliations of people in the community in which you now reside? How does the religious diversity differ from where you grew up? How would you classify the majority of groups on a scale of conservative to liberal? What influence might these religions have on what you teach in your classroom?

To answer these questions online, go to the Ask Yourself module for this chapter of the Companion Website.

Nationally, adherence to the principle of separation of church and state has been schizophrenic, at best. Oaths are typically made on Bibles and often end with the phrase "so help me God." U.S. coins and currency state "In God We Trust." We have military chaplains and congressional chaplains, and we hold congressional prayer breakfasts. This has been interpreted by some to mean that the separation of church and state simply means that there will be no state church.

Complete separation of church and state, as defined by strict constitutionalists, would have a profound effect on social-religious life. It is likely that the American public wants some degree of separation of these two institutions, but it is equally likely that the public would be outraged if total separation were imposed. Total separation would mean no direct or indirect aid to religious groups, no tax-free status, no tax deductions for contributions to religious groups, no national Christmas tree, no government-paid chaplains, no religious holidays, no blue laws, and so on. The list of religious activities, rights, and privileges that could be eliminated seems almost endless.

EDUCATIONAL IMPLICATIONS

Religious groups place different emphases on the need for education and have different expectations of what children should be taught. The Amish usually want to remove their children from formal schooling after they complete the eighth grade. The Hutterites often do not want their children to attend school with non-Hutterite students. Catholics, Lutherans, Episcopalians, Hutterites, Seventh-Day Adventists, and some Fundamentalist Christian groups have established their own schools to provide both a common education (the general, nonreligious skills and knowledge) and a religious education.

Public schools are supposed to be free of religious doctrine and perspective, but many people believe that schools without such a perspective do not provide a desirable value orientation for students. Debate about the public school's responsibility in fostering student morality and social responsibility is constant. A major point of disagreement focuses on who should determine the morals that will provide the context of the educational program in a school. Because religious diversity is so great in this country, that task is nearly impossible. Therefore, most public schools incorporate commonly accepted American values that transcend most religions. In response, some students are sent to schools operated by a religious body; other students attend religion classes after school or on Saturdays; and many students receive their religious training at Sunday School.

Although the U.S. Constitution requires the separation of state and church, this does not mean that public schools and religion have always been completely separated. Until 1962 and 1963 Supreme Court decisions determined that these practices were unconstitutional, some schools included religious worship and prayer in their daily educational practices. Although schools should be secular, they are greatly influenced by the predominant values of the community. Whether evolution, sex education, and values clarification are taught in school is determined, in great part, by the religious beliefs of a community. Educators must be cognizant of this influence before introducing certain readings and ideas that stray far from what the community is willing to accept within their belief and value structure.

Among the controversial issues that surround the efforts of the New Right and Fundamentalist religious groups are school prayer, tuition tax credits, school vouchers, and censorship.

School Prayer

Despite the 1962 and 1963 Supreme Court decisions regarding school prayer, conservative groups have persisted in their efforts to revive school prayer in the schools. The law now is, in essence, a voluntary prayer law. The law in no way precludes private prayer in school. The Supreme Court decisions do not prevent teachers or students from praying privately in school. Any teacher or student can offer his or her own private prayer of thanks before the noon meal or meditate or pray between classes and before and after school. Public group prayer is forbidden by law. Advocates of school prayer sometimes advance their efforts under the term *voluntary* prayer. The interpretation of what constitutes voluntary school prayer has become a main issue in the prayer controversy. Some proponents of school prayer advocate mandated school prayer, with individuals voluntarily choosing to participate or not participate. It is likely that if such laws were ever enacted, the considerable social pressure to participate would be particularly difficult for younger children to resist (Welch et al., 1981).

In 2000, the Supreme Court ruled against a Texas school district, which had permitted prayer at a football game over the public address system. The district maintained that the football games were extra curricular, and students were not required to attend and be a part of the prayer (*Santa Fe Independent School District v. DOE,* 2000). Prayers and invocations have been a long-standing tradition at many high school games to invoke the protection against harm for all of the football players and typically ask for good sportsmanship. Seldom has the practice been challenged in the past, because it had the support of the vast majority of students and parents. However, the Court has ruled that this is a violation of the separation of church and state. It is apparent, however, that the majority of the American public favors school prayer, with two thirds of the population supporting a constitutional amendment that would permit prayer in the schools (Gallup & Lindsay, 1999).

Tuition Tax Credits

Tuition tax credits have been a major controversy within education. Proponents of tuition tax credits support income tax credits for parents who enroll their children in private schools. Many of those who support these tax credits believe that because the children in private schools reduce the number of students in public education and thereby reduce public education costs, their parents are entitled to some tax relief. Proponents further support the tax credits as a matter of social equity, encouraging greater pluralism, diversity, and competition in the American education system. The decision to send children to private schools is usually precipitated by parental desires to provide an education coupled with a religious environment, to provide an education superior to that available in the public schools, or in some cases to segregate their children from other children in the public schools. Opponents to tuition tax credits see such legislation as weakening the public education system and encouraging some parents to abandon public education for their children in favor of the exclusiveness of the private education sector.

In 1983, in *Mueller v. Allen,* the Supreme Court upheld Minnesota's allowance of income tax deductions for the cost of tuition and related educational expenses. The Minnesota law provides for income tax deductions regardless of whether a child attends public or private school—parochial or secular. Minnesota was able to convince the U.S. Supreme Court that the purpose of the law was to ensure a well-educated citizenry and to relieve the burden on public schools. The Court applied a three-part test that it often used to determine the unconstitutional establishment of religion. The Court determined that: (a) the purpose of the tax law was not to aid religion; (b) the law did not have the primary effect of aiding religion; and (c) the law did not promote excessive entanglement between church and state (Lines, 1983). With the *Mueller* decision, it is highly likely that other groups will attempt to emulate Minnesota's success through both federal and state tax laws.

School Vouchers

Various groups raise school voucher initiatives periodically. Voucher initiatives are often strongly supported by religious factions, particularly those who send their children to private religious schools. Parents and others who support these initiatives point to the failure of the public schools to educate their children adequately. They point to the states' low national rankings in student math proficiency, reading proficiency, SAT scores, class size, teacher/student ratios, computer availability, and per pupil spending (38 YES-school vouchers, 2000). They point to falling system-wide test scores and to the moral decline in schools as evidenced by school violence, drugs, and teen pregnancies. They believe that school vouchers will make it possible to send their children to the schools of their choice.

Proponents of California's Proposition 38 argue that the voucher program will not require any further appropriations since school districts can provide vouchers to students who are not using their services, thereby decreasing their expenses. They argue that in California, it costs $7,400 to educate a student in the public school system. When parents redeem a school voucher for $4,000, the $3,400 remains in the public school (38 YES-School Vouchers, 2000). The voucher program will enable all parents to ensure the quality education that they wish for their children (38 YES-School Vouchers, 2000).

Opponents to Proposition 38 and to similar initiatives maintain that this will indeed take away needed funds from the public schools. School districts have many fixed costs and already are suffering from inadequate funding. A voucher system will indeed create a fiscal crisis in the public school system, and there will be a need for additional state support to even maintain the status quo. They further state that the $4,000 provided by the vouchers will not enable any child to go to any school of choice. Many private schools have tuitions of $12,000 to $14,000 annually and the $4,000 vouchers will not even begin to cover the cost of the full tuition. While some schools may grant partial scholarships to deserving students with financial need, it will not be possible to provide support to all. Private schools tend to be located in the more affluent areas of the community. Transportation will be a major problem for students who live in areas distant from the preferred schools. Opponents contend that the primary beneficiaries of the school voucher programs will be the wealthy who can afford the private schools and already enroll their children in them, and the few borderline families who can send their children to private schools only with the help of the vouchers.

Censorship

The discussion of censorship is included in this section because the censorship movement tends to be heavily influenced by many individuals from fundamentalist and conservative religious groups. Censorship of textbooks, library books, and other learning materials in education has become another major battleground in education for the Religious Right and other fundamentalist groups.

The impact of censorship in the public schools cannot be underestimated. It is a serious matter. Censorship or attempts at censorship have resulted in violence: involved parties have been beaten and even shot. It has resulted in the dismissal or resignation of administrators and teachers. It has split communities and in the past 30 years has created nearly as much controversy as the desegregation of schools. Few can doubt the sincerity of censors and their proponents. Most, if not all, are absolutely certain that the cause they support is just and morally right. They believe that, for the sake of all, they are obligated to continue their fight to rid schools of objectionable materials that contaminate supple minds and that contribute to the moral decay of society.

At the other end of the continuum, opponents to the censors also tend to share a conviction that they are the ones in the right and that censors infringe on academic freedom, seeking to destroy meaningful education. Opponents to the censors believe that their antagonists thrive on hard times, such as when schools come under fire because of declining Scholastic Aptitude Test (SAT) scores, rising illiteracy rates, escalating costs of education, and increasing concern about violence and vandalism in the schools. Other factors that prompt the activities of censors are the removal of school prayer; teaching methods that are branded as secular humanism; and programs such as values clarification, drug education, and sex education. Books written specifically for teenagers about subjects that are objectionable to some parents and in language that others consider too realistic are often a source of concern. The emergence of African American literature, sometimes written in the black vernacular, is sometimes the source of irritation or concern.

Targets for the censors are books and materials that are identified as disrespectful of authority and religion, destructive of social and cultural values, obscene, pornographic, unpatriotic, or in violation of individual and familial rights of privacy. Books written by gays and lesbians are frequently attacked. Among the materials attacked by censors may be those that are considered nonracist or nonsexist. In a conservative community, teachers may be surprised to find that magazines such as *Time, Newsweek,* and *U.S. News and World Report* are sometimes attacked because they publish stories about war, crime, death, violence, and sex. In this same community, a teacher can anticipate a negative reaction to the teaching of evolution without presenting the views on creationism. In addition, certain dictionaries with words and definitions described as offensive have been forced off book adoption lists.

One can understand the concern of parents who are often influenced by censors. They believe that unless they choose sides and act, their children will be taught with materials that are anti-God, anti-family, anti-authority, anti-country, anti-morality, and anti-law and order.

The failure to communicate effectively with parents is a contributing source of alienation between educators and parents. Failure to communicate the objectives of new curricula and to explain how these programs enrich the educational experience may cause suspicion and distrust. Many administrators and librarians indicate that communication with parents is more crises oriented than continuous. Information about programs, policies, and procedures tends to be offered in response to inquiries or challenges, rather than as part of an ongoing public relations effort.

Secular humanism has been one direct target of the censors, particularly those affiliated with Fundamentalist religious groups. The emphasis in secular humanism is a respect for human beings, rather than a belief in the supernatural. Its objectives include the full development of every human being, the universal use of the scientific method, affirmation of the dignity of humans, personal freedom combined with social responsibility, and fulfillment through the development of ethical and creative living (Welch et al., 1981).

The groups opposed to secular humanism cite two Supreme Court cases as evidence that secular humanism is a religion: *Torcaso v. Watkins* (1961) and *United States v. Seeger* (1965). These cases were not heard by the Court to determine whether or not secular humanism is a religion. Nevertheless, the wording in the Court findings has been frequently used to support the position that the U.S. Supreme Court recognizes secular humanism as a religion.

Secular humanism is not an organized religion like Roman Catholicism, Protestantism, and Judaism. It does not have rituals, a church, or professed doctrines. Its existence is in the minds of individuals who align themselves with these perspectives. The specific beliefs and manifestations of beliefs vary from one believer to another.

Conservatives have also attacked literature and media from the New Age movement. Often attacked as resurgent paganism or Gnosticism, target materials are censored in an attempt to remove them from the classroom and library shelves.

Teachers new to the profession or new to a community should never underestimate the determination of those involved in the censorship movement. Teachers would be well advised to make certain that they are fully aware of the climate within the community before introducing new, innovative, or controversial materials, teaching strategies, and books. Experienced colleagues and supervisors can usually serve as barometers as to how students, parents, and the community will react to the new materials or teaching techniques. With this type of information, the new teacher can proceed with a more realistic anticipation of the reception that can be expected.

To answer these questions online, go to the Pause to Reflect module for this chapter of the Companion Website.

PAUSE TO REFLECT

The faculty at your school has been working for several months on a new integrated curriculum across subject areas. For the first time, they have really collaborated in this effort. At the presentation to the school board, one member accuses them of being secular humanists and not providing proper moral direction to their students. The faculty members are shocked. Why were these accusations made by the school board member? Why do some members of the community think that secular humanism is a religion? How should the faculty have approached their new curriculum project to prevent the backlash from the community?

Classroom Implications

Although religion and public schooling are to remain separate, religion can be taught in schools as a legitimate discipline for objective study. A comparative religion course is part of the curriculum offered in many secondary schools. In this approach, the students are not forced to practice a religion as part of their educational program. They can, however, study one or more religions.

Guidelines for Teaching about Religions

The Fairfax County Schools in Virginia have provided teachers with a handout titled *Religion and Public Schools: The Path Between Too Much and Too Little.* In the handout are guidelines for teaching about religions. This important advice will assist teachers in understanding how religion can be taught while maintaining the all-important separation of church and state:

- The school may sponsor the study of religion, but may not sponsor the practice of religion.
- The school may expose students to all religious views, but may not impose any particular view.
- The school's approach to religion is one of instruction, not one of indoctrination.
- The function of the school is to educate about all religions, not to convert to any one religion.
- The school should study what all people believe, but should not teach a student what to believe.
- The school should strive for student awareness of all religions, but should not press for student acceptance of any one religion.
- The school should seek to inform the student about various beliefs, but should not seek to conform him or her to any one belief.

(Becker, undated)

As part of the curriculum, students should learn that the United States (and indeed the world) is rich in religious diversity. Educators show their respect for religious differences by their interactions with students from different religious backgrounds. Understanding the importance of religion to many students and their families is an advantage in developing effective teaching strategies for individual students. Instructional activities can build on students' religious experiences to help them learn concepts. This technique helps students recognize that their religious identity is valued in the classroom and encourages them to respect the religious diversity that exists.

At the same time, educators should avoid stereotyping all students from one denomination or church. Diversity is found within every religious group and denomination. Within each group are differences in attitudes and beliefs. For example, Southern Baptists may appear to be conservative to outsiders. Among Southern Baptists, however, some would be considered part of a liberal or moderate group, whereas others would be identified as conservative. Some Southern Baptist churches may hold services so formal in nature that they might even be described as resembling an Episcopalian service.

It is the responsibility of educators to be aware of the religious diversity and the influence of religion in the community in which they work. They must also understand the influence of religion on the school's curriculum and climate in order to teach effectively. Finally, educators must periodically reexamine their own interactions with students to ensure that they are not discriminating against students because of differences in religious beliefs. It is imperative that educators recognize how influential membership in a religious microculture is in order to help students develop their potential.

Summary

Educators should never underestimate the importance that Americans place on religion. For some individuals, their religion takes precedent over all other microcultures. People have been willing to die for their religion; some have been willing to inflict great pain on others because of their beliefs. We live in a society that has become increasingly diverse. Along with increasing ethnic diversity has come increasing religious diversity. The United States has operated under Judeo-Christian principles for more than 2 centuries. When new religions threaten established religions, however, controversies and challenges arise.

Educators would do well to inform themselves of the religious groups in their community and in their school. In doing so, they greatly enhance their ability to function in the classroom, mindful and respectful of the religious rights of all students.

One's religion has considerable impact on how one functions on a day-to-day basis. Education may be greatly influenced by religious groups. Some private schools are established on religious principles and, in those schools, religion is an integral part of the curriculum. Even in public schools, attempts by religious groups to influence the system are made regularly. The degree of religious influence in the schools varies from one community to another. Educators should not underestimate the influence and strategies of conservative religious groups and would be well advised to know their community before introducing controversial materials.

To answer these questions online, go to the Chapter Questions module for this chapter of the Companion Website.

Questions for Review

1. Discuss how the religious majority in a community can influence curriculum and instructional methodology.
2. To what extent does religion influence American life with respect to its importance to the individual and church or synagogue attendance?

3. What is the relationship of religion to public office?
4. What are the current trends with respect to membership in conservative, moderate, and liberal religious groups? What are the implications of these trends for the political and legal directions of the country?
5. What do laws permit with respect to school prayer? How does the Religious Right want to change these laws?
6. Discuss censorship in the schools, including the targets of the censors.
7. How have Protestantism, Catholicism, and Judaism influenced American culture?
8. In what ways does gender affect religion and religion affect gender issues?
9. What is the relationship of religion to race?

References

Becker, B. (undated). *Religion and public schools: The path between too much and too little.* Springfield, VA: Fairfax County Schools.

Bezilla, R. (Ed.). (1993). *Religion in America.* Princeton, NJ: Princeton Religion Research Center.

Birkholz, E. L. (Ed.). (2000, Winter). *Congressional yellow book: Who's who in congress, 25*(4). New York: Leadership Directories

Chryssides, G. D. (1999). *Exploring new religions.* London: Cassell.

Corduan, W. (1998). *Neighboring Faiths.* Downers Grove, IL: InterVarsity Press.

Gallup, G. H., Jr. (1999). *The spiritual life of young Americans.* Princeton, NJ: The George H. Gallup International Institute.

Gallup, G. H., Jr., & Lindsay, D. M. (1999). *Surveying the religious landscape.* Harrisburg, PA: Morehouse Publishing.

Gomes, P. (1996). *The good book.* New York: Morrow.

Greeley, A. M. (1982). *Religion: A secular theory.* New York: Free Press.

Groothuis, R. M. (1997). *Good news for women: A biblical picture of gender equality.* Grand Rapids, MI: Baker Books.

Hudson, W. S., & Corrigan, J. (1992). *Religion in America* (5th ed.). New York: MacMillan.

Kosmin, B. A., & Lachman, S. P. (1993). *One nation under God: Religion in contemporary American society.* New York: Harmony.

Lincoln, C. E. (1994). *The Black Muslims in America.* Grand Rapids, MI: Eerdmans.

Lincoln, C. E., & Mamiya, L. H. (1990). *The black church in the African American experience.* Durham, NC: Duke University.

Lindner, E. W. (1998). *1998 yearbook of American and Canadian churches.* Nashville: Abingdon Press.

Lines, P. M. (1983, August 24). Impact of Mueller: New options for policymakers. *Education Week.*

Marty, M. E. (Ed.). (1975). *Our faiths.* Royal Oak, MI: Cathedral Publications.

Oxtoby, W. G. (Ed.). (1996). *World religions.* Oxford, UK: Oxford University Press.

Princeton Religion Research Center. (1995). *Religion in America.* [Supplement]. Princeton, NJ: Princeton Religion Research Center.

Robinson, F. (Ed.). (1996). *Islamic world.* Cambridge, UK: Cambridge University Press.

Roof, W. C., & McKinney, W. (1985, July). Denominational America and the new religious pluralism. *Annals of the American Academy of Political and Social Science, 480,* 24–38.

Santa Fe Independent School District v. DOE (99-62) 168 F. 3d 806 (June 19, 2000).

38 YES-School Vouchers 2000. Available: http://www.vouchers2000.com.

Van Biema, D. (2000). Battle of the Baptists, *Time, 155*(26), 49.

Van Leeuwen, M. S. (1990). *Gender and grace.* Downers Grove, IL: Intervarsity Press.

Welch, D., Medeiros, D. C., & Tate, G. A. (1981, December). Education and the new right. *Educational Leadership,* 203–207.

Williams, P. W. (1990). *America's religions: Traditions and cultures.* New York: MacMillan.

Suggested Readings

Chryssides, G. D. (1999). *Exploring new religions.* London: Cassell.
This book provides an excellent overview of some of the nontraditional religions in the world. Included are religious groups such as suicide cults, new Christian movements, new forms of Buddhism, New Age, witchcraft, and paganism.

Corduan, W. (1998). *Neighboring faiths.* Downers Grove, IL: InterVarsity Press.
Written from a Christian perspective, the text covers the major non-Christian religions in the United States with a historical background of the religion and the basic belief structure of the particular group.

Gallup, G. H., Jr., & Lindsay, D. M. (1999). *Surveying the religious landscape.* Harrisburg, PA: Morehouse.
This is the successor to the *Religion in America Series* published by the Gallup organization. This publication looks the religious practices of Americans and what they believe. It provides more in-depth narrative and interpretation than *Religion in America.*

Hudson, W. S., & Corrigan, J. (1992). *Religion in America* (5th ed.) New York: MacMillan.
A look at the history of religion in this country and its profound influence on the formation of culture in America. It includes a discussion of the pluralistic nature of religion today.

Lincoln, C. E. (1994). *The Black Muslims in America* (3rd ed.). Grand Rapids, MI: Eerdmans.
This book is a close examination of a small, growing, and increasingly visible religious segment in the African American community.

Lincoln, C. E., & Mamiya, L. H. (1990). *The black church in the African American experience.* Durham, NC: Duke University.
This book is an examination of the history and role of the black church in American society.

Van Leeuwen, M. S. (1990). *Gender and grace.* Downers Grove, IL: Intervarsity Press.
This volume is an examination of gender issues in a Christian biblical context.

CRITICAL INCIDENTS IN TEACHING

Religion

Religious Discrimination

Janice Ferguson is a 5-year-old Jewish girl living in a conservative Protestant community where there are few non-Christian families. She is the only Jewish child in her kindergarten class. She is an outgoing child, and well-liked by her classmates. While playing on the playground with two of her classmates, one of them asks Janice what she expects to receive for Christmas. Janice answers by stating that her family does not observe Christmas, "Why not?" the other girls ask.

"Because we're Jewish and we have Hanukkah instead," Janice explains. The next day, Janice, visibly upset, seeks out Mrs. Tedesco, her teacher, on the playground, "Mary Ellen said that her daddy told her that Jews were bad people because they killed Jesus. I don't think she wants to be my friend anymore."

To answer these questions online, go to the Critical Incidents module for this chapter of the Companion Website.

Questions for Discussion

1. What can Mrs. Tedesco do for Janice to provide her with some immediate comfort?
2. What can or should Mrs. Tedesco do with regard to Mary Ellen?
3. How could Mrs. Tedesco stop a potential problem in bigotry from spreading? What activities can she plan for her class?

Censorship

Mitchell Aoki is a second-year English teacher in a midwestern community of 80,000. He teaches sophomore and junior English classes. A fourth-generation Japanese American, Aoki majored in English and religion and received his teaching credential from a private Southern Baptist university. His evaluations from his principal for his first year were considered excellent for a first-year teacher.

When his principal asks him to come to his office, Aoki is surprised when he is handed a letter from a parent. The letter reads:

"Suzanne came home crying in the heart. I don't know who this Mr. Aoki is, but he needs to know that it is important to respect the religious values of others even if he does not believe in our God. There will be retribution, for one cannot take the name of God in vain and not expect punishment for such blasphemy."

Stunned, Mr. Aoki asks the principal what the letter is all about. "That's what I was about to ask you," the principal replies.

"I never use profanity in front of the students. In fact, I don't use profanity at all," Mr. Aoki responds. "I don't know what this is all about. The letter implies that I'm an atheist, a non-Christian. I'm an active member of a Protestant Church. I even majored in religion."

"I know, Mitchell. That's why I'm trying to get to the bottom of this," the principal says.

Suddenly it strikes Mr. Aoki. "It was the series of poems I read to the class last week. They were examples of poetry by some contemporary writers, and in one passage an author referred to someone as a 'God damned weasel.' I read that as a direct quote to a class of high school juniors, and now I'm branded as a blasphemer! He's assuming that because of my ethnic background, I'm an atheist or Buddhist or something!"

Questions for Discussion

To answer these questions online, go to the Critical Incidents module for this chapter of the Companion Website.

1. Did Mitchell Aoki exercise poor judgment in reading the class a poem that contained words offensive to the student and her father?
2. If he did nothing wrong, should he take precautions in the future to avoid similar reactions?
3. Should the student and father be contacted by Mr. Aoki? By the principal? By both? If so, what form should the contact take? A letter? A conference? An apology? An explanation? What type of explanation?
4. Are minority group teachers at greater risk of being perceived as having values, morals, and ethics different from those of the majority of Americans?

Religious Dietary Attitudes

Allison Beller is a fourth-grade teacher in a suburban school district. The community is primarily middle class, and the children come from diverse ethnic and religious backgrounds. Part of her curriculum includes some basic lessons in cooking. Today's lesson involves the preparation of hamburgers. Beller is aware that one student is a vegetarian and that two others do not eat red meat. She has prepared burgers out of ground turkey for two and substituted what she thought was an appropriate alternative for the vegetarian child.

Beller is stunned, therefore, when the vegetarian child states before the class that eating hamburger is wrong and sinful. "My daddy says that hamburgers come from cows that are killed and that it is wrong to kill cows or anything else. He says that if you eat the hamburgers, you are as bad as the people who killed the cow."

The other children in the class are also shocked at the accusation and sit in their places, speechless.

Questions for Discussion

To answer these questions online, go to the Critical Incidents module for this chapter of the Companion Website.

1. How should Ms. Beller respond to the accusation?
2. What should she say to the class?
3. Should she go on with the lesson?
4. Should she contact the child's parent? If so, what should she say and/or do?
5. Should she consult with the principal?
6. Should she discontinue the cooking lessons?

Religious Discrimination

Nadar Hoseini is a third grader in a suburban community in northern Virginia. Nadar's parents emigrated from Iran in the mid-1970s and are now naturalized citizens. Nadar was born in Virginia, where his father is a chemist for a large manufacturer. During recess, Ms. Nash notices that Nadar is sitting alone and is visibly upset. After some probing into an apparent problem, she learns that Nadar's friends have shunned him. Michael, he tells Ms. Nash, told the group that his father says the World Trade Center was bombed by Muslims who are all fanatics trying to blow up America and kill innocent Americans. "Your friend Nadar is one of them Moslems, and you had better not let me catch you playing with him again. We ought to ship all of them Muslims back where they came from!" Michael quotes his father.

Protesting, Nadar insists that he was born in the United States and that he and his family are American. The protest falls on deaf ears as Nadar's classmates join Michael in ostracizing him. Ms. Nash is determined to help Nadar's situation but at the moment is at a loss as to how she will approach the problem.

To answer these questions online, go to the Critical Incidents module for this chapter of the Companion Website.

Questions for Discussion

1. What should Ms. Nash say to Nadar?
2. Should Ms. Nash go directly to Michael and the other boys involved?
3. How can she change the perceptions of the boys without seeming to attack Michael's father?
4. What sensitivity activities can she conduct in the class?

Religion-Based Criticism in the Classroom

Charlotte Silva is a fifth-grade teacher in a suburban school near a major city in Texas. "Ms. Silva," Deborah Smith blurts out, "Cindy Segal's sister is getting an abortion next week. That's a sin."

"It's not," protests Cindy. "My parents said it is a woman's right to do as she pleases with her body."

"She's going to have an unborn child killed. She's only 17 and she's pregnant. She's not even married. That's a sin too. My mother and daddy told me that those things are sins. They arc, aren't they? Our preacher says that you can rot in hell for sins like that, and he doesn't lie. That's true, isn't it, Ms. Silva? Will you please tell Cindy?"

The entire class has heard this outburst, and they are all staring at the teacher, waiting for her response.

To answer these questions online, go to the Critical Incidents module for this chapter of the Companion Website.

Questions for Discussion

1. Although the teacher must provide some response, should she allow a discussion on religious ethics in the classroom?

2. If she decides not to discuss the issue, how should she acknowledge the question and avoid a judgmental response to the ethics question?
3. If the teacher decides to allow a discussion of the issues, how should she proceed? What can she allow in the discussion? What must be avoided?

Religious Sensitivity

Angela and her family are devout members of a local Jehovah's Witness group. Angela tried out for and was given a small role in a high school play. Ms. Lowry, the drama teacher and director of the play, set Wednesday night for the final dress rehearsal. The Wednesday night rehearsal conflicted with Angela's evening worship services, and she told Ms. Shepherd this. Ms. Shepherd asked Angela if her parents would excuse her from the religious services for the one night and allow her to come to the rehearsal. The next day, Angela told Ms. Shepherd that she would have to go to the services and could not come to the rehearsal. Because Angela's role was very minor, Ms. Lowry told Angela that this was no problem and that they would work around her absence.

The night of the rehearsal, Angela's father, with his daughter in tow, showed up at the theater after their religious services and angrily yelled at Ms. Shepherd for being insensitive to their religion.

To answer these questions online, go to the Critical Incidents module for this chapter of the Companion Website.

Questions for Discussion

1. Should Ms. Shepherd have changed the rehearsal schedule to accommodate Angela's needs?
2. Was she out of line to ask Angela to ask her father for permission to miss religious services?
3. Can schools realistically be expected to schedule all weekday meetings and extracurricular activities at times that will please all and offend no one?
4. How should Ms. Shepherd respond to Angela's father?
5. Was Ms. Shepherd being insensitive?
6. What should Ms. Shepherd say to Angela?
7. What should Ms. Shepherd say to the other students at the rehearsal who have witnessed the father's outburst?

Chapter 7

Language

To devalue his language or to presume standard English is a better system is to devalue the child and his culture and to reveal a naiveté concerning language.

J. Baratz (1968, p. 145)

Theresa Roberts, a kindergarten teacher at Waialeale Elementary School in Honolulu, had just finished welcoming her new kindergarten class and introducing herself. As she wrote her name and the name of the school on the chalkboard, she felt a slight tug on the back of her skirt and heard a faint voice just above a whisper say, "Teacha, I like go pee pee." Turning around, she saw the pleading face of Nohea Kealoha. "What did you say?" Ms. Roberts said disgustedly. In a slightly louder voice, Nohea repeated herself, "I like go pee pee." With some in the class beginning to giggle, Ms. Roberts exclaimed, "You will go nowhere, young lady, until you ask me in proper English. Now say it properly." "I no can," pleaded Nohea. "Then you can just stand there until you do." With the students giggling and Nohea standing as ordered, Ms. Roberts proceeded with her lesson.

A few minutes later, the occasional giggle exploded in a chorus of laughing. As Ms. Roberts turned to Nohea, the child was sobbing as she stood in the middle of a large puddle of urine on the classroom floor.

Do teachers have the right to expect and demand standard English from their students? How important is it for students to be able to speak standard

English? If a student is able to communicate well enough in his or her non-standard English for others to understand, why should educators be concerned about non-standard English usage?

LANGUAGE AND CULTURE

The above incident took place in a school in Hawaii many years ago. Nohea (not her real name) is now an adult and describes the incident as one of the most painful and humiliating in her life. When she entered school, she was unable to speak standard English; she could speak only Pidgin English. The teacher knew precisely what the child was asking for. Her insensitivity, however, resulted in lasting emotional scars on a child, now a woman. This type of insensitivity, unfortunately, is not an isolated incident. Individuals in southeastern New Mexico have described similar incidents involving non-English-speaking Latino students entering school for the first time.

Most students enter school speaking standard English. Some students, however, come to school barely speaking English. Some are bilingual, some speak a nonstandard dialect, and some may use sign language to communicate. As the scene changes from school to school, the languages and dialects spoken also change. The scene, however, is indicative of the multilingual nature of the United States, a result of its multicultural heritage.

Students exhibit cultural similarities and differences related to language, as well as to gender, class, ethnicity, religion, exceptionalities, and age. Because they speak one or more languages, as well as dialects of these languages, they are part of another microcultural group. Of course, not all African American children speak Black English, nor do all Latinos speak Spanish. Within most microcultures, members will vary greatly in language or dialect usage.

Unfortunately, society often attaches a stigma to bilingual students that characterizes them as "low-income, low-status persons who are educationally at risk" (Hakuta, 1986, p. 7). Rather than value and promote the use of two or more languages, some educators expect students to replace their native languages with English as soon as possible. Movements to establish English-only policies and practices bestow "official blessing upon state residents who speak English, and a repudiation of those residents who do not" (Spencer, 1988, p. 142). Individuals who have limited English proficiency frequently suffer institutional discrimination as a result of the limited acceptance of languages other than English. Wolfram, Adger, and Christian (1999) assert that students in this group are frequently at great risk for school failure, despite the fact that they may not necessarily be categorized as disadvantaged.

Language is the means by which we communicate. It makes our behavior human. It can incite anger, elicit love, inspire bravery, and arouse fear. It binds groups of people together. Language and dialect serve as a focal point for cultural identity.

People who share the same language or dialect often share the same common feelings, beliefs, and behaviors. It provides a common bond for individuals with the same linguistic heritage.

Language shapes cultural and personal identity. It may also be the means by which one group of people stereotypes another. Language has a role in connecting individuals to each other. Language and accents can usually be altered, whereas racial and physical appearance generally cannot. Thus, through changing the style of one's language or even the language itself, an individual can express relationships to those with whom he or she interacts (Dicker, 1996).

Language is much more than just a means of communication. It is used to socialize children into their linguistic and cultural communities, developing patterns that distinguish one community from another. Thus, the interaction of language and culture is complex but central to the socialization of children into acceptable cultural patterns. Exactly how a language is learned is not known, but almost all children have the ability to learn one or more native languages. In part through imitating older persons, the children gradually learn. They learn to select almost instinctively the right word, the right response, and the right gesture to fit the situation. By age five, children have learned the syntax of their native language, and they know that words in different arrangements mean different things. This suggests that within their own communities children develop impressive language skills, although these skills may vary greatly from school requirements (Wolfram, Adger, & Christian, 1999). The average adult has 50,000 words at his or her disposal and can communicate through numerous vocal sounds and gestures.

Native speakers of a language unconsciously know and obey the rules and customs of their language community. Society and language interact constantly. A wrong choice in word selection may come across as rude, crude, or ignorant. Individuals who are learning a new language or who are unfamiliar with colloquialisms may make wrong choices or even be surprised at the use of certain words when such use is incongruent with their perceptions of what is proper. An Australian student in a Southwestern school was shocked when a girl in his class responded to his query of what she had been doing during the summer: "Oh, just piddling around." Her response was meant to convey the message that she had been passing her time in idle activities. From his frame of reference, however, the Australian student understood her to say that she had been urinating. It is important for classroom teachers to recognize that students who are new to a language may not always be able to make appropriate word selections or to comprehend the meaning of particular dialects or colloquialisms.

In the 1930s, Fiorello La Guardia was the mayor of New York City. La Guardia, of Jewish and Italian ancestry, was fluent in Yiddish and Italian as well as the New York dialect of English. When speaking Italian to Italian audiences, La Guardia used the broad and sweeping gestures characteristic of the people of southern Italy. When speaking Yiddish to Jewish audiences, he used the forearm chop identified with many Eastern European Jews. When speaking English, he used softer, less emphatic gestures more typical of English-speaking individuals. The example of La Guardia suggests not only that different ethnic groups have different

Language diversity of the United States is reflected in street signs, stores, and advertisements, as well as in the conversations of neighbors and shopkeepers in a neighborhood.

communication styles but also that individuals adjust their communication style, whenever possible, to suit the needs of the intended audience.

At an early age, a child acquires the delicate muscle controls necessary for pronouncing the words of the native language or for signing naturally if the child is deaf. As the child grows older, it becomes increasingly more difficult to make the vocal muscles behave in new, unaccustomed ways necessary to master a foreign language. For example, some Filipinos are unaccustomed to the sounds associated with the letter *f*, which makes it difficult, if not impossible, for some to pronounce the word *four* as an American does.

All this tends to inhibit people from learning new languages and encourages them to maintain the one into which they were born. Although the United States is primarily an English-speaking country, many other languages are spoken here. Spanish, Italian, and sign language are the most commonly used languages other than English. Among English-speaking individuals are numerous dialects—from the Hawaiian pidgin (technically, a creole) to the Southern drawl of Atlanta to the Appalachian white dialect to the Brooklyn dialect of New York. Each is distinctive, and each is an effective means of communication for those who share its linguistic style.

The U.S. Census Bureau estimated that there were approximately 32 million non-English speaking individuals living in the country in 1990 (U.S. Census Bureau, 1996). With 45 million more residents in 2000 than in 1990, it would be safe to assume that there are more than 40 million non-English speakers in the United States. This figure does not include the millions of English-speaking individuals whose dialects are sometimes labeled as nonstandard. The Census Bureau also identified 329 languages spoken in the United States in 1990 (U.S. Census Bureau, 1996).

The multilingual nature of U.S. society reflects the rich cultural heritage of the people. Such language diversity is an asset to the nation, especially in its interaction with other nations in the areas of commerce, defense, education, science, and technology. The advantage to being bilingual or multilingual is often overlooked because of our ethnocentrism. In many other nations, children are expected to become fluent in two or more languages and numerous dialects, enabling them to communicate with other groups and to appreciate language diversity.

ASK YOURSELF

In many countries other than the United States, citizens speak two, three, or more languages. Schools in these areas promote the use of both the native language and other local and regional languages. Two or more languages are taught from the early grades. Why do bilingualism and multilingualism not receive the same support in the United States? Are there advantages to being fluent in more than one language in the United States? Are there any disadvantages?

To answer these questions online, go to the Ask Yourself module for this chapter of the Companion Website.

THE NATURE OF LANGUAGE

As humans, we communicate to share ourselves with others. Language is our medium of exchange for sharing our internal states of being with one another. Through language, we reach out and make contact with our surrounding realities. Through language, we share with others our experiences with that reality (Samovar & Porter, 1991).

Samovar and Porter (1991) suggest that language is not simply a means of reporting experience, but rather a way of defining experience. Different languages represent different social realities. Thus, to understand what is being said, we must also understand the social context of the language itself. Language goes beyond the simple understanding of one another. It helps us understand culture itself; it represents culture. Each language provides us with a means to perceive the world and a means to interpret experiences.

Language usage is culturally determined. In addition to influencing the order of words to form phrases, language influences thinking patterns. "Time" is described differently from culture to culture. Western societies view time as something that can be saved, lost, or wasted; punctuality is highly valued. In other societies, time assumes different values and is reflected in the language of the group. The language of the Lakota, for example, has no words to convey "late" or "waiting" (Samovar & Porter, 1991).

Some Asians tend to be circular in their speaking patterns. One reason for this manner of speaking is the feeling that, for one to understand and appreciate the point to be made, a foundation or background must be fully laid out. In this manner, the point of the discussion is clearly in proper context. For those Westerners and others who are more accustomed to getting directly to the issue at hand, the point could be lost in the circular presentation of the concept.

For effective communication to take place, it is important that there are enough cultural similarities between the sender and the receiver for the latter to decode the message adequately. Even when one is familiar with a word or phrase, comprehension of the intended meaning may not be possible unless there is similarity in cultural backgrounds. In certain cultural groups, *bad* takes on an opposite meaning and may denote the "best." A *candy man* is not one who sells sweets, but one who sells drugs. *Bad* and *candy man* are examples of *argot,* a more or less secretive vocabulary of a co-culture group. In argot, a word sounds the same but the meaning is different. Co-cultures are groups of people who exist in society outside the dominant culture. They often function apart from the dominant culture. Users of argot include some working-class African Americans, homosexuals, gang members, and hobos (Samovar & Porter, 1991).

There is no such thing as a good language or a bad language from a linguistic point of view. All languages have developed to express the needs of their users. In that sense, all languages are equal. It is true that languages do not all have the same amounts of grammar, phonology, or semantic structure. It is also true that society places different levels of social status on the different language groups. These judgments are based not on linguistic acceptability, but on social grounds (Wolfram, Adger, & Christian, 1999). Languages are equal, however, in the sense that there is nothing limiting, demeaning, or handicapping about any of them. All languages meet the social and psychological needs of their speakers and, as such, are arguably equal (Crystal, 1997).

Language is very much cultural. It, together with dialects, is usually related to one's ethnic, geographic, gender, or class origins. Speakers from a particular background often downgrade the linguistic styles of others. For example, Easterners may be critical of the speech of Southerners, citing the use of slow, extended vowels and the expression "y'all." Southerners, on the other hand, may be critical of the speech and language patterns of people from Brooklyn, who seem to some to speak through their noses and to use such phrases as "youse guys." The Eastern dialect of English is appropriate in the East, the Southern dialect appropriate in the South, and Black English, or Ebonics, appropriate in many African American communities.

Language systems are dynamic like most other microcultures. They change constantly as society changes. Language change is inevitable and rarely predictable. For example, an elderly third-generation Japanese American born and raised in Maryland learned Japanese from both his grandparents and parents. On his first trip to Japan many years ago, he had no difficulty in conversing with the people, but he noticed smiles, grins, and giggles when he spoke. When he asked whether he had said anything humorous, the people politely explained that he was speaking as if he were someone out of the 1800s. His grandparents had immigrated to the United States in the 1800s and his family, insulated from modern-day Japanese, had maintained the language systems used more than 100 years ago. The language in Japan, however, had changed sufficiently to make his language patterns stand out as archaic.

In some areas, language changes are so gradual that they go unnoticed. In other circumstances, changes are more easily noted. Expressions and words tend to be identified with a particular period. Sometimes the language is related to particular microcultures for certain periods. For example, words and phrases such as *chilling, hyped,* and *def* may be a part of our language for a time, only to be replaced by other expressions. *Language is a system of vocal sounds and/or nonverbal system by which group members communicate with one another.*

LANGUAGE DIFFERENCES

Literally thousands of languages are known in the world today. Most reference books suggest 4,000 to 5,000, but estimates are as high as 10,000 languages (Crystal, 1997). In the United States, language differences ultimately reflect basic behavioral differences between groups of people. Physical and social separation inevitably leads to language differences. The constant movement and settlement patterns of people, as well as natural barriers such as mountains and rivers, isolated many of the early settlers in the United States. The lack of communication across communities in the early years of the country further contributed to the isolation. Thus, as language changes took place, different dialects of the same language developed in different communities.

Social variables also contribute to language differences. Both class and ethnicity reflect differences in language. The greater the social distance between groups, the greater the tendency toward language differences. Upwardly mobile individuals often adopt the language patterns of the dominant society because it may, at times, facilitate social acceptance.

Sign Language

A language is a system of vocal sounds and/or nonverbal systems by which group members communicate with one another. Some languages do not have a written system. Individuals who are deaf are not able to hear the sounds that make up oral languages and have developed their own language for communication. American

Sign Language (ASL) is a natural language that has been developed and used by deaf persons. Just in the past 30 years, linguists have come to recognize ASL as a language with complex grammar and well-regulated syntax. A growing number of colleges and universities will accept fluency in ASL to meet a second-language requirement. The majority of adults who are deaf in Canada and the United States use ASL. Like oral languages, different sign languages have developed in different countries.

Children who are deaf are able to pick up the syntax and rhythms of signing as spontaneously as hearing children pick up their oral languages. Both children who hear and children who are deaf who are born into deaf families usually learn ASL from birth. Most deaf children, however, have hearing parents and do not have the opportunity to learn ASL until they attend a school for the deaf, where they learn it from their peers.

ASL is the only sign language recognized as a language in its own right, rather than a variation of spoken English. With its own vocabulary, syntax, and grammatical rules, ASL does not correspond completely to spoken or written English (Heward, 2000, Smith 2001). To communicate with the hearing, those who are deaf often use signed English. It is a system of signing that parallels the English language. Rather than have its own language patterns like ASL, it translates the English oral or written word into a sign. Few hearing individuals know ASL because they rarely observe it. Individuals who are deaf use it to communicate with each other. When one sees an interpreter on television or at a meeting, it is usually signed English that is being observed (Swank, 1997).

Sign language is one component of the deaf microculture that sets its users apart from the hearing. In part because of the residential school experiences of many individuals who are deaf, a distinct cultural community has developed. As a cultural community, they are "highly endogamous, with in-group marriages estimated at between 86% and 90% percent of all marriages involving individuals who are deaf" (Reagan, 1988, p. 2). Although ASL is the major language of the deaf community, many individuals are bilingual in English and ASL.

Bilingualism

Language diversity in the United States has been maintained primarily because of continuing immigration from non-English speaking countries. In its short history, the United States has probably been host to more bilingual people than any other country. Each new wave of immigrants has brought with it its own language and then witnessed the erosion of that language in the face of the implicitly acknowledged public language, English (Hakuta, 1986, p. 166).

One fascinating aspect of bilingualism in the United States is its extreme instability, for it is a transitional stage toward monolingualism in English. The incessant move toward monolingualism, however, is a very rapid process (Hakuta, 1986). Schools have assisted in this process. Prior to World War I, native languages were used in many schools where a large number of ethnic group members were trying to preserve their language. In this country, the maintenance of native languages other than English now depends on the efforts of members of the language group through churches and other community activities. Now, even our bilingual education programs are designed to move students quickly into English-only instruction. However, a review of the research suggests that bilingual education in the United States is far more effective than a strictly monolingual approach (Corson, 1999).

Early language policies throughout this country were extremely narrow in focus, and failed to take into account the social-cultural problems inherent in language and learning (Corson, 1999). The acquisition of a second language is important when it serves one's own social and economic needs. Without English language skills, immigrants are often relegated to the most menial, lowest paying, and sometimes dangerous jobs in society.

During the civil rights movement of the 1960s, language-minority groups, especially Latinos, began to celebrate their native language traditions. Other ethnic groups decried the loss of their native languages over a few generations and blamed the school's Americanization process for the loss. The passage of federal legislation for bilingual education resulted. Many of those early advocates, however, hoped that the bilingual programs would help maintain and promote the native language while teaching English skills.

What constitutes bilingualism? It implies the ability to use two languages. People hold different opinions about the degree of fluency required. Whereas some maintain that a bilingual individual must have native-like fluency in both languages, others suggest that measured competency in two languages constitutes bilingualism (Baca and Cervantes, 1998).

Hakuta (1986) has identified two types of bilingualism: subtractive bilingualism and additive bilingualism. Subtractive bilingualism occurs when a second language replaces the first. Additive bilingualism occurs when the two languages are of equal value and one does not dominate the other. The latter has the more positive effect on academic achievement.

Accents

An accent generally refers to how an individual pronounces words. Because many monolingual Japanese speakers do not have the sound of an "*l*" in their language, many tend to pronounce English words that begin with the letter "*l*" as if they began with the letter "*r*". Thus, the word *light* may be pronounced as if it were *right*, and *long* as if it were *wrong*. Note that an accent differs from the standard language only in pronunciation. A dialect, however, may contain changes both in pronunciation and in grammatical patterns of the language system. For example, in Hawaiian Pidgin English, "Don't do that" may evolve into "No make like dat." Teachers should be aware that persons who speak with an accent often speak standard English but, at this level of their linguistic development, are unable to speak without an accent.

DIALECT DIFFERENCES

There is no agreement on the number of dialects of English spoken in the United States. There are at least eleven regional dialects: Eastern New England, New York City, Western Pennsylvania, Middle Atlantic, Appalachian, Southern, Central, Midland, North Central, Southwest, and Northwest (Owens, 1992). Social, ethnic, age, and gender considerations, however, complicate any attempt to isolate areas completely.

Dialects

In the United States, English is the primary language. Numerous English dialects are used throughout the country, however. Dialects are language rule systems used by identifiable groups that vary in some manner from a language standard considered ideal. Each dialect shares a common set of grammatical rules with the standard language and should be considered structurally equal (Wolfram, Adger, & Christian, 1999). Theoretically, dialects of a language are mutually intelligible to all speakers of the language; however, some dialects enjoy greater social acceptance and prestige. No dialect is better than any other, nor should a dialect be characterized as substandard, deviant, or inferior (Owens, 1992).

Certain languages are sometimes improperly referred to as dialects. Examples are the labeling of African languages as African dialects or the languages of the American Indians as Indian dialects. This improper practice would be synonymous with labeling French and German as dialects spoken in the different countries in Europe.

Dialects differ from one another in a variety of ways. Differences in vowels are a primary means of distinguishing regional differences, whereas consonant differences tend to distinguish social dialects. Regional and social dialects cannot be divorced from one another, however, because an individual's dialect may be a blend of both. In Northern dialects, for example, the "*i*" in words such as *time, pie,* and *side* is pronounced with a long-i sound that Wolfram and Christian (1989) describe as a rapid production of two vowel sounds, one sounding more like *ah* and the other like *ee.* The second sound glides off the first so that *time* becomes *taem, pie* becomes *pae,* and *side* becomes *saed.* Southern and Southern-related dialects may eliminate the gliding *e,* resulting in *tam* for *time, pa* for *pie,* and *sad* for *side.*

In social dialects, consonants tend to distinguish one dialect from another. Common examples of consonant pronunciation differences are in the "*th*" sound and in the consonants "*r*" and "*l.*" In words such as *these, them,* and *those,* the beginning "*th*" sound may be replaced with a "*d*", resulting in *dese, dem,* and *dose.* In words such as *think, thank,* and *throw,* the "*th*" may be replaced with a "*t*," resulting in *tink, tank,* and *trow.* Wolfram, Adger, and Christian (1999) suggest that middle-class groups may substitute the "*d*" for "*th*" to some extent in casual speech, whereas working-class groups make the substitution more often.

In some groups, particularly the African American working class, the *th* in the middle or end of the word is not spoken. The "*th*" in *author* or *tooth* may be replaced with an "*f,*" as in *aufor* and *toof.* In words such as *smooth,* a "*v*" may be substituted for the "*th,*" resulting in *smoov.* In regional and socially related dialects, "*r*" and "*l*" may be lost, as in *ca* for *car* and *sef* for *self.*

Among dialects, differences in various aspects of grammatical usage can also be found. Wolfram, Adger, and Christian (1999) suggest that nonstandard grammar tends to carry with it a greater social stigma than nonstandard pronunciation.

A common example of grammatical differences in dialect is in the absence of suffixes from verbs where they are usually present in standard dialects. For example, the *-ed* suffix to denote past tense is sometimes omitted, as in, "Yesterday we play a long time." Other examples of grammatical differences are the omission of the *s* used in the present tense to denote agreement with certain subjects. "She have a car" may be used instead of "She has a car." The omission of the suffix has been observed in certain American Indian communities, as well as among members of the African American working class. In the dialect of some African American working-class groups, the omission of the *s* in the plural form of certain words and phrases, as in "two boy" rather than "two boys," has been observed. *Two* is plural, and an *s* to show possession after *boy* is viewed as redundant. Also often omitted in these dialect groups is the possessive '*s,* as in "my friend car" instead of "my friend's car."

Variations in language patterns among groups are significant when compared by age, socioeconomic status, gender, ethnic group, and geographic region (Wolfram, Adger, & Christian, 1999). For example, individuals in the 40- to 60-year-old age group tend to use language patterns different from those of teenage groups. Teenagers tend to adopt certain language patterns that are characteristic of their age group. Slang words, particular pronunciation of some words, and certain grammatical contractions are often related to the teenage and younger groups.

Social factors play a role in the choice of language patterns. The more formal the situations are, the greater the likelihood is of more formal speech patterns being used. The selection of appropriate speech patterns appears to come naturally and spontaneously. Individuals are usually able to "read their environment" and to select, from their large repertoire, the language or speech pattern that is appropriate for the situation.

Wolfram, Adger, and Christian (1999) also indicate that although the evidence is not conclusive, the range between high and low pitch used in African American communities is greater than that found in white communities. Such differences would, of course, be the result of learned behavior. African American males may tend to speak with raspiness in their voices. American women, it has been suggested, may typically have a greater pitch distribution over a sentence than do men.

Other differences in dialects exist as well. Because educators are likely to find dialect differences in the classroom, additional reading in this area may be appropriate. The "Suggested Readings" section at the end of this chapter includes some helpful resources.

Bi-dialecticism

Certain situations, both social and professional, may dictate adjustments in dialect. Some individuals may have the ability to speak in two or more dialects, making them bi-dialectal. In possessing the skills to speak in more than one dialect, an individual may have some distinct advantages and may be able to function and gain acceptance in more cultural contexts. A large-city executive with a rural farm background may quickly abandon his three-piece suit and put on his jeans and boots when visiting his parents' home. When speaking with the hometown folks, he may put aside the standard English necessary in his business dealings and return to the hometown dialect that proves he is still the local town person they have always known.

Likewise, an African American school psychologist who speaks standard English both at home and at work may elect to include some degree of Black English in her conference with African American parents at the school. The vernacular may be used to develop rapport and credibility with the parents. This strategy may allow the psychologist to show the parents that she is African American more than just in appearance and that she understands the problems of black children and parents. However, she may choose to use little if any of the parent's dialect in order to maintain her credibility as a professional. In a conference with white parents, in contrast, the same psychologist may choose to be scrupulously careful to speak only standard English if she believes that this is necessary for effective communication.

Children tend to learn adaptive behaviors rapidly, a fact that is often demonstrated in the school. Children who fear peer rejection as a result of speaking standard English may choose to use their dialect even at the expense of criticism by the teacher. Others may choose to speak with the best standard English they possess in dealing with the teacher but use the dialect or language of the group when outside the classroom.

Educators must be aware of children's need for peer acceptance, and balance this need with realistic educational expectations. Pressuring a child to speak standard English at all times and punishing him or her for any use of dialects may be detrimental to the overall well-being of the child.

Standard English

Although standard English is often referred to in the literature, no single dialect can be identified as such. In reality, however, the speech of a certain group of people in each community tends to be identified as standard. Norms vary with communities, and there are actually two norms: informal standard and formal standard. The language considered proper in a community is the informal standard. Its norms tend to vary from community to community. Formal standard is the acceptable written language that is typically found in grammar books. Few individuals speak formal standard English.

Because no particular dialect is inherently and universally standard, the determination of what is and what is not standard is usually made by people or groups of people in positions of power and status to make such a judgment. Teachers and employers are among those in such a position. These are the individuals who decide what is and what is not acceptable in the school and in the workplace. Thus, people seeking success in school and in the job market often tend to use the standard language as identified and used by individuals in positions of power. Moreover, certain individuals may be highly respected in the community. Just as people who are respected and admired often influence hairstyles, the language of those who are admired also serves as a model. Generally speaking, standard American English is a composite of the language spoken by the educated professional middle class. With the wide variations of dialects, there are actually several dialects of standard American English (Wolfram, Adger, & Christian, 1999).

Perspectives on Black English

Black English, sometimes referred to as Vernacular Black English, African American Vernacular English (AAVE). or Ebonics, is one of the best-known dialects spoken in the United States. It becomes controversial when schools consider using it for instruction. Its use is widespread and it is a form of communication for the majority of African Americans. It is a linguistic system used by working-class African Americans within their speech community (Fairchild & Edwards-Evans, 1990; Owens, 1992; Wolfram, Adger, & Christian, 1999).

Woffard (1979) estimates that approximately 80% of African Americans use Black English consistently and that 19% use speech that, with the exception of slight differences in vocal quality and pronunciation, is indistinguishable from standard English. The remaining 1% uses other dialects.

Black English is considered by most linguists and African Americans to be a legitimate system of communication. It is a systematic language rule system of its own and not a substandard, deviant, or improper form of English. Although differences are found between Black English and standard English, they both operate with the same type of structural rules as any other type of language or dialect (Fairchild & Edwards-Evans, 1990). Wolfram, Adger, and Christian (1999) assert that when comparing the linguistic characteristics of Black English and standard English, we find far more common language features than distinctive ones. They dispute the theory by some linguists that Black English is increasingly evolving in a divergent path from other vernacular English dialects. In fact, there is considerable overlap among Black English, Southern English, and Southern white nonstandard English. Much of the distinctiveness of the dialect is in its intonational patterns, speaking rate, and distinctive lexicons (Owens, 1992).

Teacher bias against Black English is common among majority-group educators and among some African American educators as well. Although Black English is an ethnically related dialect, it is also a dialect related to social class. Dialects related to lower social classes, such as Hawaiian pidgin, Appalachian English, and Black English, are typically stigmatized in our multidialectal society. Unfortunately, many people attach relative values to certain dialects and to the speakers of those dialects. Assumptions are made regarding the intelligence, ability, and moral character of the speakers, and this can have a significant negative impact (Wolfram, Adger, & Christian, 1999). As such, the use of these dialects without the ability to speak standard American English leaves the speaker with a distinct social, educational, and sometimes occupational disadvantage. The refusal to acknowledge Black English as a legitimate form of communication may be considered Eurocentric. Insofar as teachers endorse this rejection, they are sending a message to many of their African American students that the dialect of their parents, grandparents, and significant others in their lives is substandard and unacceptable.

Dialects and Education

In December 1996, the Oakland (California) Unified School District moved into the center of controversy with their adopted policy on black English, or Ebonics. African American students comprise 53% of Oakland's 52,300-student district. Of all the ethnic groups in the district, they have, on average, the lowest grade point average (1.8), and they comprise 71% of the students enrolled in special education programs. In an attempt to remediate some academic problems of black students in the district, the school board voted unanimously to recognize black English, or Ebonics, as a second language and the primary language of its African American students.

The school board's December 18, 1996, resolution stated, "African language systems are genetically based and not a dialect of English, and . . . the interests of the Oakland Unified School District in providing equal opportunities for all of its students dictate limited-English proficient education programs recognizing the English-language acquisition and improvement skills of African-American students are as fundamental as is application for bilingual principles for others whose primary languages are other than English "(*Education Week,* 1997, pp. 1–2).

State and federal education officials had been highly critical of the district's limited-English-proficient (LEP) programs and had strongly urged the district to focus greater attention on the 16,000 LEP students. These students were primarily

VIDEO INSIGHT

Ebonics and Teaching Standard English

Have you ever spoken with someone from a different part of the country and had difficulty understanding some of his or her expressions or speech patterns?

In 1996, a school board in Oakland, California, voted to recognize black English, or Ebonics, as the primary language of many of the district's students. Since then, educators, activists, and ordinary citizens have jumped into the debate over the role of dialects and standard English in the classroom. With a group of peers, stage your own "roundtable" to try to decide whether the use of Ebonics or other dialects should be accepted or should be challenged as being detrimental to the learning of standard English. How will you address the cultural influences that are reflected in the language that your students use in your classroom?

from Cantonese-, Spanish-, and Vietnamese-speaking backgrounds. An official of the Oakland teachers' union suggested that the resolutions emanated out of feelings that African American students have not been served well and that they have not had the resources they needed (Schnaiberg, 1997a).

The resolution was seen by some as an attempt by the school district to obtain more funding from both state and federal sources for bilingual education. It was praised by some and attacked by others. Prominent African Americans such as Maya Angelou and Jesse Jackson were among the early critics. It reached the U.S. Senate, where a senator from North Carolina was quoted as saying, "This is political correctness that has simply gone out of control." Former U.S. Secretary of Education Richard Riley stated, "Elevating 'black English' to the status of a language is not the way to raise standards of achievement in our schools and for our students. . . . The use of federal bilingual-education funds for what has been called 'black English' or 'Ebonics' is not permitted. The administration's policy is that 'Ebonics' is a nonstandard form of English and not a foreign language" (Schnaiberg, 1997a, p. 3).

Responding to the maelstrom, the school board members invited Jesse Jackson to meet with them and then clarified or modified their position. The board indicated that the acquisition of standard English should be a goal of the district's students and that teachers should develop skills to work effectively with students who used Ebonics. Ebonics would be used as a means to develop standard English skills. Jackson modified his position and gave conditional support to the school board's efforts. The school board revised the wording of the resolution. Still maintaining that Ebonics is not a dialect of English, the revision no longer suggests that it is genetically based. It no longer calls for students to be taught in their "primary language" of Ebonics and emphasizes that the district should implement programs that move students from the language patterns they bring to school toward English proficiency. The Oakland controversy has calmed itself for now. What is certain, however, is that the controversy over dialects in schools will continue. Meanwhile, U.S. Representative Peter T. King (R, N.Y.) introduced a bill to bar the use of federal money to support "any program that is based upon the premise that Ebonics is a legitimate language" (Schnaiberg, 1997b, p. 2).

Lost in the Oakland School Board controversy was the fact that education literature suggested that the original decision had considerable scientific support (Wheeler, 1999). This was clearly demonstrated by the support of the Linguistic Society of America (Wolfram, Adger, & Christian, 1999) and the success of the 1977 Bridge program (Wheeler, 1999). The Bridge program consisted of a series of readings and cassette recordings using Black English in an attempt to help children learn to read. After 4 months of testing, it was established that African American students using these dialect readers demonstrated 6.2 months of progress, while the African American students using the standard English material showed only 1.2 months of progress over the same period of time (Wheeler, 1999). Although public outcry forced the cancellation of the Bridge readers, the success of the program was undeniable. Learning to read and dialect acquisition are two distinct tasks. Attempts to merge the two may contribute to children's failure in school (Wheeler, 1999).

The issue of requiring a standard American English dialect in the schools is both sensitive and controversial. Because of the close relationship between ethnic minority groups and dialects that are often considered nonstandard, this issue also has civil rights implications.

To require that standard English be spoken in the schools is considered discriminatory by some who think that such a requirement places an additional educational burden on the nonstandard-English-speaking students. The insistence on standard English may hinder the acquisition of other educational skills, making it difficult for these students to succeed. It is argued that such practice denies nonstandard-English-speaking students the same educational opportunities as others and thus morally, if not legally, denies them their civil rights.

Others argue that the school has the responsibility to teach each student standard English to better cope with the demands of society. There is little doubt that the inability to speak standard English can be a decided disadvantage to an individual in certain situations, such as seeking employment.

Dialect differences in the school may cause problems beyond the interference with the acquisition of skills. A second problem tends to be subtler and involves the attitude of teachers and other school personnel toward students with nonstandard dialects. Too often, educators and other individuals make erroneous assumptions about nonstandard dialects, believing at times that the inability to speak a standard dialect reflects lower intelligence. Wolfram, Adger, and Christian (1999) suggest that unlike prejudice based on gender or ethnicity, which may often result in litigation and positive change, language prejudices are rarely challenged and, therefore, are much less likely to change.

In a university classroom experiment by one of the authors, segments of two tape recordings in the area of language and culture were played. Neither speaker was identified by name, occupation, or ethnicity; however, both are nationally prominent individuals in the field of linguistics. Both hold earned doctoral degrees, and both are African American. One individual speaks in standard English. The other individual speaks in standard English with a slight trace of a black speech pattern. His speech leaves little doubt by his listeners that he is African American.

After the two tape segments were played, the students were asked to indicate which of the two speakers, in their opinion, was the more intelligent. The class, which included several African American students, was unanimous in selecting the individual who spoke with standard English and no accent or black speech patterns.

This simple classroom experiment suggests that most people have distinct preconceived notions about nonstandard-English-speaking individuals. If teachers and other school personnel react in this manner to students, the consequences could be serious. Students may be treated as if they are less intelligent than they are, and they may respond in a self-fulfilling prophecy in which they function at a level lower than they are capable of reaching. In cases where children are tracked in schools, they may be placed in groups below their actual ability level. This problem surfaces in the form of disproportionately low numbers of African American and Latino children being placed in classes for the gifted and talented (Office of Civil Rights, 1999). School administrators cite the inability to appropriately identify these gifted and talented ethnic minority children as one of their biggest challenges. Teachers who have negative attitudes toward children with nonstandard dialects may be less prone to recognize potential giftedness and may be less inclined to refer these children for possible assessment and placement.

Educators have several alternatives for handling dialect in the educational setting. The first is to accommodate all dialects on the basis that they are all equal. The second is to insist that only a standard dialect be allowed in the schools. This second alternative would allow for the position that functional ability in such a dialect is necessary for success in personal, as well as vocational, pursuits.

A third alternative is a position between the two extremes, and it is the alternative most often followed. Native dialects are accepted for certain uses, but standard English is encouraged and insisted on in other circumstances. Students in such a school setting may be required to read and write in standard English because this is the primary written language they will encounter in this country. They would not be required to eliminate their natural dialect in speaking. Such a compromise allows students to use two or more dialects in the school. It tends to acknowledge the legitimacy of all dialects while recognizing the social and vocational implications of being able to function in standard English.

To answer these questions online, go to the Pause to Reflect module for this chapter of the Companion Website.

PAUSE TO REFLECT

Some activists have suggested that the language of instruction should be in the dialect of students' cultures. Others argue that standard English should be the only acceptable language within the classroom. What are the advantages and disadvantages of each approach? Do you think teachers should at least be familiar with the dialects used by students in the classroom? Why or why not? How do you plan to respond to different dialects in your classroom?

The issue that seems to be at stake with some supporters of the right to use nonstandard dialects is the recognition of the legitimacy of the particular dialect. Few, if any, will deny the social and vocational implications of dialects. Some parents may prefer to develop, or have their children develop, a standard dialect. However, the arrogant posture of some school officials in recognizing standard dialects as the only legitimate form of communication is offensive to many and may preclude rational solutions to this sensitive issue.

NONVERBAL COMMUNICATION

Although most people think of communication as being verbal in nature, nonverbal communication can be just as important in the total communication process. Because it is so clearly interwoven into the overall fabric of verbal communication, nonverbal communication often appears to be inseparable from it.

Nonverbal communication can serve several functions. It conveys messages through one's attitude, personality, manner, or even dress. It augments verbal communication by reinforcing what one says: A smile or a pat on the back reinforces the positive statement made to a student. It contradicts verbal communication: A frown accompanying a positive statement to a student sends a mixed or contradictory message. Nonverbal communication can replace a verbal message: A finger to the lips or a teacher's hand held in the air may communicate "Silence" to a class.

The total meaning of communication includes not only the surface message as stated (content) but also the undercurrent (emotions or feelings associated with that content). The listener should watch for congruence between the verbal message and the message being sent nonverbally.

Research has supported the contention that definite prejudices are based on physical characteristics. For example, physical attractiveness plays a part in the way we perceive other people. If one has a bias against a particular group, individuals from that group could be perceived as unattractive, and can suffer from social rejection based on the perceptions.

Cultural differences have profound implications on how individuals interact non-verbally with one another. The differences also have implications for educators. Some cultural groups are more prone toward physical contact than others. Latinos and Native Hawaiians, for example, tend to be among the contact cultures. Consequently, one can often observe Latinos or Hawaiians greeting each other with a warm embrace. This is true among the men from these groups. As they meet their friends, it is certainly not uncommon to see these men embracing one another. On the other hand, however, it might be surprising to see Asian men embracing one another. Of course, the more acculturated Asian American men are likely to observe behaviors typical in the general society.

The usual conversational distance between white Americans is about twenty-one inches. A distance much greater than this may make the individuals feel too far apart for normal conversation and a normal voice level. Individuals of other cultural groups, such as Arabs, Latin Americans, and Southern Europeans, are accustomed to standing considerably closer when they talk. In contrast with these contact cultures, Asians and Northern Europeans have been identified as non-contact cultures and may maintain a greater distance in conversation. Students maintain differential distances in cross-cultural relationships. White Americans tend to maintain a greater distance when conversing with blacks than when conversing among themselves. Women tend to allow a closer conversational space than do men. Straight individuals distance themselves more from conversational partners they perceive to be gay (Samovar & Porter, 1991).

Educators need to be aware that different cultural groups have different expectations when it involves contact with a teacher. Some groups may view a pat on the head of a child to be a supportive gesture. However, some Southeast Asians believe that the individuals' spirit resides in the head, and a pat on the head of a child may very well be viewed as offensive by both the parents and child.

Other nonverbal issues may involve the facial expressions or behaviors of the student. American teachers typically expect a child to look at them while they are having a conversation. However, some groups consider it disrespectful for the child to look directly into the eyes of the teacher. Consequently, as a sign of respect, the child may look at the floor while either speaking to the teacher or being spoken to. The teacher, however, may view the behavior in an opposite manner than intended, and demand that the child look her or him in the eye.

Any discussion of nonverbal behavior has inherent dangers. As examples are given, the reader must realize that these are generalizations and not assume that any given behavior can immediately be interpreted in a certain way. Nonverbal communications are often a prominent part of the context in which verbal messages are sent. Although context never has a specific meaning, communication is always dependent on context.

SECOND LANGUAGE ACQUISITION

With the arrival of new immigrants annually into the United States, the resulting effect is the addition of more language minority students in our schools. Most of these students are able to move from bilingual education programs to English-only instruction. Motivation is usually high. The acquisition of English skills serves both social and economic needs. Without linguistic acculturation, assimilation into mainstream society may be impossible. This, in turn, effectively keeps non-English speakers or English language learners (ELL, previously referred to as limited English proficient [LEP]) out of many job markets.

Role of First Language in Second Language Acquisition

Most children acquire their first language naturally through constant interaction with their parents or significant others. Knowledge of their first language plays an important role in the process of acquiring and learning a second language. Some concepts acquired through their first language (e.g., Spanish) can be transferred to a second language (e.g., English) when a comparable concept in the second language

English-speaking students usually learn a second language as a foreign language in schools. Non-English speakers, in contrast, learn English in bilingual, English as a second language, or immersion programs.

exists. However, English speakers should not think of Spanish, French, Chinese, or any other language as essentially English with Spanish, French, or Chinese words that, if translated, is basically the same language. There are words and concepts in all of these languages for which there is no English equivalent. There may be no exact English translation to convey the exact same meaning.

In the study of second language acquisition, various occurrences have been observed. When an ELL child's language development is interrupted or replaced because of instruction of a second language in school prior to the development of his or her first language proficiency skills, the following may result: (a) loss of first language (Lambert & Freed, 1982); (b) mixing or combining of the first and second language, resulting in the child's own unique (idiosyncratic) communication system (Ortiz & Maldonado-Colon, 1986); (c) limited proficiency in both first and second languages (Skutnabb-Kangas & Toukomaa, 1976); or (d) an inability to develop English language proficiency in his or her school years (Cummins, 1984).

Corson (1999) argues that early brain development of young children is shaped by the signs and symbols involved in first language acquisition. The failure of schools to build on a child's first language during these early years may have serious consequences in the learning process. The implications of these observed language behaviors suggest that ELL children should be allowed to develop a firm grasp of basic concepts in their home language prior to instruction of academic concepts in an English-only environment.

Language Proficiency

Cummins (1984) found that many ELL students failed academically after completing English as a second language (ESL) training and being placed in monolingual English class settings. Many of these students were subsequently referred and placed in special education classes. In carefully studying the language characteristics of these students, Cummins found that in two years these students were able to acquire adequate English communication skills to suggest to their teacher that they were prepared to function in a monolingual English class placement. Cummins also found, however, that the basic language skills, which he labeled "basic interpersonal communicative skills" (BICS), were inadequate to function in high-level academic situations. Although two years was adequate for everyday conversational usage, an additional 5 to 7 years of school training was essential to develop the higher levels of proficiency required in highly structured academic situations. Cummins (1984) labeled this higher level of proficiency "cognitive academic language proficiency" (CALP). Cummins' framework for conceptualizing language proficiency has been widely adopted by many ESL and bilingual special education programs and has profound implications for language minorities. Cummins (2000) suggests that there are two reasons why it takes much longer for ELL students to learn academic language than it does to learn basic conversational language. First, academic language is the language of subject matter (e.g., science, math), literature, magazines, and so forth. It is very different from conversational language. As students progress through successive grades, they encounter words that Cummins characterizes as "low frequency" words. These are words with Greek and Latin derivations. In addition they are exposed to more complex syntax (e.g., passive) and abstract expressions that are seldom if ever heard in everyday conversation. Secondly, academic language is what educators develop among native English speakers who are already fluent in conversational English when they enter school. Therefore, the ELL student is learning conversational English while classmates are at a higher level, learning academic English.

OFFICIAL ENGLISH (ENGLISH ONLY) CONTROVERSY

In 1981, U.S. Senator S. I. Hayakawa, a strong and harsh critic of bilingual education and bilingual voting rights, introduced a constitutional amendment to make English the official language of the United States. The measure sought to prohibit federal and state laws, ordinances, regulations, orders, programs, and policies from requiring the use of other languages. Hayakawa's efforts were made not only in support of English but also against bilingualism. Had the amendment been adopted, Hayakawa's proposal would have reversed the efforts that began in the 1960s to accommodate linguistic minorities in this country. The English Language Amendment died without a hearing in the 97th Congress (Crawford, 1992).

In 1983, Hayakawa helped found the organization called "U.S. English" and began lobbying efforts that resulted in a reported 1.4 million-member organization and an annual budget in the millions of dollars. The movement, also referred to as "Official English" or "English Only," has mounted a major effort to lobby the U.S. Congress to pass legislation to make English the official language of the United States. By 2000, English as the official language had been adopted as statutes or state constitutional amendments in 25 states (Crawford, 1992; U.S. English, 2000).

The organization reports that, in a 1995 survey of 1,208 Americans, 86% favored making English the official language of the United States (U.S. English, 1997). U.S. English supports only the limited use of bilingual education. The organization favors sheltered English immersion, and it maintains its position that ELL students should be transitioned completely out of bilingual education and into mainstream English usage within a maximum of 1 or 2 years.

Official English has become a polarizing issue. William Bennett (1992), secretary of education during the Reagan administration, leveled an attack on the Bilingual Education Act as a failure and a waste of tax dollars. Bennett received a considerable amount of mail supporting his position. An examination of these letters by Crawford (1992), however, found that they contained little with respect to the education of non-English-speaking students. Instead, the letter writers used the opportunity to vent their frustrations about illegal immigrants on welfare, Asians and Latinos overrunning communities, and other issues such as the out-of-control birthrates of linguistic minorities. They were offended by the use of tax dollars to support what they viewed as the perpetuation of a foreign language.

For supporters of the English Only movement, English has always been the common language in the United States. It is a means to resolve conflict in a nation that is diverse in ethnic, linguistic, and religious groups. English is an essential tool of social mobility and economic advancement (Crawford, 1992).

U.S. English members have vigorously supported California Proposition 227, which passed in 1998. This proposition is often referred to as the Unz initiative after its coauthor, Ron Unz. This new law essentially puts an end to bilingual education in the state. Citing numerous examples of bilingual education failures, the proposition requires all language minority students to be educated in sheltered English immersion programs, not normally intended to exceed one year. Sheltered English immersion or structured English immersion involves a classroom where English language acquisition is accomplished with nearly all instruction in English, but with the curriculum and presentation designed for children who are learning the language. At the completion of the year, the students are transferred to English language mainstream classrooms (Unz and Tuchman, 1998). The new law allows parents to seek waivers and, if granted, the child's education may continue in a bilingual classroom. If schools or teachers fail to implement a child's education as prescribed by the law, they may be sued.

As might be expected, supporters of bilingual education have vigorously attacked the proposition with concerns that the Unz initiative will spread to other states. Proposition 227 opponents argue that the Unz initiative was not backed by research or scientific data. Rather, it was based on observations of the high failure and dropout rate of ELL students, primarily Latino. It was also based on observations that most ELL students are able to grasp the fundamentals of speaking English in a year. They support their arguments against the proposition by citing research (e.g., Cummins) which suggest that only basic conversational skills can be acquired in such a limited time and not the necessary academic language skills, which take years longer to develop adequately. They contend that the new law is a "one size fits all" approach to educating students and that it cannot have lasting benefits. Further, they argue, that during K–4 years in school, it is extremely difficult for parents to obtain waivers to keep their children in bilingual education. Parents, they contend, have no appeal rights, and the law intimidates teachers and administrators and inhibits them from doing what they know is educationally appropriate for students (NABE, 2000).

Opponents of the English Only movement readily agree on the importance of learning English. However, they view their adversaries as individuals trying to force Anglo conformity by ending essential services in foreign languages. They view the attacks on bilingual education as unjustified because good bilingual education has been shown to be effective. Bad bilingual education, they concede, is ineffective; it is seldom bilingual education, except in name. Opponents of bilingual education, they argue, have seen to it that programs fail by giving inadequate support or resources to programs, by staffing programs with unqualified personnel, by obtaining faulty test results on bilingual education students by testing them in English, and by other means that cast negative outcomes on bilingual education (Fillmore, 1992).

It is true that many earlier immigrants did not have the benefit of bilingual education programs. Thrust into sink-or-swim situations, they ended up swimming, succeeding in school, and finding their niche in society. It is also true, however, that many students were unable to swim and so sank in their efforts to acculturate in school. Since the number of language minority students today has increased dramatically, we can ill afford a sink-or-swim system, which would result in failure for massive numbers of students

In spite of their differences, the majority of the individuals who support bilingual education, as well as those who are opposed to it, are well-intentioned individuals who want to enhance the educational opportunities for immigrant children. If all interested parties would be less concerned with the politics of the issue and would base their programmatic preferences on sound, well-documented research, the students would be the ultimate winners.

EDUCATIONAL IMPLICATIONS

Language is an integral part of life and an integral part of our social system. The diversity and richness of the language systems in this country are a reflection of the richness and diversity of American culture. The ability of U.S. educators to recognize and appreciate the value of different language groups will, to some extent, determine the effectiveness of our educational system.

All children bring to school the language systems of their cultures. It is the obligation of each educator to ensure the right of each child to learn in the language of the home until the child is able to function well enough in English. This may imply the use of English as a second language (ESL) or bilingual programs for ELL children. Equally important is the responsibility to understand cultural and linguistic differences and to recognize the value of these differences while working toward enhancing the student's linguistic skills in the dominant language. Although it is important to appreciate and respect a child's native language or dialect, it is also important that the teacher communicate the importance and advantages of being able to speak and understand standard English in certain educational, vocational, and social situations.

Language and Educational Assessment

Few issues in education are as controversial as the assessment of culturally diverse children. The problem of disproportionate numbers of ethnic minority children in special education classes for children with disabilities has resulted from such assessment. The characteristics of language are directly related to the assessment of linguistically different children. Despite genuine attempts to accommodate the diverse backgrounds of students, many of the educational and intelligence tests used to assess ethnic and linguistic minority children are normed primarily on children from white, middle-class backgrounds. There is an expectation of cultural and linguistic uniformity in the development of assessment tests (Wolfram, Adger, & Christian, 1999). Therefore, such tests are often considered biased against the student who is not proficient in English or who speaks a dialect. It is unlikely that there are any completely unbiased assessment instruments being used to test achievement or intelligence.

Most intelligence tests rely heavily on language. Yet, little attempt may be made to determine a child's level of proficiency in the language or dialect in which a test is administered. For example, a Latino child may be able to perform a task that is called for in an intelligence test but may not be able to understand the directions given in English. Even if a Spanish translation was available, it might not be in a dialect with which the child is familiar. Using an unfamiliar Spanish dialect may place a student at an extreme disadvantage and may yield test results that are not a true indication of the student's abilities. The same may be true for Asians, African Americans, or Native Americans who are being tested. Rather than accurately testing specific knowledge or aptitude, all too often intelligence tests measure a student's competence in standard forms of the language (Wolfram, Adger, & Christian, 1999). Corson (1999) warns that one of the dangers of assessment tests is that they measure intelligence by those things that are valued within the dominant group and tend to exclude things that are culturally specific to minority children. Refusal to acknowledge the value of linguistic differences has resulted in inadequate services and the inappropriate placement of children through highly questionable assessment procedures.

Several successful class-action lawsuits have been brought against school boards or school districts on behalf of children placed in special education classes on the basis of low scores on IQ tests. Typically the suits argue that biased and inappropriate test instruments were used on language minority students, which resulted in inappropriate special education placement. Among the cases often cited is *Guadalupe Organization, Inc. v. Tempe Elementary School District No. 3, 587 F.2d 1022, 1030 (9th Cir. 1978)*, which was a suit filed in Arizona that resulted from the disproportionately high placement of Yaqui Indian and Mexican American children in classes for students with mental retardation. *Diana v. State Board of Education* was a suit brought on behalf of children of Mexican immigrants placed in classrooms for students with mental retardation on the basis of low IQ scores on tests argued to be discriminatory.

Bilingual Education

In 1974, a class-action suit on behalf of 1,800 Chinese children was brought before the U.S. Supreme Court. The plaintiffs claimed that the San Francisco Board of Education failed to provide programs designed to meet the linguistic needs of those non-English-speaking children. The failure, they claimed, was in violation of Title VI of the Civil Rights Act of 1964 and the equal protection clause of the Fourteenth Amendment. They argued that if the children could not understand the language used for instruction, they were deprived of an education equal to that of other children and were, in essence, doomed to failure.

The school board defended its policy by stating that the children received the same education afforded other children in the district. The position of the board was that a child's ability to comprehend English when entering school was not the responsibility of the school, but rather the responsibility of the child and the family. In a unanimous decision, the Supreme Court stated: "Under state imposed standards, there was no equality of treatment merely by providing students with the same facilities, textbooks, teachers, and curriculum; for students who do not understand English are effectively foreclosed from any meaningful education" (*Lau v. Nichols*, 1974). The Court did not mandate bilingual education for non-English-speaking or limited English-speaking students. It did stipulate that special language programs were necessary if schools were to provide an equal educational opportunity for such students. Hence, the *Lau* decision gave considerable impetus to the development of bilingual education as well as ESL programs.

In 1975, the Education for All Handicapped Children Act (amended in 1990 as the Individuals with Disabilities Education Act [IDEA]) required each state to avoid the use of racially or culturally discriminating testing and evaluation procedures in the placement of children with disabilities. It also required that placement tests be administered in the child's native language. In addition, communication with parents regarding such matters as permission to test the child, development of individualized education programs (IEPs), and hearings and appeals must be in their native language.

Throughout the 1970s, the federal government and the state courts sought to shape the direction of bilingual education programs and mandate appropriate testing procedures for students with limited English proficiency. The *Lau* remedies were developed by the U.S. Office of Education to help schools implement bilingual education programs. These guidelines prescribed transitional bilingual education and rejected ESL as an appropriate methodology for elementary students. With a change of the federal administration in 1981, a shift to local policy decisions began to lessen federal controls. Emphasis was placed on making the transition from the native language to English as fast as possible. The methodology for accomplishing the transition became the choice of the local school district. Thus, ESL programs began to operate alongside bilingual programs in many areas. Although the future level of federal involvement in bilingual education is uncertain, there is little doubt among educators that some form of bilingual education is needed.

The definition of bilingual education that is generally agreed on is "the use of two languages as media of instruction" (Baca and Cervantes, 1998). Bilingual education has been supported, in part, by federal funds provided by the Bilingual Education Act of 1968, reauthorized in 1974, 1978, and 1984. Hernandez (1989) reports, "Federal policy encourages the establishment of programs using bilingual educational practices, techniques, and methods or alternative instructional programs in school districts in which bilingual programs are not feasible" (p. 83). Thus, federal legislation defines bilingual education more broadly than do Baca and Cervantes (1998). Methods other than the use of two languages are allowed and even encouraged.

Children who speak little or no English cannot understand English-speaking children or lessons that are presented in English. Not only are these children faced with having to learn new subject matter, but they must also learn a new language and often a new culture. It is likely that many of these children will not be able to keep up with the schoolwork and will drop out of school unless there is appropriate intervention. Approximately 45% of Mexican American children drop out of school before the 12th grade, and the attrition rate of Native American students is as high as 55%. Although language differences may not be the sole contributor to the academic problems of these children, they are considered by many to be a major factor.

The primary goal of bilingual education is not to teach English or a second language per se, but to teach children concepts, knowledge, and skills in the language they know best and to reinforce this information through the use of English (Baca and Cervantes, 1998). Two philosophies currently shape programs in bilingual education: the transitional approach and the maintenance approach.

Transitional programs emphasize bilingual education as a means of moving from the culture and language most commonly used for communication in the home to the mainstream of U.S. language and culture. It is an assimilationist approach in which the ELL student is expected to learn to function effectively in English as soon as possible. The native language of the home is used only to help the student make the transition to the English language. The native language is gradually phased out as the student becomes more proficient in English.

In contrast, maintenance programs provide a pluralistic orientation. The goal is for the ELL student to function effectively in both the native language and English. The student actually becomes bilingual and bicultural in the process, with neither language surfacing as the dominant one. The student's native language and culture are taught concurrently with English and the dominant culture.

Bilingual education can be justified as: (a) the best way to attain maximum cognitive development for ELL students, (b) a means for achieving equal educational opportunity and/or results, (c) a means of easing the transition into the dominant language and culture, (d) an approach to educational reform, (e) a means of promoting positive interethnic relations, and (f) a wise economic investment to help linguistic minority students become maximally productive in adult life for the benefit of society and themselves (Baca and Cervantes, 1998).

Whereas many bilingual educators favor maintenance programs, the majority of the programs in existence are transitional. The acute shortage of trained personnel and the cost of maintenance programs are frequently cited as reasons for the predominance of transitional programs. Bilingual educators, however, strongly support the use of bicultural programs even within the transitional framework. A bicultural emphasis provides students with recognition of the value and worth of their families' cultures and enhances the development or maintenance of a positive self-image.

A 1995 study of 42,000 non-English-speaking students compared the performance of students who had 6 years of well-designed bilingual education programming with that of students who had been placed into an English-speaking environment prior to becoming fluent. The 6-year bilingual education students performed far better on standardized English tests in the 11th grade than the other group. The latter were described as being left out of the discussion in their mainstream classes. The highest achievers, the study found, were children in two-way programs in which English-language children and non-English speakers were mixed together in the same class. Half of the curriculum was taught in a foreign language, and half was taught in English (Hornblower, 1995).

Advocates of bilingual education see the advantages in being bilingual. Although bilingual education programs have primarily been established to develop English skills for ELL students, some offer opportunities for English-speaking students to develop proficiency in other languages. In addition, bilingualism provides an individual with job market advantages. As the United States becomes less parochial, the opportunity for business and other contacts with individuals from other countries increases, providing decided advantages to bilingual individuals.

Bilingual education as it currently exists has many problems and many critics. Research has provided evidence that well-developed and well-delivered bilingual education programming can deliver positive results. Critics have also provided ample evidence that some children in bilingual education programs have fared poorly and many have dropped out of school. What should be recognized is that there is an acute national shortage of qualified bilingual educators. Being bilingual does not necessarily qualify an individual as a bilingual educator. Many who fill bilingual education positions are not fully qualified in their preparation and training. When these individuals fail to deliver desired results, bilingual education is often unfairly characterized as being programmatically unsound.

English as a Second Language

English as a second language (ESL) is a program often confused with bilingual education. In the United States, learning English is an integral part of every bilingual program. But teaching English as a second language in and by itself does not constitute a bilingual program. Both bilingual education and ESL programs promote English proficiency for ELL students. The approach to instruction distinguishes the two programs. Bilingual education accepts and develops native language and culture in the instructional process. Bilingual education may use the native language, as well as English, as the medium of instruction. ESL instruction, however, relies exclusively on English for teaching and learning. ESL programs are used extensively in this country as a primary medium to assimilate ELL children into the linguistic mainstream as quickly as possible. Hence, some educators place less emphasis on the maintenance of home language and culture than on English language acquisition, and they view ESL programs as a viable means for achieving their goals.

LINK TO THE CLASSROOM

Choosing an Approach to Bilingual Education

In some urban and suburban areas, nearly 100 different languages may be used in homes within the school district. The use of English by students from these homes varies along a continuum from total English proficiency to none. How do teachers teach when one or many of their students have limited or no proficiency in English? Think about the following four options:

> *a. In some schools, limited-English-proficient (LEP) students are immersed into an English-only classroom in which they are expected to learn English on their own at the same time that they are supposed to learn the subject matter.*
> *b. Some school districts hire teacher aides who are bilingual and can assist LEP students in the learning process.*
> *c. English as a second language (ESL) is employed by some schools in teaching English.*
> *d. Some schools employ bilingual education, in which instruction is provided in both English and the native language.*

Which of these four approaches is most successful in ensuring that students learn the subject being taught? Why? Why might school districts choose different approaches on the basis of the number of LEP students in a school or school district? What courses or experiences have you had that will prepare you to effectively teach students English language learners? What courses are offered at your college/university to prepare you to work with students whose native language is not English?

Nonverbal Communications in the Classroom

Cultural differences in nonverbal communications between students and teachers can be very frustrating to both. To begin to overcome such differences, a teacher must try to analyze particular nonverbal communications when students, especially those from a different cultural background, are not responding as the teacher expects. What the teacher perceives as inattention on the part of the students, interruptions by the students at times considered inappropriate by the teacher, or even a tendency on the part of the students to look away from the teacher while being addressed may, in fact, be due to cultural differences.

In most school settings, students from subordinate groups are expected to become bicultural and adopt the nonverbal communication patterns of the dominant group while in school. A more sensitive approach is for teachers also to learn to operate biculturally in the classroom.

Teachers should reflect on what is occurring in the classroom when communications are not as expected. The first step is to become more aware of the nature of the difficulty. In the school setting, students should sometimes have access to teachers, counselors, or administrators who are from a culturally similar background. Teachers can make an effort to learn what the cultural cues of students mean and to react appropriately. A more effective approach, however, is to be able to analyze what is happening in the classroom and to respond on the basis of what is known about the student and his or her cultural background.

Summary

The *Lau* decision of 1974 ensures non-English-speaking children the right to an appropriate education that meets their linguistic needs. Even with a legal mandate, appropriate services may not always be delivered because of lack of tolerance or insensitivity to language or dialects that are not considered standard English. Because nonstandard dialects tend to have a negative stigma attached to them, some educators may refuse to view them as legitimate forms of communication. Although they may indeed be legitimate forms of communication and may serve the speaker well in certain contexts, nonstandard English dialects may preclude certain social and vocational opportunities.

Bilingual education has both its supporters and its detractors. Through proper educational programming, however, children with limited English proficiency can have the education to which they are entitled.

To answer these questions online, go to the Chapter Questions module for this chapter of the Companion Website.

Questions for Review

1. How is language a function of culture?
2. Explain why ASL is considered a language parallel to English, German, Chinese, and so on.

3. What are the advantages of being bilingual in the United States? How is bilingualism encouraged and discouraged within educational settings?

4. What are dialects? What factors generally determine whether an individual becomes bidialectal?

5. Why is Black English a controversial issue in education? How should it be handled in the classroom?

6. Why is it important to be sensitive to nonverbal communications between teacher and student and among students?

7. Why might it be unwise to assume that a student is ready for academic instruction in English as soon as he or she has some basic English conversational skills?

8. Contrast maintenance and transitional bilingual education. Which do you think is more appropriate? Why?

9. When might an ESL approach be the most appropriate strategy to use in a classroom?

10. What are some of the issues in the English Only/U.S. English controversy? Why do some individuals support California's Proposition 227, while others oppose it?

11. Is poorly delivered bilingual education better than no bilingual education at all? Why?

12. What changes in your teaching methodology should you make when a deaf student is in your classroom? What changes should you make when you have a student or students whose native language is not English?

References

Baca, L. M., & Cervantes, H. (1998). *The bilingual special education interface* (3rd ed.). Upper Saddle River, NJ: Prentice Hall.

Baratz, J. (1968). Language in the economically disadvantaged child: A perspective. *ASHA, 10,* 145–146.

Bennett, W. (1992). Bilingual education: A failed path. In J. Crawford (Ed.), *Language loyalties.* Chicago: University of Chicago Press.

Bull, P. (1983). *Body movement and interpersonal communication.* New York: Wiley.

Corson, D. (1999). *Language policy in schools: A resource for teachers and administrators.* Mahwah, NJ: Lawrence Erlbaum Associates, Inc.

Crawford, J. (Ed.). (1992). *Language loyalties.* Chicago: University of Chicago Press.

Crystal, D. (1997). *The Cambridge encyclopedia of language* (2nd ed.). Cambridge, UK: Cambridge University Press.

Cummins, J. (1984). *Bilingualism and special education: Issues in assessment and pedagogy.* San Diego: College-Hill Press.

Cummins, J. (2000*) Language, power and pedagogy: Bilingual children in the crossfire.* Clevedon, England: Multicultural Matters.

Diara v. State Board of Education, Civil Action No C-70 37 RFP (N.D.Cal. Jan 7, 1970 and June 18, 1973).

Dicker, S. J. (1996). *Languages in America: A pluralistic view.* Bristol, PA: Multilingual Matters.

Education Week. (1997, January 15). Full text of the "Ebonics" Resolution adopted by Oakland School Board.

Education Week on the Web. Available: http://www.edweek.org/ew/vol-16/16oakc.h16. April 25, 2001.

Fairchild, H. H., & Edwards-Evans, S. (1990). African American dialects and schooling: A review. In A. M. Padilla, H. H. Fairchild, & C. M. Valadez (Eds.), *Bilingual education: Issues and strategies.* Newbury Park, CA: Sage.

Fillmore, L. W. (1992). Against our best interest: The attempt to sabotage bilingual education. In J. Crawford (Ed.), *Language loyalties.* Chicago: University of Chicago Press.

Hakuta, K. (1986). *Mirror of language: The debate on bilingualism.* New York: Basic Books.

Hernandez, H. (1989). *Multicultural education: A teacher's guide to content and process.* Upper Saddle River, NJ: Prentice Hall.

Heward, W. L. (2000). *Exceptional children* (6th ed.). Upper Saddle River, NJ: Prentice Hall.

Hornblower, M. (1995). Putting tongues in check. *Time, 146*(15).

Lambert, R., & Freed, B. (Eds.). (1982). *Loss of language skills.* Rowley, MA: Newbury House.

Lau v. Nichols, 414, U.S., 563-572. (1974, January 21).

Malandro, L. A., & Barker, L. L. (1983). *Introduction to nonverbal communication.* New York: McGraw-Hill.

National Association for Bilingual Education (NABE). (2000). *The Unz intiative: extreme, irresponsible, and hazardous to California's future.* Washington, DC: Author.

Office of Civil Rights. (1999). *1997 elementary and secondary civil rights survey.* Washington, DC: Government Printing Office.

Ortiz, A. A., & Maldonado-Colon, E. (1986). Reducing inappropriate referrals of language minority students in special education. In A. C. Willig & H. F. Greenberg (Eds.), *Bilingualism and learning disabilities: Policy and practice for teachers and administrators.* New York: American Library.

Owens, R. E., Jr. (1992). *Language development.* New York: MacMillan Publishing Co.

Reagan, T. (1988, Fall). Multiculturalism and the deaf: An educational manifesto. *Journal of Research and Development in Education, 22*(1), 1–6.

Samovar, L. A., & Porter, R. E. (1991). *Communication between cultures.* Belmont, CA: Wadsworth.

Schnaiberg, L. (1997a, January 15). "Ebonics" vote puts Oakland in maelstrom. *Education Week* on the Web. Available: http://www.edweek.org/ew/vol-16/16oak.h16.

Schnaiberg, L. (1997b, January 22). Oakland board revises "Ebonics" resolution. *Education Week* on the Web. Available: http://www.edweek.org/ew/vol-16/17ebon.h16.

Skutnabb-Kangas, T., & Toukomaa, P. (1976). *Teaching migrant children's mother tongue and learning the language of the host country in the context of the socio-cultural situation of the migrant family.* Helsinki: Finnish National Commission for UNESCO.

Smith, D. D. (2001). *Introduction to special education* (4th Ed.). Needham Heights, MA: Allyn & Bacon.

Spencer, D. (1988, May). Transitional bilingual education and the socialization of immigrants. *Harvard Educational Review, 58*(2), 133–153.

Swank, L. (1997). Speech and language impairment. In P. Wehman (Ed.), *Exceptional individuals in school, community, and work.* Austin, TX: PRO-ED.

Unz, R. K. & Tuchman, G. M. (1998). Initiative statute: English language education for children in public schools. Palo Alto, CA: Author
(Available: http://www.nabe.org/unz/text).

U.S. Census Bureau. (1996). *Statistical abstract of the United States: 1996* (116th ed.). Washington, DC: U.S. Department of Commerce.

U.S. English. (1997, January 2). [Internet homepage]. Available: http://www.us-english.org/.

U.S. English (2000, September 8). Available: http://www.us-english.org/foundation/issues/otherlang.asp.

Wheeler, R. (Ed.). (1999). *The workings of language: From prescriptions to perspectives.* Connecticut: Praeger.

Woffard, J. (1979). Ebonics: A legitimate system of oral communication. *Journal of Black Studies, 9*(4), 367–382.

Wolfram, W., & Christian, D. (1989). *Dialects and education, issues and answers.* Upper Saddle River, NJ: Prentice Hall.

Wolfram, W., Adger, C., & Christian, D. (1999). *Dialects in schools and communities.* Mahwah, NJ: Lawrence Erlbaum Associates, Inc.

Suggested Readings

Baca, L. M. & Cervantes, H. (1998). *The bilingual special education interface.* Upper Saddle River, NJ: Prentice Hall.

An excellent overview of bilingual special education, this book contains basic but important information on general bilingual education, including litigation and legislation related to the rights of children with limited English proficiency.

Crawford, J. (Ed.). (1992). *Language loyalties.* Chicago: University of Chicago Press.

This excellent treatment of the "Official English/English Only" controversy contains essays, speeches, and articles for and against the "Official English" issue. Included are articles supporting bilingual education and articles against it.

Samovar, L. A., & Porter, R. E. (1991). *Communication between cultures.* Belmont, CA: Wadsworth.

An excellent treatment of language and culture, this book includes chapters on intercultural communication and the communication of a nonmainstream group.

Wolfram, W., Adger, C., & Christian, D. (1999). *Dialects in schools and communities.* Mahwah, NJ: Lawrence Erlbaum Associates, Inc.

This is an excellent overview of dialects by well-recognized authorities in the field of dialects. The text addresses language variations in the United States, and defines and explains dialects and the sources of language differences. It also addresses communicative interactions and cultural styles in the classroom, and explains why language differences do not mean language deficits.

CRITICAL INCIDENTS IN TEACHING

Ebonics

Rudolfo Chavez is the principal of Jackie Robinson Middle School. An appointment was made for him with Ms. Kermit Norton, the mother of a sixth grader. She declined to give Chavez's secretary any information on why she was coming. Chavez exchanges the customary greeting and then asks Ms. Norton what he can do for her. At this point, she calmly tells Mr. Chavez that he can tell his teachers to stop being racist and to start respecting the culture of African American students.

Mr. Chavez is feeling defensive and tried to maintain his composure as he inquires about the nature of the complaint. "This white teacher of Trayson's says to my son to stop talking this Black English stuff because it is bad English and he won't allow it in his classroom. He says it's a low-class dialect, and if Trayson keeps talking like that, he ain't never going to amount to nothing, will never get into college, and won't never get a good job. That's just plain racist. That's an attack against all black folk. His granddaddy and grandmother talk that way. All my kinfolk talk that way. I talk that way. You mean to tell me that this school thinks we're all low-class trash? Is that what your teachers think of black folk?"

Questions for Discussion

To answer these questions online, go to the Critical Incidents module for this chapter of the Companion Website.

1. What do you suppose is Mr. Chavez's response to Ms. Norton?
2. Should he arrange a meeting between Ms. Norton and Aaron Goodman, Trayson's teacher?
3. What should be the school's position on Ebonics, or vernacular Black English?
4. Is this a school district or individual school issue?
5. Is Mr. Goodman wrong to tell Trayson that his speech is a low-class dialect? Wrong to tell him that if he speaks only Black English it will have negative educational and vocational consequences?

Chapter 8

Age

If people learn to love and learn to share in early adulthood, they will be able to care for and guide the next generation effectively.

F. P. Hughes and L. D. Noppe (1991, p. 401)

Mark McKenzie was a tenth grader in an affluent school district in a Southwestern suburban community. The community is essentially a new town. The town, which 20 years ago had fewer than 20,000 residents, had grown to more than 100,000. Most homes in Mark's neighborhood were in the $250,000 to $350,000 price range. Some homes sold in excess of $500,000. Crime in this community was almost nonexistent. At least one fourth of the students in high school drove their own cars. Several drove late-model cars, two had Corvettes, and one drove a Mercedes SUV.

Mark moved into this community with his family just two years ago. His father was an engineer in a large high-tech company, and his mother was a successful realtor. He had a brother in the eighth grade and a sister in the sixth grade. Mark's parents were extremely fond of their children, but time commitments to their successful careers precluded extensive time and interactions with them. Mark had been promised a car for his next birthday. When Mark and his family moved from their previous home in the Midwest, Mark had begun to demonstrate occasional periods of depression. He had left

275

two very close friends that he had grown up with, and he had objected vehemently to the move.

Since moving to the new home, Mark had made some casual friends, but none as close as the friends in his previous community. In the fall of Mark's sophomore year, he became more withdrawn, attended no school social events, and spent most of his nonschool hours in his room, behind closed doors.

In a conversation with two classmates the next spring, he stated that death brought people the ultimate peace and tranquility. He expressed the same sentiment in two poems written for his English class. His teacher considered the poetry good and passed off his expressions as a teenager's glamorization of death.

A month after writing the poems, Mark began giving away some of his prized possessions. He gave the baseball card collection that he had started 5 years before, and had always valued, to his brother; he gave his stereo and CDs to his sister. When questioned by his parents, he replied only that he had paid for these out of his own money and thought it was his prerogative to do what he wanted with them. "Besides," he stated, "I'm no longer interested in the cards or music." Later, Mark gave his $300 guitar to his brother, along with his baseball glove. He gave other personal items to his sister and a few to friends at school.

Shortly after giving away his possessions, Mark's depression seemed to dissipate and his behavior was such that it could be described as euphoric. His parents were pleased, and his father remarked, "Mark's finally got his act together." A week later, Mark's body was found in a wooded area less than a half mile from his home. He had died of a self-inflicted gunshot wound. Mark had become one of more than 6,000 teenagers who would end their own lives that year.

Was Mark's death the fault of his parents who had forced the family move on their children? Was it the fault of the parents who seemed to be too wrapped up in their careers to spend more time with their children? What were some signs of Mark's impending action? Why had he become euphoric when he was about to take such a drastic action on himself? What should the school do after Mark's death? Should a school memorial service be held? Why? Why not?

AGE AND CULTURE

Each person who lives long enough will become a part of every age microculture. Without choice, we must all go through the various stages in life and eventually join the ranks of the aged. Like other microcultures, we feel, think, perceive, and behave, in part, because of the age group to which we belong. In this chapter, we examine the major age groups: childhood, adolescence, adulthood, and the aged. We examine how ethnicity, gender, social status, and other determinants of culture interface with these periods in an individual's life. We examine how peer pressure affects behavior in some age groups. Critical issues such as child abuse, adolescent substance abuse, and adolescent suicide are examined. Finally, we examine how an understanding of age groups can affect the educational process.

An understanding of the various childhood and adult groups is helpful in understanding and providing appropriately for the needs of students. A student's classroom behavior may be a function of his or her relationship with parents, siblings, and significant others. As these family members and significant others move through various age stages in their lives, their behavior, as well as their relationship to the student, may change. Consequently, the student's behavior may, in part, be influenced by the age changes of the significant people in his or her life.

How we behave is often a function of age. Although many adolescents behave differently from one another, the way they think, feel, and behave is at least partly because they are adolescents. At the same time, age does not stand alone in affecting the way a person behaves or functions. Ethnicity, socioeconomic status, religion, and gender interact with age to influence a person's behavior and attitudes.

An African American woman in her 80s, for example, may eat the type of food she does partly because her age and related health condition require eliminating certain foods from her diet. But her socioeconomic status may determine, to some extent, the foods she can afford to buy, and her ethnicity may determine her choices in foods. Her gender, language, disability-nondisability status, and religious background may not influence eating habits to any significant degree. These other cultural variables, however, along with her age, may influence other types of behavior and functioning. From the time of birth through the last days of life, a person's age may influence perceptions, attitudes, values, and behavior.

In this chapter, we do not attempt to examine all developmental stages of the various age groups. This information can be obtained through a human development text. Instead, we examine some critical issues related to various age groups. Because it is impossible to address all critical issues affecting each age group, we selectively address issues affecting schools directly or indirectly.

CRITICAL ISSUES IN CHILDHOOD

Social Class and Poverty

One of the most critical issues that educators routinely face is that of social class and poverty. Today, one child in five lives in poverty, and teachers in the inner city may find that nearly all of the children in their classrooms live in poverty. Poverty creates numerous problems for children. In many instances, children live with a single parent, typically the mother. When the father is absent, children often lack adequate male role models, and the mother often bears the entire burden of discipline and financial support. Single mothers living in poverty must often work outside the home to provide for their families.

Mothers from middle and upper socioeconomic groups may not need to work outside the home. Those who choose to do so can often be selective in their choice of a day care setting to ensure an environment congruent with family values. Day care settings are often important variables in the socialization process because many of a child's early behaviors are learned from peers and caregivers. Children from lower socioeconomic groups, however, may end up with a less than satisfactory day care environment. In some instances, older siblings, themselves children, may be required to assume family child care responsibilities while their parents work at outside jobs.

In 1998, 19% of children in the United States lived in poverty. This was the first year since 1980 that the poverty rates dropped below 20%. While the national poverty drop is encouraging, there is considerable disparity from one state to another. The poverty rate in New Hampshire was at a national low of 8%, while the poverty rate in Washington, DC, was at 36%. The rate was 25% or higher in 11 states (Annie E. Casey Foundation, 2000). Many of these children suffer from inadequate housing, nutrition, and medical care. Many of their homes have inadequate heating or cooling, which affects their sleep and physical well-being. Homes are often old and in neighborhoods where residents live in fear for their personal safety. Children who live in poverty are more susceptible to childhood illnesses and are less likely to be treated medically. Children who suffer from physical problems are less likely to function academically at their highest potential.

Poverty brings many associated problems that place children at risk. The nation's capitol, Washington, DC, the center of power and the leader in poverty, also leads the nation in the following at-risk areas for children:

- Low-birth-weight children
- Infant deaths per live births
- Child deaths per 100,000 children, ages 1–4
- Deaths by accident, homicide, or suicide, ages 15–19
- Teen births per 100,000, females ages 15–19
- Children living with parents without full-time, year-round employment
- Families with children under age 18, headed by single parent
- 16–19-year-olds who are not in school and not working (Annie E. Casey Foundation, 2000)

As children enter school, they begin to recognize socioeconomic differences. Although the choice of friends may or may not be a function of socioeconomic levels, the type of playmates available may be. With the exception of children transported away from their neighborhood schools, most children in their earlier years attend schools that are somewhat homogeneous in terms of socioeconomic level.

Neighborhood playmates are even more homogeneous. During this period, however, an increasing awareness develops regarding the differences in material possessions found in different homes. Children whose families lack financial resources are often unable to acquire clothing considered important to the peer group. Around the ages of six to eight, children begin to understand what is meant by rich and poor.

Immigrant Children

The immigrant child who enters an American school for the first time may experience a culture shock resulting from losing all familiar signs and symbols for social interaction (Igoa, 1995). Igoa states, "Each time I encountered an unexplained cultural difference, I would feel awkward, confused, ashamed, or inadequate." (p. 16) The beginning of school may also be a difficult time for an immigrant family. Children seeking peer acceptance may wish to become more acculturated than what is considered acceptable by parents seeking to maintain traditional cultural values. The conflicting values may emanate from teachers, as well as from peers. It is not uncommon to find immigrant children in their early school years resisting the language of the home, as well as family values related to dress and behavior. During the early school years, children begin to identify with significant adults in their lives who serve as role models. This identification allows children to strengthen, direct, and control their own behavior in such a way that it approximates the behavior of those they hold in esteem. Educators often serve as role models for children, and their influence can be profound. Educators who are sensitive to diverse cultural and family values can assist children from immigrant families in becoming bicultural, rather than in having to choose between the culture of the home and that of the school.

Children, Ethnic Awareness, and Prejudice

After years of work in improving race relations in this country, the 1980s and 1990s saw growing optimism that the United States had turned the corner on race relations. The hate crimes and racial violence that have emerged in recent years, however, remind us that the ugly head of racism continues to surface. Although we as educators expect to see racism among adults and, to some extent, adolescents, we are sometimes shocked and often dismayed when it is evidenced in the behavior of young children. Despite the overall improvement in race relations and the lower level of prejudice among parents, the level of prejudice among young children ages four to seven has not declined in the last 40 years and continues to remain high.

Aboud (1988) defines ethnic awareness as a "conscious recognition of ethnicity in individuals or groups. . . being able to assign correctly the labels to the actual faces or pictures of various people indicates a basic form of perceptual ethnic awareness" (p. 6). Among young children, ethnic awareness and prejudice tend to increase with age. At some point, prejudice may decline but ethnic awareness may remain high. Although it may be necessary for a child to be aware of ethnic differences before he or she can develop prejudice, ethnic awareness in itself is not bad in a child. Attempts to discourage children from noticing that people are different, that they have different pigmentation, have different hair and eye colorization, or speak differently denies an accurate perception of reality in children (Aboud, 1988). Nonprejudiced children are also aware of differences but respond differently to them.

To recognize differences in others, a child must also be involved in self-identification because the child must be aware of what he or she is like before recognizing how another child differs. Children as young as three are able to identify with others of the same color or racial group (Aboud, 1988).

By the age of three, children may develop an awareness of people who are different from themselves and may, because of societal influence, target those individuals for prejudicial behaviors (Sleek, 1997). At four and five years of age, a significant number of children (about 75%) are able to correctly identify ethnic groupings. By ages six and seven, children are able to make the identification at close to 100% accuracy. Some children of color demonstrate an early preference for whites, and some white children indicate a preference for their minority group peers (Aboud, 1988).

By the age of five, some children have developed high levels of prejudice toward other racial groups (Bigler and Liben, 1993; Doyle and Aboud, 1995). It is often assumed that children who hold biased attitudes toward other groups are simply reflecting their parents' attitudes. People assume that children who are prejudiced were taught these attitudes by their parents. Citing several studies (e.g., Aboud & Doyle, 1996a; Kofkin, Katz, & Downey, 1995), Aboud and Doyle (1996b) concluded that such assumptions are unjustified. There appears to be no strong evidence that children are influenced by the attitudes of parents or peers. Children under the age of seven are often more prejudiced than their parents and often do not adopt the open and unbiased attitudes of their parents. Children over the age of seven are influenced by their parents to a greater extent. However, the biases they develop are influenced by others in addition to thier parents (Aboud, 1988).

Variables Affecting Attitudes and Prejudice.   One proposed theory of prejudice in children is the social reflection theory. This theory suggests that the prejudice we see in children is a reflection of the values of society. Research studies, in general, have shown that the higher-status and in-groups in society are preferred by both white and some children of color. Whites are typically the higher-status and in-group in society. Where social stratification occurs in a community, young children develop negative attitudes toward the lower-status and out-groups. This tends to be true even if the parents hold positive or open attitudes toward minority groups who are typically the lower-status or out-groups (Aboud, 1988).

Aboud (1988) suggests that parents who are characterized as prejudiced are often authoritarian in their childrearing practices and tend to use more punitive strategies in ensuring their status as parents while curbing hostility in their children. Parents with these characteristics tend to produce prejudiced children. It has

LINK TO THE CLASSROOM

Nonracist Curriculum for Preschoolers

How early in a child's schooling should issues of race, gender, and other differences be addressed? Researchers have found that children reflect many of society's racial and gender prejudices as early as preschool. Many believe that interventions in the primary grades can reduce prejudiced attitudes. How should teachers respond when they hear students calling one another or others derogatory names? What strategies would you use as a preschool or elementary teacher to introduce topics of race, sexual orientation, and disabilities? How could positive interracial relations be promoted in the classroom and the school?
In adolescence, peers begin to be a dominant source of influence on social behavior, sometimes causing alienation from parents and other family members.

been theorized that such parental practices instill low self-esteem in children as a message is conveyed to them that they are bad. The children, in turn, project their negative qualities onto others who are the object of their parents' attacks (i.e., people of color) (Aboud, 1988).

Because prejudice appears to be somewhat prevalent among young children (ages four to seven) and because children are cognitively capable of becoming less prejudiced, it would appear to be very appropriate to develop activities that have been shown to reduce prejudice during the early years of elementary school.

Child Abuse

Child abuse is a phenomenon that has been increasing in alarming proportions. Each year, hundreds of thousands of child abuse cases are reported. In 1998, there were 903,000 victims of child abuse reported in the United States. More than half of these children (53.6%) suffered from neglect. Almost one quarter (22.7%) were physically abused, and 11.5% were sexually abused. More than one quarter of these young children (25.3%) were reported to have suffered from more than one form of abuse. It is estimated that 1,100 children died of abuse and neglect in 1998. This represents a rate of 1.6 deaths per 100,000 children in the general population. Of these fatalities 37.9% were children not yet 1 year old and 77.5% were children 3 years old or younger. Some experts believe these numbers are unrealistic and estimate that approximately 5,000 children die from child abuse each year (U.S. Department of Health and Human Services, 2000).

The incidence rates of child abuse varies from one ethnic/racial group to another. In 1998, the child abuse rate for Asian/Pacific Islanders was 3.8 per 1,000. The abuse rate for white children was 8.5 per 1,000, 10.6 for Latinos, 19.8 for American

Indians/Alaska natives, and 20.7 for African Americans. The majority (60.4%) of the perpetrators were women; and 87.1 percent of the abused children were victimized by one or both parents (U.S. Department of Health and Human Services, 2000).

Child abuse or maltreatment is usually categorized as physical abuse, physical neglect, sexual abuse, or emotional abuse. Physical abuse refers to nonaccidental injury inflicted by a caretaker. There is often a fine line between physical abuse and discipline through physical punishment. In the United States, physical punishment is common in many families as a childrearing practice. Few states have prohibitions against corporal punishment in schools. Some state statutes consider corporal punishment abusive if bruises are visible after 24 hours. Others view an act as abusive if the person intends to harm the child. Physical indicators include unexplained bruises and welts, unexplained burns, unexplained fractures, and unexplained lacerations and abrasions (Tower, 1992).

Physical neglect involves the deliberate neglect or extraordinary inattentiveness to a child's physical well-being. Tower (1992) suggests that authorities have at times cited Mexican immigrants for neglect because when Mexican parents are absent, they are typically assisted by extended family members in child care. Some immigrants to the United States may be without extended family members who can provide these services. Consequently, older siblings may be forced into child care responsibilities. When the older siblings are considered by authorities to be too young to provide responsible care, this by law is neglect. Some children who suffer from neglect may exhibit poor hygiene, may be inappropriately dressed for weather conditions, or may suffer from hunger. Children who suffer from neglect may have medical or dental needs that have not been attended to. At times, the practices of some religious groups can come into conflict with the law regarding parental decisions for addressing illness and refusing conventional medical care. The courts have, in some instances, intervened and overturned parental rights when children were considered to be at extreme risk.

Sexual abuse refers to the involvement of children or adolescents in sexual activities that they do not comprehend or to which they are unable to give informed consent. It also includes practices that violate the social mores of one's culture as they relate to family roles. Sexual abuse is usually found in familial abuse or incest; extrafamilial molestation or rape; exploitation through pornography, prostitution, sex rings, or cults; or institutional abuse (e.g., day care centers). Children who are sexually abused may become withdrawn or secretive. Some may do poorly in school. Some abused children may use school as an outlet, however, and may actually excel. They may cry without provocation, may be anorexic or bulimic, and may attempt suicide (Tower, 1992).

Children who are emotionally abused are chronically belittled, humiliated, or rejected, or they have their self-esteem attacked. Emotional abuse is a pattern of psychologically destructive behavior. "It includes acts or omissions by parents or caregivers that have caused or could cause serious behavioral, cognitive, emotional, or mental disorders." (National Clearinghouse on Child Abuse and Neglect Information, 2000). Children who are emotionally or psychologically abused may exhibit a low self-esteem by continually demeaning themselves. Some become self-destructive through the use of drugs, develop eating disorders, or even become suicidal. Some children exhibit withdrawal behaviors; others may exhibit destructive behaviors. Some, attempting to demonstrate their worth, may become overachievers. These children may also exhibit problems with asthma, hyperactivity, or ulcers (Tower, 1992).

The reasons individuals become child abusers are numerous and too extensive to elaborate in this brief section. They do include parents who were abused as children, individuals who suffer from low self-esteem, and individuals who suffer from psychological disorders (Tower, 1992).

Abusive behavior can have a long-lasting effect on a child. The scars may persist into adulthood. Greven (1990) reports that the etiology of male delinquency and criminality in adolescence is often rooted in early childhood experiences, discipline, and family life. Greven suggests that physical punishment of children consistently appears as one primary influence in the development of aggressiveness and delinquency in males. Among male children who are loved, respected, and cared for, the incidence of delinquency and antisocial behavior tends to be low.

Child abuse is everyone's problem. It is the responsibility of each teacher to report known or suspected cases of child abuse to the school supervisor. The supervisor, in turn, is responsible for reporting these problems or concerns to professionals who are mandated by state and federal laws to bring the matter to the attention of appropriate protective agencies. These professionals are referred to as "mandated reporters." Every state has mandated laws requiring the reporting of child abuse. State laws differ in that one state has no penalties for failure to report, whereas others impose fines and even jail terms. Some states stipulate that a report must be made if there is suspicion of abuse; others stipulate accountability for failure to report if there is "reasonable cause to believe." Beyond the legal mandates, educators have a professional and ethical obligation to make reports to protect children from abuse.

One of the newest concerns for parents and educators is the sexual predators who seek out children on the Internet. As children become increasingly computer literate, some begin to surf the Internet. Through this means, predators seek out potential victims and lure them into secret and illicit rendezvous. As educators train children to become proficient computer users, it is incumbent upon educators to train the children to be socially responsible in their use of technology.

CRITICAL ISSUES IN ADOLESCENCE

Adolescence is perhaps one of the most challenging times in the life of an individual and the family. It is a long transitional period (6 years or so) during which the individual is "suspended" between childhood and adulthood. During adolescence, emancipation from the primary family unit is the central task of the individual. It is a difficult period for the young person, who is attempting to be free from the role of a child but is not fully equipped to assume the responsibilities of adulthood.

In some cultures, entry into adulthood begins immediately after childhood. Adolescence as a stage of behavioral development does not exist. In Western culture, however, an individual is seldom allowed or expected to make an immediate transition from childhood to adulthood. It is interesting to note that the anticipated state of extreme disequilibrium associated with adolescence and the period of "storm and stress" does not exist in some cultures in which adolescence does not exist. Cultural definitions of the role of the adolescent, along with social attitudes, have created circumstances that cause this period of life to be what it is in Western culture.

Relationship with Parents

As the adolescent shifts emotional ties from the family to peers, a restructuring may take place in the parent-adolescent relationship. Parents may be viewed more objectively. Parents may become more concerned about peer influence as they have increasingly less interaction with their child. These changes have the potential for turning the period of adolescence into one of dissonance and alienation from parents and other members of the family. One need only observe a few adolescent-family situations, however, to realize that the degree of dissonance and alienation varies greatly.

The attitude of the parents may contribute to the alienation. Parents who expect problems with their children in the adolescent period sometimes fall into the trap of a self-fulfilling prophecy. Their expectation of alienation generates a hostile attitude on their part. The adolescents quickly sense this attitude, and a vicious cycle is started. In contrast, parents who have confidence in their children may promote a feeling of confidence and trust. These children often develop sufficient self-confidence to resist peer pressure when it is appropriate.

Alienation is disturbing to families, to adult members of the community, and to the adolescents themselves. In their efforts to achieve autonomy, sexual functioning, and identity in order to become productive, self-sufficient individuals, some adolescents think they must turn away from the family. They exhibit considerable ambivalence because young persons are usually unprepared to yield family support systems in the quest for independence. As adolescents assert their rights to assume adult behaviors, they sometimes are unable to assume complementary adult-like responsibility. Recognizing this shortcoming, parents are understandably reluctant to grant adolescents adult privileges; this further adds to the alienation.

At-Risk Youth and High-Risk Behavior

It is important to differentiate between the terms *adolescent "at risk"* and *"high-risk behaviors."* At-risk youth are those who live in a disadvantaged status. This may be due to conditions such as poverty, discrimination, family instability, genetic or constitutional factors, parental neglect or abuse, or major traumatic events. High-risk adolescent behaviors are those that youth engage in that make them or others vulnerable to physical, social, or psychological harm or negative outcomes. Not all youth deemed "at risk" engage in high-risk behaviors. These categories of high-risk behaviors include the use of harmful substances such as alcohol or other

In adolescence, peers begin to be a dominant source of influence on social behavior, sometimes causing alienation from parents and other family members.

drugs, and sexual behaviors leading to unwanted pregnancies or sexually transmitted diseases. These behaviors are initiated during adolescence, are frequently interrelated, and often extend into adulthood (Youth Risk Behavior Surveillance, U.S., 1997).

Substance Abuse.   The use of harmful substances, primarily by children and adolescents, has been one of the most problematic areas faced by parents, schools, communities, and law enforcement agencies in the past 2 decades. It will inevitably continue to be a major problem in the next decade. The problem is a national phenomenon, and many of the problems of adult substance abuse have their roots in adolescence.

Substances are abused to produce altered states of consciousness. The adolescents who use them often seek relief, escape, or comfort from stress. The social institutions to which the adolescents must relate, including family and particularly the educational system, may be perceived as unresponsive or openly hostile. Their inability to focus on long-range goals, their desire for immediate gratification, and their lack of appreciation for the consequences of their behavior may contribute to some adolescents' misuse of substances.

Research over the years has established a clear relationship between alcohol use by adolescents and negative experiences with their families (Crowe, Philbin, Richards, & Crawford, 1998). Studies indicate that while motor vehicle accidents are the leading cause of death for youth 15–24, 75% of these involve the use of alcohol. In addition, alcohol is linked to the increasing incidence of date rapes and sexual assaults against women (McLoyd & Steinberg, 1998).

There are two broad categories of adolescent drug users: the experimenters and the compulsive users. Experimenters make up the majority of adolescent drug users. A few progress from experimenters to compulsive users. Although most experimenters eventually abandon such use, the fear of progression to compulsive use is a serious concern of parents and authorities. Recreational users fall somewhere between experimenters and compulsive users. For them, alcohol and marijuana are often the drugs of choice. Use is primarily to achieve relaxation and is typically intermittent. For a few, however, the goal is intoxication, and these recreational users pose a threat to themselves and others. This is particularly problematic among some groups of college students.

The use of illicit drugs has grown steadily among teens. Among twelfth graders, a national survey of 129,560 students in 26 states found that 26.5% admitted to the use of illicit drugs once or more a month during the past year. These teens admitted that when they used the drugs, they had become increasingly more intoxicated with repeated use. Statistics further indicated that 8.4% used drugs on a

Experimentation with smoking, alcohol, and drugs often occurs during adolescence on the urging of peers.

daily basis. Weekly alcohol use was admitted by 25.8%. Another 7.1% admitted cocaine use; 11.6%, uppers; 12.1%, hallucinogens; and 3.5%, heroin (PRIDE, Inc., 1996). A study conducted in 1997 found that the number of 9-12 year olds experimenting with marijuana had increased dramatically from 334,000 in 1993 to 571,000 in 1997 (Stevens and Smith, 2001).

Numerous problems related to substance abuse affect the community at large. Intravenous drug users are one group at high risk for AIDS. The spread of the deadly HIV virus among adolescents had, by the 1990s, affected thousands of the country's youth.

Substance abuse, while a concern among all youth groups, is no more problematic for minority youth than among their majority group counterparts. The rates of alcohol and tobacco use among blacks were lower than among whites. Use among American Indian youth was slightly higher and in some cases the same as whites. Latino substance abuse was higher or lower depending on the specific group observed. When adjusted for parental education and area of residence, differences were eliminated between youth of color and their white peers.

The problem of substance abuse is a national crisis and a national tragedy. It is a complex problem that deserves more attention by educators than the brief coverage here. The problem can and must be dealt with through the home, school, and law enforcement authorities, as well as through social agencies and responsible media.

Sexual Behaviors.   African American adolescent females (59%) were more likely than white (42%) or Latino (40%) females to be sexually active by the age of 17. Among these females, whites (70%) used some form of contraception during their first sexual encounter, while Latino (32%) and African American (58%) females were less likely to do so (Dryfoos, 1990). The Centers for Disease Control and Prevention (CDC) (1994) also reported that while adolescent cases of HIV/AIDS was but a small percentage (.5%) of the total cases, males with HIV/AIDS outnumbered female adolescents with HIV/AIDS by 2 to 1. HIV/AIDS has disproportionately affected African American and Hispanic adolescents. Although African Americans comprise only 15% of the adolescent population, they account for 60% of the youth AIDS cases. Latinos comprised 14% of the adolescent population and 24% of the AIDS cases reported in 1999 (CDC, 2000c).

Despite some declines in recent years (a 12% decrease from 1991 to 1996), the birth rate for teenagers in the United States is significantly higher compared with other industrialized countries (CDC, 1997). Although the birth rate declined in all racial and ethnic groups, the birth rate for African Americans, ages 15–19 was nearly four times that of whites (CDC, 1993). Teen birth rates are closely linked to poverty. Consequently there is a higher birth rate among teens of color who are significantly impacted by poverty. When compared across poverty groups, teen birth rates among poor whites and poor African Americans are more similar. Children born to young mothers face a substantially greater risk of low birth weight, and of serious disabilities. There is a greater likelihood of premature birth with a young mother, and a greater risk for child abuse and later emotional and educational problems (Rosenheim & Testa, 1992). Adolescent mothers face a greater likelihood of birth-related medical problems, psychological problems, lower educational and occupational attainment, marital instability, and welfare dependency (Rosenheim & Testa, 1992).

VIDEO INSIGHT

Sex, Truth, and Videotape

A child psychiatrist gives parents three guidelines for raising sexually responsible children:

a. Don't wait to start talking.
b. Don't avoid the subject.
c. If you discover that your teen is sexually active, focus on what's important.

Do you agree with this advice? As a parent, what would you do to raise a sexually responsible child? As a teacher, would your responses to questions that students might have about sex or concerns you might have about a sexually active student differ from the responses you would give or the concerns you might express as a parent? Why or why not?

Adolescent Suicide.   One of the most alarming developments in adolescent behavior is the dramatic increase in teenage suicides. It is estimated that four major causes account for 73% of all deaths among our nations youth: motor vehicle crashes (30%), other unintentional injuries (10%), homicide (20%), and suicide (13%) (Youth Risk Behavior Surveillance, U.S., 1997). Every day, an average of 18 young Americans kill themselves—5,000 to 6,500 each year. Every hour, 57 children and adolescents try to take their own lives. On average, one succeeds every 80 minutes. Well over 1,000 attempts are made each day. Since 1950, adolescent suicides have increased 300%. Only accidents and homicides exceed suicide as a cause of adolescent deaths, and many of those deaths are suspected suicides (McKee, Jones, & Barbe, 1993; Sidel, 1990).

The largest group of young people who attempt or commit suicide are 15 to 19 years old. The CDC reports, however, that the 1994 nationwide suicide rate for 10 to 14 year olds has increased 120% since 1980. This group has come under increased scrutiny as the national suicide rate for females in this age range is 1 per 100,000 and for males 2.4 per 100,000. In comparison, the rate for the 15 to 19 year olds is 3.5 per 100,000 for females and 18 per 100,000 for males (Nazario, 1997).

Alarming statistics suggest that some students of color may be at greater risk than previously thought. In a state with large urban centers and many students from diverse backgrounds, there is a disproportionately high number of attempted youth suicides among some groups. Statistics indicate that 16% of Latino, 12% of Asian, and 12% of American Indian students have attempted suicide. These compare with the lower rates of 7% and 8% among African American and European

American youth, respectively. These statistics can be puzzling because both Latino and African American students have disproportionately high levels of poverty, and Asians in California are, as a group, among the more affluent. One may question the effects of poverty and the stress of urban life, but these statistics may raise more questions than they answer (Nazario, 1997). Since 1980, the suicide rates for Asian American and Latino youth has been increasing. McLoyd and Steinberg (1998) speculate that this may be a function of the many pressures inherent in immigration and acculturation.

Numerous theories have been advanced for the adolescent suicide phenomenon. Among the reasons offered is the decline in religion, tension between parents, the breakup of the nuclear family, and the competitiveness in school. Studies indicate that, in half of the cases of attempted youth suicide, the mother was reported to be depressed. Family tension and conflict were also reported in half of the cases (McKee et al., 1993). Because of their youth and lack of experience in making accurate judgments, depressed adolescents are more prone to respond to the suggestion of suicide than an adult. Adolescent depression is a function of a wide range of situations, perhaps involving failure, loss of a love object, or rejection. It can also be a function of biochemical imbalances in the brain or the loss of a parent through death, divorce, separation, or extended absence. Fewer than 38% of this country's children live with both natural parents. The loss of a parent may be viewed as parental rejection, which may lead to feelings of guilt in the adolescent. Some mental health professionals attribute adolescent suicide to the widespread availability and use of both legal prescription and illegal drugs. Some believe that the tightening of the job market and the bleak prospects for the future among the less affluent is another contributing variable (Sidel, 1990).

Alienation in the family is cited as another major contributor to adolescent suicide. Where family ties are close, suicide rates are low; where families are not close, suicide rates tend to be high. Adolescent suicide victims come from all socioeconomic backgrounds, but many are from middle- and upper-income homes. The parents in these homes are generally high-achieving individuals, and they expect similar behavior from their children. Failure to conform to parental expectations may lead to alienation. McKee et al. (1993) suggest that adolescents at risk include those who have experienced a successful family suicide, adolescents who are very concerned about their parents (particularly unhappy parents), and those who are unable to conform to expected sexual behavior patterns. It is estimated that gay and lesbian youth constitute 30% of the suicides in their age-group.

No single variable or factor can be identified as the cause of adolescent suicide, which is an apparent response to the frustrations of life. Attempted suicides may be a cry for help or a call for attention to the adolescent's profound problems. It should be noted that the ratio of suicides attempted to suicides completed is 125 to 1 among adolescents. This compares with 10 to 1 in the 25 to 64 age group, and 2 to 1 in the 65 and older group. These data clearly suggest that the attempted act is more likely a desperate attempt to be heard and understood than a true intent to end life. Those who contemplate suicide but do not follow through with an attempt often report that their plans were changed by someone's simple act of concern.

Youth Violence.   Violence is one of the greatest problems facing young Americans today. Between 1985 and 1991, the homicide rate among young males increased from 13 to 33 per 100,000. Between 1993 and 1997, there was an encouraging downward trend from 34 to 22.6 per 100,000. Despite the downward trend, the rates are still unacceptably high (CDC, 2000a). Due to media coverage, the nation has become well conditioned to school violence. In reality, less than 1% of all homicides among school-aged children (5–19 years of age) occur in or around school grounds or on the way to and from school. Since the 1992–1993 school year, incidents of school-related homicides (the majority of which involved firearms) have been on a steady decline. However the incidents involving multiple victims has been on the increase, with an average of five such occurrences per year (CDC, 2000b).

Even the most callous individuals were shocked and stunned when the images of the April 1999 shootings in Littleton, Colorado, reached their TV screens. In a few brief moments two outcast students shot and killed 12 of their classmates and a popular teacher/coach at Columbine High School, then killed themselves. The odds were certainly against such a scenario taking place at a school serving this comfortable community. Statistically black students are at greater risk at school than white students. Urban students are at greater risk than those from the suburbs, poor students at risk more than the affluent (Cannon, Streisand, & McGraw, 1999). Columbine students are overwhelmingly white, and only one of the victims was black. The school served the affluent community of Littleton, and one of the assailants drove a BMW car to the school.

Perhaps even more alarming was the intent of the two assailants, Eric Harris and Dylan Klebold, who had planted at least 30 bombs in the school with the intention of killing even more of their classmates. Fortunately the bombs never detonated.

The Littleton incident was but one of a string of violent attacks against students and teachers across the United States in recent years. Most of these high-profile shootings involved young white males, most of whom are viewed as alienated individuals or outcasts. Often, their peers had ridiculed them, and they associated with other disaffected individuals in outcast groups. This was the case of the assailant in a Pearl, Mississippi, school who complained of "mistreatment every day." Another school killer allegedly hung around with individuals involved in the occult. One of the individuals involved in the Jonesboro, Arkansas, shootings boasted openly that "individuals would die" (Cannon, Streisand, & McGraw, 1999).

Harris and Klebold had provided ample warning signs of their troubled lives and potential to do harm. They had made a video for a class, which some believe was a dress rehearsal for their final attack. Authorities apparently ignored or paid little heed when advised of a hate-filled web site and death threats against another student. Obsessed with death, they professed to despising God, dressed grungy, and held to values contrary to most of their classmates. They intensely disliked the school athletes, who allegedly mocked and harassed them. Not unlike other suicidal teens, these were individuals who were troubled, and who gave out warning signs to those who would pay heed. Unfortunately no one who might have prevented the tragedy in this instance, and in so many other situations, paid heed.

Green (1999) indicates that some of the outcast students at Columbine may have been terrorized and harassed unmercifully by mainstream students. A member of the now notorious Columbine "trench coat mafia" indicated that Klebold and Harris were not actually members of the trench coat mafia, but rather on the fringe of the group and friends of some of the members. He further described how some student athletes, or so-called "jocks," had called him "faggot," bashed him against lockers, and thrown rocks and sticky soda at him from speeding cars as he rode his bicycle. He claimed that food was thrown at him in the cafeteria forcing him to wear soiled clothing the remainder of the school day. He indicated that he would wake in the morning with a knot in his stomach at the thought of what he would have to face at school. He claimed that the other students either emulated the behavior of these athletes or were reluctant to voice dissent. He indicated that while he could not condone what Harris and Klebold had done, he knew what it was like to "be cornered and pushed every day." He added, "Tell people that eventually, someone is going to snap" (Green, 1999). However, in addressing Colorado legislators, the principal of Columbine indicated that there was no bullying on the part of athletes and that teachers and staff were not aware of any such alleged behaviors (Pankratz, 1999). Whether or not these specific allegations are accurate, every educator knows that teasing and harassment, often unmerciful, takes place daily in the schools. Every teacher and administrator can remember seeing this done, having it done to him or her, or participating in some type of student-directed hurtful behavior. Educators must not allow such behavior to go on without intervention. The stakes are far too high. The problems associated with school violence are actually greater that the reported incidents. The CDC, in a national survey, found that in the 30 days prior to the study, 4% of students missed one or more days of school because of fears for their safety in or on the way to or from school. Of the students surveyed, 7.4% indicated that in the 12 months prior to the survey, they had been threatened or injured with a weapon on school property (CDC, 2000b).

The March 2001, school shooting in Santee, California is particularly troubling since several friends and associates of the alleged shooter admitted that he had told them the weekend before that he was planning the incident. They did not report it because they said he later laughed it off as a joke, and as one said, he did not want to get his friend into trouble. It is essential that teachers, students and the community be trained to take all talk of this nature seriously and to report it to the proper authorities.

Many of these warning signs of potentially aggressive behavior overlap with the warning signs of individuals considering suicide. Whether or not the presence of these signs is indicative of suicide consideration or imminent danger to others, it is a potential warning of a troubled individual. Parents, teachers, and school authorities cannot risk taking such situations lightly.

Chua-Eoan (1999) suggests warning signs on "how to spot a depressed child":

- Difficulty in maintaining relationships
- Reduced physical activity
- Morbid suicidal thoughts

- Low self-esteem
- Problems at school
- Changes in sleep patterns

Warning signs for preschoolers:

- Frequent unexplained stomachaches, headaches, or fatigue
- Overactivity or excessive restlessness
- Sad appearance
- Low tolerance for frustration
- Irritability
- Loss of pleasure in activities
- Tendency to portray the world as bleak

Depression does not necessarily indicate the likelihood of violent behaviors; however, violent behavior is often the function of depression. If you have reason to suspect that a student is depressed, refer the individual to a school counselor or to an appropriate authority.

While the reasons for such untoward violent behaviors are multifaceted, the American Academy of Pediatrics (2000) reports that by the age of 18, the average American child will have viewed about 100,000 acts of violence on television alone. The level of violence on Saturday morning cartoons exceeds that of prime time. There are 20–25 acts of violence an hour on Saturday morning as compared to 3–5 during prime time. With such continuous exposure to violence, is it possible that our children have become desensitized to senseless violent acts? Media violence affects children in the following ways:

- Increasing aggressiveness and antisocial behavior
- Increasing the fear of becoming a victim
- Making them less sensitive to violence and victims of violence
- Increasing their appetite for more violence in entertainment and real life

Bender, Clinton, and Bender (1999) suggest a number of factors that seem to influence youth violence:

- Easy access to handguns
- Early involvement with drugs
- Involvement with gangs or other antisocial groups
- Exposure to violent acts in the media
- Weak parenting
- Absence of a father or significant male role model
- Lack of connectedness
- Dysfunctional family life

Bender et al. (1999) indicates that connectedness in school is important because students need to be positively involved emotionally, academically, and socially in school and in the home environment. Bender et al. also indicates the importance of same-sex role models. He indicates that boys and girls learn to become successful adults by observing same sex role models from their earliest years onward. This can be problematic in that 85% to 100% of the faculty in the lower grades are female, leaving a void in the area of male role models.

Palermo and Simpson (1998) suggest that the decline in the nuclear family is a contributing variable to the roots of violence. They indicate that half of the marriages now end in divorce, that one fourth of births are to single mothers, and that one in four Americans over the age of 18 never marry. Married couples with a child under the age of 18 have become a shrinking minority.

The Federal Bureau of Investigation (1994) reported that African American youth, who comprised 15% of all youth under the age of 18, accounted for 50.2% of those arrested for violent crimes. Latino youth were also more likely to be arrested for serious felony offenses than either white or Asian youth. However, Gibbs (1998) contends that African American youth receive differential treatment from the juvenile justice system. They are more likely to be arrested, convicted, and incarcerated than white youth for similar offenses. The poor typically have court appointed attorneys and the trial and subsequent incarceration is often a mere formality. Youth from middle class backgrounds may have the benefit of privately retained attorneys who may be able to secure probation or reduced sentences. Incarceration severely impacts the future of these individuals, limiting educational opportunities, employment opportunities, and income.

Today, few children are cared for by one of their parents during normal working hours. Because of the need for two incomes in the nuclear family, both parents typically work out of the home. This is also the case even when two incomes are not an absolute necessity. Women often opt (rightfully) to pursue their chosen careers. This typically results in childcare from hired sources, which is sometimes good and at other times marginal. The more affluent and professional parents often have the resources to pay for the highest quality childcare. Others must accept whatever is available, and this is sometimes the crime-filled streets (Palermo & Simpson, 1998).

Street Gangs.   Juvenile gang activity in the United States can be documented as far back as the mid-1800s. Prior to the 1980s, gang activity and violence tended to affect only those in their immediate communities. Middle-class white Americans had few concerns with respect to street gangs. By the 1970s, however, and especially the 1980s, gang organizations had become more sophisticated and their activities had begun to affect a wider range of people (Drowns & Hess, 1990; Kratcoski & Kratcoski, 1996).

For many gang members, affiliation with a gang is their means of achieving status in a community. The gangs acquire power in a community through violent behavior and the fear that such behavior generates (Drowns & Hess, 1990). Some of today's gangs are well armed. Sheley and Wright (1995) found that 86% of incarcerated youths and 30% of students in inner-city high schools owned and used guns. Among both groups, the guns were high-quality, sophisticated weapons. Gang members consider guns essential for passing through the turf of others. The problem of gun ownership is not limited to a few "bad apples"; rather, it is typical in the impoverished inner city and is spreading outward. For many, assault rifles are the weapon of choice. With weapons such as these, drive-by shootings have become commonplace among gang members struggling for turf, avenging an insult, or retaliating a rival gang's previous assault. Drive-by shootings claim the lives of almost as many innocent bystanders as intended victims. In communities such as Los Angeles, the number of innocent bystanders injured or killed each year is in the hundreds. These acts of violence generate the fear that, in turn, gives gangs power in the community. It is estimated that, in Los Angeles alone, more than 1,200 street gangs exist with more than 150,000 members (Jackson, Lopez, & Connell, 1997).

Howell (1998) summarizes the findings of several studies related to gang activities in the United States. While not all gangs are violent, violent gang activity is a growing problem in the country. These gangs draw the attention of the media, offenses have become more violent and more lethal weapons are being used, resulting in more serious injuries and death. While gangs are certainly a part of the problem, it is unclear whether the problems are primarily due to organized street gangs, law-breaking youth groups, or non-gang related youth. Gangs have moved eastward from the West Coast. Bloods and Crips have migrated from the Los Angeles area to 45 or more Western and Midwestern communities. It is uncertain if this migration is due primarily to family migration or deliberate gang relocation and expansion. Howell indicates that there is certainly ample evidence to indicate that some gang members are involved in drug use and have been involved in narcotics trafficking and drug-related killings. What is uncertain is whether the gang involvement is an organized effort, or primarily the acts of individuals who happen to be gang members. Most gang on gang violence is the result of turf disputes and some of the violence attributed to drug wars may be more related to turf wars.

The variables that contribute to gang membership and the reasons for the violent nature of many of the gangs are multifaceted. So too are the means to combat the problem. Either the solutions to ending gang membership have not yet been found, or the will to solve the problems has not yet been resolved.

Gang membership is usually structured by race or nationality. Most visible among these gangs are Latino, black, and Asian gangs, and Jamaican posses. Latino gangs tend to operate out of barrios and are some of the older gangs in existence. Some gang members belong to the same gangs that their fathers did before them. Among the best-known gangs are the African American Bloods and the Crips. The Crips began in the Los Angeles area as high school youth who extorted money from classmates and were involved in other violence. The Bloods are the primary rivals of the Crips. Both gangs have extended well beyond Los Angeles, spreading as far north as Alaska and as far east as Washington, DC, and making inroads in communities across the country.

Asian gangs are most prominent in Chinese and Vietnamese communities. Among the Chinese gangs, the Yu Li, Joe Boys, and Wah Ching are the most prominent. Asian gangs are, by their own choice, less visible but capable of the same levels of violence as the other ethnic gangs. It is believed that some Asian gangs have ties to organized crime groups in Asia, such as the Hong Kong triads. They also have spread across the United States and Canada (Dannen, 1992; Drowns & Hess, 1990).

Gang members are identifiable by their clothing, communication, graffiti, and tattoos. Bloods and Crips often wear bandannas on their heads. The color of the Bloods is red; the Crips, blue. Clothing may identify individuals as gang members. Gang-specific clothing may include jackets or sweatshirts with gang names. Tattoos on the hands, arms, and shoulders are common among Latino gang members but are not usually displayed by African American gang members. Hand signs may identify an individual with a specific gang.

Graffiti used by gangs can provide considerable information. African American and Latino gang graffiti differ from one another: Black gang graffiti often contains profanity and other expressions that are absent from Latino gang graffiti. Latino gang graffiti has more flair and more attention to detail. Gangs use graffiti to stake a claim to turf. If the graffiti is crossed out and new graffiti written, another gang is challenging the former's claim to the turf. Through careful observation, law enforcement can determine the sphere of influence a gang has. Graffiti will indicate where the gang has unchallenged influence and where challenges begin and by whom.

In inner-city schools, gang members may be involved with student extortion and teacher intimidation. Violence occasionally erupts on school campuses. The presence of several gang members in the same class may be intimidating to teachers, as well as to other students. Discipline in such classes may be a considerable challenge. In addition, some gang members are involved in the sale and distribution of cocaine and crack cocaine. This has spread across the country, and the fight for drug turf is the cause of much of the violence.

The emergence of street gangs over the past 2 decades has become a major challenge for educators. In some instances, schools have become scenes of violence resulting in the installation of metal detectors and the hiring of security guards at the schools. If law enforcement is unable to stem the growth of gang violence, it is unlikely that educators are any better equipped to do so. As with other issues related to youth, gang participation is often a function of poverty. It disproportionately affects individuals of color because they are disproportionately affected by poverty. There are white gangs as well. Some of the white gangs are involved in hate groups, such as the "skinheads." Gang membership gives the disenfranchised perceived visibility and status. It provides a sense of acceptance and, at times, a substitute for family. It may even provide the individual an income from illegal activities. Somehow, society has failed to provide better alternatives than gang membership. Perhaps that is one of the major challenges for education.

The Young African American Male: An Endangered Species

"The young African American male has become somewhat of an enigma in American society. Miseducated by the educational system, mishandled by the criminal justice system, mislabeled by the mental health system, and mistreated by the social welfare system. . . . They have come in an unenviable and unconscionable sense—rejects of our affluent society and misfits in their own communities" (Gibbs, 1992, p. 6).

Although living in representative communities throughout the United States, young African American males live primarily in urban, inner-city neighborhoods. Disproportionately represented in the lower end of the socioeconomic continuum, and failing to become an integral part of society because of rejection and continued discrimination, many have become endangered, embittered, and embattled (Gibbs, 1992).

Gibbs (1992) suggests six social indicators or serious problems experienced by African American males in our society: lack of education, unemployment, delinquency, drug abuse, teenage pregnancy, and mortality rates. Since the early 1980s, black males have sustained increases in all of these problems.

Dropout rates in inner-city schools remain disproportionately high. Among those who do graduate from high school, many are functionally illiterate and lack the basic skills necessary for entry-level jobs, military service, or postsecondary education. College enrollments for African Americans have been declining in recent years.

The unemployment rate for African American males remains disproportionately high, typically at least twice that of the general population. The unemployment rate of black males exceeds that of black females by a ratio of 2 to 1. Those who are employed are frequently working in menial, lowpaying jobs (Gibbs, 1992). Even these jobs have become increasingly difficult for African Americans to obtain because of increased competition from other groups, particularly immigrants. Coupled with this is the disposition of some employers to hire from groups other than African Americans. Unemployment statistics fail to report the problem of disproportionately high numbers of unemployed African Americans who become so discouraged that they drop out of the job-seeker's market.

Although African American youth make up less than 20% of the total youth population, they account for nearly one third of the arrests. They are arrested in greater frequency than white youth for robbery, rape, homicide, and aggravated assault. They are also more likely than white youth to be arrested for other violent personal crimes (Krisberg, Schwartz, Fishman, Eiskovits, & Guttman, 1986). The incarceration rate of black males is the highest of all groups. This finding suggests that African American youth are treated more harshly in the criminal justice system.

With the exception of inhalants and hallucinogens, nonwhite youth have an equal or higher rate of drug abuse than white youth. The related problem of AIDS among intravenous drug users is particularly problematic, with the sexually active too often infecting their partners. Although both a legal and a moral problem, drug use among African American youth is an even greater problem because they are destroying themselves physically, psychologically, and socially (Gibbs, 1992).

The pregnancy rate for African American youth is twice that of white youth (Children's Defense Fund, 1986b). White teens are more likely than black teens to terminate their pregnancies (Gibbs, 1992). Studies indicate that many African American males have negative attitudes toward the use of contraceptives and discourage their partners from such use (Children's Defense Fund, 1986a; Gibbs, 1986). Some young black males may view the birth of a child as confirmation of their virility (Gibbs, 1992); this attitude enhances both the likelihood of pregnancy and the spread of AIDS and other diseases.

Teenage mothers are more likely to drop out of school, go on welfare, and experience complications in pregnancy. As a group, children born to teens are more likely to suffer from abuse and to grow up in single-parent, welfare-supported families. They are also less likely to be academically successful (Gibbs, 1992). Young African American males who father children are more likely to attain lower levels of academic achievement and lower occupational status; they also tend to have larger families and to experience unstable marriages (Chilman, 1983).

Young African American males have an alarmingly high mortality rate, primarily because of homicides and suicides. A young black male has about a 1 in 20 chance of being murdered before the age of 25.

Gibbs (1992) suggests four variables that have contributed to the deteriorating status of African American males in the United States. The first variable is tied to historical factors, which include Roosevelt's New Deal, World War II's economic opportunities, Truman's postwar policies, and the civil rights and economic gains of the 1960s for African Americans. Throughout most of the 1960s and during some of the 1970s, liberal federal administrations were committed to increasing opportunities for minorities. A conservative attack on these advances began in the 1980s, however, with a federal administration that dismantled or diluted many of the civil rights and social welfare programs. As the economy stopped expanding and as other disadvantaged groups began to compete with blacks for the scarce resources, African Americans saw many of their short-lived gains slip away.

Meanwhile, most middle-class African Americans moved out of the inner cities and into integrated urban centers or suburbs. This left the inner cities with a lack of strong leadership and the role models that its residents needed. This is the second variable that Gibbs says contributed significantly to the demise of many inner-city, young black males. Gibbs (1992) suggests that isolation from the black middle class and alienation from the white community turned the inner cities' ghettos into "welfare reservations" where black youth lack access to positive role models, quality education, recreation, cultural facilities, job opportunities, and transportation.

Another sociocultural factor that has contributed to the declining status of African American males is the loss of influence of the black church in the inner city. It has meant that, in many instances, the church is no longer the center of activity in the community and no longer exerts the high level of influence as the monitor of norms and values. A breakdown has also occurred in traditional African American community values, such as the importance of family, religion, education, self-improvement, and social cohesion. Many inner-city residents no longer have the feelings of concern and responsibility for one another they once did. The sense of shared community and common purpose has been replaced by a sense of hopelessness, alienation, and despair (Gibbs, 1992).

Economic factors constitute the third of Gibbs' variables. Among the economic factors that contribute to the frustration and alienation of this country's black youth are the structural changes that occur when an economy that had a predominantly manufacturing and industrial base evolves to one with a high-technology and service base. With many manufacturing jobs moving out of the country and the new jobs located in the suburbs, African American youth are often at a disadvantage without adequate transportation or skills to compete (Gibbs, 1992). Many of the schools that serve poorer communities and students of color are not as well equipped with technology as the schools serving the more affluent students. Many low-income families, including African Americans, do not have computers in the home and are therefore limited in their ability to develop skills in technology.

The fourth variable contributing to the problems of African American youth is the political climate of the country. A conservative political backlash gave the conservative federal administrations of the 1980s through the early 1990s what they believed to be a mandate to dismantle the antipoverty and affirmative action policies of the Kennedy, Johnson, and Carter administrations. In the mid-1990s, the anti-affirmative action efforts were continued at state levels. Major higher education systems in both California and Texas ended affirmative action efforts. Gibbs (1992) suggests that the goal of providing all Americans with a decent standard of living through federally subsidized health and welfare programs was placed on hold. At the same time, the low-income and disadvantaged were often characterized by their critics as lacking motivation and having dysfunctional family systems dependent on welfare programs. The resulting cutbacks on programs such as Comprehensive Employment Training Act (CETA,) the Job Corps, federally subsidized college student loans, and youth employment programs had a direct negative impact on African American youth. These cutbacks resulted in reduced training and employment opportunities and, in many instances, cut off the access of young black Americans to the American dream. The discontinuance or near elimination of these programs has been costly in civil unrest and in the deterioration of cities. Perhaps the greatest cost of all has been in the loss of human spirit and dignity.

ADULTHOOD

Adulthood is of particular importance to multicultural education because adults, particularly parents, have such an important role in shaping the attitudes and behaviors of the students we see in our schools. Adulthood is a critical period in the life of an individual because it is the time when one's hopes and aspirations come into fruition or when one's dreams are shattered. For the millions of low-income and disenfranchised, the latter is often the case. In this section, we examine two major adult cohort groups: the baby boomers and the baby busters.

To some people, the adult years represent the best years of their lives. To others, it is a time of important decision making, coupled with stress and sometimes pain. Young adults are faced with some of the greatest decisions they will ever make in their lives. Some decisions are awesome because of the impact they may have on the rest of an individual's life. Decisions must be made about education beyond high school; vocational choices must be made; and decisions regarding a mate, marriage, and children are made during this period.

Physical vitality, the excitement of courtship and marriage, the birth of children, and career satisfaction can bring considerable pleasure to individuals during this period of life. At the same time, unwise choices in education or vocation along with frustration in courtship and failure in marriage can bring frustration and grief. To many Americans in poverty, adulthood brings the reality that they are among the disenfranchised in this country. If they are among the minority groups frequently targeted for discriminatory practices, life can be particularly difficult. Lack of financial resources may make the reality of a higher education elusive. Good jobs are particularly difficult to find because preference is often given to members of the dominant group and to individuals from more favored minority groups. During a recession, these individuals tend to be the most affected. They suffer from abject poverty, unemployment, and poor living conditions and are not likely to escape from this life. Frustration and anger appear to be inevitable, along with an intense feeling of impotence.

The Baby Boomers

The baby boomers, 76 million strong, are likely the most influential cohort group in the United States. Born between 1946 and 1964, the oldest of this group are now in their mid-50s. Together, the "boomers" set the moral and political tone of the country, as well as family styles and career patterns (Roof, 1990). President George W. Bush is part of this group, as are many of the advisors who surround him. Many boomers are in or approaching their professional prime and are therefore able to exert considerable influence on others.

The most educated cohort group in the history of this country, 85% of boomers have high school degrees and 36% have completed college. This generation was surrounded by the civil rights movement; issues related to the Vietnam War; and the changing moral, sexual, and familial values associated with the countercultural years. The boomers are divided into two age groups. Those born in the late 1940s tend to form a group that is different from those born in the early 1960s. The older group experienced or witnessed freedom marches, the Kennedy assassination, and the Vietnam War; they participated in or witnessed the political turmoil of the period. The younger group has experienced less social unrest and is more likely to have been affected by the gasoline shortages of 1970 and the incidents at Three Mile Island and Chernoble; they may, as a group, be more prone toward inwardness (Roof, 1990). Members of this group may have related more to the "me generation" of the 1980s than the older boomers.

Although many boomers dropped out of church involvement for two or more years, 43% of older boomers and 38% of younger boomers have returned to active involvement. The younger boomers tend to be more religious with respect to personal faith and practice. As a group, they adhere to traditional Judeo-Christian beliefs and practices more than the older group. They are more likely to be political conservatives and to hold more traditional views on moral issues than the older group (Roof, 1990).

More than most Americans, older boomers tend to endorse alternative religious beliefs, believe in reincarnation, practice meditation, and view other religions as equally viable alternatives to their own. Because more in this group are married and have children, they tend to be involved with religious institutions to a greater extent. Roof (1990) suggests that although married persons with children tend to be more involved with religious activities, the opposite is true for married persons without children. Those without children tend to have lower levels of religious involvement and to have views that are sometimes characterized as more liberal than those of singles on topics such as the legalization of marijuana, abortions, and the acceptance of alternative lifestyles.

It is apparent that the social and political views of one's youth often leave an indelible imprint that affects one's attitudes, beliefs, and religious involvement. The children in our schools today are, for the most part, those of the youngest baby boomers, and these attitudes and experiences are being communicated to *them*. Consequently, these beliefs are likely to become evident in our schools.

Generation X

After the baby boomers come the "busters"! Forty-one million in number and born between 1965 and 1976, this cohort group has been tagged the "baby busters" or the "X generation." Whereas the average number of babies born during the 1946 to 1964 boomer years was 4 million per year, the average number of children born per year during the buster years was 3.4 million. It should be noted that some define the Generation X years through 1977, and some even as late as 1981.

Susan Mitchell (1993) of American Demographics described the busters as resentful of the boomers. These young adults believed that the boomers had a party and didn't clean up their mess. They ran the country into a huge deficit and job scarcity in the early 1990s. However, by the beginning of the new millennium, the U.S. economy had prospered, and the busters found a highly favorable job market. Those with skills in technology found many opportunities, and some have become extremely wealthy in the high-tech industries.

Born into a more diverse world, the busters tend to be more accepting than older Americans in matters related to ethnicity, family structure, and lifestyle. They have grown up in an age of AIDS, latchkey children, divorce, economic decline, and increased violence. They realize that danger is always present and that stability may be difficult to come by (Mitchell, 1993).

Drury (1998) suggests some typical characteristics of this group. He indicates that the Xers have been burned by their parents' divorces and consequently have a higher view of marriage than the previous generation. As a group, they are willing to delay marriage until the "right person" comes along. They view sex as disconnected from marriage. They view living together prior to marriage, or safe sex, as normal. They are tolerant of almost everything except intolerance. They are more open to non-Judeo-Christian spirituality and are more prone than the earlier generation to embrace Hinduism, Buddhism, and new age philosophy mixed with forms of Christianity. Some are contemptuous of organized religion.

Many of the Xers have been paying into the Social Security fund for 15 or more years. They see an unfair burden placed on them to maintain the system with minimal assurances that it will be there for them when they retire (Political Action Committee for Generation X, 2000). The Xers account for 33.6% of the nation's work force. As a group, they tend to be self-confident, which was learned by fending for themselves. They have grown up in the age of information and technology, and are comfortable and function well in it. They have seen family and friends who were loyal to their work lose their jobs due to corporate downsizing in the 1990s. Consequently they tend to look for day-to-day dividends for their efforts (Tulgan, 1997).

Politically, nearly 50% of busters identify themselves as independent, compared with only 38% of other Americans. They are often more liberal on social issues than those who are older—including the boomers. They are less likely than others to support book bannings from libraries or the firing of gay teachers. They tend to be accepting of interracial dating and have a more positive view of the women's movement. They are more likely than other Americans to support affirmative action for minorities (Mitchell, 1993).

As a group, the busters were counted on more heavily by Bill Clinton than by George Bush in the 1992 presidential election. The efforts apparently paid off for Clinton that year. The youngest of the busters became eligible to vote in the 1996 elections, as did the oldest of the post-buster group, many of whom believed that Clinton, the boomer, was more in touch with their views than was Robert Dole, the older of the candidates.

The Aged

All individuals who live into their mid-60s become members of the microculture of the aged, along with their membership in other microcultures. As with other minority groups, the aged are often discriminated against. But unlike discrimination

VIDEO INSIGHT

A Closer Look

In this video segment you will see that according to the census bureau, 34 million people over the age of 65 are still working, and 50,000 of those are over the age of 90 and still cashing a paycheck. If medicine and technology continue at the rate they are moving now, by the year 2030, one third of our lifetimes will be spent in retirement. Right now, individuals who make it past the age of 65 can expect to live until they are approximately 83.

Often in our culture, the aged are seen as useless, noncontributing burdens for their younger family members and society to shoulder. How will the changing demographics and lifestyles of retirees alter the face of our country? How might it alter our perception of the aged?

against minority groups, the individuals who discriminate will also someday become part of the aged group and may become victims of discrimination. Butler and Lewis (1991) describe **ageism** as "aversion, hatred, and prejudice toward the aged and their manifestation in the form of discrimination on the basis of age" (p. 557). They further suggest that the aged are stereotyped as senile, rigid in thought and manner, garrulous, and old-fashioned in morality and skills.

In U.S. society, little value is placed on nonproduction. Because of the decrease in some basic capacities (sensory, motor, cognitive, and physiological), aging does have a detrimental effect in a variety of professional fields (Schulz & Salthouse, 1999). Airline pilots, for example, are prohibited from flying commercial aircraft after the age of 60. Despite the passage of the Age Discrimination Employment Act in 1978, similar limitations are placed on occupations such as law enforcement and

One of the misconceptions regarding the elderly is that most cannot be productive.

firefighting. It is understandable, then, why some individuals who view the aged as nonproductive may adopt an ageist attitude. Also contributing to the prevalence of ageism is the emphasis placed by U.S. society on physical beauty. The physical ideal is associated with youth, and the aging process only serves to move an individual farther from the accepted norms of physical beauty.

In 1900, 1 in 25 Americans was over age 65. Three million elderly lived in the United States that year. In 2000, one in eight Americans or 12.65% of the population, an estimated 34,848,000 people, were 65 years of age or older (U.S. Census Bureau, 2000). Projections suggest nearly 70 million elderly by 2030, when all of the baby boomers will be over age 65. The percentage of elderly will increase to an estimated 20.2% of the population in 2030 (Taeuber, 1993). People 85 years of age and older, one of the fastest-growing segments of society, make up 1.6% of the population today, but that is expected to increase to 5% by 2050. The number of centenarians was estimated to be 65,000 in 2000 (Schulz & Ewen, 1993; Treas, 1995, U.S. Census Bureau, 2000).

The aged resemble other oppressed minority groups in that they suffer from prejudice, discrimination, and deprivation. As the aged increase in numbers and in percentage of the population, it is likely that resentment toward them will increase. As with immigrant bashing, segments of our society already perceive the elderly as a drain on resources. There are legitimate concerns regarding society's ability to pay for pensions, to finance health care for the chronically ill elderly, and to provide the personal assistance that the elderly with disabilities require. Will Social Security, Medicare, and Medicaid remain solvent given the increasing numbers of older adults? Providing adequate support for the aged will be a significant challenge in the future.

The rest of society tends to have three basic misconceptions regarding the aged:

1. *Most elderly people are sick or infirm.* The reality is that only 20% of persons over age 65 are in this category and only 10% are unable to engage in normal activity.
2. *Most elderly people are senile.* The fact is that fewer than 10% of the aged have incapacitating mental illness or senility.
3. *Most elderly people cannot be productive.* The reality is that, as a group, the elderly are as productive as young workers, are less prone to job turnover, and have lower accident and absentee rates.

The aged are discriminated against in many areas that affect their well-being and lifestyles. For example, many employers discriminate against them in hiring and retention. In addition, many medical personnel admit that they prefer not to treat the elderly, while some younger people, because of their prejudices, appear to avoid the elderly.

As a microculture, only some of the aged seem to have a sense of group identity. Some use chronological indices to determine the advent of old age; the remainder generally uses functional criteria, such as retirement or health conditions. Some are ashamed of old age and resist identification with the elderly. At the same time, some among the aged have adopted a militant posture, forming groups to protest and promote the rights of the elderly.

As a group, the aged make up a potent political force. As the federal and state governments move toward balancing their budgets, social and welfare programs have often been cut. With many of the elderly living on fixed incomes, they are rightfully fearful of cuts that directly affect the quality of their lives. Consequently, as a group, they typically exercise their right to vote to a greater extent than other age groups. The recognition of their voter influence has been evident in recent political campaigns, during which candidates openly courted the votes of this group, pledging to support their interests.

The aged are understandably concerned about voter issues related to the maintenance or enhancement of Social Security and health care benefits. They are more likely than other groups to support "taxpayer revolts" and to resist any efforts toward revenue enhancement that will affect their incomes. Because they typically are no longer involved in their education or that of their children, they often resist attempts to increase school revenues through taxes. Efforts such as California's Proposition 13, which rolled back property taxes but had a negative impact on education, have had wide support. As the ranks of the aged grow and as they successfully lobby for a greater share of available resources, they are at greater risk of ageist attacks. The working population is increasingly aware that larger amounts of their paychecks are being deducted to provide for Social Security benefits and other programs for the elderly. In addition, younger workers may perceive older workers who hold higher-paying supervisory positions as obstacles to their own advancement. They want the elderly to retire so that there will be greater opportunity for advancement for the young. Yet, when the aged do retire, younger workers may resent them because Social Security taxes must be deducted from their paychecks to fund their retired colleagues' pensions.

Poverty is a very serious problem with the aged. In 2000, the poverty threshold for a single individual 65 or older was $7,900, and for a couple in which the head of the household was 65 or older, $10,075 (U.S. Census Bureau, 2000). With this criterion, 9.7% of the elderly in 2000 were living in poverty, an all-time low percentage. The figure almost doubles, however, if the "near poor" are included. This category includes those whose income is no greater than 150% of the official poverty level (Treas, 1995). We must also remember that there are significant differential rates of poverty when one's racial or ethnic group is factored in. Socioeconomic status tends to be a major factor in the adjustment to old age. As with the earlier years in life, income influences longevity, health status, housing, and marital status for the aged. Middle- and high-income individuals typically have Social Security, pension plans, savings, and medical plans that ease their transition into their retirement years. The pensions and Social Security incomes of low-income individuals tend to be limited and, in some instances, nonexistent. Many of these individuals must continue working well beyond usual retirement years in order to survive.

More than half of African American and Latino elderly tend to depend on Social Security as their sole source of income. Fewer elderly Latinos are eligible for

Social Security benefits than their white counterparts. Social Security benefits of African American and Latino recipients tend to be lower than those of whites because of their frequently lower income levels during their working years.

Elderly persons with high incomes have advantages associated with their greater financial resources. During their earlier years, they were able to maintain better living conditions and better health care, which often translates into better health in the advanced years. Their financial resources enable them to maintain these higher living and health care standards. This advantage, in turn, may result in extended, quality leisure activities, such as travel, which makes the retirement years more pleasurable. It is understandable, therefore, that individuals from high socioeconomic backgrounds tend to view old age more favorably than those from low socioeconomic backgrounds.

As people mature in age, they move through different age groups and become members of different microcultures. As individuals join new age-group cultures, they bring with them other aspects of culture, such as ethnicity, socioeconomic status, and gender. As these various cultures interface with one another and blend their individual, unique qualities, they add to the rich pluralistic nature of American society.

EDUCATIONAL IMPLICATIONS

As with other microcultures, the various age-groups of the U.S. population contribute greatly to the pluralistic nature of this society. Some basic educational considerations should be examined in the study of age groups as a function of culture. American society in general has not always been viewed as particularly supportive or positive in its perception of all age groups. The discussion on adolescence noted that this period is often viewed as a time of storm and stress, whereas in some cultures this period passes with few crises. In American society, the former view tends to prevail. In addition, advancing age is not viewed by the U.S. macroculture with the respect or reverence that is found in many other cultures. Ageism does exist and is, regretfully, as much a part of our social system as racism and handicapism.

For these reasons, it is critically important that students be exposed to age as it relates to culture. Moreover, studying age and its relation to culture is important because students, if they live to full life expectancy, will become members of each age group. Thus, unlike the study of different ethnic groups, students can learn to understand and appreciate microcultures of which they have been members, are presently members, or will eventually become members. By addressing the issues of various age groups in the classroom, educators can help students to better understand their siblings, parents, and other important persons in their lives. Knowledge can eliminate fear of the unknown as students begin to move into different age groups at different times in their lives. It is important that issues related to age groups be appropriately introduced into the curriculum because students need to understand the concept of ageism. Just as the school assists students in understanding the problem of racism, the school should be responsible for helping students understand the aged and dispel the myths related to this group. Field trips to retirement homes or visits to the class by senior citizens may provide useful experiences. As students become aware of the nature and characteristics of each age group, they will develop perceptions of each individual, regardless of age, as being an important and integral part of society.

It is critically important for educators to understand age as it relates to both students and their parents. Understanding the particular age-group characteristics and needs of students can assist the educator in better understanding and managing age-related behavior, such as reactions or responses to peer-group pressure. Understanding the nature of parents, siblings, and other important individuals (e.g., grandparents) will assist the educator in parent-teacher relationships and in helping students cope with their interactions with others. For example, as an elderly grandparent moves into the family setting, this event may affect a child and his or her classroom behavior.

The school is perhaps in the best position of any agency in the community to observe the effects of child abuse. The classroom teacher is an important agent in detecting and reporting abuse and in all states is required by law to do so. To do this, the teacher must be aware of the problem of abuse, the manifestations of abuse, and the proper authorities to whom abuse is reported. If the teacher's immediate supervisor is unresponsive to the reporting of a potential abuse problem, the teacher should then continue to seek help until competent and concerned individuals in positions of authority provide it.

The single most important factor in determining possible child abuse is the physical condition of the child. Telltale marks, bruises, and abrasions that cannot be adequately explained may provide reason to suspect abuse. Unusual changes in the child's behavior patterns, such as extreme fatigue, may be reason to suspect problems. The parents' behavior and their ability or lack of ability to explain the child's condition and the social features of the family may be reason to suspect abuse. Although physical abuse or neglect may tend to have observable indicators, sexual abuse may occur with few, if any, obvious indicators. Adults may be unwilling to believe what a child says and may be hesitant to report alleged incidents. There is no typical profile of the victim, and the physical signs vary. Behavioral manifestations are usually exhibited by the victims but are often viewed as insignificant or attributed to typical childhood stress. Chronic depression, isolation from peers, apathy, and suicide attempts are some of the more serious behavioral manifestations of the problem (Sarles, 1980).

The number of children and youth infected by the HIV virus and other sexually transmitted diseases is a national tragedy. Prevention efforts must be multifaceted if these diseases are to be eradicated. The school has a major role to play, and there are specific steps which can be taken. School-based programs are critical in reaching youth before they engage in risky behaviors. Topics such as HIV, STDs, unintended pregnancy, and tobacco and other drug abuse should be integrated into the curriculum and should be an ongoing program for all students, kindergarten through high school. The development of these programs should be done carefully and should take into consideration parent and community values.

The majority of suicides are planned and are not committed on impulse, and most suicide victims mention their intentions to someone. Of adolescents who commit suicide, 80% make open threats beforehand (Griffin & Felsenthal, 1983). Often, a number of warning signs can alert teachers, other professionals, and parents. The following are some of the danger signals (Griffin & Felsenthal, 1983):

- Aggressive, hostile behavior
- Alcohol and drug abuse
- Passive behavior
- Changes in eating habits
- Changes in sleeping habits
- Fear of separation
- Abrupt changes in personality
- Sudden mood swings
- Decreased interest in schoolwork and decline in grades
- Inability to concentrate
- Hopelessness
- Obsession with death
- Giving away valued possessions
- Euphoria or increased activity after depression

If teachers or other school personnel suspect trouble, friendly, low-key questions or statements may provide an appropriate opening: "You seem down today"or "It seems like something is bothering you." If an affirmative response is given, a more direct and probing (but supportive) question may be asked. If there is any reason whatsoever to suspect a possible suicide attempt, teachers and other school staff should alert the appropriate school personnel. Teachers should recognize their limitations and avoid making judgments. The matter should be referred to the school psychologist, who should, in turn, alert a competent medical authority (psychiatrist) and the child's parents. Assistance can also be obtained from local mental health clinics and suicide prevention centers. Prompt action may save a life.

Our coverage of adolescent substance abuse has been brief. But the importance of the problem is such that every educator should be aware of the problem and work toward providing children at an early age with appropriate drug education. No agency, group, or individual can wage an effective campaign against substance abuse alone. Only with a united effort can an effective battle be waged.

Hafen and Frandsen (1980) indicate danger signs for drug or alcohol ingestion that may place an individual at life-threatening risk:

- *Unconsciousness.* The individual cannot be awakened or, if awakened, lapses back into deep sleep.
- *Breathing difficulties.* Breathing stops altogether, may be weak, or weak and strong in cycles. Skin may become bluish or purple, indicating lack of oxygenated blood.
- *Fever.* Any temperature above 100°F (38°C) is a danger sign when drugs are involved.

- *Vomiting while not fully conscious.* If a person is in a stupor or in a semiconscious or unconscious state, vomiting can cause serious breathing problems.
- *Convulsions.* Twitching of face, trunk, arms, or legs; muscle spasms or muscle rigidity may indicate impending convulsions. Violent jerking motions and spasms likely indicate a convulsion.

In the event these signs are observed in the classroom, the school nurse should be summoned immediately. If none is available, then someone trained in CPR should be summoned. It would be advisable for a list of all personnel with CPR training to be made available to all teachers and other staff.

As parents hurry children into adulthood, educators may also contribute to the hurrying process. Teachers, administrators, and support personnel should be cognizant of the fact that the children they teach and work with are children, and not miniature adults. Children have but one opportunity to experience the wonders of childhood. In comparison with adulthood, childhood and adolescence are relatively short periods of time, and these young people should have every opportunity to enjoy these stages of their lives to the fullest extent possible.

Summary

The study of age as a microculture is important to educators because it helps them understand how the child or adolescent struggles to win peer acceptance and to balance this effort with the need for parental approval. In some instances, the pressures from peers are not congruent with those from the home.

As each child develops into adolescence, we observe a growing need for independence. Adolescence for some is a time of storm and stress; for others, it passes with little or no trauma.

Young adulthood is one of the most exciting times in life. It is a time for courtship, marriage, children, and career choices. It is a time when individuals reach their physical and occupational prime. Young adulthood can also be a threatening time because choices made at this time often have a lifetime impact on the individual. Adulthood is the time when dreams are either fulfilled or become forever elusive. With the latter can come bitterness, resentment, and anger.

With life expectancy increasing each year, those in the aged cohort increase in numbers daily. More than half a million advance into the ranks of the aged each year. Like the ethnic minorities and those with disabilities, the aged face discrimination and prejudice in the form of ageism. Those who discriminate will someday become aged, perhaps to face the treatment that they themselves imposed on others.

To answer these questions online, go to the Chapter Questions module for this chapter of the Companion Website.

Questions for Review

1. Explain why child abuse is a problem, and cite some of the signs of child abuse.
2. When does ethnic identification begin in children, and how is it manifested?

3. Describe some variables that contribute to prejudice in children.
4. What are the sources of alienation between adolescents and their families?
5. What is the extent of substance abuse among adolescents, and what are some of the underlying causes of substance use in this age group?
6. What are the causes of adolescent suicide, and what are the warning signs?
7. What are some primary differences between the younger and the older baby boomers?
8. In what ways do the baby busters differ from the baby boomers?
9. What factors have contributed to some African American males being considered at risk in our society?
10. How does old age relate to ethnicity and socioeconomic status?
11. What are the roots of ageism?

References

Aboud, F. (1988). *Children and prejudice.* Cambridge, MA: Basil Blackwell.

Aboud, F., & Doyle, A. B. (1996a). Does talk of race foster prejudice or tolerance in children? *Canadian Journal of Behavioral Science, 28*(3), 1–14.

Aboud, F., & Doyle, A. B. (1996b). Parental and peer influence on children's racial attitudes. *Internationd Journal of Intercultural Relations, 20* : 371-383.

American Academy of Pediatrics. (2000). *Some things you should know about media literacy.* Available: http://www.aap.org/advocacy/childhealthmonth/media.htm.

Annie E. Casey Foundation. (2000). *Kids count.* Baltimore, MD: Author.

Bender, W. N., Clinton, G., & Bender, R. L. (Eds.) (1999). *Violence prevention and reduction in schools.* Austin, TX: Pro-Ed.

Bigler, R., & Liben, L. (1993). A cognitive development approach to racial stereotyping and reconstructive memory in Euro-American children. *Child Development, 64,* 1507–1519.

Butler, R. N., & Lewis, M. I. (1991). *Aging and mental health: Positive psychosocial and biomedical approaches* (4th ed.). New York: MacMillan.

Cannon, A., Streisand, B., & McGraw, D. (1999, May 3). Why? *U.S. News and World Report, 26* (17), 16-19.

Centers for Disease Control and Prevention. (1993). Advanced report of final natality statistics, 1991. *Monthly Vital Statistics Report* [suppl., Sept. 9], *42*(3), 34–37.

Centers for Disease Control and Prevention. (1994, June). *HIV/AIDS surveillance report,6*(1), 1–26.

Centers for Disease Control and Prevention. (1997). State specific birthrates for teenagers—United States, 1990–1996. *Morbidity and Mortality Monthly Report, 46*(36), 837–841.

Centers for Disease Control and Prevention. (2000a). *Youth violence in the United States.* Available: http://www.cdc.gov/ncipc/factsheets/yvfacts.htm.

Centers for Disease Control and Prevention. (2000b). *Facts about violence among youth and violence in schools.* Available: http://www.cdc.gov/ncipc/factsheets/schoolvi.htm.

Centers for Disease Control and Prevention (2000c). *HIV/AIDS surveillance in adolescents: AIDS cases in 13 to 19 year olds by race/ethnicity, U.S.* Available: http://www.cdec.gov/hiv/graphics/images/1265/1265-7.htm.

Children's Defense Fund. (1986a). *Building health programs for teenagers.* Washington, DC: Author.

Children's Defense Fund. (1986b). *Welfare and pregnancy: What do we know? What do we do?* Washington, DC: Author.

Children's Defense Fund. (1990). *SOS America: A children's defense budget.* Washington, DC: Author.

Chilman, C. (1983). *Adolescent sexuality in a changing American society.* New York: Wiley.

Chua-Eoan, H. (1999). Escaping from the darkness. *Time, 153* (21), 44–49.

Crowe, P., Philbin, J., Richards, M. H., & Crawford, I. (1998). Adolescent alcohol involvement and the experience of social environments. *Journal of Research on Adolescence, 8*(4), 403–422.

Dannen, F. (1992, November 16). Annals of crime: The revenge of the Green Dragons. *New Yorker,* 76–99.

Doyle, A. B., & Aboud, F. E. (1995). A longitudinal study of white children's racial prejudice as a social cognitive development. *Merrill-Palmer Quarterly, 41,* 210–220.

Drowns, R. W., & Hess, K. M. (1990). *Juvenile justice.* St. Paul, MN: West.

Drury, K. (1998). *15 Characteristics of Generation X.* CompuCoach. Available: http://www.churchsmart.com/compucoach/01056.htm.

Dryfoos, J. (1990). *Adolescents at risk: Prevalence and prevention.* New York: Oxford University.

Federal Bureau of Investigation. (1994). *Uniform crime report: Crime in the United States, 1993.* Washington, DC: U.S. Department of Justice.

Gibbs, J. T. (1986). Psychosocial correlates of sexual attitudes and behaviors in urban early adolescent females: Implications for intervention. *Journal of Social Work and Human Sexuality, 5,* 81–97.

Gibbs, J. T. (1992). Young black males in America: Endangered, embittered, and embattled. In M. S. Kimmell & M. A. Messner (Eds.), *Men's lives* (2nd ed.). New York: MacMillan.

Gibbs, J. T. (1998). High–risk behaviors in African American youth: Conceptual and methodological issues in research. In V. C. McLoyd & L. Steinberg (Eds.), *Studying minority adolescents.* Mahwah, NJ: Lawrence Erlbaum Associates, Inc.

Green, S. (1999, April 24). Trench coat mafia teen describes school life filled with taunts, abuse. *Denver Post,* p. A-01.

Greven, P. (1990). *Spare the child: The religious roots of punishment and the psychological impact of physical abuse.* New York: Knopf.

Griffin, M. E., & Felsenthal, C. (1983). *A cry for help.* Garden City, NY: Doubleday.

Hafen, B. Q., and Frandsen, K. J. (1980). Drug and alcohol emergencies. Center City, MN: Hazelden Foundation.

Howell, J. C. (1998). Recent gang research: Program and policy implications. In P. M. Sharp & B. W. Hancock (Eds.). *Juvenile delinquency* (2nd ed.). Upper Saddle River, N. J. : Prentice Hall.

Hughes, F. P., & Noppe, L. D. (1991). *Human development across the life span.* New York: Macmillan.

Huizinga, D., & Elliot, D. (1985). *Juvenile offenders prevalence, offender incidence, and arrest rates by race.* Boulder, CO: Institute of Behavioral Science.

Igoa, C. (1995). *The Inner World of the immigrant child.* Mahwah, N. J.: Lawerence Erlbaum Associates, Inc.

Jackson, R. L., Lopez, R. J., & Connell, R. (1997, January 12). Clinton puts priority on curtailing gang crime. *Los Angeles Times,* pp. A1, A12.

Kofkin, J. A., Katz, P. A., & Downey, E. P. (1995). *Family discourse about race and the development of children's racial attitudes.* Paper presented at the meeting of the Society for Research in Child Development, Indianapolis, IN.

Kratcoski, P. C., & Kratcoski, L. D. (1990). *Juvenile delinquency* (3rd ed.). Upper Saddle River, NJ: Prentice Hall.

Krisberg, B., Schwartz, I., Fishman, G., Eiskovits, Z., & Guttman, E. (1986). *The incarceration of minority youth.* Minneapolis: University of Minnesota, H. H. Humphrey Institute of Public Affairs.

McKee, P. W., Jones, R. W., & Barbe, R. H. (1993). *Suicide in the school.* Horsham, PA: LRP.

McLoyd, V. C., & Steinberg, L. (1998). *Studying minority adolescents.* Mahwah, NJ: Lawrence Erlbaum Associates, Inc.

Mitchell, S. (1993, May 23). The baby busters. *San Jose Mercury News*, pp. 1L, 5L.

National Clearinghouse on Child Abuse and Neglect Information (2000). "What is Maltreatment?" July 2000. Available : www.calib.com/nccanch/pubs/factsheets/childmal/htm.

Nazario, S. (1997, March 9). Children who kill themselves. *Los Angeles Times*, pp. A1, A28–A30.

Newman, B. M., & Newman, P. R. (1986). *Adolescent development.* Upper Saddle River, NJ: Merrill/Prentice Hall.

Palermo, G. B., & Simpson, D. (1998). At the roots of violence: The progressive decline and dissolution of the family. In P. M. Sharp & B. W. Hancock, (Eds.), *Juvenile delinquency: Historical, theoretical, and societal reactions to youth* (2nd Ed.). Upper Saddle River, NJ: Prentice Hall

Pankratz, H. (1999, August 25). Jock culture theory a myth: Principal defends Columbine staff. *Denver Post*, p. A-01.

Political Action Committee for Generation X (2000). Gore and Bush not the same on Social Security. Available: http://www.xpac.org.

PRIDE, Inc. (1996). *Student use of most drugs reaches highest level in nine years: More report getting "very high, bombed, or stoned"* [Press release]. Chamblee, GA: National Parents' Resource Institute for Drug Education.

Roof, W. C. (1990). Return of the baby boomers to organized religion. In C. H. Jacquet, Jr. (Ed.), *1990 yearbook of American and Canadian churches.* Nashville: Abingdon Press.

Rosenheim, M., & Testa, M. (Eds.). (1992). *Early parenthood and the transition to adulthood.* New Brunswick, NJ: Rutgers University Press.

Sarles, R. M. (1980). Incest. *Pediatric & Review*, 2(2) 51-54.

Schulz, R., & Ewen, R. B. (1993). *Adult development and aging* (2nd ed.). New York: MacMillan.

Schulz, R., & Salthouse, T. (1999). *Adult development and aging: Myths and emerging realities* (3rd ed.). New Jersey: Prentice Hall.

Sheley, J., & Wright, J. (1995). *In the line of fire: Youth, guns, and violence in urban America.* New York: Aldine de Gruyter.

Sidel, R. (1990). *On her own: Growing up in the shadow of the American dream.* New York: Viking.

Sleek, S. (1997, October). People's racist attitudes can be unlearned. *APA Monitor*, 38.

Stevens, P., & Smith, R. L. (2001). *Substance abuse counseling.* Upper Saddle River, NJ: Merrill/Prentice Hall.

Taeuber, C. M. (1993). *Sixty-five plus in America* (U.S. Bureau of the Census, Current Population Reports, Special Studies, P23–178RV). Washington, DC: U.S. Government Printing Office.

Tower, C. C. (1992). Child abuse and neglect. In N. A. Cohen (Ed.), *Child welfare.* Needham Heights, MA: Allyn & Bacon.

Treas, J. (1995). *Older Americans in the 1990s and beyond.* Washington, DC: Population Reference Bureau.

Tulgan, B. (1997). *The manager's pocket guide to Generation X.* Amherst, MA: HRD Press.

U.S. Census Bureau (2000). *Resident population estimates of the United States by age and sex.* Available : http://www.census.gov/population/estimates/nation/untfile2-1.txt.

U.S. Department of Health and Human Services (2000). *Child abuse and neglect national statistics.* Available : http://www.calib.com/nccanch/pubs/factsheets/canstats/htm.

Youth Risk Behavior Surveillance—United States, 1997. (1997). Calverton, MD: National Center for Chronic Disease Prevention and Health Promotion. Available: http://www.cdc.gov/epo/mmwr/preview/mmwrhtml/00054432.htm.

Suggested Readings

Bender, W. N., Clinton, G., & Bender, R. L. (Eds.). (1999). *Violence prevention and reduction in schools.* Austin, TX: Pro-Ed.
  A very good overview of school violence, causes, and preventative measures. Nine chapters.

Gibbs, J. T. (1992). Young black males in America: Endangered, embittered, and embattled. In M. S. Kimmell & M. A. Messner (Eds.), *Men's lives* (2nd ed.). New York: MacMillan. This is an excellent discussion of African American males in the United States and the variables that have placed them at risk in our society.

McLoyd, V. C., & Steinberg, L. (Eds.) (1998). *Studying minority adolescents.* Mahwah, NJ: Lawrence Erlbaum Associates, Inc.
  A very good overview of the research on minority adolescents. Includes four sections: (a) research on the minority adolescent and families, (b) advancing our understanding of the influence of race and ethnicity in development, (c) responding to methodological challenges in the study of ethnic minority adolescents and families, and (d) integration of research and provision of services. Fourteen chapters.

CRITICAL INCIDENTS IN TEACHING

Age

Cultural Attitudes Toward the Aged

"That is really stupid!" exclaims Keith to Michael Wong. "You have the neatest room of anyone in the class, with your own stereo, TV, and computer. Now you have to share it with your grandfather! Why do you have to share your bedroom with an old man? It isn't fair." "Because he's too old to care for himself, and he can't share my sister's room. She's a girl," Michael explains to his best friend, Keith.

"Why don't your parents put him in an old people's home as my parents did with my grandmother?" Keith protests. "When they get old, they're useless. They just get in your way. Old people just don't have the right to interfere with other people's lives. When I get too old, I want someone like Dr. Death, that guy in Michigan, to just help me go away—peaceful like. Old people are a pain in the butt to everyone. I'm not going to be a bother like that to anyone. Besides, it'll be a zillion years before I'm ever that old. Ha!"

Trying to explain, Michael says to Keith, "My grandfather really isn't a bother. He's a neat guy. He may be old, but he's very wise, you know. Really smart. Besides, we Chinese don't like to put our parents and grandparents in nursing homes. It's kind of a disgrace to the family. Sure, I'd rather have my own room to myself, but it's okay. I really don't mind."

Hearing the discussion, Mr. Fitzpatrick, Michael and Keith's sixth-grade teacher, is trying to decide whether he should intervene.

Questions for Discussion

To answer these questions online, go to the Critical Incidents module for this chapter of the Companion Website.

1. Should Mr. Fitzpatrick intervene in the discussion or let the boys work it out themselves?
2. Should the teacher discuss attitudes toward the aged? If so, what should be discussed?
3. Should the teacher discuss how different cultures perceive old age differently?
4. Should the teacher address the ageist attitudes of Kevin? If so, how?

Ageism

Medgar Evers High School is in the inner city and is attended primarily by students of color. The physical plant and equipment have suffered from years of neglect and inadequate funding. In one of the girls' bathrooms, two of the toilets do not flush. The hot water has been turned off in all of the lavatories, and some do not work at all. Paint is peeling from the walls and ceilings. Ceilings that are supposed to be covered with tiles have a fourth to a third missing. The custodial staff has been decreased by half in recent years. Trash often goes uncollected, and weeds grow all over the campus lawn. The computer class has but eight Apple IIe's for 26 students. The few other computers are broken beyond repair, and there are no funds to buy Power Macs or Pentium-equipped PCs.

There is hope, however. A school bond initiative will give all of the schools in the district funds to make repairs and upgrade equipment. Cory Andrews' government class has been following the school bond issue carefully. They have studied and discussed the importance of an informed electorate and the importance of exercising one's right to vote. They have urged their parents and relatives to vote and to support the school bond. A community voters' rights group comprised primarily of retired senior citizens is strongly against the school bond initiative. They have been vocal and outspoken against any efforts to increase their taxes.

On Tuesday night, several students from the government class gather at Maximino Apodaca's house to watch the election returns. They are interested in many of the issues and candidates, but the school bond issue is the one they are watching closely. Finally, the projections are in and the bond initiative has been defeated by a 60% to 40% margin. On Wednesday morning, several in the government class are openly angry. "This school will be a pigsty as long as we are students here, and probably forever," says Tyrone Wheatley. "It's all because of those blood-sucking old people. They want more Social Security. They want more health care. Hell, they haven't paid in but a fraction from what they have collected, and they still want more. And they are the ones who caused the bond issue to be voted down. I really hate old people. They're greedy, and they don't contribute anything to society. All they do is take, take, take." Many in the class echo the same sentiments.

Questions for Discussion

To answer these questions online, go to the Critical Incidents module for this chapter of the Companion Website.

1. Should Mr. Andrews allow the students to continue to vent their frustration and anger?
2. Should he use this as an opportunity to open a meaningful discussion?
3. The discussion has degenerated into an attack on the aged. Should he try to change the students' perceptions of the aged?
4. What strategies or activities can Mr. Andrews provide to develop more positive understanding about the aged?
5. What positive activities can Mr. Andrews and his students create to develop understanding about the aged?

Weapons at School?

First grader Sharlene Moennich's favorite cartoon character is Tweety Bird. Pleased with her new gift from her father, she proudly showed her plastic Tweety Bird, which was attached to her backpack by a small six-inch chain. Kin Lo, Sharlene's teacher, was very much aware of the new school board's strictly enforced zero tolerance policy to protect students against violent attacks. The policy called for the immediate expulsion of any student carrying firearms, knives, sharp instruments, and chains to school. There were no exceptions, and Mr. Lo is aware that a student earlier in the month was expelled for carrying a nail clipper to school. It would be almost impossible to injure anyone with the tiny chain. However, the zero tolerance policy did not define the length or size of prohibited chains. A chain was a chain, and Sharlene's chain would be treated in the same manner as carrying a firearm to school. To compound the dilemma for Mr. Lo was the stipulation on the zero tolerance policy that any district employee who knowingly fails to report a violation would himself/herself be suspended without pay.

Kin Lo knows that the chain is harmless. He is aware that Sharlene, a model student, and her parents are unaware that this constitutes a weapon. He is also aware that ignorance of the policy is not considered a valid excuse, and that Sharlene will be expelled if she is reported. Lo is also aware that other students have seen the chain and know that he, too, has seen it. He faces certain suspension, and an entry into his personnel file that he failed to report a student's possession of a banned weapon.

Questions for Discussion

To answer these questions online, go to the Critical Incidents module for this chapter of the Companion Website.

1. What should Kin Lo do?
2. Should he quietly ask Sharlene to give him the Tweety Bird to hold, call her parents, and explain the problem?
3. Should he, as required by policy, turn the innocent Sharlene into the principal, knowing that she will be expelled?
4. Are there any other options?

Perceived Peer Pressure

For most of the school year, Karen Apoliana's sixth grade class in Honolulu had been planning a year-end excursion to the Island of Hawaii. They had already studied many of the scenic and historical wonders of this land, from the 300-foot Akaka falls, to the Kilauea Crater at Volcano National Park. In their science lessons, they had studied volcanoes. Now they would see an active volcano's lava flow into the sea at Kamoamoa. The tickets had been purchased: necessary clothing, flashlights, and other accessories were packed or ready to be packed. For the last time, Ms. Apoliana reviewed the rules for the trip. Any violation of the rules would result in a student being sent home on the plane by him or herself. The parents signed the rules document and so did each student.

John Freitas was never part of the in-crowd or group in the class. He wanted very much to be accepted and had tried unsuccessfully on several occasions to do things that would draw attention to himself and make the others in the class think that he was a tough guy. The first day in the Hilo hotel where the group was staying, John shoplifted some postcards, gum, and other merchandise from the hotel gift shop, which he planned to give to other students, thinking that this would enhance his image among his classmates. Several of his classmates saw him take the items, and so did the gift shop clerk. She called the hotel manager, who escorted an embarrassed John out of the gift shop and directly to Ms. Apoliana. Stealing was on the list of offenses that was punishable with an immediate return trip home on the plane. From a distance, the students who had witnessed the event watched as Ms. Apoliana spoke with John.

To answer these questions online, go to the Critical Incidents module for this chapter of the Companion Website.

Questions for Discussion

1. What should Ms. Apoliana do?
2. John is contrite, acknowledging his guilt, and promising to be a model student if she will let him stay and not send him back on the plane.
3. If she allows John to stay, she is confident that he will keep his word and not engage in further untoward behaviors. But the other students will also know that she did not maintain her own rules for discipline.
4. If Ms. Apoliana allows John to stay, what should she say to the other students?
5. If she sends John home, what should she say to the other students?
6. What should she say to John's parents if he stays? If he has to leave?

A Half Truth

Eric "Rocky" Young was another student in Karen Apoliana's class. He was running with a bad crowd in school and was defiant to both his parents and to his teachers. A teacher in the restroom caught him and his friends allegedly defacing the wall with graffiti. They were taken to the principal's office who in turn, called the police. The boys were all to be arrested. A frightened and crying Rocky assured Ms. Apoliana that he was innocent of writing the graffiti that the principal had identified. Ms. Apoliana was touched by Rocky's apparent sincerity and intervened with the principal. Because of her efforts, the arrest was called off. Later, however, another student told Ms. Apoliana that Rocky was indeed innocent of the graffiti he had been accused of, but that he had marked up the walls elsewhere in the restroom. Feeling betrayed by Rocky, she questioned him, and this time he confessed to his guilt.

To answer these questions online, go to the Critical Incidents module for this chapter of the Companion Website.

Questions for Discussion

1. What should Ms. Apoliana do? Had she been betrayed and used?
2. Should she tell the principal so that he could call the police again?
3. Should she suggest an alternative punishment for Rocky?

Chapter 9

Education That Is Multicultural

We must be the change we wish to see in the world.

Mahatma Gandhi

Natisha Loftis had not said a word to any of her teachers since the beginning of school. It's not that she was a "bad" student; she turned in assignments and made Bs. She certainly didn't cause her teachers trouble. Therefore, the high school counselor, Mr. Williams, was somewhat surprised to hear that she was dropping out of school. He had been Natisha's advisor for more than 2 years, but he didn't really remember her. Nevertheless, it was his job to conduct interviews with students who were leaving school for one reason or another.

Natisha described her school experiences as coming to school, listening to teachers, and going home. School was boring and not connected at all to her real life, in which she had the responsibility for helping her father raise five brothers and sisters. She might even be able to get a job with the same *cleaning firm that her dad worked for. For sure, nothing she was learning in school could help her get a job. And she knew from more than 10 years of listening to teachers and reading textbooks that her chances of becoming a news anchorwoman or even a teacher were about the same as winning the lottery. The last time a teacher had even asked about her family was in the sixth grade, when her mom left the family. The only place anyone paid attention to her was in church.*

School had helped silence Natisha. Classes provided no meaningful experience for her. The content may have been important to the teachers, but she could find no relationship to her own world. Why has Natisha decided to drop out of school? How can the curriculum be made more meaningful to students who are not white and middle class? How can teachers make a student like Natisha excited about learning?

MULTICULTURAL EDUCATION

It is no easy task to incorporate cultural knowledge throughout teaching. In the beginning, teachers must consciously think about it as they interact with students and plan lessons and assignments. They should approach teaching multiculturally as an enthusiastic learner with much to learn from students and community members who have cultural backgrounds different from their own. Teachers may need to remind themselves that their way of believing, thinking, and acting evolved from their own culture and experiences, which may vary greatly from that of the students in their school. Teachers will need to listen to the histories and experiences of students and their families and integrate them into their teaching. Students' values need to be validated within both their in-school and out-of-school realities—a process that is authentic only if teachers believe the cultures of their students are as valid as their own.

Educators are often at a disadvantage because they do not live, or have never lived, in the community in which their students live. Too often, the only parents with whom they interact are those who are able to attend parent-teacher meetings or who have scheduled conferences with them. In many cases, they have not been in their students' homes or been active participants in community activities. How do we begin to learn other's cultures? Using the tools of an anthropologist or ethnographer, we could observe children in classrooms and on playgrounds. We can listen carefully to students and their parents as they discuss their life experiences. We can study other cultures. We can learn about the perspectives of others by reading articles and books written by men and women from different ethnic, racial, socioeconomic, and religious groups. Participation in community, religious, and ethnic activities can provide another perspective on students' cultures.

Our knowledge about our students' cultures should allow us to make the academic content of our teaching more meaningful to students by relating it to their own experiences and building on their prior knowledge. It should help us make them and their histories the center of the education process in our effort to help them reach their academic, vocational, and social potentials. In the process, students should learn to believe in their own abilities and to become active participants in their own learning. Students should be able to achieve academically without adopting the dominant culture as their own. They should be able to maintain their own cultural identities inside and outside the school.

Teaching multiculturally requires the incorporation of diversity throughout the learning process. If race, ethnicity, class, and gender are not interrelated in the curriculum, students do not learn that these are interrelated parts of a whole called *self.* Although Chapters 2 through 8 addressed membership in these microcultures separately, they should be interwoven throughout one's own teaching. For example, if activities are developed to fight racism but continue to perpetuate sexism, we are not providing multicultural education. At the same time, we should not forget women of color and women in poverty when discussing the impact of sexism and other women's issues.

All teaching should be multicultural and all classrooms should be models of democracy, equity, and social justice. To do this, educators must do the following:

1. Place the student at the center of the teaching and learning process.
2. Promote human rights and respect for cultural differences.
3. Believe that all students can learn.
4. Acknowledge and build on the life histories and experiences of students' microcultural memberships.
5. Critically analyze oppression and power relationships to understand racism, sexism, classism, and discrimination against the disabled, gay, lesbian, young, and elderly.
6. Critique society in the interest of social justice and equality.
7. Participate in collective social action to ensure a democratic society.

Teachers and other school personnel can make a difference. Making one's teaching and classroom multicultural is an essential step in empowerment for both teachers and students.

Public Support

One sometimes has the impression that diversity in either schools or society has few advocates. However, public opinion polls show otherwise. A majority of students think they should study the history and culture of diverse groups (Metropolitan Life Insurance Company, 1996a). Nearly 90% of adult respondents to a national poll endorsed the teaching of diversity in the public schools (National Conference for Community and Justice, 1994). Yet, one in four students reported that no such courses were offered in their schools.

The public also values diversity in the workforce and teaching profession. More than 80% of the respondents to a survey by the Business Higher Education Forum believe that diversity is a valued asset. They said "it is important to have employees of different races, cultures, and backgrounds in the workplace, while 85 percent noted the importance of diversity to the future of the economy" (Survey, 2000, p. 1). Ninety percent of the respondents thought that diversity is "important to the quality of higher education." In a survey on the public's perception of the teaching profession, "nearly 60 percent thought that it was very or somewhat important for students to have teachers from different ethnic/cultural backgrounds than their own" (Recruiting New Teachers, 1998, p. 24).

The public does not believe that the same educational opportunities are being provided to white students and students of color. More than three fourths of the respondents in the Recruiting New Teachers (1998) survey believe that affluent students have more opportunities than students in low-income neighborhoods. At the same time, 80% believe that equal educational opportunity is possible and should be pursued as a national goal.

Supporting Dispositions

Education that is multicultural requires teachers and other school personnel to have dispositions that support learning for students from diverse backgrounds. Dispositions are the values, commitments, and professional ethics that influence teaching and interactions with students, families, colleagues, and communities. An educator's dispositions affect student learning, motivation, and development as well as the educator's own professional growth. They are guided by beliefs and attitudes related to values such as caring, fairness, honesty, responsibility, and social justice (National Council for the Accreditation of Teacher Education, 2000). If a teacher's interaction with students is disrespectful and disparaging of the student's culture and experiences, the teacher will be incapable of delivering multicultural education.

Teachers must receive a license from the state in which they plan to work. Many states have adopted licensure standards that outline expectations for knowledge, teaching skills, and dispositions. These states expect teachers to demonstrate the following dispositions, which stress the importance of diversity and culture in student learning.

- The teacher believes that *all* children can learn at high levels and persists in helping all children achieve success.
- The teacher appreciates and values human diversity, shows respect for students' varied talents and perspectives, and is committed to the pursuit of "individually configured excellence."
- The teacher respects students as individuals with differing personal and family backgrounds and various skills, talents, and interests.
- The teacher is sensitive to community and cultural norms.
- The teacher makes students feel valued for their potential as people, and helps them learn to value each other.

- The teacher appreciates multiple perspectives and conveys to learners how knowledge is developed from the vantage point of the knower.
- The teacher has enthusiasm for the discipline(s) she or he teaches and sees connections to everyday life. (Interstate New Teacher Assessment and Support Consortium, 1992)

Educators with these dispositions will be able to build on the cultures and experiences of students from diverse backgrounds to support and extend academic learning. The remainder of this chapter will focus on the knowledge and skills needed to make one's teaching, classroom, and school multicultural.

Multiculturalizing the Curriculum

Curriculum is more than the composite of courses that students are required to take—the so-called official curriculum. It is political. It "not only represents a configuration of particular interests and experiences; it also represents a site of struggle over whose versions of authority, history, the present, and the future will prevail in schools" (McLaren & Giroux, 1995, p. 40). Whose story, whose culture, and whose values will be reflected in the curriculum being taught and the supporting textbooks and readings that are assigned?

Regardless of the grade level or subject being taught, the curriculum should be multicultural. It should be directed toward all students. It is as important for students in a homogeneous setting as for those in more diverse settings to acknowledge and understand the diversity in the United States and the world. Because students in settings with limited diversity do not have the opportunities to interact with persons from other cultural backgrounds, they should learn to value diversity, rather than fear it. They should come to know that others have different perspectives on the world and events that are based in different experiences. The Internet could facilitate interacting with and getting to know persons from other cultures.

Although communities are not always rich in ethnic diversity, they all are diverse. Educators need to determine the microcultures that exist in the community. Schools that are on or near Native American reservations will include students from the tribes in the area, as well as non-Native Americans. Urban schools typically include multiethnic populations and students from different socioeconomic levels; inner-city schools have a high proportion of low-income students. Rural schools include low-income and middle-class families. Teachers who enter schools attended by students from different cultural backgrounds will need to adjust to that setting; otherwise, both students and teachers could suffer.

The current traditional curriculum is based on the histories, experiences, and perspectives of the dominant group. The result is the marginalization of the experiences of other groups. Multicultural teaching tells it as it is. Diversity existed in the United States when Europeans arrived and became greater with each passing century. To teach as if only one group is worthy of inclusion in the curriculum is not to tell the truth. It suggests that only one group is important and that if you belong to another group, you are inferior to the one being taught. How would you feel if you never saw yourself, your family, or your community in the curriculum? What groups discussed earlier in this book seldom, if ever, make it in to textbooks or class discussions?

Instructional materials and information about different groups are available to students and teachers. It may be more difficult to find resources on microcultures where the membership is small or somewhat new to the United States, but it is not impossible. Both students and teachers can use the Internet to locate information, including personal narratives, art, music, and family histories. Although teachers cannot possibly address each of the hundreds of ethnic and religious groups in this country, they should attempt to include the groups represented in the school community, whether or not all of them are represented in the school.

For example, in western Pennsylvania, a teacher should include information about and examples from the Amish. This approach will help Amish students feel a valued part of the school and will signal to other students that cultural diversity is acceptable and valued. In schools in the Southwest, the culture of Mexican Americans and Native Americans should be integrated throughout the curriculum. In other areas of the country, the curriculum should reflect the histories, experiences, and perspectives of Mormons, Muslims, Vietnamese Americans, Lakotas, Jamaican Americans, African Americans, Chinese Americans, Puerto Ricans, and other groups as appropriate. Students should find themselves in the curriculum; otherwise, they are marginalized and do not see themselves as an integral part of the school culture.

Educators are cautioned against giving superficial attention to cultural groups. Multicultural education is much more than food, festival, and fun, or heroes and holidays. Even celebrating African American history only during February is not multicultural education. It is much more complex and pervasive than setting aside an hour, a unit, or a month. It becomes the lens through which the curriculum is presented.

The amount of specific content about different groups will vary according to the course taught, but awareness and recognition of the nation's diversity can be reflected in all classroom experiences. No matter how assimilated students in a classroom are, it is the teacher's responsibility to ensure that they understand diversity, know the contributions of members of both dominant and other groups, and hear the voices of individuals and groups who are from cultural backgrounds different from the majority of students.

Multiculturalism is not a compensatory process to make others more like the dominant group. As an educator integrates diversity into the curriculum, the differences across groups must not become deficits to be overcome. Teachers who believe that their own culture is superior to students' cultures will not be able to build the trust necessary to help all students learn.

When one first begins to teach multiculturally, extra planning time will be needed to discover ways to make the curriculum and instruction reflect diversity. With experience, however, this process will be internalized. The teacher will begin to recognize immediately what materials are not multicultural and will be able to expand the standard curriculum to reflect diversity and multiple perspectives.

CULTURALLY RESPONSIVE TEACHING

Culturally responsive teaching is an essential component of education that is multicultural. This pedagogy affirms the cultures of students, views the cultures and experiences of students as strengths, and reflects the students' cultures in the teaching process. It is based on the premise that culture influences the way students learn (Smith, 1998). In her study of successful teachers of African American students, Gloria Ladson-Billings (1994) identified six practices that define culturally responsive teaching:

- Students whose educational, economic, social, political, and cultural futures are most tenuous are helped to become *intellectual* leaders in the classroom.
- Students are apprenticed in a learning community rather than taught in an isolated and unrelated way.
- Students' real-life experiences are legitimized as they become part of the "official" curriculum.
- Teachers and students participate in a broad conception of literacy that incorporates both literature and oratory.
- Teachers and students engage in a collective struggle against the status quo.
- Teachers are cognizant of themselves as political beings. (pp. 117–118)

In this section we will explore elements of the teaching-learning process that should be considered and developed to become a culturally responsive teacher. Begin now to incorporate these practices into your own lesson plans. Look for evidence of these practices as you observe teachers in schools and identify others that support culturally responsive teaching.

High Teacher Expectations

Unfortunately, some teachers respond differently to students because of the students' microcultural memberships. Researchers have found different expectations and treatment of students, based on race, gender, and class. Some educators have low expectations for the academic achievement of students of color and those from low-income families. Teacher expectations are often based on generalizations about a group. When these generalizations are applied to all or most students from those groups, grave damage can be done. Students tend to meet the expectations of the teacher, no matter what their actual abilities are. Self-fulfilling prophecies about how well a student will perform in the classroom are often established early in the school year, and both student and teacher unconsciously fulfill those prophecies.

Educators should develop strategies to overcome negative expectations they may have for certain students and plan classroom instruction and activities to ensure success for all students. Ethnicity, gender, race, class, or disability cannot become an excuse for students' lack of academic achievement. Empathy

VIDEO INSIGHT

Minority Education Support

*According to psychologist Claude Steele, all groups, including members of culturally dominant groups, are susceptible to **stereotype threat.** Stereotype threat, he explains, is a kind of self-fulfilling prophecy in which people's low expectations for a group of learners tend to fill the learners with self-doubt, causing their level of performance to drop.*

In an ongoing program designed by Steele at the University of Michigan, students and professors engage in behavior designed to help eliminate the grade gap between white and minority students that is caused, in part, by stereotype threat. The teachers communicate to students that they have high expectations for them and that they believe the students can achieve those goals; the students work in racially diverse groups, taking the same classes, living in the same dorms, and studying together. What can you do in your own classroom to replicate the dramatic results of the Michigan program? How can you use cooperative learning groups in your classroom to communicate the same high expectations for learning success to all students?

with a student's situation is appropriate, but we must prevent it from subsequently lowering our expectations for achievement.

Upper middle-class students are placed disproportionately in high academic tracks, whereas low-income students are disproportionately placed in low academic tracks. Even when students have no differences in ability, academic tracks reflect race, gender, and class differences. Students who end up in the low-ability classes have limited academic mobility; they rarely are perceived to achieve at a level high enough to move them to the next highest level (Weinstein, 1996). Teaching behavior for high-ability groups is much different than for low-ability groups; middle-ability groups usually receive treatment more similar to that of high-ability groups. Students in the lowest tracks are often subject to practice and review drills. At the high end of the track, students are engaged in interesting and motivating intellectual activities.

To a large degree, students learn to behave in the manner that is expected of the group in which they are placed. Through tracking, educators have a great influence not only on directing a student's potential but also on determining it by their initial expectations for that student. The sad reality is that tracking does not appear to work, especially if the goal is to improve learning.

Heterogeneous grouping is more helpful in improving academic achievement for students from low-income and oppressed groups. Contrary to popular belief, such grouping does not limit the academic achievement of the most academically talented students, especially when the instruction is geared to challenging them.

All students in the class benefit (Weinstein, 1996). The students who suffer the most from tracking practices are those from groups who are disproportionately placed in the low-ability groups. Compared with students in other tracks, these students develop more negative feelings about their academic potential and future aspirations. Educational equity demands a different strategy. It requires that all students be academically challenged with stimulating instruction that involves them actively in their own learning.

Reflecting Culture in Academic Subjects

Knowledge about students' cultures is important in teaching subject matter in a way that students can learn it. The challenge for educators is to facilitate the learning process for all students. Culturally responsive teaching increases academic achievement because the subject matter is taught within the cultural context and experiences of the students and the communities served. In this approach, the subject begins to have meaning for students as it is related to their lives.

Researchers at the Institute for Research in Teaching found a relationship among teachers, learners, and subject matter that can be improved with knowledge and understanding of culture and diversity. McDiarmid (1991) argues that teachers need to do the following:

- Know how school knowledge is perceived in their learners' cultures. Resistance to school authority and knowledge among low-income, working-class, and minority youngsters limits their engagement with academics, especially when they do not see the relevance to their own lives.
- Know what kind of knowledge, skills, and commitments are valued in students' cultures. Such knowledge is critical to developing representations of subject matter that either bridge or confront the knowledge and understandings that students bring with them.
- Know about students' prior knowledge of, and experience with, the subject matter. The frameworks of understanding, based on prior experience, that students use to make sense out of new ideas and information are also critical if teachers are to make their subject matter meaningful to students.
- Understand that how a given subject matter is taught and learned determines, in part, the kinds of opportunities that teachers create for students to understand.
- Have a repertoire of different representations for a given idea, concept, or procedure. Teachers' abilities to generate or adapt representations, and their capacity to judge the appropriateness of representations for different students depends probably equally, on their understanding of their subject matter and their knowledge about their students.
- Understand the relationship of their subject matter to the world to help students understand these connections. Such connections are critical to the students' need to see the relationship between what they are studying in

school and the world in which they live. Such connections are critical if teachers are to help oppressed students increase their control over and within their environment.

- Understand the role that teachers and schools play in limiting access to vital subject matter knowledge by addressing what they define as individual differences through organizational arrangements such as individualization, tracking, and ability grouping.
- Know that, for students, they are representatives of their subject matter. If teachers represent mathematics as repetitious drill and practice and if they express negative attitudes toward mathematics, their students are likely to develop similar beliefs and attitudes.
- Consider their role in the classroom and how that role shapes the roles that students assume. If students are to explore problems and ideas with classmates, teachers need to consider how their behavior facilitates or inhibits such collaboration.

Teachers must know a subject well to help students learn it. Subject matter competence alone, however, does not automatically translate into student learning. Without an understanding of students' cultures, teachers are unable to develop instructional strategies that can be related to students' life experiences. Interviews with African American teachers who have successfully taught mathematics to black students who speak a dialect confirmed that the use of cultural context and students' prior experiences is essential in helping students learn. One teacher interviewed by Delpit (1995) reported:

> He found that the same problem that baffled students when posed in terms of distances between two unfamiliar places or in terms of numbers of milk cans needed by a farmer, were much more readily solved when familiar locales and the amount of money needed to buy a leather jacket were substituted. (p. 65)

Students' cultural backgrounds must be reflected in the examples used to teach academic concepts. Rural students do not relate to riding a subway to school or work, nor do inner-city students easily relate to single-family homes with large yards. If students seldom see representations of themselves, their families, or their communities, it becomes difficult to believe that the academic content has any meaning or usefulness for them. It will appear to them that the subject matter has been written and delivered for someone else. At the same time, they can still *learn* about other lifestyles based on different cultural backgrounds and experiences, but not as the only ones to which they are ever exposed. The teacher's repertoire of instructional strategies must relate content to the realities of the lives of students.

The teacher who understands the experiences of students from different cultural backgrounds can use that knowledge to help students learn subject matter. A teacher's sensitivity to those differences can be used to make students from oppressed groups feel as comfortable in the class as those from the dominant culture.

To answer these
questions online,
go to the Pause to
Reflect module for
this chapter of the
Companion
Website.

PAUSE TO REFLECT

Making Your Discipline Multicultural
   *Teaching that is culturally responsive requires changes in the curriculum to
build upon the cultures of diverse groups, no matter the subject being taught. Think
about a lesson you observed a teacher or professor in your discipline recently teach.
How were the lesson and the teaching of it culturally responsive? How might they
have been culturally responsive?*

Multiple Perspectives

It is important for students to learn that individuals from other ethnic, religious,
and socioeconomic groups often have perspectives on issues and events that are
different from their own. Most members of the dominant group have not had the
negative and discriminatory experiences that people of color have had with
schools, with the police, in government offices, or in shopping centers. They do not
understand the privilege they experience based solely on their skin color. These
experiences and the histories of groups provide the lens for viewing the world.
Thus, perspectives vary for good reasons. Understanding the reasons makes it easier to accept that most other perspectives are just as valid as one's own. At the same
time, perspectives and behaviors that degrade and harm members of specific
groups such as those of the Ku Klux Klan and Nazis are not considered valid by
the authors of this text.
   Culturally responsive teaching requires examining sensitive issues and topics.
It requires looking at historical and contemporary events from the perspective of
white men, African American women, Puerto Ricans, Japanese Americans, Central
American immigrants, Jewish Americans, and Southern Baptists. Reading books,
poems, and articles by authors from diverse cultural backgrounds is helpful because it exposes students to the perspectives of other groups.
   The community and students may view as untrustworthy teachers and others
who are unable to accept alternate perspectives. An example is the inability of
whites to see racism in almost everything experienced by African Americans. Even
when African American students point out a racist action, many white teachers
and students cannot see it, in part, because they have no experience of knowing or
feeling racism. Instead of acknowledging it, they often argue that the reporter mis-
interpreted the action or that the action was not meant to be racist. As a result,
many African Americans learn that whites are really not interested in eliminating
racism because they never recognize it or choose to ignore it (Tatum, 1997). Immigrant students, other students of color, students with disabilities, and girls and
young women have similar narratives that are given little or no credit by many
members of the dominant group.

Student Voices

Culturally responsive teachers seek, listen to, and incorporate voices of students, their families, and communities. Students are encouraged to speak from their own experiences, to do more than regurgitate answers that the teacher would like to hear. Teaching that incorporates the student voice allows students to make sense of subject matter within their own realities. Listening to students helps teachers understand their prior knowledge of the subject matter, including any misinformation or lack of information that suggests future instructional strategies. Student voices also provide important information about their cultures. Teaching must start from the students' life experiences, not the teacher's life experiences or the experiences necessary to fit into the dominant school culture.

Most schools today legitimate only the voice of the dominant society—the standard English and world perspective of the white middle-class. Many students, especially those from oppressed groups, learn to be silent or disruptive, and/or they drop out, in part because their voices are not accepted as legitimate in the classroom. Culturally responsive teaching requires educators to recognize the conflict between the voice of the school and the voices of students. Success in school should not be dependent on the adoption of the school's voice.

Teachers should position themselves "as less masters of truth and justice and more as creators of a space where those directly involved can act and speak on their behalf" (Lather, 1991, p. 137). One approach is the use of *dialogic inquiry*, in which instruction occurs as a dialogue between teacher and students. It requires that teachers have a thorough knowledge of the subject being taught. Rather than depend on a textbook and lecture format, the teacher listens to students and directs them in the learning of the discipline through dialogue. It incorporates content about the diverse backgrounds of students, as well as those of the dominant society. It requires discarding the traditional authoritarian classroom to establish a democratic one in which both teacher and students are active participants.

Introducing student voices to the instructional process can be difficult, especially when teacher and students are from different cultural backgrounds. The teacher may face both anger and silence, which will in time be overcome with dialogue that develops tolerance, patience, and a willingness to listen. Although this strategy increases the participation of students in the learning process, some teachers are not comfortable with handling the issues that are likely to be raised. Too often, teachers ignore students' attempts to engage in dialogue and, as a result, halt further learning by many students.

In addition to dialogue between students and teacher, student voices can be encouraged through written and artistic expression. Some teachers ask students to keep journals in which they write their reactions to what is occurring in class. The journals make the teacher aware of learning that is occurring over time. To be effective, students must feel comfortable writing whatever they want without the threat of reprisal from the teacher.

The dialogues developed through these approaches can help students understand the perspectives brought to the classroom by others from different cultural backgrounds. It helps them relate the subject matter to their real world and perhaps take an interest in studying and learning it.

Student and Teacher Interactions

Although the development and use of culturally responsive materials and curricula are important and necessary steps toward providing multicultural education, alone they are not enough. The interactions between teachers and students determine the quality of education. Teachers send messages that tell students that they have potential and that they can learn. Teachers who know their subject matter, believe that all students can learn, and care about students as individuals can have a great impact on students and their learning.

In an ethnographic study of eight African American and white teachers who had been identified as successful by the parents of African American students, Ladson-Billings (1994) found the following to be true:

> Teachers who practice culturally relevant [responsive] methods can be identified by the way they see themselves and others. They see their teaching as an art rather than as a technical skill. They believe that all of their students can succeed rather than that failure is inevitable for some. They see themselves as a part of the community and they see teaching as giving back to the community. They help students make connections between their local, national, racial, cultural, and global identities. Such teachers can also be identified by the ways in which they structure their social interactions: Their relationships with students are fluid and equitable and extend beyond the classroom. They demonstrate a connectedness with all of their students and encourage that same connectedness between the students. They encourage a community of learners; they encourage their students to learn collaboratively. Finally, such teachers are identified by their notions of knowledge: They believe that knowledge is continuously re-created, recycled, and shared by teachers and students alike. They view the content of the curriculum critically and are passionate about

VIDEO INSIGHT

Survival Lessons

Kids are faced with more and more violence and tragedy everyday. To combat this, some schools across the country have set up full-time mental health programs to identify and help troubled children before the trouble gets out of control.

Francis Scott Key Elementary and the other schools mentioned in this video segment present models for helping troubled youth. What else can be done to help these children deal with some of the challenges of today's society? What do you think the role of the teacher should be in helping students handle problems such as drugs, bullying, suicide, and violence?

it. Rather than expecting students to demonstrate prior knowledge and skills they help students develop that knowledge by building bridges and scaffolding for learning (p. 30).

The teacher who is enthusiastic about culturally responsive teaching will be more likely to use multicultural materials and encourage students to develop more egalitarian views. Research studies have found that warmer and more enthusiastic teachers produce students with greater achievement gains. These teachers solicit better affective responses from their students, which leads to classrooms with a more positive atmosphere. Students from low-income families and students of color "do especially well with teachers who share warm, personal interactions with them but also hold high expectations for their academic progress, require them to perform up to their capabilities, and see that they progress as far and as fast as they are able"(Brophy, 1998). Teachers need to carefully assess the needs of individual students in the classroom, however, to develop effective teaching strategies. They should not generalize these research findings to all students.

Teachers do make a difference in student learning. They can make students feel either very special or incompetent and worthless. In a year-long study of schools, researchers found that "students, over and over again, raised the issue of care. What they liked best about school was when people, particularly teachers, cared about them or did special things for them" (Institute for Education in Transformation, 1992, p. 22).

To provide the greatest assistance to all students, teachers cannot provide the same treatment to each student, because they should be working toward meeting individual needs and differences. Teachers must be sure they are not treating students differently, however, based solely on students' membership in a microcultural group. With the elimination of bias from the teaching process and the emergence of proactive teachers who seek the most effective strategies to meet the needs of individual students, the classroom can become a stimulating place for most students, regardless of their cultural background and experiences.

How can teachers analyze their own classroom interactions and teaching styles? At least two types of data could be collected: (a) how much talking is done by the teacher and individual students and (b) the nature of the interactions (e.g., giving praise, criticizing, asking questions, initiating discussion). Researchers have developed several instruments to assist in this process, and data may be collected by several methods (see the Link to the Classroom in Chapter 4 for an example). If equipment is available, teachers can videotape or audiotape a class and then systematically record the interactions as they view or listen to the tape later. An outside observer could be asked to record the nature of a teacher's interaction with students. An analysis of the data would show teachers how much class time they spend interacting with students and the nature of the interactions. These data would show any differences in interactions based on gender, ethnicity, or other characteristics of students. Such an analysis would be an excellent starting point for teachers who want to ensure that they do not discriminate against male or female students or students from different ethnic or socioeconomic groups.

Every effort must be made to ensure that prejudices are not reflected in these interactions. Teachers must continually assess their interactions with boys, girls, and students from dominant and oppressed groups to determine whether the interactions provide different types of praise, criticism, encouragement, and reinforcement based on the cultural backgrounds of the students. Only then can steps be taken to equalize treatment.

Student and Teacher Communications

Lack of skill in cross-cultural communications between students and teachers can prevent learning from occurring in the classroom. This problem is usually the result of misunderstanding cultural cues when students are from cultural backgrounds different from that of the teacher.

Just as cultures differ in the structure of their language, they also differ in the structure of oral discourse. Moves made in teaching-learning discourse, who is to make them, and the sequence they should take vary from culture to culture. These rules are not absolute laws governing behavior; in fact, they are closer to expectations and norms by which participants make sense of conversation and behavior. But when these patterns differ from the culture-of-teacher to culture-of-child, serious misunderstandings will occur as the two participants try to play out different patterns and assign different social meanings to the same actions.

These differences are likely to prevail in schools with large numbers of students from oppressed groups. Miscommunications occur when the same words and actions mean something different to the individuals involved. When students are not responding appropriately in the classroom, teachers should consider the possibility of communication cues being read differently on the basis of culture.

Effective cross-cultural communications between students and teachers promote student learning. When the cultural cues between students and teacher are not understood, communications and learning often are affected adversely.

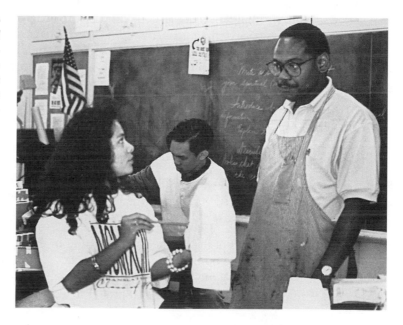

Direct and continuous participation in cultures that are different from our own can improve our competency in other communication systems and should help us be more sensitive to differences in cultures with which we are not familiar. Teachers who are aware of these differences can redirect their instruction to use primarily the communications that work most effectively with students. At the same time, the teacher can begin to teach students how to interact effectively in the situations with which they are uncomfortable. This approach will assist all students in responding appropriately in future classroom situations that are dominated by interactions with which they are not familiar.

CROSSING BORDERS

Unknowingly, educators often transmit biased messages to students. For example, lining up students by gender to go to lunch reinforces the notion that boys and girls are distinct groups. Why not line them up by shoe colors or birth dates instead? What messages do students receive when girls are always asked to take attendance and boys are asked to move chairs; when upper middle-class students are almost always asked to lead small-group work; or when persons of color are never asked to speak to the class? Most educators do not consciously or intentionally stereotype students or discriminate against them; they usually try to treat all students fairly and equitably. We have learned our attitudes and behaviors, however, in a society that is ageist, handicapist, racist, sexist, and ethnocentric. Some biases have been internalized to such a degree that we do not realize we have them. When educators are able to recognize the subtle and unintentional biases in their behavior, positive changes can be made in the classroom.

Traditionally, teachers have been part of the socialization process that teaches different male and female behaviors based on gender. Although boys are often more aggressive than girls, many of the differences observed in the way teachers treat the two groups are based on their own beliefs about male and female behavior. Teachers have more interactions with boys through both discipline and instruction (Brophy, 1998).

Students of color are often treated significantly different from white students. Because many white students share the same European and/or middle-class culture as the teacher, they also share the same cultural cues that foster success in the classroom. Students who ask appropriate questions at appropriate times or who smile and seek attention from the teacher at times when the teacher is open to such gestures are likely to receive encouragement and reinforcement from the teacher. In contrast, students who interrupt the class or who seek attention from the teacher when the teacher is not open to providing the necessary attention do not receive the necessary reinforcement.

As a result of the teacher's misreading of the cultural cues, students begin to establish ethnic boundaries within the classroom. This situation is exacerbated when students from the dominant group receive more opportunities to participate in instructional interactions and receive more praise and encouragement. Low-

LINK TO THE CLASSROOM

Two Perspectives on Who is Responsible for Learning a Second Culture

Students from the same cultural background as the teacher have little trouble understanding the rules that govern student-teacher interactions. Students from other cultural backgrounds often experience different interactional patterns with adults and do not understand the cues provided by the teacher. Some educators suggest that the rules that govern classroom interactions should be taught to students so that all are able to operate under the same rules somewhat equally. Others believe that teachers should learn to be bicultural or multicultural so that they interact appropriately with students from different backgrounds. What are the rules that govern classroom behavior and interactions with teachers? Which students have the advantage in these interactions? Why are these patterns unfamiliar to some students? What are the advantages of each of these approaches to students of color? Which approach would you consider using in your classroom?

income students and students of color receive fewer opportunities to participate, and the opportunities usually are of a less-substantive nature. They also may be criticized or disciplined more frequently than white students for breaking the rules. Delpit (1995) suggests:

> The clash between school culture and home culture is actualized in at least two ways. When a significant difference exists between the students' culture and the school's culture, teachers can easily misread students' aptitudes, intent, or abilities as a result of the difference in styles of language use and interactional patterns. Secondly, when such cultural differences exist, teachers may utilize styles of instruction and/or discipline that are at odds with community norms. A few examples: A twelve-year-old friend tells me there are three kinds of teachers in his middle school: the black teachers, none of whom are afraid of black kids; the white teachers, a few of whom are not afraid of black kids; and the largest group of white teachers, who are *all* afraid of black kids. It is this last group that, according to my young informant, consistently has the most difficulty with teaching and whose students have the most difficulty with learning (p. 168).

Unless teachers can critically examine their treatment of students in the classroom, they will not know whether they treat students inequitably because of cultural differences. Once that step has been taken, changes can be initiated to ensure that cultural background is not a factor for automatically relating differently to students. Teachers may need to become more proactive in initiating interactions and in providing encouragement, praise, and reinforcement to students from cultural backgrounds different from their own.

Race

Many teachers have a difficult time addressing the issue of race in the classroom. Yet, it affects the work of schools. Most white students probably don't believe that racism is a factor in their lives; they may even question its existence. Most persons of color, on the other hand, feel the pressure of racism all around them. They don't understand how their white peers and teachers could possibly miss it. To ignore the impact of racism on society and our everyday worlds is to negate the experiences of students and families who suffer from its negative impact. Can we afford to ignore it because it is complex, emotional, and hard for some to understand and handle? As teachers incorporate diversity throughout the curriculum, there should be opportunities to discuss the meaning of race in this country and the debilitating effect racism (as well as sexism, classism, etc.) has on large numbers of people in this country and the world.

There is value in racial and ethnic groups working together to overcome fears and correct myths and misperceptions. This *healing* cannot occur if educators are unwilling to facilitate the dialogue about race. Discussions of race often challenge "unconscious and deeply held beliefs about society, self, and social relations" (Griffin, 1997, p. 292). Some students react with anger; others are defensive and guilty.

VIDEO INSIGHT

Children and Race

It has been more than forty years since school desegregation was mandated by the U.S. Supreme Court. Is this nation any closer to integrating children of different backgrounds in its schools? Do the generations of children who are growing up in schools today experience less prejudice than past generations? Is the nation any closer to melding relationships of racially and ethnically diverse people in this pluralistic society?

Do some independent reflective research by interviewing school-age children and recording their answers to the following question: "Have you ever had any good friends who are of a different race than you?" If the answer to this initial question is yes, ask, "What kinds of activities do you and this friend participate in together? How is this friendship the same or different from any of your other friendships? What do you value most about this friendship?" If the answer to the initial question is no, ask, "Would you be a friend to someone who is of a different race or ethnic background than you if you had the opportunity? Why or why not?"

Consider the children's answers. What do your data reveal? Using this knowledge, how will you make a difference by helping students develop as citizens in a global community who tolerate, respect, and accept all others?

At the beginning, many white students resist reexamining their world views, acknowledging the privilege of whiteness, and accepting the existence of discrimination. Griffin (1997) suggests the following:

> Students need to be able to express resistance without fear of negative sanctions from the teachers or other students in the class. Unless students feel comfortable about expressing their honest reactions, class discussions are likely to be shallow and forced. Remind students about participation guidelines and rely on the use of questions and contradictions rather than dogmatic or didactic teaching to challenge students' thinking (p. 292).

These changes do not occur overnight; they take months, and sometimes years, of study and self-reflection. Some people never accept that racism exists and needs to be eliminated. The dialogue about race and racism should occur in all schools, not just those with diverse populations.

Numerous studies show that interactions and understandings among people from different racial and ethnic groups increase as they work together on meaningful projects inside and outside the classroom. Teachers should ensure that students are not segregated in cooperative groups and group work. They can establish opportunities for cross-cultural communications and learning from each other (Pillsbury & Shields, 1999).

Teachers also should take a critical look at their own interactions with students and communities of color. Many teachers have not critically examined the meaning of race and racism and their role in maintaining the status quo. If educators are unable to acknowledge the existence of racism and understand the effect it has on their students, it will be difficult to serve communities of color effectively and nearly impossible to eliminate racism in either schools or society.

Poverty

Another difficult topic to analyze critically is poverty, especially its causes. Too often, families and individuals are blamed for their own poverty. It is difficult for many, especially those advantaged by the current economic conditions, to acknowledge that our system does not provide the same opportunities for all whites and persons of color. Chapter 2 described the growing gap between the incomes of the wealthy, the middle class, and persons in poverty.

Teachers can help students explore the contributions of the labor class as well as the rich and powerful. They can examine various perspectives on eliminating jobs in one area of the country and moving them to cheaper labor markets in another part of the country or world. Students could examine the changing job markets to determine the skills needed for future work. They could discuss why companies are seeking labor outside the United States for high-tech jobs as well as low-paying jobs in meat processing companies. They could critique different perspectives on seeking labor outside the country rather than ensuring that U.S. students have the necessary skills for the growing technology fields.

The question of whether inequity can be reduced through education continues to be asked. Many argue that the gaps of academic achievement based on low-income and ethnicity can be eliminated. Culturally responsive teachers are successful in teaching all students, but far too many teachers do not know enough about the cultures and experiences of their students to teach effectively. These teachers have only their own cultural backgrounds and experiences on which to draw; unfortunately, these practices may not be based on the learning styles of students and may sometimes lead to resistance and opposition to learning. When teaching focuses on learning within the students' cultures, schools can have a powerful impact on the educational success of all children.

Schools with large numbers of low-income students are generally not funded at the same levels as other schools. Robert Slavin (1997/1998), the founder of *Success for All Schools*, argues that the achievement gap could be decreased:

> "By giving high-poverty schools the resources typical of suburban schools, and focusing these new resources on proven, replicable programs and practices, we could make profound changes in the achievement gaps that so bedevil our educational system and our society" (p. 10).

One of the problems with increasing the equity of school funding is that communities with higher incomes and wealth are not always willing to provide public support at the levels necessary to ensure achievement in schools with high concentrations of poverty or near-poverty.

TEACHING IN URBAN, RURAL, AND SUBURBAN SCHOOLS

The cultural context of a community is influenced by the location of the school. Cultural groups adapt to the *place* in which they are located in different ways. The way we live changes as we move from one area of the country or world to another. So do the schools. In this section, we will explore some of the differences and challenges of teaching in rural, urban, and suburban schools.

Rural Schools

Schools in rural areas are generally smaller than in suburban and urban areas. A few one-room schools still exist in sparsely populated areas west of the Mississippi. An advantage of lower enrollments is a relatively low student-to-teacher ratio, allowing more individual attention for students. One of the problems in small schools is that they probably do not offer more than one course in physics, chemistry, and biology. Instead of a specialist to teach each of those areas, they need a science teacher who is qualified to teach all of them. Not all rural schools have the resources or an adequate number of students to offer foreign languages, technology education, music, art, or advanced placement. Satellite connections in some rural areas have allowed students to take these courses via distance learning. Rural schools may also have fewer computers and be less well served by telecommunications than other schools (Howley & Barker, 1997).

Incomes in rural areas are generally lower than in other parts of the country. The rural workforce earns less than its urban counterparts, and the poverty rate is higher than in other places. More than one fourth of working rural residents earn only enough to place them just above the poverty line. The rural economy is sensitive to changes in manufacturing and export rates. Farm production can fluctuate with the weather and prices controlled by the world economy. Multinational corporations have moved manufacturing jobs that were once available in rural areas to cheaper labor markets in other parts of the country and world (Haas & Nachtigal, 1998). Processing plants for meat and fish continue to be located near the source of the raw product, but the work is dangerous and laborers are poorly paid. New immigrants have been filling a number of these jobs in areas that have had little diversity in the past.

Rural communities have lost many of their sons and daughters to cities where jobs are more plentiful and incomes higher. Some ask if schools have forsaken the best traditions of rural living as an integral part of the curriculum. Some would argue that students should be prepared for college and satisfying work, but maintain a commitment and support for the place where they were raised.

Urban Schools

Not all schools in a city are equal. Parents of students in upper middle-class neighborhoods are able to donate funds to hire teachers of art and music. They can pay for tutors to ensure that their children have the knowledge and skills necessary for entrance into desirable colleges and universities. These and many low-income parents are actively engaged in their children's education. They talk with teachers; they try to ensure that their children are in classes with the best teachers; they encourage their children to be involved in extracurricular activities; and they monitor their children's performance to ensure that they are performing well on standardized tests.

Enrollment in the largest 100 schools in the country ranged from 47,000 in Alpine School District in Utah to 1.1 million in New York City (U.S. Department of Education, 1999). The majority of students in the largest cities are not white; Figure 8.5 shows the ethnic and racial diversity in these school districts. Almost 60% of the students are eligible for free lunch; 12% have one or more disabilities; and 120 different languages are spoken. Even in schools with diverse student bodies, segregation within the school is common. White students are much more likely to be in classes for the gifted and talented. African American students, low-income students, and students who have limited English skills are overrepresented in special education classes. Advanced placement classes are often not available in inner-city schools.

Urban schools are characterized as highly centralized, state-sponsored, authoritative, and bureaucratic (Rury & Mirel, 1997). Over the past decade, a growing number of urban schools have created elected school boards, reduced the bureaucracy, become decentralized, and allowed the establishment of charter schools. Teacher shortages in major cities are common. Classrooms are filled at the last

Figure 9–1

Diversity of Students in the Largest U.S. Cities in the 1997–1998 School Year.

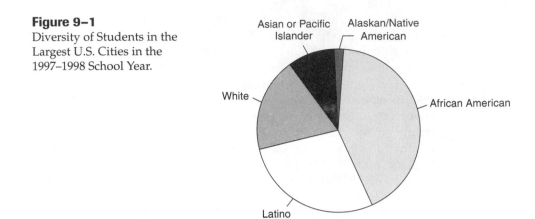

minute with teachers who are not fully licensed and have had no or little teacher preparation. "In schools with the highest minority enrollments, students have less than a 50 percent chance of getting a science or mathematics teacher who holds a license and a degree in the field he or she teaches" (National Commission, 1996, p. 16). Hiring practices in many urban districts are very bureaucratic. It sometimes takes months to process applications from qualified teachers, many of whom give up and find jobs elsewhere (National Commission, 1996).

Inequalities exist between most urban and suburban schools (Kozol, 2000). Decisions about how to spend a city's funds have an impact on school spending. Today, a number of cities and states spend much more on incarcerating the population than educating it. Jonathan Kozol (2000), who has spent years investigating the inequalities of schools, reports the following:

> The city [New York] spends $64,000 yearly to incarcerate an adult inmate on the prison island. It spends $93,000 yearly to incarcerate a child on the prison barge or in the very costly and imposing new detention center built on St. Ann's Avenue. That's about eleven times as much as it is spending, on the average, for a year of education for a child in the New York City public schools during the last years of the 1990s—*eighteen* times what it is spending in a year to educate a mainstream student in an ordinary first-grade classroom in the schools of the South Bronx (p. 155).

The teacher-to-student ratio in inner city classes is generally higher than in rural and suburban schools, even though the students in inner-city schools have the greatest need for support and care in society. They may have a sick grandmother at home for whom they are responsible; a father who could help them learn to navigate the community and school, but is in jail; a mother who is too sick to work; or an unmarried sister who has just learned that she is pregnant. These are major problems that children do not usually face in economically advantaged communities. Small classes are probably more critical in the inner city than any other area, and yet there are often 35 to 50 students per teacher. Some classes meet in noisy places such as basement corridors or storerooms without windows. Would we allow our children to be educated in these settings? Jonathan Kozol (2000) reminds us that, "There should not be a narrow gate for children of the poor, a wide and open gate for children of the fortunate and favored. There should be one gate. It should be known to everyone. It should be wide enough so even Pineapple [a low-income student] can get in without squeezing" (p. 296).

Suburban Schools

Schools in wealthy suburbs are more likely to have the latest technology, qualified teachers, advanced-placement courses, gifted-and-talented programs, and numerous extracurricular activities. Sometimes, high schools have sprawling campuses in park-like settings. Not all suburban schools, however, are of this high quality. Those that serve predominantly English, language learners, and students from low-income families and backgrounds other than Europe, are likely to be the older schools in the region. One school district near Washington, DC, for example, has had a very difficult time recruiting qualified and licensed teachers, usually beginning the school year with far too many teachers on emergency licenses. In this case, teacher salaries are not competitive and school conditions such as class size are not conducive to the most effective teaching. This district serves a very diverse, but working-class, population. On the other side of the city is a school district in one of the wealthiest counties in the United States. Qualified teachers are waiting for jobs, often substituting for several years before a full-time job becomes available.

The problems of urban schools are found in many suburban schools as well—especially drugs, student-on-student harassment, and lack of attention to students who may need it the most. Not all suburban schools have the resources to adequately support counselors, social workers, and others who can help students deal with the complexities of today's life. Some may not have the computers and technology that are important in preparing students for the future work world, but overall they are more likely to have these resources than their urban and rural counterparts.

More suburban parents are satisfied with their schools than are their urban counterparts (Carnevale & Desrochers, 1999). Many migrants from the city have moved to the suburbs to provide their children with greater opportunities for success in the suburban schools. For many families, these schools are successful in that graduates are more likely to attend and complete college than graduates of schools in other areas. Does this occur because most suburban school districts are better funded, have qualified teachers, and expect students to achieve at high levels? Is it because family income is higher in the suburbs or because a larger percentage of the parents have finished high school and college? Even with higher achievement scores in the suburbs, not all students are well served.

TEACHING FOR DEMOCRACY AND SOCIAL JUSTICE

As education that is multicultural matures in its application, teachers and their students begin to confront inequities in schools and communities. Then they take steps to eliminate existing inequities within the classroom and school and, sometimes, in the community. Two approaches interact in this process: teaching for social justice and democratic classrooms.

Teaching for social justice requires a disposition of caring and social responsibility for persons who are less advantaged than oneself. Socially just educators believe that the country's resources should be somewhat equitably distributed. They also believe that all people have the right to decent housing, health insurance, education, and adequate food and nutrition, regardless of their ethnicity, race, socioeconomic status, sexual orientation, or disability. They confront inequity by critically analyzing oppression in society (Bell, 1997). Herbert Kohl (1998) describes the teacher for social justice as "one who cares about nurturing all children and is enraged at the prospects of any of her or his students dying young, being hungry, or living meaningless and despairing lives . . . they go against the grain and work in the service of their students" (p. 285).

Democratic classrooms engage both students and teachers in learning to lead and follow and to be teachers and learners together. Power relations between students and teachers are enacted in classrooms. Teachers and other school officials can use their power to develop either democratic settings in which students are active participants or autocratic settings controlled totally by adults. Establishing a democratic classroom helps overcome the power inequities that exist. It challenges the authoritarianism of the teacher and breaks down the power relationships between teacher and stu4dents. Students become active participants in governing the classroom and in critically analyzing school and societal practices related to equity and social justice.

Critical Thinking

As a result of being taught multiculturally, students learn to think critically about what they are learning and experiencing. Shor (1996) defines critical thinking as "a holistic, historically situated, politically aware intervention in society to solve a felt need or problem, to get something done in a context of reflective action" (p. 163). Students should be supported in questioning the validity of the knowledge presented in textbooks and other resources. They should be encouraged to explore other perspectives. Developing the skills to think critically about issues helps students make sense of the events and conditions that affect their own lives.

Multicultural teaching requires students to investigate racism, classism, and sexism and how societal institutions have served different populations in discriminatory ways. Even though we may overcome our own prejudices and eliminate our own discriminatory practices against members of other cultural groups, the problem is not solved. It goes beyond what we individually control. The problem is societal and is imbedded in historical and contemporary contexts that we must help students understand.

Educators can help students examine their own biases and stereotypes related to different cultural groups. These biases often surface during class discussions or incidents outside the classroom. They should not be ignored by the teacher. Instead, they should become one of those *teachable moments* in which issues are confronted and discussed. Accurate information can begin to displace the myths that many hold about others.

Student Engagement

The curriculum for democratic classrooms and teaching for social justice encourages student participation, critical analysis, and action. Projects focus on areas of interest to students and the communities in which they live. As they participate in these activities, they apply and extend the mathematics, science, language arts, and social studies that they have been learning. Teachers and students in these classrooms have developed a vision for a more egalitarian and socially just society. Projects often engage students in collective action to improve their communities.

After conducting research and collecting and analyzing data, students sometimes move their recommendations through the democratic processes of their local communities to make changes for improving conditions. In one Midwest school, students and their teacher became very concerned about the treatment of new immigrants in the local community and businesses. They drafted a legislative bill requiring the study of race in social studies across the state. Facing opposition from some, they lobbied the state legislature on behalf of the bill and were successful in having it adopted. Students in this social studies class not only were able to affect school curriculum through their actions, but also learned the legislative process of their state through hands-on experience.

SCHOOL CLIMATE

Another area in which commitment to multicultural education can be evaluated is the general school climate. Three factors were identified by students as having a positive role in promoting good relations among students and adults: (a) the quality of teachers' relationships with students, (b) the quality of education, and (c) the social skills that teachers impart to students (Metropolitan Life Insurance Company, 1996b). "When teachers support students by treating them with respect and caring about their futures, and encourage students by helping them to succeed, students are more likely to respect and get along with one another; when taught how to be more tolerant of others, students exhibit greater tolerance" (p. 3). A disturbing finding of the survey was that a majority of students do not think that teachers, parents, and other adults treat students of color and low-income equally.

Visitors entering a school can usually feel the tension that exists when cross-cultural communications are poor. They can observe whether diversity is a positive and appreciated factor at the school. If only students of color or only males are waiting to be seen by the assistant principal in charge of discipline, visitors will wonder whether the school is providing effectively for the needs of all of its students. If bulletin boards in classrooms show only white characters, visitors will question the appreciation of diversity in the school. If the football team is comprised primarily of African Americans and the chess club of whites, they will wonder about the inclusion of students from a variety of cultural backgrounds in extracurricular activities. If school administrators are primarily men and most teachers are women, or if the teachers are white and the teacher aides are Latino, the visitors will envision discriminatory practices in hiring and promotion procedures. These are examples of a school climate that does not reflect a commitment to multicultural education.

Staffing composition and patterns should reflect the cultural diversity of the country. At a minimum, they should reflect the diversity of the geographic area. Women, as well as men, should be school administrators; men, as well as women, should teach at preschool and primary levels. Persons of color should be found in the administration and teaching ranks, not primarily in custodial and clerical positions.

When diversity is valued within a school, student government and extracurricular activities include students from different microcultural groups. Students should not be segregated on the basis of their membership in a certain microculture. In a school where multiculturalism is valued, students from various cultural backgrounds hold leadership positions. Those roles are not automatically delegated to students from the dominant group in the school.

If the school climate is multicultural, it is reflected in every aspect of the educational program. In addition to those areas already mentioned, assembly programs reflect multiculturalism in their content, as well as in the choice of speakers. Bulletin boards and displays reflect the diversity of the nation, even if the community is not rich in diversity. Cross-cultural communications among students and between students and teachers are positive. Different languages and dialects used by students are respected. Both girls and boys are found in industrial arts, family science, calculus, bookkeeping, physics, and vocational classes. Students from different cultural groups participate in college preparatory classes, advanced placement classes, special education, and gifted education at a rate equal to their representation in the schools.

The school climate must be supportive of multicultural education. When respect for cultural differences is reflected in all aspects of students' educational programs, the goals of multicultural education are being attained. Educators hold the key to attaining this climate.

To answer these questions online, go to the Pause to Reflect module for this chapter of the Companion Website.

PAUSE TO REFLECT

The school climate is an indicator of whether diversity and equality are respected and promoted in a school. Take an inventory of: (a) a school that you may be observing; (b) the school, college, or department of education that is responsible for preparing teachers at your college or university; or (c) the college or university itself. What is the diversity of the faculty? How diverse is the student body? How does the diversity differ between administrators and faculty? In what activities do white students and students of color participate? How reflective of diversity are displays on the walls and in display cases? What is the diversity of students on the honor roll or dean's list? What positive and negative characteristics do you observe?

The Hidden Curriculum

In addition to a formal curriculum, schools have a hidden curriculum that consists of the unstated norms, values, and beliefs about the social relations of school and classroom life that are transmitted to students. Because the hidden curriculum includes the norms and values that undergird the formal curriculum, it must also reflect diversity if education is to become multicultural. Although the hidden curriculum is not taught directly or included in the objectives for the formal curriculum, it has a great impact on students and teachers alike. It includes the organizational structures of the classroom and the school, as well as the interactions of students and teachers.

Elements of the hidden curriculum are shaped by crowds, praise, and power (Jackson, 1990). As members of a crowd, students must take turns, stand in line, wait to speak, wait for the teacher to provide individual help, face interruptions from others, and be distracted constantly by the needs of others. They must develop patience in order to be successful in the school setting. They must also learn to work alone within the crowd. Even though they share the classroom with many other students, they usually are not allowed to interact with classmates unless the teacher permits it. These same characteristics will be encountered in the work situations for which students are being prepared. They are not part of the formal curriculum but are central to the operation of most classrooms.

Praise can be equated with evaluation. Teachers usually evaluate students' academic performances through tests and written and oral work. Much more than academic performance is evaluated by teachers, however. Student misbehavior probably receives the most punishment, usually when classroom rules are not adequately obeyed. For example, teachers' "words of encouragement or feedback directed to boys tend to focus exclusively on their achievement striving and accomplishments, but some of what is said to girls in parallel situations focuses instead on neatness, following directions, speaking clearly, or showing good manners" (Brophy, 1998, p. 237). Similarly, students who have been assigned a low-ability status often receive negative attention from the teacher because they are not following the rules, rather than because they are not performing adequately on academic tasks.

In addition to evaluations based on academic performance and institutional rules, teachers often make evaluations based on personal qualities (Jackson, 1990). Teachers sometimes group students according to their clothes, family income, cleanliness, and personality, rather than academic abilities. This practice is particularly dangerous because most tracking perpetuates inequities; it does not improve academic achievement.

Another aspect of the hidden curriculum is that of unequal power. In many ways, this is a dilemma of childhood. By the time students enter kindergarten, they have learned that power is in the hands of adults. The teacher and other school officials require that their rules be followed. In addition to the institutional rules, teachers may require that students give up their home languages or dialects to be successful academically or at least to receive the teacher's approval. Instead, students should be encouraged to be bicultural, knowing both their home and dominant cultural language and patterns.

How can the hidden curriculum reflect multicultural education? A first step is to recognize that it exists and that it provides lessons that are probably more important than the academic curriculum. Students' curiosity must be valued and encouraged. Too often, the requirements of the classroom place more value on following the rules than on learning. Trying hard is sometimes more important than being able to think and perform. Our interactions with students should be evaluated to ensure that we are actually supporting learning, rather than preventing it.

Parent Involvement

After working in Alaska, in historically black and predominantly white universities, and in the South Pacific country of Papua, New Guinea, Delpit (1995) concluded, "If I want to learn how best to teach children who may be different from me, then I must seek the advice of adults—teachers and parents—who are from the same culture as my students" (p. 102). Parents expect teachers to help their children learn academic skills. A well-known educational psychologist, Jere Brophy reports the folowing:

> Most parents care about their children's success at school and will respond positively to information sharing and requests from teachers. Furthermore, one of the distinctive features of the teachers and schools that are most effective with students at risk for school failure is that they reach out to these students' families, get to know them, keep them informed of what is going on at school, and involve them in decision making (pp. 240–241).

Not all parents feel welcome in schools, in part because most schools reflect the dominant culture and language, rather than their own. Therefore, school personnel may need to reach out to the parents, rather than simply wait for them to show up at a meeting. A true collaboration requires that parents and teachers become partners in the teaching process. Teachers need to listen to parents and participate in the community to develop a range of teaching strategies that are congruent with the home cultures of students (Neuman, Hagedorn, Celano, & Daly, 1995). Parents can learn to support their children's learning at home but may need concrete suggestions, which they will seek from teachers who they believe care about their children.

Educators must know the community to understand the lived cultures of the families. In a school in which a prayer is said every morning regardless of the Supreme Court's decision forbidding prayer in public schools, one should not teach evolution on the first day of class. In that school setting, one may not be able to teach sex education in the same way it is taught in many urban and suburban schools. In another school, Islamic parents may be upset with the attire that their daughters are expected to wear in physical education classes and may not approve of coed physical education courses. Jewish and Islamic students wonder why the school celebrates Christian holidays and never their religious holidays.

Because members of the community may revolt against the content and activities in the curriculum does not mean that educators cannot teach multiculturally. It does suggest that they must know the sentiments of the community before introducing concepts that may be foreign and unacceptable. Only then can educators develop strategies for effectively introducing such concepts. The introduction of controversial issues may need to be accompanied by the education of parents and by the presentation of multiple perspectives that place value on the community's mores.

Adults in the community can be valuable resources in discussions of cultural differences. When community members trust school officials, they become partners with teachers in improving student learning.

In addition, the community becomes a resource in a multicultural classroom. We can learn much about cultures in the community through participation in activities and by inviting community members into the school. Community speakers and helpers should represent the diversity of the community. Speakers also should be selected from different roles and age groups.

PROFESSIONAL GROWTH

Educators should undertake a number of actions to prepare to deliver education that is multicultural. First, they should know their own cultural identity and the degree to which they identify with the various microcultures of which they are members. The degree of identification will probably change over time. Second, they should be able to accept the fact that they have prejudices that may affect the way they react to students in the classroom. When they recognize these biases, they can develop strategies to overcome or compensate for them in the classroom.

Becoming Multicultural

Educators need to learn about cultural groups other than their own. They might read about different cultural groups, attend ethnic movies or plays, participate in ethnic celebrations, visit different churches and ethnic communities, and interact with members of different groups in a variety of settings. Teachers who enjoy reading novels should select authors from different cultural backgrounds. The perspective presented may be much different from their own. Novels may help the reader understand that other people's experiences may lead them to react to situations differently from the way the reader would. It is often an advantage to discuss one's reactions to such new experiences with someone else to clarify and confront one's own feelings of prejudices or stereotypes.

Educators should make an effort to interact with persons who are culturally different from themselves. Long-term cultural experiences are probably the most effective means for overcoming fear and misconceptions about a group. One must remember, however, that there is much diversity within a group. One cannot generalize about an entire group on the basis of the characteristics of a few persons. In direct cross-cultural contacts, one must learn to be open to the traditions and ways of the other culture in order to learn from the experience. Otherwise, one's own traditions, habits, and perspectives are likely to be projected as better, rather than as just different.

If individuals can learn to understand, empathize with, and participate in a second culture, they will have a valuable experience. If they learn to live multiculturally, they are indeed fortunate. Welch (1991) describes one way that teachers from the dominant group can earn respect from members of other groups:

> For those with more areas of commonality, a different sort of work enables genuine conversation to occur. A genuine conversation between those who are privileged by way of class, gender, or race and those who have experienced oppression or discrimination

on the basis of those characteristics is possible when those who are privileged work to end the oppression or discrimination they denounce. As we do more than vote for those opposed to racism, challenging racism directly in our workplaces, in our families, in our own lives, we can be trusted in a way that enables those oppressed because of race to speak with us more honestly. In our work, we see more clearly the costs of racism and the intransigence of structures of oppression. Men who work against rape or domestic violence, who are involved in challenging the value systems that lead to such violence, are able to hear the voices of women, and women are able to trust them in a way impossible if the only form of relation is a dialogue (pp. 98–99).

Teaching as a Political Activity

Teachers who have made their teaching multicultural confront and fight against racism, sexism, and other discrimination in schools and society. They develop strategies to recognize their own biases and overcome them. They use their knowledge and skills to support a democratic and equitable society. They may work with their students "to act politically, to advocate both individually and collectively for themselves and for other marginalized people. Young people can learn to affect their social world quite powerfully" (Sleeter, 1996, p. 240).

Politically active teachers become advocates for children who have been marginalized by society. They may become active in political campaigns, supporting candidates who have an agenda for children, and for adults with the greatest needs. They become involved in local political action to improve conditions in the community. They are teachers who work for equity, democracy, and social justice.

Summary

Multicultural education is a means for using cultural diversity positively in the total learning process. In the process, classrooms become models of democracy and equity. To do this requires that educators: (a) place the student at the center of the teaching and learning process; (b) promote human rights and respect for cultural differences; (c) believe that all students can learn; (d) acknowledge and build on the life histories and experiences of students' microcultural memberships; (e) critically analyze oppression and power relationships to understand racism, sexism, classism, and discrimination against the disabled, young, and elderly; (f) critique society in the interest of social justice and equality; and (g) participate in collective social action to ensure a democratic society.

Culturally responsive teachers help students increase their academic achievement levels in all areas, including basic skills, through the use of teaching approaches and materials that are sensitive and relevant to students' cultural backgrounds and experiences. The voices of students and the community are valued and validated in the process. No longer can we afford to teach all students the same knowledge and skills in the same way. Teachers must make an effort to know all of their students, to build on their strengths, and to help them overcome their weaknesses.

The curriculum must incorporate the culture of the community and students in the classroom. Students should learn to think critically, deal with the social and historical realities of U.S. society, and gain a better understanding of the causes of oppression and inequality, including racism and sexism. Multicultural education starts *where people are,* builds on the histories and experiences of the community, and incorporates multicultural resources from the local community.

Positive student and teacher interactions can support academic achievement, regardless of gender, ethnicity, age, religion, language, or exceptionality. Oral and nonverbal communication patterns between students and teachers can be analyzed and changed to increase the involvement of students in the learning process. Teachers must be sure, however, that they do not treat students differently solely on the basis of the students' membership in a group. Teachers should regularly evaluate their academic expectations for students and their biases to ensure that they are helping all students learn.

The communities and students with whom one works will differ based on the school location. Schools in urban areas generally have more resources than those in rural and urban areas. The conditions supportive of learning differ among these schools as well. Class sizes, the number of qualified teachers, and resources available to students and teachers are often not conducive to learning in many urban schools.

Educators face a tremendous challenge in the next decade to effectively build on the culture and diversity students bring to the classroom. Every subject area can be taught in ways that reflect the reality of cultural differences in this nation and the world. Skills to function effectively in different cultural settings can also be taught. For students to function effectively in a democratic society, they must learn about the inequities that currently exist. Otherwise, our society will never be able to overcome such inequities.

As educators, we must teach all children. The ultimate goal of multicultural education is to meet the learning needs of each student. This goal has not been reached in the past, partly because educators have been unable to effectively use the cultural backgrounds of students in providing classroom instruction. One important goal of education that is multicultural is learning for all students. Acceptance of the challenge to multiculturalize our schools is vital to the well-being of all citizens.

Questions for Review

To answer these questions online, go to the Chapter Questions module for this chapter of the Companion Website.

1. How do multicultural education and culturally responsive teaching interact?
2. How can a student's culture be used to teach academic content? Give examples that apply to the subject area that you plan to teach.
3. If the textbook you have been assigned to use includes no information or examples pertaining to groups other than European, what can you do to provide a balanced and realistic view of society to students?
4. How can you incorporate student voices into the subject that you plan to teach?
5. Identify teacher behaviors and attributes that should positively support the delivery of education that is multicultural.

6. How might you structure group work in your class to facilitate cross-group interactions?
7. What are the characteristics of democratic classrooms and why are most classrooms not democratic?
8. Why is teaching for social justice controversial in some school systems?
9. What characteristics would determine that a school is committed to multicultural education?
10. What do you need to do to prepare yourself to understand and use the culture of students in your own teaching.

Web Resources

To link to the following websites go to the Web Resources module for this chapter of the Companion Website.

A website for people opposed to tougher standards and widespread standardized testing. The website was established by Alfie Kohn, author of *The Schools Our Children Deserve: Moving Beyond Traditional Classrooms and "Tougher Standards."*

The website of the Association of Supervision and Curriculum Development includes a number of resources related to teaching diverse students and multicultural education.

This website has a collection of cross-cultural world creation myths that can be used to compare cultures around the world.

The website of the Center for Applied Linguistics provides resources for scholars and educators who use the findings of linguistics and related sciences in identifying and addressing language issues.

The website of the Commission on Research in Black Education includes lessons on African language and history, and papers on the education of black children.

The website for middle school and high school students to inspire them to become involved in action to end hunger and poverty in their local communities, their country, and the world.

The website of the National Association for Bilingual Education, which promotes educational excellence and equity through bilingual education. It includes legislation, policies, and research related to language diversity.

The website of the National Association for Multicultural Education (NAME) connects users to others who are working in the field of multicultural education.

The National Conference of Community and Justice is a human relations organization dedicated to fighting bias, bigotry, and racism in America. It promotes understanding and respect among all races, religions, and cultures through advocacy, conflict resolution, and education.

The website of the National Parent Teacher Association includes information on building home–school relationships.

This website was designed by a group of teachers who wanted to improve education in their own classrooms and schools as well as to help shape school reform that is humane, caring, multiracial, and democratic.

The website of NECA promotes social and economic justice through transformative, quality education for all learners.

References

Bell, L. A. (1997). Theoretical foundations for social justice education. In M. Adams, L. A. Bell, & P. Griffin (Eds.), *Teaching for diversity and social justice: A sourcebook.*(pp. 1–15). New York: Routledge.

Brophy, J. E. (1998). *Motivating students to learn.* Boston: McGraw-Hill.

Carnevale, A. P., & Desrochers, D. M. (1999). *School satisfaction: A statistical profile of cities and suburbs.* Princeton, NJ: Educational Testing Service.

Delpit, L. (1995). *Other people's children: Cultural conflict in the classroom.* New York: New Press.

Griffin, P. (1997). Facilitating social justice education courses. In M. Adams, L. A. Bell, & P. Griffin (Eds.), *Teaching for diversity and social justice.* (pp. 279–298). New York: Routledge.

Haas, T., & Nachtigal, P. (1998). *Place value: An educators' guide to good literature on rural lifeways, environments, and purposes of education.* Charleston, WV: ERIC Clearinghouse on Rural Education and Small Schools.

Howley, C., & Barker, B. (1997, December). The national information infrastructure: Keeping rural values and purposes in mind. *ERIC Digest* (EDO-RC-97-4). Charleston, WV: Clearinghouse on Rural Education and Small Schools.

Institute for Education in Transformation. (1992). *Voices from the inside: A report on schooling from inside the classroom.* Claremont, CA: Author.

Interstate New Teacher Assessment and Support Consortium. (1992). *Model standards for beginning teacher licensing and development: A resource for state dialogue.* Washington, DC: Council of Chief State School Officers.

Jackson, P. W. (1990). *Life in classrooms.* New York: Teachers College Press.

Kohl, H. (1998). Afterword: Some reflections on teaching for social justice. In W. Ayers, J. A. Hunt, and T. Quinn (Eds.), *Teaching for social justice.* (pp. 285–287). New York: Free Press and Teachers College Press.

Kozol, J. (2000). *Ordinary resurrections: Children in the years of hope.* New York: Crown.

Ladson-Billings, G. (1994). *The dreamkeepers: Successful teachers of African American children.* San Francisco: Jossey-Bass.

Lather, P. (1991). *Getting smart: Feminist research and pedagogy with/in the postmodern.* New York: Routledge.

McDiarmid, G. W. (1991). What teachers need to know about cultural diversity: Restoring subject matter to the picture. In M. M. Kennedy (Ed.), *Teaching academic subjects to diverse learners* (pp. 257–269). New York: Teachers College Press.

McLaren, P., & Giroux, H. A. (1995). Radical pedagogy as cultural politics: Beyond the discourse of critique and anti-utopianism. In P. McLaren (Ed.), *Critical pedagogy and predatory culture* (pp. 29–57). New York: Routledge.

Metropolitan Life Insurance Company. (1996a). Students voice their opinions on: Learning about multiculturalism. *The Metropolitan Life Survey of the American Teacher: Part 4.* New York: Louis Harris.

Metropolitan Life Insurance Company. (1996b). Students voice their opinions on: Violence, social tension, and equality among teens. *The Metropolitan Life Survey of the American Teacher: Part 1.* New York: Louis Harris.

National Commission on Teaching & America's Future. (1996). *What matters most: Teaching for America's future.* New York: Author.

National Conference for Community and Justice. (1994). *Taking America's pulse: A summary report of the National Conference Survey on Intergroup Relations.* New York: Author.

National Council for the Accreditation of Teacher Education. (2000). *NCATE 2000 Standards.* Washington, DC: Author.

Neuman, S. B., Hagedorn, T., Celano, D., & Daly, P. (1995, Winter). Toward a collaborative approach to parent involvement in early education: A study of teenage mothers in an African American community. *American Educational Research Journal, 32*(4), 801–827.

Pillsbury, G., & Shields, C. M. (1999, October). Shared journeys and border crossings: When *they* becomes *we. Journal for a Just and Caring Education, 5*(4), 410–429.

Recruiting New Teachers, Inc. (1998). *The essential profession: A national survey of public attitudes toward teaching, educational opportunity and school reform.* Belmont MA: Author.

Rury, J. L., & Mirel, J. E. (1997). The political economy of urban education. *Review of Research in Education, 22,* 49–110.

Shor, I. (1996). *When students have power: Negotiating authority in a critical pedagogy.* Chicago: The University of Chicago Press.

Slavin, R. E. (1997, December/1998, January). Can education reduce social inequity? *Educational Leadership, 55*(4), 6–10.

Sleeter, C. E. (1996). *Multicultural education as social activism.* Albany NY: State University of New York Press.

Smith, G. P. (1998). *Common sense about uncommon knowledge: The knowledge bases for diversity.* Washington, DC: American Association of Colleges for Teacher Education.

Survey reveals strong support for diversity in ed, business. (2000, February 28). *Higher Education and National Affairs, 49*(4), 1, 4.

Tatum, B. D. (1997). *Why are all the black kids sitting together in the cafeteria? And other conversations about race.* New York: Basic Books.

U.S. Department of Education. National Center of Educational Statistics. (1999). *Characteristics of the 100 largest public elementary and secondary school districts in the United States: 1997–98.* Washington, DC: U.S. Government Printing Office.

Weinstein, R. S. (1996, November). High standards in a tracked system of schooling: For which students and with what educational supports? *Educational Researcher, 25*(8), 16–19.

Welch, S. (1991). An ethic of solidarity and difference. In H. A. Giroux (Ed.), *Postmodernism, feminism, and cultural politics: Redrawing educational boundaries* (pp. 83–99). Albany: State University of New York Press.

Suggested Readings

Ayers, W., Hunt, J. A., & Quinn, T. (1998). *Teaching for social justice.* New York: The New Press and Teachers College Press.

The chapters in this volume provide hands-on activities for classrooms and historical and inspirational writing on social action, writing and community building, and adult literacy.

Banks, J. A., & Banks, C. A. M. (Eds.). (1995). *Handbook of research on multicultural education.* New York: Macmillan.

This major reference document includes chapters on the history, goals, status, and research issues related to multicultural education. Drawing on the expertise of national leaders in the field, it addresses knowledge construction, ethnic groups, immigration, language issues, academic achievement, intergroup education, and international perspectives.

Delpit, L. (1995). Other people's children: Cultural conflict in the classroom. New York: New Press.
The author of this book, a winner of several book awards, proposes that an understanding of the culture and language patterns of students and their communities is key to overcoming the power differentials between schools and families. The narrative includes numerous examples from different cultures in which the author has taught or conducted ethnographic studies.

Derman-Sparks, L., & A.B.C. Task Force. (1989). Anti-bias curriculum: Tools for empowering young children. Washington, DC: National Association for the Education of Young Children.
These recommendations for creating an anti-bias curriculum and environment include how to deal with children's stereotyping and discriminatory behaviors. This handbook provides guidelines and activities to help children learn about cultural differences, including race, disabilities, and gender identity.

Fletcher, S. (2000). Education and emancipation: Theory and practice in a new constellation. New York: Teachers College Press.
The author explores the contributions and limitations of liberalism, critical theory, postmodernism, and care-theory to education for all students. He describes the tensions and conflicts in opposition to the agenda set by neo-conservatives.

Hollins, E. R., & Oliver, E. I. (Eds). (1999). Pathways to success in school: Culturally responsive teaching. Mahwah NJ: Lawrence Erlbaum Associates, Inc.
This volume provides strategies for making the curriculum and pedagogy culturally responsive. It addresses the teaching of mathematics, science, communications, history, literature, and music.

Ladson-Billings, G. (1994). The dreamkeepers: Successful teachers of African American children. San Francisco: Jossey-Bass.
This ethnographic study describes the differing dispositions, philosophies, and practices of eight teachers who were identified as successful by parents of African American students. Culturally responsive pedagogy becomes meaningful with the examples from the group of teachers.

McNergney, R. F., Ducharme, E. R., & Ducharme, M. K. (Eds.). (1999). Educating for democracy: Case-method teaching and learning. Mahwah, NJ: Lawrence Erlbaum Associates, Inc.
The cases in this book promote democratic teaching and learning in elementary and secondary schools.

Meier, D. R. (1997). Learning in small moments: Life in an urban classroom. New York: Teachers College Press.
This chronicle of coteaching by two first-grade teachers provides a first-person account of the ups and downs of teaching in an urban public school.

Multicultural Perspectives. (Published by the National Association for Multicultural Education, 733 15th Street, NW, Suite 430, Washington, DC 20005; nameorg@nameorg.org).
This quarterly magazine features articles by scholars and practitioners in the field of multicultural education. It also includes promising practices, multicultural resources, and book and film reviews.

Rethinking Schools. (Published by Rethinking Schools, 1001 E. Keefe Ave., Milwaukee, WI 53212; RSBusiness@aol.com).

Advocating the reform of elementary and secondary schools, this quarterly newsletter promotes educational equity and supports progressive educational values. Teachers, parents, and students are the regular contributors.

Rethinking Schools. (1994). Rethinking our classrooms: Teaching for equity and justice. Milwaukee: Author.

This collection of articles from classrooms and schools includes creative ideas, compelling classroom narratives, and hands-on examples of ways teachers can promote values of community, justice, and equality. Poems, student handouts, lesson plans, and teaching tips are integrated throughout the book.

Teaching Tolerance. (Published by the Southern Poverty Law Center, 400 Washington Ave., Montgomery, AL 36104).

This semiannual magazine provides teachers with ready-to-use ideas and strategies to help promote harmony in the classroom. Contributions address politics, race, economics, abilities, culture, and language.

Subject Index

AAVE (African American
   Vernacular English),
   253–256
Abuse
   child, 281–283, 306
   emotional, 282–283
   physical, 281, 282, 306
   sexual, 281, 282, 306
   substance, 285–287,
      307–308
Accents, 249–250
Acculturation, 14
ADA (Americans with
   Disabilities Act), 171
Adolescents
African American males, 107,
   295–298
   birth rates, 287
   relationship with parents,
      284
   sexual behaviors, 287–288
   substance abuse, 285–287,
      307–308
   suicide, 288–289, 307
   violence, 290–293
Adulthood, 298–301
Affirmative action, 22
Affluence, 27, 41, 42–43
African American
   Vernacular English
   (AAVE), 253–256
African Americans, 59,
   79–80, 85, 87
   male students, 107,
      295–298
   students, 101, 256
   women, 145
   youth, 293
Afrocentric curriculum, 107
Age
   and culture, 277
   educational implications,
      305–308
   and inequality, 62–63
Age Discrimination
   Employment Act, 302
Aged, 63, 301–305

Ageism, 301–302, 303
AIDS, 287
Alienation, 284, 289
American Association of
   University Women, 155
American Indians, 78–79, 80
   religions, 217
   schools, 107
American Muslims, 95
American Printing House for
   the Blind, 175
American Sign Language
   (ASL), 247–248
Americans with Disabilities
   Act (ADA), 171
Anti-Defamation League, 114
Anti-Semitism, 210–211, 222
Antifeminists, 128
Appalachia, 45
Argot, 246
Asian American students, 101
ASL (American Sign
   Language), 247–248
Assimilation, 14–15, 56
Association of Supervision
   and Curriculum
   Development, 351
"At risk" adolescents, 284
Athletics and gender,
   153–154
Attempted suicides, 289

Baby boomers, 299–300
Baby busters, 300–301
Baha'ism, 218
Basic interpersonal
   communicative skills
   (BICS), 261
Bell Curve, The (Hernstein
   and Murray), 109
Bi-dialecticism, 252–253
Biculturalism, 17–18
Bilingual education, 261–263,
   265–268
Bilingual Education Act, 262,
   266
Bilingualism, 248–249, 267

Biological differences
   between genders,
      128–130
Birth rates for teenagers, 287
Black English, 253–256
Black Muslims, 213–214
Blaming the victim, 38, 50,
   201, 337
Bloods (gang), 294, 295
Blue-collar workers, 51–52
Board of Education of the
   Hendrick Hudson School
   District v. Rowley, 172
Branch Davidians, 219
Bridge reading program, 256
Brown v. Board of Education of
   Topeka, 111, 169, 187
Buddhism, 214–216
Bureau of Indian Affairs, 79,
   114, 217
Business Week, 42

CALP (cognitive academic
   language proficiency),
   261
Case studies. See Critical
   Incidents in Teaching
Catholicism, 209–210
CDF (Children's Defense
   Fund), 32
Censorship, 230–231
Center for Applied
   Linguistics, 351
Charter schools, 107
Child abuse, 281–283, 306
Children
   and class, 277–279
   and depression, 291–292
   and ethnic awareness,
      279–281
   and poverty, 62–63,
      277–279
   and prejudice, 279–281
Children's Defense Fund
   (CDF), 32
Christian Science Monitor, 216
Christian Scientists, 216

Class
   and children, 277–279
   differences, 46–56
   educational implications,
      64–71
   and gender, 144
   structure, 38–39
Co-cultures, 246
Cognitive academic language
   proficiency (CALP), 261
Columbine High School
   shootings, 290–291
Commission on Research in
   Black Education, 351
Communication
   with exceptional children,
      183
   nonverbal, 9, 258–259, 269
   student-teacher, 333–334
Conflicts between groups, 11
Conversational distance,
   258–259
Council for Exceptional
   Children, 170
Creationism, 225
Crips (gang), 294, 295
Critical Incidents in Teaching
   age, 313–316
   class, 74
   ethnicity, 119–122
   exceptionality, 192–195
   gender, 158–159
   religion, 236–239
Critical thinking, 342–343
Crowds, 345
Cults, 218–219
Cultural borders, 16, 334–338
Cultural discontinuity
   theory, 102–103
Cultural identity, 20–21
Cultural pluralism, 15–16
Cultural relativism, 10–11
Culturally responsive
   teaching, 325–334
Culture, 6–11
   characteristics, 7–9
   definition, 6

and gender, 130–132
manifestations, 9
Culture of poverty thesis, 50
Curriculum
 Afrocentric, 107
 dominant culture as
  center, 106–107
 ethnocentric, 107
 hidden, 345–346
 multiculturalizing, 323–324
 multiethnic, 107–109
 as reflection of culture,
  13–14, 68–69,
  327–329

Deaf and hearing impaired
 people, 178, 248
Delinquent behaviors,
 180–181
Democracy and Education
 (Dewey), 22
Democratic classrooms, 342
Depression, 291–292
Desegregation, 111–113
Detracking, 47, 326–327. *See
 also* Tracking
Dialects, 250–252, 254–258
Dialogic inquiry, 330
*Diana v. State Board of
 Education*, 168, 265
Disabilities
 history of treatment,
  165–166
 labeling of students with,
  163–165
 learning, 164
Discrimination, 92–93
 gender, 136–140
 homosexuality, 141–143
Diversity
 in the classroom, 4–6
 ethnic and racial, 78–83
 religious, 5
Dominant culture, 11–15, 16

Eastern Orthodox Church, 216
Ebonics, 253–256
Education and
 socioeconomic status,
 44–45
Education for All
 Handicapped Children
 Act, 171, 265
Education Watch, 109
Education Week, 102, 254
Elderly, 63, 301–305
ELL (English language
 learners), 259–261, 263,
 266, 267, 268
Emotional abuse, 282–283
Emotional disturbances,
 180–181
Enculturation, 7
English as a second language
 (ESL) programs, 260–261,
 263, 265–266, 267–268
English Language
 Amendment (1981), 261

English language learners
 (ELL), 259–261, 263, 266,
 267, 268
"English only" movement,
 261–263
Equal educational
 opportunity, 24
Equal Rights Amendment
 (ERA), 127, 128
Equality, 24–28
ESL (English as a second
 language) programs,
 260–261, 263, 265–266,
 267–268
Ethnic and racial diversity,
 78–83
Ethnic awareness, 279–281
Ethnic differences, 104–106
Ethnic groups, 83–85
Ethnic studies, 106–107
Ethnicity
 educational implications,
  102–113
 and gender, 144–145
 and mathematics, 152
 and occupations, 59
 and poverty, 57–59
 and science, 152
 and technology, 151
 and tests and other
  assessments, 109–111
Ethnocentrism, 10. *See also*
 Discrimination; Prejudice
Evaluation of students by
 teachers, 345
Evolution, 200, 207, 225
Exceptionality
 definition, 162–163
 educational implications,
  181–184
 microcultures, 175–181
 needs of exceptional
  children, 183–184
 and society, 173–175
Eye contact, 259, 269

Fairfax County Schools, 232
First Amendment, 197, 200.
 See also Separation of
 church and state
Freedom, 12–13
Funding for schools, 69–70

Gangs, 293–295
Gay, Lesbian, and Straight
 Education Network, 155
Gays. *See* Homosexuality
Gender
 and athletics, 153–154
 and biology, 128–130
 and class, 144
 and culture, 130–132
 and discrimination,
  136–140
 educational implications,
  146–154
 and ethnicity, 144–145
 and intelligence, 129–130

and jobs and wages, 61,
 138–140
and mathematics, 130,
 151–153
and physical differences,
 128–129
and poverty, 60–62
and religion, 145–146,
 219–220
and salaries, 61
and science, 151–153
and socialization, 132–133,
 134, 137
and society, 126–128
and spatial abilities, 130
and technology, 151
and tests and other
 assessments, 146–147
and verbal abilities, 130
vs. sex, 130
Gender discrimination,
 136–140
Gender identity, 132–136
Gender inequality, 60–62
Gender sensitive education,
 148–150
Gender stereotyping,
 134–136
Generation X, 300–301
Gifted and talented, 175–177
*Guadalupe Organization, Inc.,
 v. Tempe Elementary
 School District No. 3 et al.*,
 264–265

Haitian students, 17
Handicapism, 174–175
Hate groups, 95–97, 295
Hate on Campus, 96
Health impairments, 179–180
Hearing impairments, 178,
 248
Heaven's Gate, 219
*Hendrick Hudson School
 District v. Rowley*, 172
Hidden curriculum, 345–346
High-risk behavior, 284–285
HIV/AIDS, 287, 306
Homeless people, 48–50
Homophobia, 143–144
Homosexuality, 141–143, 150,
 220–221
Hostile Hallways (American
 Association of University
 Women), 143

IDEA (Individuals with
 Disabilities Education
 Act), 171–172, 185, 186,
 265
Identity
 cultural, 20–21
 gender, 132–136
 racial and ethnic, 97–102
 religious, 223–224
Illegal immigrants, 79, 82
Immigrant children, 279
Immigration to U.S., 78–83

Inclusion, 186
Income and socioeconomic
 status, 41–42
Individualism, 12, 18, 22,
 23–24
Individuals with Disabilities
 Education Act (IDEA),
 171–172, 185, 186, 265
Intelligence
 and gender, 129–130
 tests, 264–265
Interethnic conflict, 89–90
Intergroup relations, 89–97,
 111–113
Internet, 283, 323, 324
*Irving Independent School
 District v. Tatro*, 172
Islam, 212–214

Jainism, 217
Jobs and wages
 and gender, 138–140
Joe Boys (gang), 294
Johnson-Reed Act, 81
Jonesboro (Ark.) school
 shootings, 290
Judaism, 210–212

Kentucky Industries for the
 Blind, 175
Kentucky School for the
 Blind, 175

Language
 and culture, 9, 242–245
 differences, 247–250
 and educational
  assessment, 264–265,
  267
 educational implications,
  263–269
 nature of, 245–247
 prejudices, 256–257
 and socialization, 243
Larry P. v. Riles, 168
Lau v. Nichols, 265
Lead poisoning, 168
League of United Latin
 American Citizens, 114
Learning disabilities, 164
Least restrictive environment
 (LRE), 185
Lesbians. *See* Homosexuality
Limited English proficient.
 See English language
 learners (ELL)
Linguistic Society of
 America, 256
Link to the Classroom
 choosing an approach to
  bilingual education, 268
 crossing a border, 17
 ethnic and racial groups,
  105
 is it discrimination?, 94
 nonracist curriculum for
  preschoolers, 281
 power limits detracking, 47

Link to the Classroom, *(cont.)*
  programs for the gifted, 176
  teacher-student
    interactions by gender,
    150
  two perspectives on who is
    responsible on
    learning a second
    culture, 335
Littleton (Colo.) school
  shootings, 290–291
LRE (least restrictive
  environment), 185

Magazines, 135
Mainstreaming, 185–188
Maintenance programs
  (bilingual education),
  266–267
Male liberation, 127
Mandated reporters, 283
Mathematics
  and ethnicity, 152
  and gender, 130, 151–153
Mensa, 176–177
Mental retardation, 163–164,
  165, 174, 177
Meritocracy, 23–24
Mexican Americans, 80
Microcultures, 16, 18–21
  exceptional, 175–181
Middle class, 52–53
Mills v. Board of Education,
  170
Monolingualism, 248–249
Mueller v. Allen, 228–229
Multicultural education
  characteristics, 30–31
  definition, 5
  history, 28–29
  public support, 321–322
  supporting dispositions,
    322–323
  underlying concepts, 30

NAME (National Association
  for Multicultural
  Education), 32, 351
NARC (National Association
  for Retarded Children),
  170
Nation of Islam, 213–214
National Association for
  Bilingual Education, 351
National Association for
  Multicultural Education
  (NAME), 32, 351
National Association for
  Retarded Children
  (NARC), 170
National Association for the
  Advancement of Colored
  People, 115
National Conference of
  Community and Justice,
  351
National Congress of
  American Indians, 115

National Gay and Lesbian
  Task Force, 141
National Organization for
  Women (NOW), 127, 156
National Parent Teacher
  Association, 351
National Urban League, 115
Native Americans. *See*
  American Indians
Nativism, 81, 86
Navajo Indians, 18
NECA (Network of
  Educators on the
  Americas), 351
Net worth, 42–43
Network of Educators on the
  Americas (NECA), 351
New Age movement, 218
New Christian Right, 224–226
Newspapers, 135
Newsweek, 230
Nonsexist education, 148–150
Nonverbal communication,
  9, 258–259, 269
Normalization, 185–188
NOW (National
  Organization for
  Women), 127

OAAU (Organization of Afro-
  American Unity), 213
Oakland (California) Unified
  School District, 254–256
Occupations
  by ethnicity, 59
  by gender, 61
  and socioeconomic status,
    43–44
"Official English"
  movement, 261–263
Oklahoma City bombing, 95,
  96
Olympics, 135
Organization of Afro-
  American Unity
  (OAAU), 213

Pan-ethnic classification,
  86–87, 98–99
*PARC v. Commonwealth of
  Pennsylvania,* 169–170
Parent involvement in
  schools, 346–348
Passage of St. John (Bach), 222
Passing of the Great Race, The
  (Grant), 86
Pause to Reflect
  AIDS and homosexuality,
    142
  cultural discontinuity, 7
  dialects in the classroom,
    257
  equality in society and
    schooling, 26
  jobs held by men and
    women, 62
  making your discipline
    multicultural, 329

perceptions of others by
    class, 53
  race as a social construct, 89
  school climate, 344–345
  secular humanism,
    231–232
  segregating students with
    disabilities, 187
Pearl (Miss.) school shooting,
  290
*Pennsylvania Association for
  Retarded Children v.
  Commonwealth of
  Pennsylvania,* 169–170
People's Temple, 219
Performance assessments,
  110–111
Physical abuse, 281, 282, 306
Physical contact, 259
Physical differences by
  gender, 128–129
Physical impairments,
  179–180
Physical neglect, 281, 282, 306
Pluralism
  cultural, 15–16
  religious, 203–206
Plyer v. Doe, 82
Political leadership
  and religious affiliation,
    207–209
Poor. *See* Poverty
Poverty, 27, 56–57
  and age, 62–63
  and children, 62–63,
    277–279
  in the classroom, 337–338
  educational implications,
    64–71
  and gender, 60–62
  and race and ethnicity,
    57–59
  and special education,
    167–168
Power
  in the classroom, 342, 346
  as part of racism, 93
  and socioeconomic status,
    45–46
Praise, 345
Prayer in schools, 200, 207,
  227–228
Prejudice, 90–91, 93, 95,
  279–281
Preschoolers, 292
Privilege, 13–14
Proposition 13 (California),
  304
Proposition 38 (California),
  229
Proposition 227 (California),
  262
"Protecting Students from
  Harassment and Hate
  Crimes," 155
Protestantism
  branches, 206–207
  political influence, 207–209

Public Law 101-336
  (Americans with
  Disabilities Act), 171
Public Law 94-142
  (Education for All
  Handicapped Children
  Act), 171, 265
Public Law 105-17 (IDEA
  Amendments), 172
Public Law 101-476
  (Individuals with
  Disabilities Education
  Act), 171–172, 185, 186,
  265
Public Law 93-112 (Vocational
  Rehabilitation Act), 161,
  170–171

Race
  educational implications,
    102–113
  and poverty, 57–59
  and religion, 221–223
  and tests and other
    assessments, 109–111
Racial and ethnic diversity,
  78–83
Racial and ethnic identity,
  97–102
Racial groups, 85–89
Racism, 93–94, 336–337
Refugees, 82
Religion
  and African Americans,
    222
  and culture, 198–201
  and education, 223
  educational implications,
    227–233
  and gender, 219–220
  and homosexuality,
    220–221
  and race, 221–223
  and slavery, 221–222
  and socioeconomic class,
    223
  as a way of life, 201–203
Religion and Public Schools
  (Becker), 232
Religions
  American Indian, 217
  teaching about, 232–233
Religious diversity, 5
Religious group membership
  in U.S., 204–205
Religious identity, 223–224
Religious pluralism, 203–206
Religious preference among
  Americans, 203–204
Religious Right, 224–226
Roe v. Wade, 224
Rural schools, 338–339

Salaries and gender, 61
San Francisco Board of
  Education, 265
*Sante Fe Independent School
  District v. DOE,* 228

Santee (Calif.) school
   shooting, 291
School busing, 25
School climate, 343–348
School funding, 69–70
School prayer, 200, 207,
   227–228
School shootings, 290–291
School vouchers, 229
Schools Our Children Deserve
   (Kohn), 351
Science
   and ethnicity, 152
   and gender, 151–153
Scopes trial, 207
Second language acquisition,
   259–261
Section 504, Public Law 93-
   112 (Vocational
   Rehabilitation Act), 161,
   170–171
Secular humanism, 231–232
Self-fulfilling prophecies, 66,
   67, 257, 284, 325, 326
Separation of church and
   state, 200, 201, 224, 226,
   227, 228, 232
SES (socioeconomic status),
   40–46, 65–68
Sex education, 200
Sex roles, 130–132
Sex *vs.* gender, 130
Sexism, 136–144
Sexual abuse, 281, 282, 306
Sexual behaviors of
   adolescents, 287–288
Sexual harassment, 143–144
Sheltered English immersion,
   262
Shootings in school, 290–291
Sign language, 247–248
Signed English, 248
Sikhism, 217
Single-sex classes, 152–153
Skinheads, 295
Slavery and religion, 221–222
Social justice, 26–27
Social reflection theory, 280
Social role valorization, 185
Social Security, 300–301,
   304–305
Social stratification, 40
Socialization
   definition, 7
   by gender, 132–133, 134, 137
   and language, 243
Socioeconomic status (SES),
   40–46, 65–68
Southern Baptists, 221, 233
Southern Poverty Law
   Center, 115
Spatial abilities, 130
Special education
   disproportionate
      placements, 166–173
   and language, 264–265
   law, 168–173

and poverty, 167–168
   referrals, 168
Standard English, 253
Stereotype threat, 326
Stereotyping of gender roles,
   134–136
Sterilization, 165, 174
Street gangs, 293–295
Structural assimilation, 14, 15
Structural inequalities
   theory, 103
Structured English
   immersion, 262
Student achievement and
   assessment, 109–111
Student engagement, 343
Student-teacher
   communication, 333–334
Student-teacher interactions,
   331–333
Subcultures, 16, 18–21
Substance abuse, 285–287,
   307–308
Suburban schools, 341
Suicide, 288–289, 307
Suicide Cults, 219

Teacher expectations, 65–68,
   325–327
Teachers
   becoming multicultural,
      348–349
   communication with
      students, 333–334
   and homosexuality, 150
   interactions with students,
      331–333
Teaching
   culturally responsive,
      325–334
   as a political activity, 349
   for social justice, 342
Teaching Tolerance (Southern
   Poverty Law Center), 115
Technology, 151
Teenagers. *See* Adolescents
Television, 134–135
Tests and other assessments
   bias, 110
   and ethnicity and race,
      109–111
   and gender, 146–147
   and language, 264–265, 267
   standardized, 109–110
Textbooks, 135
38 YES-School Vouchers, 229
Thousand Pieces of Gold
   (McCunn), 105
Time, 230
Title IX, 1972 Education
   Amendments, 153–154
Torcaso v. Watkins, 231
Tracking, 65–68, 326–327,
   345. *See also* Detracking
Transitional programs
   (bilingual education),
   266, 267

Tuition tax credits, 228–229
Turner Diaries, The
   (McDonald), 96

Underclass, 48–51
Unitarian Universalists,
   216–217
United States v. Seeger, 231
University of Michigan, 326
Upper class, 54–56
Upper middle class, 53–54
Urban schools, 339–341
U.S. News and World Report,
   230
U.S. Office of Civil Rights,
   155
U.S. Office of Education, 265

Values, 9, 12–13
Verbal abilities, 130
Vernacular Black English,
   253–256
Video Insights
   America in black and
      white, 91
   American spoken here, 250
   Billy Golfus, 163
   children and race, 336
   a closer look, 301
   denying school to children
      of illegal immigrants,
      79
   Ebonics and teaching
      standard English, 255
   the fairer sex?, 140
   God and evolution in
      Kansas classrooms, 225
   a life without limits, 179
   looking for a chance in
      Appalachia, 45
   minority education
      support, 326
   my child, 174
   school busing, 25
   secret life of boys, 129
   sex, truth, and videotape,
      288
   smart kid, tough school, 46
   survival lessons, 331
   teen's video of growing up
      in the city, 6
Vietnamese Americans,
   99–100
Violence, 290–295
Visual impairments, 164, 175,
   178
Vocational Rehabilitation
   Act, 161, 170–171
Voucher initiatives, 229

Wah Ching (gang), 294
Wealth, 27, 41, 42–43
Web resources
   Alfie Kohn, 351
   American Association of
      University Women,
      155

Anti-Defamation League,
   114
Association of Supervision
   and Curriculum
   Development, 351
Bureau of Indian Affairs,
   114
Center for Applied
   Linguistics, 351
Children's Defense Fund,
   32
Commission on Research
   in Black Education, 351
Gay, Lesbian, and Straight
   Education Network,
   155
League of United Latin
   American Citizens, 114
for middle school and high
   school students, 351
National Association for
   Bilingual Education,
   351
National Association for
   Multicultural
   Education, 32
National Association for
   Multicultural
   Education (NAME),
   351
National Association for
   the Advancement of
   Colored People, 115
National Conference of
   Community and
   Justice, 351
National Congress of
   American Indians, 115
National Organization for
   Women, 156
National Parent Teacher
   Association, 351
National Urban League,
   115
Network of Educators on
   the Americas (NECA),
   351
Southern Poverty Law
   Center, 115
U.S. Office of Civil Rights,
   155
Women's Educational
   Equity Association, 155
White-collar workers, 52–53
Women's Educational Equity
   Association, 155
Women's movements,
   126–127
Women's studies, 147–148
Working class, 51–52
Worship service attendance,
   202–203

Youth and Hate (Southern
   Poverty Law Center), 96
Yu Li (gang), 294

Name Index

A.B.C. Task Force, 83
Abernathy, Ralph, 222
Aboud, F., 279, 280, 281
Adams, John, 216
Adams, John Quincy, 216
Adger, C., 242, 243, 246, 250,
    251, 252, 253, 254, 256,
    264
Algozzine, B., 168, 186, 187
American Academy of
    Pediatrics, 292
American Association of
    University Women, 143,
    146, 147, 152
Anderson, D., 141
Anderson, S., 42, 55
Angelou, Maya, 255
Annie E. Casey Foundation,
    278
Anthony, Susan B., 125
Anyon, J., 64
Applewhite, Marshall, 219
Auletta, K., 48

Baca, L. M., 249, 266, 267
Bach, J. S., 222
Ballenger, C., 17
Baratz, J., 241
Barbe, R. H., 288
Barker, B., 339
Bates, P., 111
Battistich, V., 69
Becker, B., 232
Bell, L. A., 342
Bellah, R. N., 12
Bender, R. L., 292, 293
Bender, W. N., 292, 293
Bennett, William, 262
Berends, M., 67, 101
Bernstein, J., 55
Bezilla, R., 201, 205, 223
Biddle, B. J., 69
Bigler, R., 280
Binet, Alfred, 129
Birkholz, E. L., 208
Boyd, D., 13

Brophy, Jere E., 332, 334, 345,
    346
Bryant, William Cullen, 216
Bush, George, 171, 209, 225,
    226, 301
Bush, George W., 299
Business Higher Education
    Forum, 322
Butler, R. N., 302

Cannon, A., 290
Carnes, J., 95
Carnevale, A. P., 341
Carnoy, M., 64
Carolina Environment, Inc.,
    168
Carter, Jimmy, 203, 298
Cavanagh, J., 42
Celano, D., 346
Centers for Disease Control
    and Prevention, 287, 288,
    290, 291
Cervantes, H., 249, 266, 267
Chen, X., 143
Children's Defense Fund,
    296
Chilman, C., 297
Chinn, P.C., 183, 184
Christensen, L., 105
Christian, D., 242, 243, 246,
    250, 251, 252, 253, 254,
    256, 264
Chryssides, G. D., 218, 219
Chua-Eoan, H., 291
Clawson, D., 82
Clinton, Bill, 225, 301
Clinton, G., 292
Collins, C., 42
Connell, R., 294
Cookson, P. W., 55, 56
Corduan, W., 203, 205, 213,
    214, 215, 217, 218, 219
Corrigan, J., 209, 216, 217,
    224, 225
Corson, D., 249, 260, 264
Crawford, I., 285

Crawford, J., 261, 262
Croninger, R. G., 143
Cross, W. E., Jr., 94
Crowe, P., 285
Crystal, D., 246, 247
Cummins, J., 260, 261, 262

Daly, P., 346
Dannen, F., 294
Darwin, Charles, 207
Daskal, J., 49
Davenport, E. C., 152
Davison, M. I., 152
Day, M., 182
de Beauvoir, S., 134
Delpit, L., 328, 335, 346
Deno, 168
Derman-Sparks, L., 83
Desrochers, D. M., 341
Dewey, John, 22, 26
Dicker, S. J., 243
Ding, S., 152
Dole, Robert, 209, 225, 301
Donato, R., 112
Douglass, Frederick, 126
Downey, E. P., 280
Doyle, A. B., 280
Drew, C. J., 165, 167, 177, 185
Drew, Timothy, 213
Drowns, R. W., 293, 294
Drury, K., 300
Dryfoos, J., 287
Dunn, L., 166, 167

Eck, D. L., 5, 95
Education Trust, The, 110
Edwards-Evans, S., 253, 254
Eiskovits, Z., 296
Erickson, F., 6, 11, 16
Escalante, Jamie, 110
Ewen, R. B., 303

Fairchild, H. H., 253, 254
Falwell, Jerry, 224
Fard, W. D., 213
Farrakhan, Louis, 214

Federal Bureau of
    Investigation, 293
Felsenthal, C., 307
Fillmore, L. W., 263
Fishman, G., 296
Fordham, S., 101
Frandsen, K. J., 307
Freed, B., 260
Furstenberg, F. F., Jr., 52

Gallup, G. H., Jr., 201, 202,
    203, 204, 206, 209, 228
Gamoran, A., 67
Gandhi, Mahatma, 217, 319
Gay, Lesbian, and Straight
    Education Network, 143,
    144
Gelfand, D. M., 167
Gibbs, J. T., 293, 296, 297, 298
Gibson, M. A., 101, 102, 103
Giroux, H. A., 13, 16, 323
Gliedman, J., 173
Gomes, P., 220, 221, 222
Goodenough, W., 6, 17
Gordon, M. M., 14, 83
Graden, J., 168
Grant, Madison, 86
Greeley, A. M., 202
Green, S., 291
Greenwald, R., 70
Greven, P., 283
Griffin, M. E., 307
Griffin, P., 336, 337
Grissmer, D. W., 109
Groothuis, R. M., 220
Guttman, E., 296

Haas, T., 339
Hacker, A., 58
Hafen, B. Q., 307
Hagedorn, T., 346
Hakuta, K., 242, 248, 249
Hardman, M. L., 165, 167,
    177, 185
Harris, Eric, 290–291
Harry, B., 182

Hartman, C., 42
Hayakawa, S. I., 261
Hedges, L. V., 70
Hernandez, H., 266
Hernstein, R. J., 109
Hess, K. M., 293, 294
Heward, W. L., 162, 164, 248
Higher Educational
    Opportunity, 44, 58
Hoffman, D. M., 20
Hornblower, M., 267
Houston, B., 147
Howell, J. C., 294
Howley, C., 339
Hudson, W. S., 209, 216, 217,
    224, 225
Hughes, F. P., 275
Hyde, J. S., 130

Igoa, C., 279
Institute for Education in
    Transformation, 332
Institute for Research in
    Teaching, 327
Interstate New Teacher
    Assessment and Support
    Consortium, 323

Jackson, Jesse, 203, 222, 255
Jackson, P. W., 345
Jackson, R. L., 294
Jefferson, Thomas, 216
Jenson, W. R., 167
Johnson, D., 50
Johnson, Lyndon, 298
Jones, Jim, 219
Jones, R. W., 288
Jovanovic, J., 149

Kahir, 217
Kalyanpur, M., 182
Karp, S., 69
Katz, P. A., 280
Kelley, M., 79
Kennedy, John F., 225, 298
Kim, D., 69
Kim, S., 152
King, Martin Luther, Jr., 222
King, Peter T., 256
King, S. S., 149
Kinsey, Alfred Charles, 141
Kirby, S. N., 109
Klebold, Dylan, 290–291
Kofkin, J. A., 280
Kohl, Herbert, 342
Kohn, Alfie, 351
Koresh, David, 219
Kosmin, B. A., 213, 214
Kozol, Jonathan, 37, 340
Kratcoski, L. D., 293
Kratcoski, P. C., 293
Krisberg, B., 296
Kuang, H., 152
Kwak, N., 152

La Guardia, Fiorello, 243
Lachman, S. P., 213, 214

Ladson-Billings, Gloria, 104,
    106, 325, 331
Laine, R. D., 70
Lambert, R., 260
Lasch, C., 39
Lasley, T. J., 18
Lather, P., 330
Lee, V. E., 143
LePore, P. C., 67
Levin, H. M., 64
Levin, J., 95
Lewis, M. I., 302
Liben, L., 280
Liebow, E., 50
Lincoln, C. E., 213, 222
Lindner, E. W., 205
Lindsay, D. M., 201, 202, 203,
    204, 206, 209, 228
Lines, P. M., 229
Linn, E., 143
Little, Malcolm, 213
Longfellow, Henry
    Wadsworth, 216
Lopez, R. J., 294
Lorde, A., 13, 93, 137
Lowell, James Russell, 216

Madsen, R., 12
Maldonado-Colon, E., 260
Mamiya, L. H., 222
Marty, M. E., 216, 217, 224
Maslow, Abraham, 181
Massey, D., 20
McCunn, Ruthann Lum, 105
McDevitt, J., 95
McDiarmid, G. W., 327
McDonald, Andrew, 96
McGraw, D., 290
McKee, P. W., 288, 289
McKinney, W., 207, 224, 225
McLaren, P., 11, 323
McLoyd, V. C., 286, 289
McVeigh, Timothy, 96
Meier, K. J., 112
Menchaca, M., 112
Mercer, J., 166
Metropolitan Life
    Insurance Company,
    321, 343
Mirel, J. E., 339
Mishel, E., 55, 57
Mitchell, Susan, 300, 301
Mondimore, F. M., 141
Montalto, N. V., 28
Mowder, B. A., 167
Muhammad, Elijah, 213
Muhammad, Wallace Deen,
    213
Murdock, S. H., 57
Murray, C., 109

Nachtigal, P., 339
National Association for
    Bilingual Education, 263
National Board for
    Professional Teaching
    Standards, 111

National Clearinghouse on
    Child Abuse and
    Neglect Information, 282
National Coalition for the
    Homeless, 48, 49
National Commission on
    Teaching & America's
    Future, 340
National Conference for
    Community and Justice,
    89, 91, 321
National Council for the
    Accreditation of Teacher
    Education, 322
National Law Center on
    Homelessness and
    Poverty, 48
National Low Income
    Housing Coalition, 49
Nazario, S., 288, 289
Neuman, S. B., 346
Nguyen, My Lien, 77
Nirje, B., 185
Noppe, L. D., 275
Nystrand, M., 67

Oakes, J., 101
Ogbu, J., 100, 101
Olson, L., 82, 102
Omi, M., 92
Ortiz, A. A., 260
Ortner, S. B., 130, 131
Owens, R. E., Jr., 250, 253,
    254
Oxtoby, W. G., 212

Pai, Y., 18
Palermo, G. B., 293
Pang, V. O., 87
Pankratz, H., 291
Patton, J. M., 167
Payne, K. J., 69
Persell, C. H., 55, 56
Philbin, J., 285
Pierce, William, 96
Pillsbury, G., 337
Political Action Committee
    for Generation X, 301
Poole, Elijah, 213
Porter, R. E., 245, 246, 259
Pratte, R., 15
President's Committee on
    Mental Retardation, 164
PRIDE, Inc., 287
Princeton Religion Research
    Center, 209, 223, 225, 226

Radziewicz, C., 186
Randolph, A. Philip, 3
Reagan, Ronald, 209, 225
Reagan, T., 248
Recruiting New Teachers,
    Inc., 322
Redlener, I., 50
Richards, M. H., 285
Riley, Richard, 255
Rist, R. C., 66, 67

Rivkin, S. G., 111
Robertson, Pat, 203, 224
Robinson, F., 212
Roof, W. C., 207, 224, 299,
    300
Rose, S. J., 43, 47, 48, 52, 53,
    54, 63
Rosenheim, M., 287
Roth, W., 173
Rury, J. L., 339
Rynkiewich, M. A., 9

Sadker, D., 146
Salend, S., 186, 187
Salthouse, T., 302
Samovar, L. A., 245, 246, 259
Sandall, S. R., 167
Sarles, R. M., 306
Schaps, E., 69
Schmitt, J., 55
Schnaiberg, L., 255, 256
Schnalberg, L., 82
Schofield, J. W., 111, 112
Schulz, R., 302, 303
Schwartz, I., 296
Sears, J. T., 141, 142
Serna, L., 47
Sheley, J., 293
Shields, C. M., 337
Shinn, M., 49
Shor, I., 342
Sidel, R., 288, 289
Simpson, D., 293
Sirotnik, K. A., 26
Skutnabb-Kangas, T., 260
Slavin, R., 70
Slavin, Robert, 338
Sleek, S., 280
Sleeter, C. E., 28, 29, 30, 91,
    349
Smith, D. D., 248
Smith, Dan, 43
Smith, G. P., 325
Smith, R. L., 287
Solomon, D., 69
Solomon, R. P., 101
Southern Poverty Law
    Center, 95, 96
Spencer, D., 242
Spencer, R., 58
Spradley, J. P., 9
Steele, Claude, 326
Stein, N., 143
Steinberg, L., 286, 289
Stevens, P., 287
Stewart, J., Jr., 112
Streisand, B., 290
Stronge, J. H., 50
Sullivan, W. M., 12
Swank, L., 248
Swidler, A., 12

Taeuber, C. M., 303
Tafoya, S. M., 87
Taft, William Howard, 216
Takaki, R., 101
Tatum, B. D., 88, 94, 329

Testa, M., 287
Thorne, B., 132, 133
Thurlow, M. L., 168, 186, 187
Tiegerman-Farber, E., 186
Tipton, S. M., 12
Toukomaa, P., 260
Tower, C. C., 282, 283
Treas, J., 303, 304
Treisman, Philip Uri, 110
Tuchman, G. M., 262
Tulgan, B., 301
Turnbull, A., 186
Turnbull, R., 186

UNESCO, 58
University of Chicago, 70
University of Pennsylvania, 250
Unks, Gerald, 142

Unz, Ron K., 262
Urban Institute, 48, 49
U.S. Bureau of the Census, 44, 47, 51, 52, 56, 58, 59, 60, 63, 81, 86, 103, 138, 139, 140, 245, 303, 304
U.S. Department of Education, 49, 58, 104, 146, 339
U.S. Department of Health and Human Services, 281, 282
U.S. English, 261, 262
U.S. Office of Civil Rights, 166, 167, 257

Valencia, R. R., 112
Van Leeuwen, M. S., 220
Viadero, D., 107

Walsh, M. R., 130, 131, 132
Walters, R. H., 183
Warren, Earl, 169
Watson, M., 69
Weinstein, R. S., 326, 327
Weis, L., 101
Weitzman, B., 49
Welch, S., 228, 231, 348
Wells, A. S., 47
Wesson, C., 168
Wheeler, R., 256
Widerstrom, A. H., 167
Williams, P. W., 211, 212, 213
Williamson, S., 109
Willis, P. E., 101, 134
Winant, H., 92
Winn, J., 182
Woffard, J., 253

Wolfensberger, W., 185
Wolfram, W., 242, 243, 246, 250, 251, 252, 253, 254, 256, 263
Wright, J., 293

X, Malcolm, 213

Yell, M. L., 170, 172
Yeskel, F., 42
Young, Andrew, 222
Young, R. L., 87
Youth Risk Behavior Surveillance, 285, 288
Ysseldyke, J. E., 168, 186, 187

Zandy, J., 68
Zia, H., 127